God on Our Side

God on Our Side

Religion in International Affairs

Shireen T. Hunter

ROWMAN & LITTLEFIELD
Lanham • Boulder • New York • London

Published by Rowman & Littlefield
A wholly owned subsidiary of
The Rowman & Littlefield Publishing Group, Inc.
4501 Forbes Boulevard, Suite 200, Lanham, Maryland 20706
https://rowman.com

Unit A, Whitacre Mews, 26-34 Stannary Street, London SE11 4AB,
United Kingdom

Copyright © 2017 by Rowman & Littlefield

All rights reserved. No part of this book may be reproduced in any form or by any electronic or mechanical means, including information storage and retrieval systems, without written permission from the publisher, except by a reviewer who may quote passages in a review.

British Library Cataloguing in Publication Information Available

Library of Congress Cataloging-in-Publication Data
Names: Hunter, Shireen, author.
Title: God on our side : religion in international affairs / Shireen T. Hunter.
Description: Lanham : Rowman & Littlefield, 2016. | Includes bibliographical references and index.
Identifiers: LCCN 2016031937 (print) | LCCN 2016033688 (ebook) | ISBN 9781442272576 (cloth : alk. paper) | ISBN 9781442272583 (pbk. : alk. paper) | ISBN 9781442272590 (electronic)
Subjects: LCSH: Religion and international relations—Case studies. | Religion and politics—Case studies. | Religion and state—Case studies.
Classification: LCC BL65.I55 H86 2016 (print) | LCC BL65.I55 (ebook) | DDC 201/.727—dc23
LC record available at https://lccn.loc.gov/2016031937

∞ ™ The paper used in this publication meets the minimum requirements of American National Standard for Information Sciences Permanence of Paper for Printed Library Materials, ANSI/NISO Z39.48-1992.

Printed in the United States of America

Contents

Preface	xi
Note	xiii
Introduction	1
Religion as the New Defining Paradigm of International Relations	3
Restoring the Balance or Shifting the Emphasis?	5
Has There Been a Secular Bias in the Study of International Relations?	8
The Need for a Rigorous Definition of Religion	11
Religion, Secularism, and Other Values	12
What Is Religion?	13
Religion as Ideology or the Ideologization of Religion	13
What Is Secular and How Is It Different from Religion?	15
The Shifting Boundaries of Religious and Secular Spheres	15
Secularism, State, and Political Power	17
Secularism and Religion: Inevitable Conflict or Accommodation?	19
Religion as Motivation, Justification, and Instrument of Policy	21
Channels for Transmission of Religion's Influence	22
Differentiating the Impact of Religion on Different International Actors	23
Religion and International Relations Theory	23
The Theoretical and Methodological Framework	25
Notes	27
1 The Range and Characteristics of International Actors	31
The Evolution of the International System and Its Actors	31
Has the Nation-State Become Obsolete?	33

The Resilience of States and the State-Centric International System	35
States and Supranational Organizations	35
States and Regional Organizations	37
States and Transnational Organizations	39
Non-Governmental Organizations and States	41
Defining the NGOs	41
Violent Non-State Actors: Terrorist Entities	44
Hizbullah and Iranian Support	45
Reasons for Hizbullah's Creation: Religion, or Socio-Economic Deprivation and Political Disenfranchisement?	46
The Taliban and Pakistan	47
Global Politics: Impact on the Emergence of the Taliban	49
Regional and International Consequences of the Soviet Invasion	50
Support for the Mujahedin	51
Struggle for the Control of Eurasia: Another Cause of the Taliban's Emergence	52
Consequences of the USSR's Demise	52
The United States and the Taliban	53
Lesser Terrorist Groups	54
Conclusions	55
Notes	56
2 Determinants of Behavior of International Actors	**61**
Determinants and Motivations of State Behavior	63
The Impact of Geography	64
Historical Experience: Impact on States' Self- and World-views	65
Religion and States' Views of Their Exceptionality	66
Resource Base	68
Changing Internal Determinants	69
The Impact of Leaders' Personalities	70
Value Systems/Ideology/Ideas	72
Religion as Ideology	74
External Determinants	74
Motivations and Goals behind State Behavior	76
Self-Preservation	76
Territorial Integrity and Preventing Aggression	76
Economic Well-Being/Prosperity	77
Prestige	77
Autonomy and Independence	78
Power/Interest versus Values/Ideals: Real or False Dichotomy?	78

Motivation in Specific Cases	78
Ends, Means/Instruments, Intentions, Capabilities	81
Intentions and Capabilities	81
Motivations of Violent Non-State Actors	82
The Taliban	83
Hizbullah	85
Conclusions	87
Notes	88

3 Russia's Policy toward the Yugoslav Crisis: The Role of Religion   93

The USSR and the Yugoslav Crisis: Gorbachev's Approach	94
Fear of the Contagious Impact of the Yugoslav Crisis	95
The Impact of Domestic Politics	97
Post-Soviet Period: The Russian Federation and the War in Bosnia	98
Forging a Post-Soviet Russian Identity: Impact on Russian Foreign Policy	98
Historical Foundations of Russian Nationhood and Statehood	99
Orthodox Christianity and the Birth of the Russian State	101
Slavism and the Russian Identity	103
Russia as the Leader of Slavs	104
The Western Challenge, Russian Reforms, and Debates on Identity and Values	105
Peter's Reforms and Their Consequences	105
Post-Soviet Russian Identity and Foreign Policy: The Return of Old Debates	107
Reassertion of Orthodoxy	108
Reassertion of Ethnic Identities: Impact on Russian Slavism	109
Russia as a Great Power/Russia as Civilization Creating and Civilizer	111
Serbia in the Context of Russia's Self-Image	112
Russian Foreign Policy Debates and the Bosnian War	114
The Characteristics of the Westernizers/Euro-Atlanticist School	115
Eurasianist School/Advocates of a Multipolar International System	116
Yeltsin and the Bosnian War	117
Increased Importance of Domestic Context of Foreign Policy	118
The Dominant Foreign Policy Thinking of the Yeltsin Era: Impact on Bosnia Policy	118
The Impact of Domestic Politics	120
Serb Intransigence: Limits on Russian Influence	123
Russian Civil Society and Public Opinion: Attitudes on the Bosnian War	123

	Russian Volunteers in the Yugoslav Conflict	124
	The Role of the Orthodox Church	125
	Conclusions	126
	Notes	129
4	Turkey's Policy toward the Bosnian War	135
	Turkish National Identity: Foundations and Evolution	137
	Religion, Ethnicity, Political Legitimacy, and Foreign Policy	139
	End of Empire, Establishment of the Turkish Republic, and Islam's Eclipse	139
	Limits to Atatürk's Project, Islam's Resilience, and Its Reappearance in Identity Debates	140
	Turkey's Political Developments: Impact on Islam's Position	142
	Parliamentary Politics	142
	Anti-Leftist Struggle	143
	Other Causes of Islam's Rise in the 1980s	143
	Atatürk's Vision for Turkey's Foreign Policy	145
	Unraveling of the USSR: Impact on Turkish Debates	146
	Turkey's Identity Debate: Renewed Interest in Islam	147
	International Repercussions of Soviet Collapse and Turkey's Foreign Policy Debates	148
	A New Foreign Policy Framework	149
	The 1991 Persian Gulf War: Reassertion of Turkey's Strategic Importance	149
	New Horizons beyond Europe	150
	Reconciling Western and Turko-Islamic Visions	151
	Turkey's European Ambitions	153
	Islam's Growing Role: Dilemmas for Turkish Foreign Policy	153
	Turkey's Ottoman Legacy in the Balkans: Advantages and Liabilities	154
	Turkish Citizens of Balkan Origins: Impact on Turkey's Approach to the Yugoslav Crisis	156
	Turkish Domestic Politics and Public Opinion	157
	The Yugoslav Crisis: Balancing Conflicting Interests and Pressures	159
	Old Alliances, New Ambitions	161
	Components of Turkey's Bosnia Policy	161
	Non-Governmental Assistance and Activism	164
	The Impact of Public Opinion	165
	Conclusions	165
	Notes	167
5	European Policy toward Turkish Membership in the EU	173
	Turkey's Long Quest to Join Europe	173

Reasons for the EU's Rejection of Turkey	177
Political Issues: The Cyprus Problem	179
Greek-Turkish Territorial Disputes	180
Domestic Politics and Human Rights	180
Economic Barriers	184
More Intractable Obstacles: Geography	186
Cultural Differences as the Real Obstacle?	190
European Identity and EU Identity: Are They the Same?	191
Universalism, Europeanism, Deepeners, Wideners	193
Foundations of EU Identity: Can It Be Different from Those of European Identity?	194
Religion as Culture: Christianity and European Culture	197
Christian Roots of Europe's Secular Values	200
Christianity as the Foundation of the European Way of Life and Historical Memory	201
The Role of the "Other" in European Identity	202
East as the Inferior Other	203
EU Expansion, Muslim Immigration, and Return of Religion to the European Political Scene	204
Impact on the Debate on Turkish Membership	207
Islam, Turkish Identity, Historical Memory, and Turkey's View of Its International Role	208
Islam and Turkish Identity	208
Popular Views on Turkey's Membership: The Impact of Cultural/Religious Factors	210
The Evolution of the EU and Its Identity	211
Conclusions	212
Notes	214
Conclusion	221
Importance of Agency	222
Continued Importance of State Actors	222
Importance of Identifying Principal Determinants of International Actors' Behavior	222
Importance of Focusing on Specific Cases	222
Fallacy of International Relation's Secular Bias	223
Adequacy of Existing Theoretical Schools of International Relations	223
Continued Primacy of Security and Material Interests	223
Central Role of Capabilities	224
Religion Is More Effective if Used as Ideology	224
Indirect Nature of Religion's Influence	225
Internal Politics as the Principal Conduit for Religion's Influence	225

Importance of Domestic Structures of Actors as Channels of Influence	226
Civil Society and Public Opinion as Channels for Religion's Influence	227
Political Leaders' Proclivities	227
Religion as Instrument of Policy	228
Religion's Comparatively Limited Role as a Determinant of Actors' Behavior	228
The Need for More Analysis of Religion's Role as a Determinant of International Actors' Behavior and as an Influence in International Affairs	228
Note	229
Appendix: Yugoslavia's Unraveling and Its Internecine Wars	231
Fragility of State: Cultural Divisions	232
Economic Divisions	233
Emerging Ideological Vacuum	234
Elections of 1990: Road to Independence and War	234
The War in Bosnia	235
Stages of the Conflict	235
Notes	238
Bibliography	241
Books	241
Journal Articles / Reports / Analyses	245
Index	249
About the Author	259

Preface

The idea of writing a book on the role of religion in international affairs first presented itself to me when I taught a course on this topic for several semesters at Georgetown University's School of Foreign Service. I searched for appropriate reading material to assign to students, some of whom had no experience in studying international affairs. I hoped to find a text which could introduce students to basic concepts in international relations, its historical evolution, the development of the modern international system and its global expansion, the range and character of the principal actors in the current international system, an analysis of the range of factors which shape the behavior of international actors, and, finally, an assessment of religion's relative role as compared to other determinants of these actors' behavior.

I found many high-quality works and made good use of them in preparing my reading lists. However, none addressed the problem the way I thought was needed to present a balanced and comprehensive view of religion's role as a factor in determining the behavior of various international actors. Some of these works dealt mostly with religion's role in the internal politics of state actors, in civil wars and other intra-state conflicts, and the contributions made by religious non-state actors to resolving (or not) such conflicts.[1]

Meanwhile, a number of scholarly articles focused on religion's impact on the behavior of a particular country or leader. For example, I found many excellent and highly instructive articles on the role of religion in the making of U.S. foreign policy, in general, and on that of the administration of President George W. Bush, in particular, as well as articles on how the religious beliefs of President George W. Bush and British prime minister Tony Blair contributed to their decision to invade Iraq in 2003. But none of the articles I came across analyzed religion's role in the context of other factors, such as security considerations, economic interests, or the pursuit of idealistic goals, such as the global spread of democracy. Yet these factors had significantly influenced American policies in the past as well as those of the Bush administration. Nor had any of these articles assessed religion's policy impact compared to those of other determinants of state behavior in shaping America's and the Bush administration's policies. Yet both the Bush administration's policy vis-à-vis Iraq in 2003 and the British were essentially motivated by security and economic considerations and interests. The Bush administration also wanted to reshape the Middle East political landscape and to mold the character of the post-Soviet international system according to American preferences.

I also discovered that some authors approached the study of religion's role in shaping the character of international affairs with already formed opinions, such as the anti-religion bias of the international relations discipline or religion's either negative or positive effect on international affairs in general. More important, these studies did not look at religion's role within specific contexts and by focusing on case studies. Yet a proper assessment of religion's role can only be done by analyzing specific cases. That approach would also clarify how and through what channels religion influences international actors' behavior and thus helps shape the dynamics of international relations.

Further, most of the works I referenced were written under the influence of the Cold War's end and the events of September 11, 2001 (9/11). As a result, they tended to exaggerate religion's impact in regard to the aftermath of the Cold War and to 9/11 and to play down evidence that showed the continued importance of non-religious factors as main determinants of state actors' behavior on that occasion and in the subsequent Global War on Terrorism.

In short, I could find little commentary that linked the study of religion with the nature and development of the international system, overall, much less providing valuable analysis of this linkage and interrelationship.

The present work is therefore an effort to contribute both to existing literature and to provide an accessible introduction to the topic of religion's role in international affairs, especially for students and others who are not especially familiar with various aspects of international affairs or with processes of policy making. This work lays no claim to theoretical innovation or to offering a particular thesis on the topic. It rather aims to provide tools needed for understanding religion's role in international affairs and for placing it in the context of other determinants of international actors' behavior. It performs this task by focusing on specific cases. In this way, it hopes to help avoid the neglect of religion's potential and actual impact on international affairs, but also warns against exaggerating its influence.

This work was made possible by a grant from Carnegie Corporation of New York. I express my thanks to the corporation and especially to its president, Dr. Vartan Gregorian. I also thank the Prince Al Waleed bin Talal Center for Muslim-Christian Understanding (ACMCU) and especially its founding director, Professor John Esposito, plus the Edmund E. Walsh School of Foreign Service of Georgetown University, for making it possible for me to complete this work at Georgetown. And I thank my research assistants, Maria Mikey and Ahmet Tarik Çaşkurlu, who provided me with valuable primary material in Turkish and Russian.

In accomplishing this study, I benefited from the works of many scholars. I am grateful to all of them. I also benefited from conversations with scholars and practitioners here in the United States, in Europe, and elsewhere. Despite all this help, all errors of fact and judgment are all mine. Finally, I benefited from the constant and unfailing support and sound advice of my husband, Robert Hunter. To him go my sincerest thanks.

Shireen T. Hunter
March 2016

NOTE

1. See for example, Jeffrey Haynes, *Religion, Politics and International Relations: Selected Essays* (London: Routledge, 2011). Also, K. R. Dark, *Religion and International Relations* (London: Macmillan, 2001).

Introduction

In the post-Soviet and post–Cold War eras, religion's potential and actual capacity to influence international actors' behavior and hence to shape the dynamics and character of international relations became of great interest to scholars of international affairs, foreign policy and opinion-making circles, and the informed public. Even as early as the late 1970s, religion as a potentially significant factor in international relations was attracting attention.

This interest was first ignited by political developments and cultural shifts in several Muslim countries during the 1970s and ensuing changes in the character of regional politics of Muslim-inhabited areas, especially those of the Middle East and South Asia. Most consequential of these politico-cultural developments, with the most far-reaching and long-term ramifications for the character of regional and international relations, were the 1979 Islamic Revolution in Iran; the rising influence of political Islam in the rest of the Muslim world in the 1980s and beyond; and the use of Islam in the Soviet-Afghan War (1979–1989) as an instrument to mobilize resistance to the USSR.

These developments demonstrated that in many societies religion remained a potent social and political force and continued to influence their overall evolution. In addition, religion exerted a critical influence in shaping the world views and self-perceptions of these societies and that of the states that represented them and hence their external behavior. Through the intermediary of this category of international actors, religion thus influenced the character and dynamics of international relations.

By triggering two developments, the Soviet Union's dissolution in December 1991 further intensified interest in religion's role in international relations.

1. The End of the Cold War. The Soviet Union's demise ended the Cold War and eliminated the paradigm of an existential struggle between socialism and capitalism/liberalism and between states representing the two systems. The belief in such an existential conflict and the ensuing Cold War for half a century had dominated most of the discourse of international relations, explained its dynamics, and to a major degree permeated all aspects of international politics and inter-state relations. Therefore, the end of the Cold War inevitably caused a paradigmatic vacuum in international relations.

2. The Discrediting of Communism. The Soviet Union's collapse also seriously eroded the credibility of Communism and thus also social and political systems and identities built upon its principles. The result was an ideological vacuum in the post-Soviet space and in those Third World countries where socialist ideas had been popular with intellectual elites. In the USSR's former constituent republics these twin developments also produced an identity vacuum or at least crisis. The main culprits were the USSR's failure to eliminate pre-existing ethnic and religious identities within its constituent republics, including in those that had been part of the Tsarist Empire since the eighteenth and nineteenth centuries; and the stunting of the development of strong national identities in these republics, partly because of the Soviet Union's strategy of forging a union-wide identity transcending local allegiances based on loyalty to socialist ideals and to the USSR.

Paradoxically, however, the Soviet Union's desire to portray itself as a voluntary unification of diverse peoples and not a new version of the Tsarist Empire led it to encourage the cultural development of various titular nationalities, including their local languages, and thus helped them retain their separate identities. Because of this internally contradictory Soviet nationality policies, although a certain sense of a union-wide identity emerged among the USSR's diverse peoples, local identities also survived, and the two coexisted within the same space.

After the Soviet Union's dissolution, the union-wide identity disappeared, forcing its former constituent republics, including the Russian Federation, to forge new national identities. In their search for new values upon which to build their post-Soviet societies and to forge new identities Soviet successor states increasingly looked to their pre-communist history, traditions, and value systems as guidelines for the future. They discovered that religion was a key component of both their pre-Soviet national identities and their value systems.[1] Thus in the Muslim-majority post-Soviet independent republics, mostly located in Central Asia, many mined their Islamic traditions and values as the foundation of their post-Soviet social and political systems and national identities. In the Russian Federation, Orthodox Christianity—an important component of Russia's pre-Soviet identity, values, and culture—was increasingly viewed as the best, or at least a very important, basis upon which to build Russia's post-Soviet value system and national identity. The outcome of these developments was the simultaneous enhancement of religion's social and political profile throughout the post-Soviet space and the emergence of new religion-based notions of collective identity and social and political theories.

RELIGION AS THE NEW DEFINING PARADIGM OF INTERNATIONAL RELATIONS

The paradigmatic vacuum resulting from the end of the Cold War could not last long because, as a power vacuum is inevitably filled, so too a paradigmatic vacuum has eventually to be filled. At any rate attempts will be made to do so, which is exactly what occurred shortly after the Soviet Union's collapse and the end of the Cold War: new overarching concepts and paradigms were advanced as replacements for the ideological battles of the Cold War era. They were intended to explain the nature of post-Soviet international relations and to identify the new forces that would shape them.

The most influential of these new paradigms was introduced by Samuel P. Huntington, in a 1993 article published in the journal *Foreign Affairs*, aptly entitled "The Clash of Civilizations." He later expounded his ideas in a book of the same title.[2] Three ideas underpinned Huntington's theory: First, he believed that serious and even unbridgeable civilizational divides exist in the world. Because all civilizations are built upon some religious foundations, therefore global cleavages are mainly rooted in religion or at least have a significant religious dimension. Second, in the absence of existential ideological battles, these religious and civilizational divisions and the ensuing conflicts will replace past ideological conflicts. Third, religion and religio-civilizational divides will constitute the new defining paradigm of international relations.

According to Huntington, the deepest civilizational divide is between the West and the Muslim world. But he also perceived civilizational incompatibility and hence potential conflict between the West and Asian cultures, as well as civilizational fault-lines within Christianity, especially between Eastern and Western Christianity. Nevertheless, for Huntington, the most significant looming clash is that between Western cultures and Islam.

However, he did not originate the idea of a looming conflict between the West and Islam. Even before the USSR's dissolution, Bernard Lewis had first advanced this idea in a 1990 article for the *Atlantic,* entitled "The Roots of Muslim Rage."[3] But Lewis had not proposed that civilizational conflicts on all fronts between the Western world and other cultures would be the new defining paradigm of international relations.

At first, many scholars viewed Huntington's ideas with skepticism. But events during the 1990s and beyond gave greater credence to his theory.

These included the outbreak of at least partly religiously motivated civil war in Afghanistan, following the 1989 Soviet withdrawal, and the wars in Bosnia and Chechnya in the 1990s and in the early 2000s. All these conflicts had considerable religious and sectarian dimensions. Therefore, they served as evidence of religion's importance as a source of dispute and conflict and thus a significant element in shaping the dynamics of international affairs. They seemed to confirm the validity of Huntington's thesis.

In this context, the most consequential event of the first decade of the twenty-first century was the terrorist attacks on the World Trade Center in New York City, on the Pentagon in Washington, DC, and in Pennsylvania on September 11, 2001 (9/11), by a group of Muslim militants, as they largely prompted the U.S. decision to launch wars on Afghanistan in 2001 and on Iraq in 2003. Those responsible for the 9/11 attacks were affiliated with the *Al Qaeda* terrorist group and its leader, Osama bin Laden. It is difficult to ascertain whether the attackers were primarily motivated by religion or whether they acted under the influence of a mixture of religious and other impulses. Most likely, in addition to religious sentiments, the terrorists were inspired by resentment over the West's domination of the Middle East and by anger over some American policies and actions in the region. For example, Osama bin Laden had spoken of his resentment at the 1991 attack on Iraq by the United States and a coalition of Western and Muslim states, in response to Saddam Hussein's invasion of Kuwait. This attack and earlier actions intended to prevent aggression by Iraq toward other Persian Gulf Arab states had necessitated the stationing of American troops in Saudi Arabia. Even after Iraqi forces were expelled from Kuwait, U.S. forces remained in Saudi Arabia. Strict Muslims, such as bin Laden, considered the presence of American troops in the Saudi Kingdom where Mecca, Islam's holiest site, is located, as sacrilegious.[4]

Regardless of the true nature of the perpetrators' motives, the events of 9/11 exacerbated religious divisions in some Middle Eastern and South Asian countries, worsened regional conflicts and rivalries that had a religious dimension, and intensified the conflictual aspects of the West's relations with some Muslim states and with large segments of Muslim populations.

The immediate outcome of 9/11 was the U.S. invasion of Afghanistan in October 2001. The principal purpose was to punish the *Al Qaeda* terrorist organization for masterminding 9/11. Its headquarters were in Afghanistan and Osama bin Laden resided there when the invasion began. In addition to retaliating against *Al Qaeda,* U.S. forces aimed to bring down the Taliban government in Kabul which had ties to *Al Qaeda.*

The second outcome of 9/11 was the U.S. decision to invade Iraq in March 2003. Unlike Afghanistan, the *Al Qaeda* connection was not a key factor, although some commentators claimed that Saddam Hussein's regime had links to *Al Qaeda,*[5] a claim disputed by many experts at the time and later disproved.[6] It appears, however, that some U.S. officials did believe that there was a link between Iraq and *Al Qaeda,* although later even American officials denied the existence of such a connection.[7] Regardless, unlike the case of Afghanistan where a major U.S. goal was to retaliate against *Al Qaeda,* the American decision to invade Iraq was determined by its broader strategic and security considerations, including its suspicion that the Iraqi regime possessed nuclear and other weapons of mass destruction.

The U.S. invasions of Afghanistan and Iraq significantly sharpened religious divides within these two countries, especially between the Sunnis and the Shias representing the two principal branches of Islam, as well as throughout the Middle East and South Asia. These two wars, especially that in Iraq, dramatically altered the balance of regional power and thus intensified regional rivalries and power struggles, including that between Iran and Saudi Arabia and to a lesser extent between Iran and Turkey. Moreover, because of these wars and their consequences the hitherto largely classical power struggles acquired a sectarian character[8] and they became catalysts for the emergence of new and at least partially religiously motivated, violent non-state actors. These new actors were added to the existing ones, such as Hizbullah in Lebanon whose origins date back to the mid-1980s, and the Taliban in Afghanistan, which was founded in the early 1990s. The latest of these new non-state actors is the Islamic State (IS). It was originally called the Islamic State of Iraq and the Levant or Syria (ISIL/ISIS). It is referred to as *Al Dawla al Islamiya fil Iraq VA al Sham* (DAESH) in Arabic.[9]

Most important, the notion of an existential struggle between the West and militant Islam, or Islamo-fascism as some have termed it, gained more credence. According to some commentators, this struggle is expected to go on for as long as a hundred years.[10] In a nutshell, 9/11 and its consequences intensified the belief (right or wrong) that religio-civilizational cleavages and the ensuing conflicts were to become the dominant paradigm of the twenty-first century, and hence a key factor in shaping the dynamics of international relations.

RESTORING THE BALANCE OR SHIFTING THE EMPHASIS?

In response, many scholars of international relations expressed regret that, in the past, religion's role in shaping the dynamics of international relations had received insufficient attention, and they emphasized the need to factor in religion's role and impact in future studies. Some scholars attributed this neglect to the international relations discipline's "secular bias."[11] They, notably Scott Thomas, maintain that this neglect derived from the dominance in the 1950s and 1960s of the modernization theory with its premise of inevitable secularization of all societies in the fields of political science and international relations.[12] Other scholars believe that the shortcomings of the existing theoretical schools of international relations are responsible for this neglect. They claim that existing theoretical schools do not allow for adequate analysis and assessment of religion's impact on international affairs. They advise that in order to remedy these shortcomings, in future studies' excessively secular outlooks should be avoided and new theoretical tools better suited to incorporate the religious variable in the study of international relations should be developed.

In the last decade or so, this renewed interest in religion's impact internationally resulted in a substantial increase in the number of books published on the subject of religion and international affairs. At least the titles of these books, if not always their content, suggested this surge. However, despite their high quality and contribution to elucidating many aspects of religion's role in politics in general and in international affairs in particular, these works do not directly address how and through what channels religion affects international relations. Many deal with religion's place in internal politics of states or with its role in causing intra and inter-state conflicts. Some explore how religion can be used to facilitate conflict resolution or help to advance the goals of economic development. Consequently, they leave some fundamental questions unanswered or provide only partial answers. Some scholars also make categorical statements regarding aspects of the topic which need closer examination. In short, despite all the often excellent work done on this topic, there is still much room left for further study and analysis of religion's role in and impact on international affairs. The following are some areas which could benefit from further inquiry:

1. The presumed secular bias of the international relations discipline. None of the scholars who have raised the issue of the existence of a secular bias in international relations discipline have answered the following question: Has this presumed bias resulted from a conscious choice by scholars of the field, or has what has been interpreted as bias in fact reflected prevailing conditions in the world since the emergence of the discipline?
2. The need for a precise definition of religion in the context of international relations. At times, many scholars treat religion as interchangeable with culture and broader societal values and even with different secular ideologies. They do not define clearly what can be or should be characterized as religious and what should be seen as secular. Nor do they state what separates the two. Consequently, existing literature does not clearly answer the question whether religion is a category separate from a society's other values, belief systems, and cultural attributes and, therefore, whether its role in determining international actors' behavior should be addressed separately from that of the for-

mer. In other words, they do not state clearly whether religion should be treated as an additional determinant of behavior. Or should religion's role be analyzed in the context of evaluating the role of broader value-related and ideational determinants of international actors' behavior? How one answers these questions is important both for determining the methods of analyzing religion's role in international affairs and for assessing its relative impact compared to other determinants of behavior. For instance, if religion is seen as being part of various actors' overall value, belief, and ideational systems, then its influence can be analyzed and assessed as part of ideational determinants of their behavior. But if religion is viewed as a separate category from other ideational systems, then it must be determined what makes religion and its influence on behavior different from that of other values and beliefs.

3. Inadequate attention in most works to the channels and mechanisms through which religion's influence is transmitted. They do not address the question whether religion's influence is principally channeled through the actions of states or non-state actors. In general, the issue of agency is not adequately and systematically treated. The following questions have also received inadequate treatment: Is religion's influence felt a) principally through its role in shaping national or group identities of state and non-state actors? b) by influencing the actors' world-views and self-perceptions? c) through its role in the internal politics of states? or d) by shaping international actors' understanding of where their interests lie, who are their friends and enemies, and ultimately what are their goals and objectives or what they should be?

4. Inadequate distinction between religion's role as motivator of behavior and determinant of policy and its function as an instrument to advance and justify policies adopted on the basis of other considerations. Current studies do not adequately address this question. Yet this distinction is very important for a relatively accurate assessment of religion's role as a motivator of international actors' behavior and therefore its influence on international affairs in general.

5. An excessively generalized approach in most works to the subject, thereby addressing the topic in very broad terms. Instead of analyzing religion's role and assessing its impact in the context of specific cases, most existing works focus on religion's role as a building block of world civilizations or as foundation of national cultures and, at times, identities.[13] These are important matters. But to gain a full understanding of religion's role in international relations and measure its impact as compared to other factors, such as power and interest, it is necessary to address it within the framework of specific cases.

6. Current literature mostly deals with religion's role in various actors' domestic politics and in causing intra- and inter-state conflicts. Other works recommend that it receive more attention in diplomatic relations.[14] But none address the question of how domestic political developments affect actors' behavior and pay insufficient attention to the interplay of internal and external settings of foreign policymaking, which ultimately shapes international actors' actions and their responses to external developments and to challenges to their interests and ideals.

In short, because of these underlying approaches to the topic, little systematic work has been done to demonstrate how and in what ways religion impacts the behavior of specific state and non-state actors and to assess its relative role compared to other determinants of their actions. Most works proclaim how important religion's role is in international affairs, but fail to demonstrate why and how. Therefore, they tend to exaggerate religion's role in contrast to the past when it was underestimated. But, this approach, too, has its own drawbacks, as has religion's neglect.

HAS THERE BEEN A SECULAR BIAS IN THE STUDY OF INTERNATIONAL RELATIONS?

Despite statements to the contrary by some scholars, there has not been a secular bias in the international relations discipline which has caused religion's role in international affairs to be neglected or has prevented it from being considered as an independent variable influencing international actors' behavior separate from other value related and ideational factors.

Nevertheless, it is true that for nearly fifty years, political scientists and development experts tended to ignore religion's role in the domestic evolution of both advanced and developing societies and held a rather deterministic view regarding religion's future place in human societies. They adhered to the dominant view of the 1950s and 1960s which maintained that, as a result of modernization and gradual secularization, religion's role in all societies' evolution will steadily and inexorably decline. The title of Daniel Lerner's book, *The Passing of Traditional Society,* best reflects this mindset.[15] Similarly, writing in 1958 about a Middle East in transition, Walter Laqueur predicted that religion (Islam) would have no role in the Middle Eastern countries' social and political evolution.[16] Their views reflected the pervasive influence of the modernization theory with its belief in the inevitable global expansion of modernization and its outcome, secularization.[17]

Therefore, when in the late 1960s and 1970s, religio-political movements emerged, mostly but not exclusively in the Muslim world, political scientists and development experts were surprised and even shocked. The assumptions of the adherents of the modernization paradigm proved to have been incorrect or at least not applicable to all societies. Nevertheless, their judgments in the 1950s and 1960s reflected the dominant global trends at the time, including in Muslim-majority countries, rather than betraying a secular bias on their part. The fact is that since the late nineteenth century, secular theories of nationalism in its ethnic variants, socialism, liberalism, and developmentalism/modernization had emerged as the dominant discourses, not only in the West but also in non-European countries, including those with Muslim majorities and among their intellectual and political elites. Moreover, in the last-named countries, between the 1920s and the 1970s, religion's role in public discourse had steadily declined and was replaced by that of nationalism, constitutionalism, anti-colonialism, and socialism. However, religion retained its hold on the masses and mass culture.

The rise of politico-religious movements, especially in the Muslim countries, demonstrated that dismissing religion as a social and political force was premature. When some of these movements succeeded in altering the political systems of their countries, as happened in Iran with the 1979 revolution, and with it their external behavior and hence the dynamics of regional and international relations, it became clear that neglecting religion's role in international relations had also been misguided. It had resulted in an incomplete understanding of forces that animate global relations. The consciousness of the drawbacks of ignoring the religious factor either in the study of internal dynamics of societies or those of international affairs convinced political scientists, development experts, and scholars of international relations that there should be more thorough investigation of the various ways in which religion affects societies' social and political evolution, the character of various societies' politics and governments, their external behavior, and hence the dynamics of international affairs.

Yet throughout the 1980s, there was no systematic effort to address religion's role in international affairs, either through its function as a motive behind international actors' actions or as an instrument for achieving their policy objectives. Nor was there any apprehension of how important an instrument of policy religion would become for a variety of international actors, although by the late 1970s, the United States had found religion, in this case Islam, to be a potent instrument to resist and roll back the Soviet Union's advances in Afghanistan, to contain its influence in other Muslim states, and even to promote change within the USSR. Throughout the 1980s the United States encouraged the spread of Islamic sentiments in the Soviet Union's Muslim-inhabited republics, which after the Soviet Union's collapse affected their political evolution.[18] Saudi Arabia and Pakistan also used religion as an instrument of their policies in Afghanistan. In this way, they enhanced religion's role not only in the Afghan society and politics, but also, often inadvertently, within their own societies and in their approach to foreign policy issues even beyond Afghanistan.

Following the Soviet withdrawal from Afghanistan in 1989 and throughout the 1990s, religion's role in Afghanistan's domestic politics and in those of neighboring states such as Pakistan was further enhanced. Furthermore, key regional actors, such as Saudi Arabia and Pakistan, increasingly used religion as an instrument of their regional policies. For example, Saudi Arabia used religion in its competition with Iran in the Middle East and in South Asia. Because Saudi Arabia is Sunni and Iran is majority Shia, regional politics increasingly acquired a sectarian tinge. The growing sectarian dimensions of regional politics of the Middle East and South Asia can be seen in the Taliban's extremely anti-Shia philosophy and in its diverging approach toward Saudi Arabia and the other Gulf Arabs and Iran, respectively, as well as in Iran's and the Gulf Arabs' treatment of the Taliban.[19] The U.S. invasions of Afghanistan in 2001 and Iraq in 2003 exacerbated sectarian tensions and lent regional rivalries an even more pronounced sectarian character.

Nevertheless, as was the case with development experts, international relations scholars' tardiness in adequately accounting for these changes was not due to their secular bias. On the contrary, they too reflected the conditions of the times. The inescapable reality is that for three centuries religion's influence in the lives of societies was in decline, albeit to varying degrees and at varying speeds in different parts of the world. Religion's decline first began in the mid-seventeenth century in West European countries, triggered by the beginning of the Age of Reason and the Enlightenment, plus the emergence of new creeds and values, such as liberalism, progress, and nationalism. Gradually, religion also lost its role as the legitimizer of power and the justifier of political action. In the West, over time popular will replaced the religious basis of political legitimacy. At the level of state behavior, ideas, such as the "reason of state," replaced old religion-based justifications. The Western societies' secularization has thus far continued, albeit in different forms and at different speeds.[20]

In the non-European world, too, by the 1890s secular discourse had made inroads, becoming influential among the non-European countries' intellectual and, to some degree, political elites. By the 1920s, modernization (or Europeanization as it was called then) and with it secularization became the dominant discourse at the elite level. In the Muslim world, this dominance lasted at least until the early 1970s. Therefore, in the non-Western world, from Japan to Egypt and Turkey, ideas of progress, nationalism, nation-building, socialism, modernization, and democracy, along with notions such as the reason of state (*raison d'état*) and national interest, became popular and affected the behavior of states and non-state actors, as represented by independence-seeking and anti-colonial movements.

In short, for nearly a hundred years, in the non-European world, too, religion was in retreat at least at the elite level. Consequently, it had little impact on the external behavior of the governments of most non-European, including Muslim, countries or, with few exceptions, on the actions of various non-state actors, especially independence-seeking movements. Even after the rise of religio-political movements in the Muslim world, most Muslim countries continued to be ruled by secular, albeit autocratic, rulers who were not much influenced by religious considerations in their external behavior.

By the mid-twentieth century, the international political system and the secular rules governing it, which had first emerged in Europe following the signing of the Treaty of Westphalia in 1648, had extended to most of the rest of the world. All non-European states desiring to join the international system had to accept its rules. Because the post-Westphalia international system was essentially secular or at least became so, inevitably those who studied and analyzed its workings reflected its predominantly secular character rather than displaying a significant secular bias.

Clearly, in future studies of international relations, religion's role should receive more attention. However, this should not be done at the expense of proper consideration of the impact of other factors, such as security, conflicting interests, and power ambitions of various actors, both at internal and external levels.

THE NEED FOR A RIGOROUS DEFINITION OF RELIGION

If religion is to be considered as a separate variable in shaping actors' behavior, it needs to be defined rigorously and less expansively. This more restricted definition of religion is needed to distinguish it as a set of theological and spiritual beliefs which connects human beings to a supernatural power from other social, political, and cultural values and beliefs. Otherwise, all ideational, cultural, and value-related factors could become subsumed under the rubric of religion. This is not an easy task, largely because religion has been defined differently by scholars of various disciplines and performs multiple functions, some of which lack any spiritual or divine dimension. For example, sociologists, including pioneers in the field like Émile Durkheim and Max Weber, have focused on religion's social functions and see it mainly as a set of symbols, rules, and rituals which binds society together, although Durkheim emphasizes religion's spiritual dimension as its distinguishing feature. Anthropologists, especially cultural anthropologists, also tend to stress religion's social functions. A good example is Clifford Geertz.[21] Some scholars and thinkers, like Karl Marx, have seen religion as essentially a political phenomenon and as an instrument of the domination of the powerful over ordinary people. Marx called religion variously the opium of the masses or the sigh of the oppressed creature.[22] Others, meanwhile, have characterized as religion any type of belief system that enables humans to make sense of their surroundings and forces which animate them and are often beyond their comprehension and control, and which provide a set of values to live by and goals to pursue.

In this expansive definition of religion, its spiritual and/or divine dimension is not sufficiently stressed. According to this definition, any all-embracing and often totalitarian secular ideology, such as socialism or fascism, could be characterized as religion. Recently, some scholars have actually suggested that these political ideologies constitute a sort of "secular religion."[23] If so, any value or ideational system could qualify as religion. More to the point, in that case the claim that religion's role has been neglected in the study of international relations would become invalid, largely because the impact of ideas, values, and ideologies in shaping the behavior of international actors and the dynamics and character of international relations has been adequately addressed, although some theoretical schools do not view these variables as the most influential.

By contrast, theologians and some philosophers have seen religion as the outward manifestation of humans' need to find meaning and purpose in their lives and to come to terms with the transitory nature of life. For example, the theologian Paul Tillich defined religion as "the state of being grasped by an ultimate concern which qualifies all other concerns as preliminary and which itself contains the answers to the question of the meaning of life."[24] In this sense, religion is deeply personal and private rather than social and public, although all religions have and do perform social functions, as well.

Religion, Secularism, and Other Values

Many analyses of religion's role in international relations define it in an expansive way and therefore conflate many other values, beliefs, and cultural traits with religion. Yet if religion should be considered as a separate category of determinants of international actors' behavior distinguishable from other ideational factors, it must be made clear how and in what ways it is different from various societies' broader value systems and cultures. In other words, the boundaries between what is secular and what is religious need to be clearly established. In short, a correct understanding of how religion impacts the behavior of international actors requires *a priori* a rigorous and less expansive definition of religion and the setting of some boundaries between the religious and secular values.

What Is Religion?

This study will use a narrow definition of religion. It will be defined as a spiritual system of belief based on the presumption of the existence of some form of divine power. Even in this narrow sense, religion has both a general and a specific definition. In its general sense, religion has been variously defined as: 1) "a set of beliefs concerning the cause, nature, and purpose of the universe, especially when considered as the creation of a superhuman agency or agencies, usually involving devotional and ritual observances, and often containing guidelines for the conduct of human affairs"[25]; or 2) as "belief in, worship of, or obedience to a supernatural power or powers considered to be divine or to have control of human destiny."[26] Because of the belief in some supernatural force or entity, by this definition religions have a sacred character and are considered as such by their adherents.[27]

Defined more narrowly, religion is "a specific set of beliefs and practices generally agreed upon by a number of persons or sects," or "any formal or institutionalized expression of such belief."[28] This definition reflects the multiplicity of belief systems generally known as religion. In short, religions' distinguishing feature, as opposed to other belief systems, is their supernatural or divine dimension and their sacred nature. Therefore, non-divine or secular systems of belief, such as nationalism and socialism, cannot be characterized as religion, although they may be capable of performing some of religion's functions, such as legitimation of power and justification of actions; further, at times they may elicit from their adherents' feelings of loyalty and willingness to sacrifice.

Religion as Ideology or the Ideologization of Religion

Historically, despite religions' divine or sacred nature, once they have been established within communities they have generally performed non-sacred functions, such as providing guidelines and rules for the conduct of worldly affairs. By so doing, they have conferred a degree of sanctity on such activities. In other words, in addition to their sacred aspects, all religions also have a profane and worldly dimension. This non-sacred aspect is particularly important in the communal religions, such as Judaism and Islam. Islam, for example, has rules for conducting commerce, organizing society's economic life, regulating family relations, and even determining what is permissible to eat and drink and what is prohibited. It has also general guidelines about dealing with non-Muslims. In short, if one defines ideology as a set of instructions on how to conduct life, how to discern good from evil, and how to relate to other communities, then religions have been the earliest and oldest types of ideologies. If religion is to be seen as also performing the role of ideology, then there is no reason why the impact of religion on international affairs should not be analyzed in the context of the role of ideational factors in shaping international actors' behavior and, hence, the character of international relations.

In the last three hundred years, the rise of rationalism, secularism, and, in parallel with them, the development of secular ideologies has obscured religion's worldly aspects. By the early 1970s, however, religion's potential to be once more turned into an all-embracing ideology covering all aspects of societies' social, economic, and political life was rediscovered. This was reflected in such politico-religious theories as Liberation Theology and in the works of Muslim intellectuals such as the Egyptian, Seyyed Muhammad Qutb, and the Iranian, Ali Shariati, and in slogans such as "Islam is the Solution" (*Al Islam Howe Al Hal*).

In particular, the Iranian intellectual Ali Shariati consciously set out to ideologize religion in order to make it a potent competitor to such secular ideologies as socialism and liberalism. He consciously sought to turn the Shia version of Islam into a potent and modern ideology. He himself has admitted to doing so and has called his clearest and greatest ideological and political achievement "*the transformation of religion from culture to ideology*" [emphasis added]. Shariati maintained that "*religion is an ideology because it has its own blueprint for life and its own world-view*" [emphasis added].[29] However, Shariati's ideologized religion was developed under the influence of secular ideologies, in particular Marxism, and in significant ways departed from traditional Shiism. He used religious symbols and vocabulary to make his message accessible to the religious masses, who viewed Marxism as equivalent to atheism. Shariati's Islam-based political ideology had very little to do with traditional, theological, or spiritual Islam. It could even be said that his ideologized Islam was in fact a secularized form of Islam.

The same was true of the Islamic Left (*Al Yassar Al Islami*) which developed in Egypt in the 1960s and 1970s.[30] This is why the Iranian clerical establishment viewed Shariati with suspicion, although they found him a useful ally in the struggle against the Shah's secular government.[31] For the same reasons, Egypt's Sunni clerics were suspicious of leftist interpretations of Islam.

In the Christian world, the melding of Catholicism and Marxism occurred even sooner under the impetus of Cuba's socialist revolution in 1960 and produced Liberation Theology.[32] Because of this mixing of Catholicism and Marxism, the Vatican disapproved of Liberation Theology[33] just as Muslim clerics disapproved of mixing Islam and Marxism to produce a new Islamo-leftist synthesis.[34] These observations raise two questions: Is it correct to consider this particular version of religion as being the same as the traditional understanding and, by observing its political consequences, to exaggerate religion's role in international affairs? Or is it not more appropriate to treat ideologized religion in a similar vein as other political ideologies?

What Is Secular and How Is It Different from Religion?

The word "secular" derives from the Latin *saecula*. It means concerned with this world and therefore with the passing or temporal realm, as opposed to *aeterna*, eternal, which is outside the realm of this passing/temporal world. In its modern understanding, too, the term "secular" means concerned with this world. The *Merriam-Webster Dictionary* defines secular as "not spiritual, of or relating to the world and not the spiritual world."[35] The *Oxford English Dictionary* defines it as "denoting attitudes, activities or other things that have no spiritual basis: secular buildings, secular moral theory contrasted with sacred."[36] In short, secular refers to worldly and profane matters whereas religion's domain is essentially otherworldly, sacred, and spiritual.

THE SHIFTING BOUNDARIES OF RELIGIOUS AND SECULAR SPHERES

Historically, boundaries between the secular and religious or sacred and profane have shifted and overlapped. For most of human history, boundaries between spiritual and temporal realms were blurred and various religions, notably Judaism and Islam, concerned themselves with both worldly and otherworldly affairs. Religions also formed societies' ethical and legal foundations and served as both motivation for and justification of collective action; and they provided the guidelines about how to interact with other collectivities, including political entities. Religious rules were not always observed, nor did religion determine all human actions. Nevertheless, religion and its edicts provided the principal component of societies' value systems and their views of what constitutes good and what is evil. Even in many societies, today, especially in the Islamic world, religious and secular spheres exist side-by-side, either peacefully or in an adversarial posture.

Historically, religion was also the principal source of knowledge about the world, its origins and its end, and about the human destiny. In monotheistic religions, divine revelation through God's prophets and contained in their holy books provided this knowledge. Followers of pagan belief systems found their knowledge about the world, life, and human destiny in their reliance on supernatural myths. Despite the monopoly of religion as a source of knowledge, even in ancient times humans endeavored to gain knowledge by reasoning and observation as evidenced by Greek, Roman, Christian, and Islamic histories and those of other civilizations. Moreover, in reality, ancient and medieval societies were not excessively religious.[37] Nevertheless, until the dawn of the Ages of Enlightenment and Reason, revelation and not reason was the main source of knowledge, and religion was the foundation of law, ethics, and culture.

With the onset of the Ages of Enlightenment and Reason, the search for knowledge and truth outside the boundaries set by religion and through the use of reasoning and observation and by the application of rational and empirical methods accelerated. Through application of these methods, life was demystified or, as Max Weber put it, its enchantment was ended. The result was a reduction in religion's influence and the expansion of the temporal realm at the expense of the spiritual.[38] As religion's hegemony over intellectual and ethical discourses of societies was reduced, even in the dogmatic religions questions of faith gradually became less a matter of compulsion and more a matter of personal choice. In short, a basic characteristic of a secular system is that, in it, knowledge is based essentially on rational thinking rather than on revelation. As such, secular and religious phenomena are fundamentally different. By the same token, a secular society is one in which religion does not exert a hegemonistic influence on its ethics and laws.

The emergence of the rationalist age, however, did not mean religion's disappearance from private and collective life. On the contrary, religion continued to influence both private and public spheres of life, and for many believers of different religions, including Islam, Judaism, and Christianity, it still does. Nevertheless, at least in Western societies religion's role has continued to decline.[39] In recent years, even in some Muslim countries there has been a decline in religiosity. Ironically, this decline has been greatest in the Islamic Republic of Iran where the political system and regime legitimacy are still based on religion.[40]

Moreover, secularism per se is not anti-religion. It merely does not recognize religion's hegemony over societies' ethical, legal, and political discourses by virtue of representing God's word, thus excluding other views. In a secular system, religion can compete in the marketplace of ideas, but it cannot demand exclusive control over societal discourse. Nevertheless, there are versions of secularism which are anti-religion and do not recognize any place for religion in the public sphere. However, most existing secular systems allow religion a role, but not a dominant and hegemonic one.[41]

In sum, in the last three centuries the boundaries of the secular and religious spheres have shifted, and the secular sphere has expanded at the expense of the religious domain, even in the non-Western world, including Muslim countries. Unlike a century or so ago when religion had a hegemonistic hold over Muslim societies, today there are societal divides along religious-secular lines in almost all Muslim countries, either openly or in hidden ways, and a large minority of Muslims favor a basically secular social and political system. The existence of this secular-religious divide became obvious during the popular uprisings in 2010–2011 in a number of Arab countries, which was known as the Arab Spring; some protesters were asking for a religion-based political system while others were demanding a democratic and secular alternative.

SECULARISM, STATE, AND POLITICAL POWER

For most of history, religion influenced all aspects of private and public life. It also constituted the foundation of political legitimacy in various societies, even if real power and authority was often based on coercion. Moreover, historically, religious and political power, or sacred and profane authority, were often combined either in a single individual, as in the prophet kings of the Old Testament and Muslim Caliphs, or in an institution like the Roman Catholic Church. In those systems within which spiritual and temporal power was not combined in a single individual or institution, authority and legitimacy of lay leaders derived from a religious source. The continuation of the leaders' authority and legitimacy also often depended on their upholding the society's dominant religion and its principles. In many societies, religion also determined the function of the government. For example, in the Islamic context, according to the famous Muslim theologian and jurist Imam Abu Hamed Muhammad ibn Muhammad al Ghazali, government's main raison d'être was to uphold peace and thus provide conditions under which the faithful could practice their religion in comfort. In ancient Iran, the king would lose his "divine light" (*Far e Yazdani*) if he neglected the teachings of the Zoroastrian faith. Even in the Greco-Roman world, religion and state were intertwined. In Rome the priest was "a government official whose task was to win the favor of gods, for they alone could guarantee the city's survival."[42]

In short, for most of human history, religion and politics and state/government were intertwined, although the relative balance of power between the two tended to shift according to circumstances. At times, as often was the case in the Muslim world, the government controlled religion and religious leaders and used them for its own worldly ends.[43] The situation in the Christian world was more complicated because of Christ's statement that "My Kingdom is not of this world" and his advice to his followers to "Render unto Caesar the things that are Caesar's and unto God the things that are God's." These dicta have often been interpreted as making a clear distinction between the realms of temporal and spiritual power. However, in Christendom, too, historically the boundaries between religious and temporal spheres were not always clear, and representatives of religious and temporal powers competed and fought as well as cooperated, while theologians and religious scholars debated the question of relations between the temporal and spiritual spheres and whether the former should be subject to the latter's control. It was not until the late seventeenth century that the boundaries between the two were gradually set.

The drawing of a distinction between the temporal and spiritual realms was partly the result of religion's dominance over politics in the Christian world between 400–1300 C.E. and its real or perceived negative consequences. The Christian world's rediscovery of the ancient world's philosophical and other legacies over time contributed to intellectual developments which resulted in the delineation of spiritual and temporal realms. The works of Muslim philosophers, most notably Avicenna (Abou Ali Sina), the Persian philosopher, and Averroes (Ibn Rushd), the Andalusian, played a significant role in the Christian world's rediscovery of its ancient heritage, especially that of Greece. Islamic philosophical discussions, notably by Avicenna, on the relative roles of reason and revelation as sources of knowledge and on how to reconcile the two encouraged similar debates in the Christian world. St. Thomas Aquinas, who was familiar with Avicenna's works, took up this issue and advanced it further. These early discussions paved the way for the coming of the Renaissance and eventually the rational age.[44]

Further contributing to a trend toward a clearer separation between spiritual and temporal realms and a greater emphasis on personal choice on matters of faith was the Protestant Reformation.[45] It was at least partly an act of revolt against the perceived religious authoritarianism of the Catholic Church.[46] The support given to the movement by some secular leaders, in turn reflected their desire to come out from under the dominant Church's tutelage. The sectarian wars which followed the Reformation further strengthened both trends. They ultimately enhanced secular leaders' power by altering the ethical and legal foundations of political power. New theories, such as the divine right of kings and, eventually, liberal and revolutionary theories which located the source of power in the people, eroded and finally eliminated religious foundations of political power in the West. In time, the wars of religion increased support in much of Christianity for the idea that matters of faith should be left to personal choice. For example, John Locke's views on this issue were influenced by Britain's sectarian wars.[47]

For nearly a hundred years, it appeared that the same process would also take place within other religious zones. In some, such as parts of East Asia, the secularization of societies and polities has advanced. But in the Muslim world, religion has made a significant political comeback.[48] A leading example of the reestablishment of the religious basis of power and political legitimacy is Iran's post-revolution government and political system, which is based on Islam and in which God is considered the source of sovereignty, political legitimacy, and law, thus limiting legislation only to matters not covered by religious laws. Saudi Arabia is another country where religion has remained the principal instrument to legitimize the ruling House of Al Saud. Nevertheless, as noted earlier, secularism has made inroads in Muslim societies and a secular-religious divide exists in most Muslim societies. Moreover, most Muslim-majority countries are ruled by secular, albeit generally authoritarian, governments.

SECULARISM AND RELIGION: INEVITABLE CONFLICT OR ACCOMMODATION?

Secularism is often defined as the antithesis of religion and thus inevitably hostile to any form of religiosity. Some people, especially in the Muslim world, view secularism as being synonymous with atheism and irreligion. Some understandings of what secularism is or should be are clearly anti-religion. A system of thought such as Marxism is obviously anti-religion, because it is based on a totally materialistic understanding of the world, dismisses revelation as a source of knowledge about the universe and the human condition, and sees religion as a means of oppression. By contrast, an understanding of secularism as being limited to the separation of the domains of the spiritual and the temporal, of the state and the church, and of politics and religion, plus the denial of any special place to religion in politics and its relegation to the private sphere, is not per se anti-religion. Similarly, certain understandings of religion and its role in society is irreconcilable with secularism. For example, any political system, such as those of the Islamic Republic of Iran or the Kingdom of Saudi Arabia, which bases its legitimacy and laws on religion, is clearly incompatible with a secular system, within which the source of political legitimacy and law is either the people's will or where authoritarian leaders rule through coercion. However, even such leaders often resort to sham elections in order to give their rule some semblance of popular legitimacy.

The distinction between these two types of understanding of secularism and religion, respectively, dates back to the early periods of Christian European societies' secularization. For example, the English philosopher John Locke's secularism and that of the eighteenth-century French revolutionaries were significantly different. Locke essentially relegated religion to the private sphere, while the latter wanted to eliminate religion from society altogether. Today, most European countries adhere to a Lockean understanding of secularism, while France's secularism (*Laïcité*) approaches that of the eighteenth-century revolutionaries. Therefore, in contemporary Europe, governments do not suppress religion, and in some countries they even help religion. Many European governments provide financial assistance to schools run by religious institutions. But throughout Europe, religion is kept closely out of politics and governance. This attitude was in display when the European Union rejected Pope John Paul II's recommendation that the EU Constitution should refer to Europe's Christian roots.[49]

In the Muslim world, the largely elite-level secularism that emerged by the early twentieth century was not opposed to religion. On the contrary, at least legally religious edicts limited secular governments' freedom of action and even the scope of legislation. When governments acted against these edicts, they often faced opposition and dissent from both the people and religious establishments. Thus Muslim countries' secularism has always been limited, even when staunchly secularizing leaders have been in power.[50] Today, this situation is reflected in the fact that, in virtually all countries that are majority Muslim, Islam is the official religion. Until the last decade, Turkey was viewed as the only example of French-style secularism in a predominantly Muslim country. However, beginning in the 1940s, Turkish secularism has undergone a gradual process of dilution. Since the coming to power of the Justice and Development Party (*Adalat Va Kalkinma Partisi*-AKP) in 2003, Turkish secularism has further eroded and the rights of religiously observant peoples have been highlighted. Currently, Turkey is a secular country in the sense that power cannot be justified in terms of religion and Muslim organizations legally cannot demand special privileges in the political arena because of religious considerations.[51] In other Muslim countries, too, with the exception of Iran and Saudi Arabia, political power is in reality secular in the sense that political leaders are not hemmed in by religion or by religious establishments. In some countries, such as Egypt, Jordan, and Morocco, among others, certain political expressions of religion are actively suppressed. Yet at the same time, they cannot be characterized as completely secular. In these countries, the principle of separation of religion and politics and government and religious establishments is not clearly, legally, and unequivocally established. On the contrary, even in countries whose political leaders oppose the intermingling of religion and politics, because of society's religiosity their constitutions cite Islamic law and jurisprudence as the principal or at least one of the sources of legislation.

In short, since the erosion of religion's centrality in people's collective lives and the consequent rise of secularism, there have always been various gradations and types of secularism. However, the term "multiple secularisms" is as newly coined as is that of "multiple modernities." The term, moreover, is not an accurate description of prevailing conditions. While secularism is a single phenomenon, it appears in different shades and types. A better way of distinguishing among various forms of secularism is to recognize the existence of legal and actual, and elite and mass, secularisms. In Western countries, secularism is both legal and actual, and it largely prevails both at the elite and mass levels. In the Muslim world, however, secularism is only actual and not legal and exists mostly at the elite level. Meanwhile, because the populations of Muslim states are still quite religious, even secular governments have to be mindful of their people's religious sensitivities and to factor them into their political calculations and actions, including in the realm of foreign policy.

Finally, secularization of politics and government has not ended religion's influence in societies and hence also on states in their political manifestation. By virtue of its function as the legitimizer of power, secularization has only ended religion's hegemony of discourse, its monopoly over different societies' lives and its domination over politics and governments. Consequently, religion has become one of many ideas competing in the public sphere for adherents and supporters. In the meantime, by being turned into a political ideology in some instances, religion has become secularized by losing its purely theological/spiritual dimension.

Ideologized religions have had the greatest impact on various countries' internal political developments. In some instances, such religions have produced changes in some countries' political structures. For example, Shariati's ideologized and revolutionized version of Islam, which was inspired by Marxism, rather than Khomeini's theological and clerical Islam, acted as the inspiration for Iran's Islamic Revolution. It was Shariati's discourse which popularized the concept of revolution and not that of Ayatullah Rouhollah Khomeini, although the latter became the symbol of the Iranian Revolution. The impact of Shariati's ideologized Islam on Iran's post-revolution external behavior has also been greater than that of theological Islam.[52] Similarly, the Saudi government's use of the Wahhabi version of Islam as state ideology and as the basis of the ruling family's legitimacy has made it influential both in the Kingdom's life and in the formation of its foreign policy. In sum, it has been the transformation of religion from a spiritual creed and a cultural phenomenon into ideology that has most impacted the dynamics of international relations.

RELIGION AS MOTIVATION, JUSTIFICATION, AND INSTRUMENT OF POLICY

Religion can and does perform multiple functions as both motivation behind policy and as an instrument of its implementation. In this respect, it is similar to other value and ideational systems. This dual aspect of religion's functions has not been adequately analyzed in the existing literature. The question whether religion's role is more important as an instrument of policy or as a motivation for behavior has also been left largely unanswered. Yet like other value and ideational systems, rather than determining policy and behavior, religion often justifies and legitimizes them. Moreover, often it is used as an instrument to advance policy objectives primarily determined by other and more worldly considerations.

This tension between religion's diverse functions existed even in those eras when it dominated all aspects of life. Historians have pondered the extent to which the Crusades were motivated by the religious beliefs of the parties involved and to what degree by their appetite for conquest, riches, and glory, with religion used primarily to garner support for these essentially worldly adventures.[53] The same could be said of the Muslim armies that conquered vast lands and destroyed large empires. Were they moved by a desire to spread Islam or were they motivated mainly by the lure of vast riches and war booty (*Ghanima*)?

In short, it is important to differentiate between religion's dual functions in order to make an accurate assessment of its impact. Viewed in this light, discussions regarding religion's role become similar to debates on the relative roles of power/interest on the one hand, and ideology/value and ideational systems on the other in shaping international actors' behavior and, hence, also the character of international relations. These debates also echo similar discussions regarding tensions between the pursuit of interests versus ideals. Scholars of international relations and foreign policy remain divided on the relative roles of power and interest versus ideas/values/ideology as the principal motivator of various actors' behavior. In all likelihood, similar debates on religion's impact would also remain inconclusive. Nevertheless, such debate could help clarify religion's role in international affairs, as similar discussions have helped elucidate the relative role of other ideologies and value systems.

CHANNELS FOR TRANSMISSION OF RELIGION'S INFLUENCE

It is also necessary to identify and study the channels through which ideals, values, ideology, and religion influence international actors' behavior. A single broad theory of international relations cannot accomplish this task because various theoretical schools tend to emphasize a particular set of factors such as power and security, ideas/ideology, or those related to the structure of the international system. A more appropriate approach should draw on insights from different theoretical schools and focus on analysis of processes through which various influences, including that of religion, are brought to bear on international actors. An important element of this approach is the study and analysis of the characteristics of the internal and external contexts within which various actors operate, interactions between the two, and their combined impact on behavior. The study of the internal setting of decision-making will shed light on the main channels of transmission of ideational influences, including religion. For example, in an authoritarian country, the ideological and ideational proclivities, including religious, of the leader or of a particular institution, such as the military, will constitute the principal channel for the transmission of such influences. By contrast, in a democratic system, the principal channels for the transmission of ideational and religious influences are the relative popularity of various ideas and values, including religion, the comparative strength of political parties and civic organizations embracing them, and their ability to influence the outcome of domestic elections.

DIFFERENTIATING THE IMPACT OF RELIGION ON DIFFERENT INTERNATIONAL ACTORS

International actors constitute a wide range with diverse organizations and objectives. It is thus important to determine whether religion affects them all in the same way and to the same extent, or whether its influence on different types of actors varies. For example, are state and non-state actors equally susceptible to religion's influence? Which type of non-state actors are most likely to be influenced by religion? How does religion affect the behavior of some inter-governmental organizations as a category of international actors? Are violent non-state actors more susceptible to religion's impact? Answering these questions is important because any idea or belief system, including religion, exerts its influence through various agents, and it is through the agency of actors that their influence is apprehended.

RELIGION AND INTERNATIONAL RELATIONS THEORY

Some scholars have attributed the relative neglect of religion's role in international affairs in the past to the inadequacies of existing principal theoretical schools of international relations. According to Jack Snyder, "The foundational statements of the three leading paradigms—Kenneth Waltz for Realism, Michael Doyle and Robert Keohane for Liberalism, and Alexander Wendt for Constructivism—offer no explicit guidance on how to do this [factor in the religion variable]."[54] Certainly, so far, none of the principal theoretical schools of international relations have specifically addressed religion's role, and other theoretical disciplines, such as foreign policy analysis, have also failed to incorporate religion as a separate factor.

As noted earlier, several factors, including the excessive influence of the modernization theory in political science studies, plus the gradual decline of religion's role in the past few hundred years as an influential determinant of international actors' behavior compared to other factors such as power, security, and ideology, contributed to the neglect of religion's role in the study of international affairs. Another contributing factor has been the difficulty of accounting separately for every single ideational/value-related motivation behind actors' behavior. For instance, it is difficult accurately to estimate the extent to which a particular actor's behavior is determined by nationalism, political ideology, some other ideational system, or religion, because all these influences operate on actors and influence their behavior.

Although they do not directly address the question of religion's role in international affairs, all theoretical schools of international relations, including the realist school, have dealt with the role of ideational factors as part of the determinants of international actors' behavior. For example, Hans Morgenthau, one of the most prominent representatives of the realist school characterized by its emphasis on the role of power as the main driver of international relations, also acknowledged the close relationship between ideology and power. He recognized the connection between ideology which he defined broadly as "a system of thought which rationalizes or justifies a particular social position," and political reality.[55] Religion stripped of its divine and spiritual aspect fits this definition. Moreover, the pursuit of power needs the support of an ideological or value/ideational system because it often requires popular backing and even sacrifice. Therefore, the pursuit of power nearly always must be justified in terms of some higher values rooted either in a specific political ideology or in a society's traditional values and culture.

Even in internal political contests for power, rivals justify their pursuit of power in terms of higher ideals. In other words, power has always needed the cover of ideals. Historically, religion was the highest of such ideals and thus proved a most effective instrument for mobilizing popular support and eliciting sacrifice for actions essentially determined by considerations of power and other material interests. It still performs the same functions in some parts of the world.

In short, international actors' behavior has always been determined by a close interplay between power and idea-based impulses. By analyzing this interaction, international relations theories have addressed religion's role at least indirectly. Moreover, some more recently developed theories of international relations, especially constructivism, heavily emphasize the role of ideas and norms in the processes that they characterize as the social construction of external realities. They also consider identities, which they believe are largely socially constructed, as having significant influence on various actors' behavior.[56] Because religion is clearly one of the most important and the oldest of social norms and constitutes a major component of individual and collective identities, a theory such as constructivism can accommodate religion in any study of its role in international affairs.

Recently, some scholars have approached this issue more systematically and have attempted to show how the study of religion's role in international relations can be accomplished within the existing theoretical schools. For example, Nukhet A. Sandal and Jonathan Fox, in their book *Religion in International Relations Theory*,[57] convincingly demonstrate how this goal can be achieved. In their view, even classical realism can accommodate the study of religion's impact if power is defined in a more flexible fashion. In this sense, in the context of the realist school "religion may be seen as a form of social power that brings people together for a certain cause."[58] This fits the notion promoted by the realist school that the pursuit of power is not possible without the use of ideas because such a pursuit requires popular support which can only be mobilized by the use of ideas and ideals. The English School of international relations, with its inclusion of diplomatic culture as part of determinants of the behavior of state actors, can also accommodate religion's study because various diplomatic cultures are the product of "interactions among different faith traditions."[59]

THE THEORETICAL AND METHODOLOGICAL FRAMEWORK

The foregoing discussion has shown that what some scholars have characterized as the secular bias of the international relations discipline has in effect been a reflection of existing realities, although some of these realities have undergone changes in the last three decades. Therefore, the neglect of religion's role in international affairs cannot be attributed to the discipline's secular bias. Moreover, it has shown that existing theories of international relations, or better yet a combination of them, provide adequate tools for the study of religion's role in international affairs, partly because the issues surrounding religion's impact on international actors' behavior are similar to debates on the relative roles of ideology/ideas/ideals versus power and interests. These similarities have increased because religions increasingly have become ideologized and in the process have lost many of their divine/spiritual dimensions. Thus they can and should be treated as part of other value/ideational determinants of international actors' behavior.

In light of these observations, the best way to analyze and assess religion's role is to focus on specific cases and to use the tools applied to the study of decision-making processes. Although general theories can supply guidelines for understanding fundamental dynamics of international relations, they cannot adequately explain specific cases of behavior. In general, applying theoretical tools should be accompanied by observation, interpretation, and analysis of actual events. A foreign policy analysis approach is also better suited for assessing the relative impact of various factors in specific cases and for clarifying interactions between the internal and external settings of foreign policy-making. Certain theses elaborated in this study are close to modified realism as defined by Sandal and Fox and to neo-liberalism, which does not view power solely in military terms. These theses include assuming the continued centrality of state actors, despite some erosion in their power, especially in the case of weak states, plus the continued importance of power, interest, and security in determining actors' behavior. The influence of the constructivist school is reflected in the emphasis on the roles of identity, world-view, and ideals in shaping international actors' views of their security and interests and threats to them, plus focusing on the interactions among these diverse and sometimes conflicting ideas and identities and how they affect the transformation and/or reconstruction of values and identities of various actors.

Within this overall framework, this study will focus on the following areas:

1. *Identifying Principal Agents.* The study will establish the range of state and non-state international actors and will assess their relative position within the current international system. It will question the validity of the thesis of nation-states' irrelevance. It will ask whether all states' positions as principal international actors have been eroded to the same degree, or whether only the weaker states have succumbed to forces corrosive of their power. It will analyze and assess non-state actors' roles in shaping the dynamics of international relations. It will ask how independent of states these non-state actors are.
2. *Identifying Principal Determinants of International Actors' Behavior.* The study will establish the factors which shape international actors' behavior and will assess their relative influence.
3. *Specific Case Studies.* The study will focus on three specific cases and will demonstrate how various factors interact and ultimately determine international actors' behavior. In the context of these case studies, this work will analyze religion's role as both motivator of behavior, through its function as part of national and, in the case of non-state actors, group identities, and as part of their value/ideational systems. It will thus assess religion's role as a determinant of behavior in comparison to other factors.

The case studies are chosen carefully so as to include different religions. The study of Russian policy toward the Bosnian War will analyze the impact of Orthodox Christianity on Russia's approach, while the chapter dealing with Turkish policy toward this war will discuss Islam's influence on Turkish policies. The chapter dealing with the question of Turkish membership in the European Union will address and assess religion's role in the EU's approach toward Turkish membership, in light of it being an inter-governmental regional organization, whose membership consists of countries where Protestant and Catholic Christianity predominate. (The impact of Turkish religious debates and developments on its EU membership considerations will also be considered.) The findings of these case studies will contribute to a better understanding and assessment of religion's role in determining international actors' behavior and hence in shaping the character of international relations. These case studies were chosen because they posed most clearly the dilemmas inherent in responding to demands of security, interests, pressures of internal and external contexts of policy, and demands of identity-related and cultural and religious factors.

Finally, the concluding section will offer some thoughts on when and under what circumstances religion's impact is strongest; what the channels are through which this influence is most effectively transmitted; and which actors are most likely to be affected by it and under what circumstances.

NOTES

1. Even during the Soviet era, traditional values and religions had not disappeared. They had only become submerged by the official discourse of socialism.
2. Samuel P. Huntington, "The Clash of Civilizations," *Foreign Affairs*, Summer 1993. Also, *The Clash of Civilizations and the Remaking of the World Order* (New York: Touchstone, 1997).
3. Bernard Lewis, "The Roots of Muslim Rage," *The Atlantic*, 1990.
4. These troops were moved into Saudi Arabia in order to prevent a potential attack by Saddam Hussein on the Kingdom in the context of Operation Desert Shield. But Bin Laden and many Muslims believed that non-Muslims should not enter the Kingdom.
5. Laurie Mylroie, "The Saddam-9/11 Link Confirmed," *FRONTPAGEMAGAZINE.Com*, 11 May, 2004, at: http://www.archive.frontpagemag.com/readArticle.aspx?ARTID=13077.
6. Jeffrey Smith, "Hussein's Prewar Ties to Al Qaeda Discounted," *Washington Post*, 6 April 2007.
7. According to some sources, Deputy Secretary of Defense Paul Wolfowitz was one such official. See Ralph G. Carter (ed.), *Contemporary Cases in US Foreign Policy: From Terrorism to Trade* (Washington, DC: CQ Press, 2011), 73.
8. Shireen T. Hunter, "The Regional and International Politics of Rising Sectarian Tensions in the Middle East and South Asia," *ACMCU Occasional Paper*, July 2013.
9. IS was originally known as ISIL and stood for The Islamic State of Iraq and the Levant, and later was called ISIS (Islamic State of Iraq and Sham/Levant) and finally IS.
10. The term Islamo-fascism was first used by President George W. Bush after 9/11. Then, Senator John McCain said that the United States will be engaged in a war with Islamo-fascism at least for a hundred years. See Stephen Schwartz, "What Is Islamofascism?" *The Weekly Standard*, 17 August, 2006, at: http://www.weeklystandard.com/print/Content/Public/Articles/000/000/012/593ajdua.asp;also, Christopher Hitchens, "Defending Islamofascism," *Slate*, 27 October, 2007, at: http://www.slate.com/articles/newsadn- politics/fighting_words/2007/10/defending_islamofascism.html; also, Helen Thomas, "McCain Foresees 100-Year War," *The-BostonChannel.com*, 13 February 2008, at: http://www.freerepublic.com/focus/news/1972773/posts.
11. Elizabeth Shakman Hurd, *The Politics of Secularism in International Politics* (Princeton: Princeton University Press, 2008).
12. For a full explanation of his ideas see Scott M. Thomas, *The Global Resurgence of Religion and the Transformation of International Relations* (New York: Palgrave Macmillan, 2005).
13. See, for example: Timothy Samuel Shah & Daniel Philpot, "The Fall and Rise of Religion in International Relations," in ed. Jack Snyder, *Religion and International Relations Theory* (New York: Columbia University, 2011), 24–59.
14. A good example of such works is the study produced by the *Transatlantic Academy* in 2015, entitled "Faith, Freedom and Foreign Policy: Challenges to Transatlantic Community."

15. Daniel Lerner, *The Passing of Traditional Society: Modernizing the Middle East* (Glencoe, IL: Free Press, 1958).

16. Walter Z. Laqueur (ed.), *The Middle East in Transition* (New York: Fredrick A. Praeger, 1958).

17. For a full discussion see Thomas, *The Global Resurgence of Religion*, 47–52.

18. The United States also where possible fostered nationalism in Central and Eastern Europe for geopolitical ends.

19. This was even the case during the Afghan-Soviet war to some degree. For example, Iran supported Afghanistan's Shias and later the alliance of the Shias and the Persian-speaking Tajiks, while Pakistan and Saudi Arabia supported the Sunni-Pashtuns.

20. This narrative has in recent years been challenged by some scholars. see Thomas, *The Global Resurgence of Religion*, 53.

21. Geertz defines religion in the following ways: "A religion is a system of symbols which acts to establish powerful, pervasive, and long-lasting moods and motivations in men formulating conceptions of a general order of existence and clothing these conceptions with such an aura of factuality that moods and motivations seem uniquely realistic." Clifford Geertz, *The Interpretation of Cultures* (New York: Basic Books, 1973), 90.

22. See http://www.age-of-the-sage.org/quotations/marx_opium_people.html.

23. Elizabeth Shakman Hurd is one such scholar. See "Secularism and International Relations Theory," in *Religion and International Relations Theory*, 60–90.

24. See L. Scott, Smith, "What Is Faith: An Analysis of Tillich's Ultimate Faith," *Quodlibet Journal*, 5, 4, October 2003, at: http://www.quodlibetjournal.net/articles/smith-tillich.shtml.

25. *Dictionary.com*, at: http://dictionary.reference.com/browse/religion.

26. *Collins English Dictionary*, at: http://www.collinsdictionary.com/dictionary/english/religion.

27. For a more detailed analysis of these issues, see among others: Thomas A. Idinopulos & Brian Courtney Wilson, *What Is Religion: Origins, Definitions and Explanations* (Champaign, IL: Human Kinetic Books, 1998). Also, Peter L. Berger, *Sacred Canopy: Elements of a Sociological Theory of Religion* (New York: Anchor Books, 1990); and M. E. Spiro, *Anthropological Approaches to the Study of Religion* (London: Tavistock Publications, 1978).

28. *Dictionary.com*, Idinopulos and Wilson, *What Is Religion*.

29. See Shireen T. Hunter, "Islamic Reformist Discourse in Iran: Proponents and Prospects," in ed. Shireen T. Hunter, *Reformist Voices of Islam: Mediating Islam and Modernity* (Armonk, NY: M. E. Sharpe, 2008) 52.

30. Hassan Hanafi, the Egyptian scholar, is a principal representative of the Islamic Left in Egypt.

31. Hunter, "Islamic Reformist Discourse in Iran," 52.

32. On the origins and development of Liberation Theology, see Gustavo Gutierrez, *Liberation Theology* (English translation), (Mary Knoll, New York: Orbis Books, 1973). Also "Liberation Theology and Struggle for Socialism," at: http://windinthetower.wordpress.com/liberation-theology-and-struggle-for-socialism/

33. See Michael Iafrate, "Pope Benedict on Liberation Theology . . . Again," *Vox Nova*, 21 December 2009.

34. Many prominent clergy in Iran, notably Ayatullah Murteza Mutahari, a close confidant of Ayatullah Khomeini, did not approve of Shariati's views based on a synthesis of Islam and Marxism.

35. *Merriam-Webster Dictionary*, at: http://www.merriam.webster.com/dictionary/secular.

36. *Oxford English Dictionary*, at: http://www.oxforddictionaries.com/us/definition/american_english/secular.

37. See Will Durant, *The Age of Faith, the Story of Civilization*, Vol. IV (New York: Simon & Schuster, 1950).

38. Max Weber, *The Sociology of Religion* (5th edition), (Boston: Beacon Press, 1969).

39. According to a report published in 2011, religion may become extinct in eight countries, namely, Australia, Austria, Canada, the Czech Republic, Finland, Ireland, the Netherlands, New Zealand, and Switzerland. See Jason Palmer, "Religion May Become Extinct in Nine

Nations, Study Says." *The BBC*, 22 March 2011, available at: http://www.bbc.com/news/science-environment-12811197.

40. For a discussion of this issue, see Shireen T. Hunter, *Iran Divided: The Historical Roots of Iranian Debates on Identity, Culture and Governance in the 21st Century* (Lanham, MD: Rowman & Littlefield, 2014).

41. There remain major exceptions, especially in the last of the rigid communist systems, North Korea; while China, which is Westernized in many respects, still faces major societal and political tensions over the extent to which religion is to be tolerated. Both Cuba and Vietnam have been coming to terms with a duality of communism and acceptance of religious belief and practice.

42. Emmett Kennedy, *Secularism and Its Opponents: From Augustine to Solzhenitsyn* (New York: Palgrave Macmillan, 2006), 1.

43. See Nazih Ayubi, *Political Islam: Religion and Politics in the Arab World* (New York: Routledge, 1991).

44. For an excellent discussion of these issues, see: Kennedy, *Secularism and Its Opponents*, also Tamara Sonn, "Islam and Modernity: Are They Compatible?" in eds. Shireen T. Hunter & Huma Malik, *Modernization, Democracy and Islam* (Westport, CT: Praeger, 2005).

45. The beginning of the Reformation is generally dated to 1517 and the publication of Martin Luther's ninety-five theses. However, its completion took nearly a hundred years. See Euan Cameron, *The European Reformation* (2nd) edition, (Oxford: Oxford University Press, 2012).

46. Cameron, *The European Reformation*. However, some scholars maintain that, initially, the Protestant Reformation created greater linkage between religion and state as most protestant-inhabited lands came under the rule of protestant princes and kings. See Daniel Nexon, "Religion, European Identity and Political Contention in Historical Perspective," in eds. Timothy A. Byrnes and Peter J. Katzenstein, *Religion in an Expanding Europe* (Cambridge: Cambridge University Press, 2006), 257.

47. Kennedy, *Secularism and Its Opponents*, 93–95.

48. Some scholars such as Peter Berger have characterized this trend as the de-secularization of the world. See *Desecularization of the World: Resurgent Religion and World Politics* (Grand Rapids, MI: Eerdmans, 1997).

49. Jason Horowitz, "Europe Seeking Unity Stumbles over Issue of Religion," *New York Times*, 7 November 2004, at: http://www.nytimes.com/2004/11/07/international/Europe/07italy.html?_e=0.

50. Examples include Atatürk in Turkey, Reza Shah in Iran, Habib Bourghiba in Tunisia, Nasser in Egypt and the Baathist governments of Saddam Hussein and Hafiz al Assad.

51. However, politicians do sometimes resort to religion to prove their fitness for office. For example, in the 2015 parliamentary elections Recep Tayyip Erdoğan reportedly used a Qur'an and said that he was brought up according to its teaching whereas his opponents were not. Arid Takdel, "Erdoğan Exploits Religious Symbols, Uses Quran as prop in Election Rallies," *Today's Zaman*, 9 May 2015, at: http://www.todayszaman.com/anasayfa_erdogan-exploits-religious-symbols-uses-quran-as-prop-in-election- rallies_38022.html.

52. Shariati's world-view is strongly permeated by Marxist concept, thus giving it a strongly anti-capitalist and anti-Western tinge. See "Reformist Discourse in Iran: Proponents and Prospects," 53.

53. See Christopher Tyerman, *The Crusades* (New York: Sterling Publishing Company, 2007); also, G. Vicari Jr. "The Secular Motivations of the First Crusade," 2 April 2001, at: http://www.medievalists.net/2011/07/25/the-secular-motivations-of-the-first-crusade/.

54. Jack Snyder, "Introduction," in *Religion and International Relations Theory*, 1.

55. Hans J. Morgenthau, "The Organic Relationship between Ideology and Political Reality," in George Schwab (ed.), *Ideology and Foreign Policy: A Global Perspective* (New York: Cyro Press, 1978), 117.

56. On the centrality of the identity in the Constructivist school, see Stefano Guzzini, "A Reconstruction of Constructivism in International Relations," *The European Journal of International Affairs*, 6. 2 (2000).

57. Nukhet A. Sandal and Jonathan Fox, *Religion in International Relations Theory* (London: Routledge, 2013).
58. Sandal and Fox, *Religion in International Relations Theory*, 175.
59. Sandal and Fox, *Religion in International Relations Theory*, 175–76.

Chapter One

The Range and Characteristics of International Actors

Assessing religion's impact on international affairs can only be done by first evaluating its influence on the behavior of international actors. This requires that the range and characteristics of international actors be identified, and their relative weight and influence within the international system and, hence, their comparative role in shaping the dynamics of international relations be evaluated. For example, it is important to determine whether nation-states are still the principal actors within the international system, or whether their centrality in the system has been irremediably eroded, thus making non-state actors more influential and therefore also transforming the very nature of international relations. Only after answering these questions would it be possible to evaluate the relative impact of principal determinants of international actors' behavior, including that of religion.

In short, assessing religion's impact on international affairs requires that the question of *agency* first be settled.

THE EVOLUTION OF THE INTERNATIONAL SYSTEM AND ITS ACTORS

In the course of more than three centuries that has elapsed since the time when the notion of a modern international system first emerged following the signing of the Treaty of Westphalia in 1648, the range and characteristics of international actors and thus the nature of the international system and the character of international relations have undergone significant transformation.[1] The international system which took shape at Westphalia had three principal characteristics: 1) it was limited to Europe; 2) it was state-centered;

and 3) it reflected Europe's new realities in the aftermath of the Thirty Years War (1618–1648).

In this new Europe, the nation-state emerged as the main political and territorial unit and the principal component of the emerging international system. The concept of nation-state implied a greater coincidence of ethnic, cultural, and political boundaries, although, in reality, many European states remained as multi-ethnic empires. These included Russia, the Austria-Hungarian Empire, and the Ottoman Empire after it was admitted to the Europe-centered international system.

Over the next three centuries, the Europe-centered international system expanded and incorporated non-European peoples and countries. The globalization of the system was first prompted by the expansion of European colonial empires in Asia, Africa, and the Americas, and later by the process of decolonization. The first significant non-European country to join the system was the United States of America following the successful completion of its revolutionary war of independence. However, until the end of World War II, the international system was still West-centered. It was only after the breakup of the European empires, the emergence of new states in Africa and Asia, and their incorporation in the international system that it became truly global. Joining the international system required that the newcomers accept its norms and principles, which were essentially based on European concepts and traditions. Therefore, these norms were also universalized.[2]

The nation-state has remained the main unit of the international system, although by the mid-nineteenth century other types of international actors had appeared. Today, they are referred to as "non-state actors." These non-state actors cover a wide range and include inter-governmental international and regional organizations, businesses operating across national borders, known as trans-national or multi-national corporations, and non-governmental organizations (NGOs). The latest category of non-state actors is the violent group, some of which have semi or para-statal structures.[3]

The emergence of new actors resulted from the expansion of international relations and their growing complexities, which required more efficient management and necessitated the establishment of new institutions. The expansion of international communications led to the creation of the Universal Postal Union (UPU) and increased maritime trade and travel resulted in establishment of the International Maritime Organization (IMO). Other specialized agencies were created by the Treaty of Versailles in 1919 in the aftermath of World War I, which also established the League of Nations. The United Nations, which replaced the League of Nations in 1945 after the end of World War II, added to the number and range of specialized organizations.[4]

The horrendous human and material costs exacted by the two world wars served as the main impetus behind the creation of both the League of Nations and the United Nations. The main goal of both institutions was to prevent other devastating wars through establishing the rule of law in international affairs and providing mechanisms for the peaceful settlement of international disputes, in part by curbing the expansionist impulses of larger and more powerful states. The League of Nations failed to prevent World War II. The United Nations, too, has not been able to prevent large-scale wars in different parts of the globe, and the rule of law in international relations is at best very fragile. Other institutions with similar objectives were created at regional levels; their numbers increased after the end of World War II as new independent states emerged in Asia and Africa.

The membership of both functional and security-related international and regional organizations consists of states, and therefore, they are called Inter-Governmental Organizations (IGOs). Because of the government-based nature of these institutions, some observers have questioned whether IGOs should be included in the category of non-state actors. However, because they are not states and their identity is separate from those of their constituent members, they are generally characterized as non-state actors.

Multinational and transnational corporations were a response to the expansion of global international trade and economic relations, which ensued from the accelerated rate of Europe's and America's industrialization in the nineteenth and twentieth centuries, thus increasing Europe's and eventually America's need for new sources of raw materials and export markets. The handling of the increased volume of international trade and the satisfaction of the growing need for sources of supply and export markets necessitated the establishment of large organizations capable of operating internationally and, later, globally.

The anti-colonial and independence-seeking movements which emerged in Asia and Africa following the end of the world wars added another category to the range of non-state actors. These movements mostly operated in a single country, but their actions were directed against other states, the colonial powers, and at times they received assistance from other states. Therefore, their activities had international ramifications. Some of them engaged in violent acts, which today are generally, but sometimes erroneously, referred to as terrorism.[5]

HAS THE NATION-STATE BECOME OBSOLETE?

By the late 1960s and early 1970s, the appearance of these non-state actors generated the impression that the centrality of states as the main international actors had been severely eroded. As a result, some scholars questioned the position of nation-states as the principal units of the international system and its main actors and, therefore, the continued validity of state-centric analysis of international relations. Stanley Hoffmann wrote one of the earliest articles on the topic: "Obstinate or Obsolete? The Fate of the Nation-State and the Case of Western Europe."[6]

Some scholars concurred with the thesis of states' increasing irrelevance and the outmodedness of a state-centric analysis of international relations. They suggested that new concepts should replace the state-centric model and new methods of analysis which they believed were better suited to new realities of international life. For example, Joseph Nye and Robert Keohane advanced the concept of "complex interdependence" as an appropriate replacement.[7] Others recommended that "as the world has grown smaller, the mutual dependence of nation-states and other trans-national political actors has grown,"[8] and thus the term "transnational system" should henceforth be used to explain the existing state of affairs.[9]

In the following decades, the trend continued toward the emergence of new types of non-state actors, especially of the more violent variety. Notable examples have been the Lebanon-based Hizbullah, which appeared in the 1980s, and the Afghanistan-based Taliban, which emerged in the 1990s. The latest to appear is the Islamic State (IS) in 2014. At first, it operated mainly in Syria and Iraq, but by mid-2015 it had expanded its operations to South Asia, North and Central Africa, the Russian Federation, especially the North Caucasus, and even engaged in terror acts in Western Europe.[10]

These non-state actors have more complex structures than regular terrorist groups and can be characterized as para- or semi-statal. Other groups, such as *Al Qaeda*, with branches in the Middle East and North Africa, and the Nigerian group *Boko Haram* fall more into the category of traditional terrorist groups. Because the larger violent non-state actors with complex structures justify their actions and define their goals in religious terms, although often other factors have more impact on their behavior, they are especially important from the perspective of this study.

The appearance of violent non-state actors added new complexities to international relations and gave greater credence to the view that the state-centric understanding of international relations is insufficient or even obsolete. In other words, the idea that the role of the nation-state has been eroded was transformed into the thesis that it has become obsolete. Proponents of this thesis maintain that because of the rise of violent non-state actors and the emergence of multinational corporations, states' ability to control their territory, to establish security, and to manage their economies has been severely undermined[11] thus eroding their sovereignty and their capacity to determine their own destinies. The failure of many post-colonial states to consolidate their statehood and to develop viable political and economic structures, their entanglement in civil wars and other forms of strife, and their vulnerability to internal and external challenges to their authority further contributed to the popularity of the thesis of nation states' obsolescence. The emergence of the globalization phenomenon in the post-Soviet era was seen as another challenge to the nation state and its continued relevance. In a globalized world, it is argued, predatory market forces prevent national governments from shielding their economies from forces beyond their control, which, in turn, undermines an important function of the nation-state, namely to ensure its people's economic well-being.[12] Meanwhile, ease of communications renders nation-states more permeable to forces beyond their control and can affect their ability to provide for national security and discharge some other key functions.

THE RESILIENCE OF STATES AND THE STATE-CENTRIC INTERNATIONAL SYSTEM

Despite the emergence of many challengers to its power, the nation-states, "often inchoate, economically absurd, administratively ramshackle, and impotent and yet dangerous, remain the basic unit despite all the remonstrations and exhortations." A main reason for states' longevity has been that, as pointed out by Auguste Comte, "One cannot destroy something unless one can replace it."[13] This conclusion by Stanley Hoffmann fifty years ago is still valid today. Neither international organizations nor the multinational corporations and a variety of violent non-state actors have been able to replace states. The process of globalization also has so far failed to render the nation-state obsolete. On the contrary, as put by Martin Wolf, for people to benefit from globalization, "they need states at both ends of their transactions."[14]

STATES AND SUPRANATIONAL ORGANIZATIONS

Supranational inter-governmental institutions (IGOs) of either an international or regional variety are the oldest category of non-state actors. They are created by states through treaties and generally reflect the ideas, preferences, and objectives of more powerful states. As such, the IGOs are not substitutes for states but rather complement them and enable them to achieve goals which they cannot obtain individually. At their best, the IGOs help reduce inter-state tensions and provide venues and mechanisms for cooperation, communication, and the peaceful settlement of disputes, as well as in dealing with a whole range of economic, health, and other challenges.[15] They influence states' behavior through a complex interplay of inducements and disincentives and thus also shape the dynamics of international relations. Decisions within IGOs are made by their member states through negotiations, compromises, and voting. The IGOs, however, lack the means of forcing states to join them or preventing them from leaving. However, leaving certain IGOs, such as the United Nations or its specialized agencies has tangible and intangible costs for states, which in reality limits their ability to abandon their membership.

IGOs can be differentiated from one another on the basis of either their geographical scope or their function. Geographically, they are divided into international and regional organizations. The most important international organization in terms of membership and the geographical scope of its mandate is the United Nations. Prominent regional organizations include the European Union (EU),[16] the Organization of African Unity (OAU), the Organization of American States (OAS), the North Atlantic Treaty Organization (NATO),[17] and the Organization of Islamic Cooperation (OIC). Major functional institutions include those connected with the UN, such as the World Health Organization (WHO) and the International Labor Organization (ILO). Other important functional organizations not connected with the UN are the International Bank for Reconstruction and Development (IBRD/World Bank) and the International Monetary Fund (IMF).

As a general rule, functional organizations operating at the global level and those dealing with economic issues have been relatively more successful in achieving their goals than those dealing with security and political issues.[18] The IGOs, generally but not always, have more influence over weaker states than on the major economic and political powers. However, even the strongest powers cannot be oblivious to their influence.[19]

The emergence of international IGOs such as the United Nations and a variety of specialized agencies has not undermined the role of states because, in reality, these organizations have no independent existence outside of their members.[20] In joining international organizations, states have to accept certain conditions and to adhere to the charters of these organizations, which lay out the rights and duties of member states. However, in its essentials this is similar to individuals agreeing to observe the rules of a club they wish to join. International organizations may refuse membership to certain states, but as noted before, there is no way they can force them to become members. Similarly, the option of leaving an organization is open to states, although the cost of withdrawal at times might be prohibitive.

International organizations, including the UN, are also incapable of enforcing their decisions on recalcitrant states. For instance, the United Nations neither has a police nor a military force[21] although, when it takes decisions under Chapter VII of the UN Charter, it has organized many peacekeeping forces, based on contribution of fighters and equipment from member states.[22] Therefore, especially if they are big and strong enough, states often defy the UN's decisions, including those of its Security Council. If there is a price to be paid by a state because of some wrongdoing, it is often exacted by one or several members of the organization, with or without the consensus of members or even by the explicit permission of the organization. For example, the United States attacked Iraq in March 2003 without the specific permission of the Security Council. It argued that UN Security Council Resolution (UNSCR) 1441, which had allowed for inspections in Iraq to determine the existence of weapons of mass destruction (WMD), also allowed for military attack on Iraq. Or more pertinent, even if the UN had prohibited the United States from attacking Iraq, which it could not have done because of America's veto power in the Security Council, it would not have had the ability to enforce its decision. Israel, too, has ignored a number of UN Security Council resolutions without incurring any significant security or economic costs.[23]

These observations illustrate that what has been called the erosion of the role of the nation-state is in reality largely about the inequality of states in terms of their power.[24] Despite the creation of various international institutions to regulate inter-state relations according to law and not force, in the current international system power rather than law ultimately determines the character of inter-state relations. What most deters states from ignoring the rules of even the most important of international organizations is their relative power and hence the degree of their vulnerability to retaliatory measures. The continued importance of power in determining the character of international relations does not mean that even powerful states do not pay a price for ignoring international rules or for acting in their defiance. Nor does it imply that powerful states do not take other factors into consideration. At times they do, especially in terms of the impact that ignoring international norms might have on their prestige and global image or, in some cases, their desire not to set a precedent for ignoring the mandate of an organization whose actions it might wish to call upon on a later occasion. But they often find the price acceptable, especially when they believe that their vital interests are at stake.

In short, international organizations have not replaced states. Nor have they eroded states' centrality as principal actors within the international system. This principle especially applies to the case of economically and militarily more powerful states.

STATES AND REGIONAL ORGANIZATIONS

States also occupy the central place in regional organizations, which are formed by their voluntary coming together. Nevertheless, generally one or two states take the initiative in their creation, as France and Germany did in the case of the European cooperative arrangements which culminated in the European Union.[25] Ironically, the United Kingdom played a critical role in fostering the European Movement in the late 1940s. However, by 1955 when the Treaty of Rome, which created the European Economic Community (EEC), was signed, Britain concluded that the ambitions of the six originating Continental powers in terms of European unity and pooling of aspects of national sovereignty were proceeding beyond what it considered acceptable. Therefore, it took Britain nearly two decades before it joined the EEC.

The degree to which regional organizations can limit their member states' freedom of action often depends on what kind of organization they desire to establish. For instance, if prospective members aim for a tightly knit organization resembling a federation, they would have to cede substantial powers, as is the case with the European Union. By contrast, if they want a looser framework of cooperation, they will cede far less powers to such an organization. Thus far, experience has shown that, with limited exceptions, in general, states are not willing to accept significant limitations on their freedom of action by virtue of their membership in regional organizations especially in areas related to their security. Consequently, decision-making in most regional organizations, especially those dealing with security issues, is based on consensus or requires large rather than simple majority. For example, decisions of the North Atlantic Treaty Organization are taken by consensus and those of the Organization of Security and Cooperation in Europe are taken by consensus minus one member (presumably the target of any action). In the European Union there is a variated system of voting in the sense that some decisions require consensus while others can be reached by majority vote or a form of weighted voting.

This approach to decision making ensures that no organization can impose any important rules and decisions on states without their agreement.[26] States also retain the option of withdrawing from such organizations if they conclude that the balance of benefits and disadvantages of membership does not meet what they perceive to be their needs. A good example is Britain's decision in 2016 to put its continued membership in the EU to a national referendum, known as the Brexit debate.[27] In June 2016, the British people voted in favor of leaving the EU. Moreover, regional organizations, including the most successful of them in terms of some pooling of sovereignty, the European Union, have not been able to replace the nation-state as the focus of identity and loyalty.[28] Nor has a pan-European identity transcending individual national identities yet been developed.[29] The rise of nationalist and often anti-EU parties in a number of European countries in the last decade, as manifested in some of the results in 2014 elections to the European Parliament, has shown the vitality of national identities.[30] These trends were further strengthened in 2015 and 2016, as evidenced by the British vote to withdraw from the EU and the existence of similar tendencies in some other European states.

In summary, regional organization, too, has failed to replace the nation-state, although at times, as with the EU, complete retention of sovereignty can be reduced,[31] and their impact on the international system and relations is also through their member states.

STATES AND TRANSNATIONAL ORGANIZATIONS

Multinational and transnational corporations are another category of non-state actors. These corporations are similar in their nature and operations, while also differing in subtle but important ways.[32] For instance, multinational corporations (MNCs) are registered in one country and have their headquarters there, but they operate in several countries through their subsidiaries. In essence, they are national companies that also operate elsewhere. Transnational corporations (TNCs), by contrast, do not identify with a single state and spread their operations in several countries.

Since the nineteenth century, through their activities in places far away from their home countries, these organizations have played important roles in international affairs. Traditionally, they have been mostly active in places rich with natural resources needed by the growing industries of their home countries and also serving as potential markets for their products. As such, they acted as the European empires' agents and later as instruments of American influence. Increasingly, however, these corporations have pursued their own interests, which sometimes coincide with, but occasionally differ from, those of governments, including those of countries in which they are at least formally based for legal reasons.

From about the 1950s onward, these transnational actors have tried to influence the policies of their governments more systematically and in directions which serve their parochial interests. For example, the Anglo-Persian Oil Company played a role in the British-American 1953 decision to bring down the government of Iran's prime minister, Mohammad Mossadegh, because it was unhappy about his nationalization of Iran's oil industry. The United Fruit Company is believed to have been instrumental in the 1954 U.S.-supported coup d'état against the government of Jacobo Arbenz in Guatemala because it suspected him of having nationalist and/or socialist tendencies, and ITT was implicated in the coup d'état against the Chilean government of Salvador Allende in 1973, for largely similar reasons.[33]

In addition to influencing the policies of the governments of countries in which they are based, the MNCs and the TNCs often also exert considerable influence on the economic and political decision making of the governments of countries in which they operate. In this way, they limit, sometimes severely, their autonomy in economic and political decision making. This function of these corporations has been used by some scholars to argue that, because of their operations, "one of the traditional rationales [ability to decide on economic policy] for modern sovereignty is undermined,"[34] and therefore has made the nation state irrelevant and even obsolete.

Yet despite their increased influence, the MNCs have not replaced states. Their impact on their home countries' policies is undeniable. Yet in all of the cases cited, it is extremely unlikely that, had other real or perceived strategic concerns not been in play, the UK and U.S. governments would have become involved in such operations. In the era being considered here, the most important determining factor in these cases was the Cold War, the perceived threat of Communism and hence that of Soviet influence, rather than the mere economic interests of the companies mentioned. In the context of the Cold War, nationalization of foreign-owned companies was seen as indicating the rise of leftist influence, rather than that of economic nationalism and the desire for autonomy. Nationalist movements were also seen as a challenge to the regional influence of both America and some other Western countries, notably Britain and also France. In short, if such acts did not threaten states' other interests, it is unlikely that they would have been persuaded by the MNCs to act. A more fundamental point is that to obtain their objective these corporations had to enlist the cooperation of states, and could not have achieved their goals on their own.

The multi/trans national companies exert greater influence on the politics and policies of weaker states.[35] Through a variety of means, the more powerful states often manage to prevent the most harmful effects of their activities. Even moderately powerful countries, through their trade and investment policies and other measures, limit the undesirable aspects of these corporations' activities. In weaker states, by contrast, a large multinational company which controls a significant part of the economy can have major and in some cases decisive influence on local politics. The activities of Royal Dutch Shell in Nigeria, for example, are often cited as a case of a company exerting undue influence over a state.[36]

Such influence, coupled with the frequent lack of MNC concern for the broader interests of the countries within which they operate, has generated resentment on the part of the host countries' populations toward them as well as toward their countries of origin.[37] Yet these countries also know that they need the investment and job creation that the MNCs bring.

In the final analysis, however, because the MNCs have to exert their influence through the intermediary of states—by influencing the policies of their home countries or those of countries where they operate—they have not become substitutes for states.

Meanwhile, there are other entities, such as big financial concerns and individual financiers with large resources at their disposal that control global financial flows. These entities are more difficult to control than the MNCs. But they are not totally immune to states' actions. For example, during the Asian financial crisis of 1998, Malaysia managed to avoid its worst effects by imposing exchange controls and preventing large-scale capital flight,[38] while Indonesia failed to take similar measures and suffered large losses.

These observations mean that the impact of the MNCs' activities in determining states' behavior, along with some limits on their freedom of action, need to be analyzed as part of factors that affect states' behavior and hence the character of international relations. The same applies to the consequences of globalization. In general, strong and efficient states can benefit from positive aspects of globalization without suffering excessively from its negative dimensions. However, even in the case of strong states, the benefits of globalization are often distributed in an unequal fashion, and some segments of a society might even incur losses because of it.

NON-GOVERNMENTAL ORGANIZATIONS AND STATES

Non-Governmental Organizations (NGOs) constitute another category of non-state actors. The label "NGO" applies to a wide array of organizations which differ from one another both in their membership and in the field and scope of their activities. The history of the emergence of the NGOs dates from the mid-nineteenth century. The International Committee of the Red Cross (ICRC), established in 1863, was the first important NGO, although it was not known as such at the time. The number and variety of such organizations increased in the following century. After the Soviet Union's collapse, NGOs operating in the former Soviet space and Central Europe burgeoned and became a focus of study and analysis by scholars of international relations.

The growing prominence of the NGOs as international actors has been first due to increased Western, especially American, governmental and private activism in the post-Soviet space. The goal of many of these activities has been to encourage the establishment of democratic governments and market economies. Later, as it had done during the Cold War, the U.S. government fostered NGOs for similar purposes in other parts of the world and at times also as a means of pressure on those governments of which it disapproved. However, the United States is not alone in creating NGOs, nor are all or even most U.S.-sponsored NGOs designed to achieve political or economic objectives. A wide variety of NGOs from other countries, primarily Western, operates in foreign countries, with eleemosynary purposes and usually without specific political objectives beyond generalities like the promotion of good governance and human rights, with "good will" being an intangible benefit.

Defining the NGOs

The first formal reference to NGOs, as such (though not with this term) is found in the United Nations Charter. Article 71 provides a space for those organizations "which are neither governments nor member states," and offers them a consultative status. In 1950, the UN's Economic and Social Council (ECOSOC) defined what came to be known as an NGO as "any international organization that is not founded by an international treaty."[39] However, "precise definitions vary as to what constitutes an NGO and the challenge of analyzing the phenomenon of NGOs remains surprisingly difficult."[40] This difficulty partly derives from the "high degree of flexibility of the NGO as an institutional form."[41] What is clear is that NGOs are not governmental organizations, even if governments benefit, directly or indirectly, from their activities or even are behind their creation.

NGOs vary widely in regard to their size, resources, focus of activity, and geographical scope of their operations. They can be national, if their membership is drawn from one country, or multinational if their membership consists of citizens of several countries or if they operate in more than one country. Their activities include developmental, humanitarian, and charity work, as well as political, social, and environmental activism. They can be secular or religious. Religious NGOs also engage in humanitarian and developmental as well as evangelical activities. The balance between their religious and other activities varies in the case of different groups: some religious NGOs engage mostly in humanitarian and developmental activities and others are more engaged in evangelizing.

In the last several decades, NGOs have become major actors in many areas of international relations. Their activities, including their advocacy function for certain causes and their lobbying of governments and international institutions, can influence the latter's decisions and behavior. Therefore, the NGOs' roles as factors in international relations cannot be ignored. What is more difficult to prove is the claim that their emergence has significantly undermined the state's centrality as the principal actor within the international system.

A closer examination of NGOs' structures, the sources of their financial resources, and the nature of their relations with states, both at home and abroad, shows that not only have they not replaced states, but that their functioning often depends on state support. For example, many NGOs, especially those operating in developing countries, depend on financial and other support from either Western governments or Western private sources. This is especially true of those NGOs which engage in social and political activism. They often oppose the existing governments of their own countries, which themselves are frequently also at odds with Western governments. As such, these NGOs promote the policy objectives of their sponsors. Some, which mushroomed in the countries of the post-Soviet space, were funded by groups like George Soros's Open Society Foundations or by institutions funded by Western governments, in whole or in part, such as the United States' National Endowment for Democracy and the German *Stiftungen,* both of which antedated the end of the Cold War, although at the time their operations were limited in scope to communist states.[42] The main goals of many of these NGOs included helping to advance their sponsors' objectives of promoting free market economies and political and social liberalism.

Many NGOs involved in development work receive funding from governments and international organizations, such as various UN agencies and the World Bank. Some NGOs are actually set up by governments as "fronts" for covert activities that they do not want to be identified with, especially in sensitive geopolitical regions. This particular brand of NGO is referred to as a government-organized NGO or GNGO.[43] The last category is what one scholar has called "briefcase" NGOs. These can also include institutions "set up by individuals for purely personal gain."[44]

A more convincing argument against the view that the appearance of the NGOs has undermined states is that, in the final analysis, NGOs can achieve their goals only by convincing states, whether their own or others. Some NGOs in the past have been successful in changing their countries' political system. However, thus far no NGO has tried to abolish the state structure. For example, the activities of Solidarity (*Solidarność*) in Poland contributed to the Communist regime's fall, but Solidarity did not abolish the Polish state.[45]

In the absence of other conditions, the ability of NGOs to produce change is limited. For instance, without fundamental changes in Soviet policies under Mikhail Gorbachev, along with the USSR's weakness, it is questionable whether Solidarity would have been successful in its efforts to bring down Poland's Communist regime.

NGOs influence state action mostly by mobilizing public opinion and enlisting influential personalities in their campaigns. However, if the state considers their goals as being against its security or national interests, their chance of success severely diminishes. As an example of the limits of NGOs' ability to affect decisions on national security, Sami Cohen cites the case of failed efforts by NGOs to prevent the stockpiling of, and illicit trade in, light weapons because states did not consider it to be in their interest to do so. By contrast, NGO activism succeeded when 122 states signed the Convention on the Total Ban of Anti-Personnel Landmines. Cohen attributed this NGO success to the fact that most states were themselves convinced of the need for such a convention, and did not need much persuasion. Even so, a number of countries, such as the United States, Russia, China, India, Pakistan, Egypt, and Finland did not sign the convention. This clearly shows that ultimately states are free to decide whether or not to respond positively to NGO activism.[46]

In sum, the ability of NGOs to replace states has been less than that of some other non-state actors. As often as not, NGOs have been more tools of states' policies than their determinants.

VIOLENT NON-STATE ACTORS: TERRORIST ENTITIES

Violent non-state actors, including terrorist organizations as such, have a long history. In the past, their activities were mostly limited to a single state and their goals focused mainly on affecting a particular state's political dynamics and structures, in order to achieve certain objectives. Various anarchists, revolutionary and nationalist groups in Europe in the eighteenth, nineteenth, and twentieth centuries represented this type of violent non-state actors. The anti-colonial and national liberation movements, which emerged in the 1940s, 1950s, and 1960s in Africa and Asia, and later the leftist revolutionary movements in the same regions and in Latin America, represented other forms of this type of non-state actors. Many of these movements received assistance from states, which were rivals/enemies of the states which were the targets of these violent groups.

In reality, violent non-state actors could not have long survived without such assistance. The Palestine Liberation Organization (PLO), which at certain times engaged in violent acts, plus the more radical Palestinian groups such as Black September, which committed the terror act at the 1972 Munich Olympics, could not have survived without the financial and other support of Arab countries. During its early existence, the PLO was heavily dependent on support from Egypt. The USSR, too, through various means, supported the radical Palestinian groups and the revolutionary movements of the developing world, while the West generally supported the existing states and their governments. In more recent times, some Palestinian groups such as HAMAS (*Harakat Al Muqawama Al Islamiyya*) have received assistance from Iran as well as some Arab states, notably Qatar, and lately even Turkey.[47] Iran's relations with HAMAS, however, became strained when the organization, which had enjoyed Syria's support in the past and had its headquarters in Damascus, refused to support Bashar Al Assad in the Syrian Civil War which began in 2011 and was still continuing in 2016. As a result, Iran reduced and, according to some sources, stopped its financial assistance to the organization.[48] Nevertheless, Iran retains its links to the military wing of the organization and still supports it financially, although it is not clear to what extent. Meanwhile, because of HAMAS' anti-Assad posture, its relation with Saudi Arabia improved, and Saudi assistance to the organization increased.[49]

In the last four decades, new types of terrorist groups/violent non-state actors have emerged. These groups often have semi-statal status and operate across national borders. The two earliest and most complex of this type of actors are the Taliban and Hizbullah. Their emergence, survival, and continued functioning would not have been possible without the support of state actors, notably Iran in Hizbullah's case and Pakistan and, to some degree, Saudi Arabia in the case of the Taliban.

Hizbullah and Iranian Support

There is no agreement on the exact date of Hizbullah's establishment. Some analysts date its founding to 1982–1983, and some to 1985. But nearly all see its roots in the Lebanese Shias' movement for social, economic, and political enfranchisement, beginning in the early 1960s.[50] A key figure in this movement was the Lebanese-origin and Iranian-born cleric Musa Sadr. A charismatic personality, he organized the first effective Shia social and political movement in Lebanon, which was known as *Harakat Al Mahrumin* (Movement of the Deprived).[51] Musa Sadr's involvement in the Lebanese Shias' movement was quite natural. His family originally hailed from Lebanon and there had been a five-hundred-year-old tradition of relations between Iran and Lebanon's Shias.[52]

Early Shia movements in Lebanon were peaceful. Their main concern was to improve the community's social and economic conditions. The 1979 Iranian Revolution changed the dynamics of Shia politics in Lebanon and added a political dimension to their aspirations. However, it was Israel's 1982 invasion of Lebanon that completely transformed the trajectory of Shia politics, first by radicalizing the Shias and second by offering Iran's newly established Islamic regime the opportunity to become closely involved in Lebanese politics; it eventually helped to create Hizbullah. It was only after the Israeli invasion that members of Iran's newly established Revolutionary Guards were dispatched to Lebanon and established links with like-minded groups and individuals.

For a long time, Hizbullah was not the dominant Shia group in Lebanon, and it had to compete with another Shia movement, AMAL (*Afwaj al Muqavemata al Lobnaniah*). Its origins also go back to Imam Musa Sadr's *Harakat Al Mahrumin*. It was the militia associated with the movement of the deprived. AMAL originally was created principally to help promote the Shias' enfranchisement and improve their economic conditions. Initially, it also sought to serve all of Lebanon's deprived people. It was more secular than religious, and its early members were mostly former members or sympathizers of the Lebanese Communist Party. Moreover, throughout the 1980s and the early 1990s, Syria exerted greater influence in Lebanon and over the Shia movements than did Iran. For instance, AMAL had close links to Syria and its then-president, Hafiz al Assad.[53] In the 1980s, AMAL battled with Hizbullah for influence in Lebanon and often won.[54] Their rivalry, in part reflected Syrian-Iranian competition over influence in Lebanon. It was only in the mid-1990s that Hizbullah emerged as the main Shia actor in Lebanon and Iran became its patron. Since that time and, despite some reports that Hizbullah has managed to diversify its sources of financial support by cultivating Lebanese Shias living abroad, Iran has remained Hizbullah's principal financial and military supporter. Therefore, it is unlikely that, without Iran's support, Hizbullah could have emerged, survived, and evolved into its present shape and power.

Hizbullah's emergence has undermined the Lebanese state's authority and has limited its government's freedom of action in some areas. However, Hizbullah's emergence has not been the main cause of the Lebanese state's weakness and limited authority. On the contrary, it was the prior weakening of the Lebanese state as a result of actions of other state and non-state actors, including Arab states like Jordan that created conditions which led to the emergence of the Hizbullah. For example, when Jordan in 1972 expelled the PLO from its territory and forced it to move to South Lebanon, it sowed the seeds of a long civil war, which greatly undermined Lebanon's state structure. The final blow was dealt by Israel's 1982 invasion, which shattered Lebanon's remaining state structures, exacerbated its divisions, and ushered in an even fiercer civil war.

The ensuing Lebanese civil war also increased the involvement of regional states in Lebanon's affairs: they competed to carve out their own spheres of influence. To obtain their goals, these competing states either created non-state actors or supported existing ones. Iran helped establish Hizbullah, and Saudi Arabia has sponsored several Sunni militant non-state actors that operate in Lebanon. The number of Sunni non-state actors increased during the so-called Cedar Revolution in 2005. The events thus named were triggered by the assassination of the country's Prime Minister Rafiq Hariri, who was close to Saudi Arabia and opposed Syria's military presence in Lebanon.[55] The Syrian Civil War also increased their numbers.[56] Yet neither Hizbullah nor other militant groups have replaced the Lebanese state. Despite its fragility, it represents Lebanon internationally and all official contacts must be established through the state and its representatives.

In short, Hizbullah's emergence has resulted from the weakness of the Lebanese state, instead of Hizbullah's being responsible for the erosion of the Lebanese state's power.

Reasons for Hizbullah's Creation: Religion, or Socio-Economic Deprivation and Political Disenfranchisement?

The emergence of entities such as Hizbullah is often cited as evidence of religion's growing role in international affairs. Yet, to what extent has religion been responsible for Hizbullah's emergence? To the extent that the persistence of sectarian identities and Lebanon's failure to develop a strong and trans-sectarian national identity contributed to Hizbullah's creation and before AMAL's, religion certainly played a key role in their development. But even without a strong sectarian identity, because of their economically, socially, and politically disadvantaged position, the Lebanese Shias were bound to establish some form of organization to help them vindicate their rights. In the past, like other Shia minorities in the region, the Lebanese Shias had seen in socialist ideas and parties a way to escape from their inferior position. This is evidenced by the fact that, as referred to earlier, in the past many AMAL members had belonged to the Lebanese Communist Party.

Imam Musa Sadr was aware of this fact. Therefore, he first focused on the issue of improving the Shias' economic conditions. He used socio-economic rather than religious arguments to justify the need for Shia cooperation and activism. This helps explain why his discourse appealed to secular Shias as well as to the faithful. Nevertheless, especially in the form of Shia cultural traditions, religion was a major factor in the emergence of AMAL and especially Hizbullah. Paramount among these traditions are emphasis on justice and the necessity of struggling against injustice (*Zulm*) and supporting the oppressed and those who have been wronged (*Mazlum*).

These Shia traditions partly shaped Hizbullah's outlook and even more so its discourse. They also contributed to its appeal to the Shia community. However, Hizbullah's role in addressing the Shias' socio-economic problems and advocating a fairer political representation has been equally important in attracting support within the Shia community.[57] Hizbullah's role is reflected in the vast network of social and economic services it has developed, plus the greater political voice it has given to the Shias. In the last ten years, Hizbullah's role in defending Lebanon against Israeli attacks, as during the 2006 Israel-Lebanon war, has even gained it broad support in the country and in the rest of the Arab world.[58] Since the outbreak of the Syrian Civil War and Hizbullah's siding with Bashar Al Assad, its influence with other Muslims has declined. In short, religion has been an important but not the only impetus for Hizbullah's creation and success.

The Taliban and Pakistan

The Taliban represents another non-state actor that owes its emergence, growth, and survival to support from other states, especially Pakistan, followed by Saudi Arabia. Some scholars even believe that the Taliban is a creature of Pakistan. For example, Amin Saikal, the Afghan-origin scholar, holds Pakistan directly responsible. He maintains that Pakistan created the Taliban in order to advance its ambitions in the post-Soviet states of Central Asia. He believes that the creation of a new force to achieve this purpose had become necessary because Pakistan had concluded that its long-time protégé, Gulbudin Hekmatyar, a radical Islamist Mujahid, had become unreliable. Saikal cites Pakistan's other major motive: its desire to create a Pashtun-dominated and -ruled Afghanistan. Pakistani officials believed that by melding the identities of Pakistan's and Afghanistan's Pashtun populations, they could create an entity which would be under their own influence and even subservient to the government in Islamabad, and in this way in effect Pakistan could control the course of Afghan politics and its external behavior.[59] Like many other scholars and observers of Pakistan and Afghanistan, Saikal considers Benazir Bhutto's minister of interior, Naseerullah Babar, Taliban's "godfather."[60] According to Saikal, Babar initially "recruited, trained and armed a number of Madrassa (religious schools) students to join a few former Mujahedin fighters from southern Afghanistan, in order to provide protection to a convoy en route to Central Asia through Afghanistan." The mission was successful and led the ISI (Pakistan's Inter-Services Intelligence Service) to take over the project and transform the nascent Taliban into "a credible ideological and fighting force. It lavished the militia with training, arms, fighters, logistics support, and money."[61]

To create the Taliban, Pakistan looked to those former Mujahedin, who after the Soviet withdrawal had gone to study at religious seminaries, but, as put by the Pakistani journalist and author Ahmed Rashid, these former warriors could not be satisfied by mere religious studies and soon became engaged in political discussions about Afghanistan's future.[62] From the start, some of them were not interested in religious studies and had joined the discussions largely out of boredom. Interestingly, a number of Pashtun Communists, belonging to the *Khalq* faction of the Afghan Communist Party and who were not religious, joined the Taliban. They were prompted to do so because they were angry that the Tajiks dominated Afghanistan's first post-Soviet government.[63] According to some accounts, Pakistani Pashtuns also joined the group, most likely encouraged by the Pakistani government. Pakistan clearly was moved by state interests rather than any religious considerations. The diversity of the recruits also indicates that most who joined the movement did so for reasons other than religion.

Regardless of the members' real motivations, Pakistan provided the group with military training and sought international diplomatic support and funding for them. According to some sources, this training was done "by Pakistan army instructors on Pakistani soil as during the anti-Communist Jihad."[64] Amin Saikal contends that the Taliban benefited from direct Pakistani military support in their conquest of Kabul. He writes "the fall of Kabul to the Taliban was achieved with Pakistan's generous logistic and combat assistance, including night vision binoculars—a contraption which had not been provided to the Mujahedin to fight the Soviets."[65]

The Pakistani military took part in subsequent Taliban operations, such as the August 1998 attack in Mazar Sharif, including on Iran's consulate, which killed a number of its diplomats. Pakistani pilots carried out the operations. Saikal puts the number of Pakistani military who took part at 1,500.[66] Ahmed Rashid describes the extent of Pakistan's support for the Taliban: "Maulana Fazlur Rahman (the chairman of the National Assembly's Standing Committee for Foreign Affairs) went to Washington and Europe to lobby for the Taliban. More importantly, he went often to Saudi Arabia and other Gulf states to enlist their financial and military help for the Taliban. He was successful and Arab help was forthcoming."[67] He adds that after Prince Turki Bin Faisal Bin Saud became head of Saudi Arabia's intelligence services, Saudi Arabia became "the principal financial backer of the Taliban."[68] This claim is supported by the fact that, after the Taliban captured Kabul in 1996 and ousted the government of Burhaneddin Rabbani, only three countries, namely Pakistan, Saudi Arabia, and the United Arab Emirates, recognized the new government.

Saudi Arabia's role was even more important in shaping the Taliban's religio/ideological outlook. As early as the late 1960s, partly because of competition with Iran which was close to Pakistan and was improving its ties with Afghanistan, Saudi Arabia decided to expand its influence in South Asia. One of its instruments was systematically to spread the Saudi brand of conservative Islam (Wahhabism) to Afghanistan and Pakistan. The Saudis believed that spreading Wahhabism would enhance their overall influence because, in general, the spread of a state's values/ideology tends to enhance its political influence. The Saudis were helped by the fact that Wahhabism, the Islamic school adhered to by the Saudi royals, had been influential in the Subcontinent as early as the late eighteenth century. It had thus helped strengthen the more conservative Sunni School (Deobandi) in pre-partition India.

Following the weakening of the Hanafi schools of Central Asia under Soviet rule, notably the Mir Amir School in Bukhara, the Deobandi School also made inroads in Afghanistan. But it was the Soviet invasion of Afghanistan and the ensuing wars that provided Saudi Arabia with a golden opportunity to change the religious landscape of Afghanistan and Pakistan. During the Soviet-Afghan War, the Saudis closed Hanafi religious schools in Afghanistan and Pakistan and replaced them with Wahhabi schools.[69] The reaction of other international actors to the Soviet invasion, notably the United States, further facilitated the Saudi strategy's success.

GLOBAL POLITICS: IMPACT ON THE EMERGENCE OF THE TALIBAN

The Afghan wars triggered by the USSR's invasion in 1979 produced significant social and cultural transformations in Afghanistan and Pakistan, preparing the ground for the eventual creation of the Taliban. However, it was the Soviet Union's collapse and ensuing changes in the character of the international and regional systems that permitted Pakistan to implement its Afghan strategy. Essentially, that was to establish a government in Afghanistan receptive to Pakistani wishes and interests. In view of its close relations with Pakistan, Saudi Arabia, too, preferred an Afghan government closely connected to Pakistan. The Saudis hoped that a pro-Pakistan-Afghan government would act as a barrier to Iran's influence. However, Pakistan and Saudi Arabia could not have achieved their plans for Afghanistan without America's support, or at least acquiescence. This was true during the Soviet-Afghan War, and even more so after the USSR's demise.

Despite the significant role played both by Saudi Arabia and Pakistan in the course of the Soviet-Afghan War, including the creation, arming, and financing of the Mujahedin, American support was the decisive factor in the USSR's defeat. After its collapse, as well, U.S. support or at least acquiescence enabled Pakistan and Saudi Arabia to implement their Afghan strategy. The coincidence of their interests with those of the United States enabled them to pursue their ideological and geopolitical ambitions in Afghanistan. The logic of the Cold War and great-power rivalry had led to the Soviet-Afghan War and unleashed developments that eventually culminated in the emergence of the Taliban. Similarly, after the Soviets withdrew from Afghanistan in January 1989 and, more important, after the Soviet Union's collapse in 1991, U.S. policies and objectives in the Middle East and South and Central Asia greatly contributed to the Taliban's appearance.

Regional and International Consequences of the Soviet Invasion

The Soviet invasion of Afghanistan led to the formation of a number of resistance movements there. Their salient characteristic was their religious, namely Islamic, leanings. Consequently, they also framed their resistance in Islamic religious terms: they called their struggle *Jihad* (Holy War) and themselves *Mujahid* (Holy Warrior), and their goal as the defense of Islam through Afghanistan's independence. However, although they emphasized Islam as the force binding them together, various resistance groups were organized along ethnic and sectarian lines and often competed. Moreover, the level of their religiosity also differed.

For example, Tajiks gathered around their famed commander, Ahmad Shah Masood, in the framework of *Jamiat e Islami*. This party was founded by Burhaneddin Rabbani, who was a Tajik, and who later headed the first post-Soviet Afghan government which lasted from 1992 to 1996. The Uzbeks were organized around General Abdul Rashid Dostum. He was totally secular and his followers were the least religious group among the Mujahedin. The Shia Hazaras, meanwhile, formed the *Hizb e Vahdat*. Those Mujahedin belonging to the Pashtun ethnic group, the largest of Afghanistan's various ethnicities, were the most religious. They had several major leaders, notably Gulbudin Hekmatyar, the founder of *Hizb e Islami*. This party later split in two when Maulavi Muhammad Yunus Khalis parted company with Hekmatyar.[70]

The organization of Afghan resistance movements along ethnic lines, coupled with the power ambitions of their leaders and the impact of regional and international politics, led to outbreak of conflict among them after Soviet forces withdrew. Eventually these conflicts were transformed into all-out civil war which is still continuing. Paramount among regional political factors were Pakistan's desire to have a subservient government in Afghanistan and Saudi Arabia's determination to prevent Iranian influence in post-Soviet Afghanistan. Among the international factors, the U.S. policy of containing Iran played the most significant role. In this context the Taliban were born.

Support for the Mujahedin

By the logic of the Cold War, when the Soviet Union invaded Afghanistan, the United States felt compelled to roll it back. It mobilized international support for the Afghan resistance and provided the bulk of the military and a significant share of the financial assistance to the Afghan Mujahedin. The United States also concluded that Islam could be a useful antidote to communism in Afghanistan and beyond and thus a convenient ideological tool to combat Communism in the region as well as to undermine the USSR by creating disturbances in its Muslim-inhabited republics. America supported the recourse to Islam and Islamic concepts, such as Jihad, as means of resistance against the USSR. Indeed, the Soviet-Afghan War popularized the concept of Jihad, which had been dormant in the Muslim world for several centuries.

As a key American ally with significant security interests in Afghanistan, Pakistan became the main conduit for American aid to the Afghan Mujahedin. Pakistan's importance for the United States was enhanced because of U.S.-Iranian estrangement after the Islamic Revolution. One outcome of this close Pakistani cooperation was establishment of the Inter-Services Intelligence (ISI). As the institution gradually grew more powerful and pursued its own particular interests, which at times diverged from those of the government, it played a key role in the creation of the Taliban.

Saudi Arabia was America's other important partner in the fight against Soviet aggression, providing a substantial portion of the Mujahedin's financial needs and supplying volunteers to fight in Afghanistan. They were joined by other volunteers from several Arab countries and came to be known as Arab Afghans.[71] Saudi Arabia's involvement in the Afghan Jihad and its close cooperation with Pakistan, coupled with its active promotion of Wahhabi Islam, dramatically changed their traditional religious and cultural beliefs in a far more conservative direction. This religious and cultural transformation thus created the right ideological environment for the rise of the Taliban.

Struggle for the Control of Eurasia: Another Cause of the Taliban's Emergence

It took five years after the USSR's withdrawal from Afghanistan in 1989 for the Taliban to burst onto the regional scene in 1994. During the first years of the Afghan civil war, which began immediately after the 1989 Soviet withdrawal, there was no sign of the Taliban. However, the long war with the USSR had produced changes in Afghanistan that had exacerbated inter-ethnic and sectarian animosities and rivalries and struggles for power. Following Soviet withdrawal, fierce competition began among different groups for control of the country and its government. This struggle for power was inevitable, yet it need not have led to a bloody civil war and the appearance of a phenomenon such as the Taliban. But the Soviet Union's collapse and the changes it caused in regional and international dynamics exacerbated Afghanistan's problems and contributed to the brutal nature of its civil war.

Consequences of the USSR's Demise

The Soviet Union's disintegration in December 1991 shifted the balance of global power in favor of the West, especially the United States, and thus transformed the character of the international political system. This great shift in the global balance of power was interpreted as the end of the bi-polar world order and its replacement with a unipolar international system, based on America's global supremacy or even hegemony.[72] As a result, the United States was encouraged to pursue a transformative policy internationally, especially in a vast region extending from the Middle East to South and Central Asia, sometimes referred to as the Greater Middle East.

As early as January 1992, a principal aspect of this new U.S. strategy was to contain Iran and prevent it from spreading its influence in Afghanistan and in post-Soviet Central Asia and the Caucasus. During a trip to Central Asia in January 1992, U.S. secretary of state James Baker clearly stated this U.S. goal.[73] The Clinton administration (1993–2000), further developed and expanded this policy and presented it in the form of its dual-containment strategy for the Persian Gulf.[74] In addition, by 1994–1995, U.S.-Russian relations had lost their earlier warmth. Thus preventing the reestablishment of Russian influence in the same regions became another American policy priority.

Meanwhile, by 1993, the opening up of the USSR's previously sealed-off republics to foreign investment, especially in their energy resources, had triggered intense rivalries among energy companies and their governments. Competition, which came to be known as pipeline wars, had also begun among regional states over transit routes for these resources.

The USSR's collapse also enhanced the competitive dimensions of regional relations, which in the past were mitigated by the common Soviet-

Communist threat. For example, Iranian-Pakistani relations deteriorated throughout the 1990s and beyond, as did Saudi-Iranian relations, which were already tense.[75] Regional countries such as Pakistan which were allies of the United States feared that in the post-Soviet era their value for the United States would diminish. To avoid this outcome, they tried to find new ways of making themselves useful to America; this included helping the United States to contain Iran's influence in Afghanistan and Central Asia. The emergence of the Taliban was, therefore, partly the outcome of changing regional and global geopolitics and the shifting priorities of U.S. foreign policy.

The United States and the Taliban

The extent of the U.S.'s role in the creation of the Taliban is not clear. It is not even certain whether America played any direct role. Most likely, the U.S. government was not directly engaged in the Taliban's creation, although the late prime minister of Pakistan, Benazir Bhutto, claimed that "weapons were supplied to the Taliban by the United States and Britain with money from Saudi Arabia."[76] Some influential players in the United States, especially some oil companies such as UNOCAL, supported the Taliban. UNOCAL's main objective was to gain access to Turkmen gas and export it through Afghanistan. But the Argentine oil company Bridas had already signed an agreement with the Rabbani government for the same purpose.[77] This meant that for UNOCAL to attain its objective, the Afghan government had to change. Some observers have suggested that, for UNOCAL to achieve its purpose, a "Pax Talibanica" needed to be established throughout Afghanistan.[78] The statement by the famed Tajik commander, Ahmad Shah Masood, as related by Saikal, also points to the fact that economic and political considerations by various players, rather than religion, were behind the Taliban's creation. Ahmad Shah spoke as follows: "As always it is the question of money. Western companies are interested in the resources of northern Afghanistan. They also want to penetrate the adjacent countries of Central Asia: Tajikistan, Turkmenistan, and Uzbekistan [and gain access to their sources of] gold and uranium, but most importantly oil and gas. All of these, [Central Asian resources] according to the true instigators of the war must go through the shortest route through Afghanistan—to the Pakistani port of Karachi. This is the essence of the war, not the struggle for 'true faith.' *The Holy Quran and Jihad are, unfortunately, only covers in this dirty war*" [emphasis added].[79]

The oil companies' plan also suited Pakistan's interests. It intended to become the main export route for Central Asian energy. To achieve this goal, it needed a friendly government in Kabul, hence the establishment of the Taliban as a tool against the existing Afghan government. By helping U.S. oil companies, by containing Iran and preventing the export of Central Asia energy through Iran, Pakistan could also show its continued usefulness to America. According to one Pakistani journalist, in his meeting with U.S. secretary of defense William Perry, General Naseerullah Babar, architect of the Benazir Bhutto government's Afghan policy, told him he would make sure that Iran would be barred from the region.[80] In this regard, too, a viscerally anti-Iran and anti-Shia group like the Taliban would be a valuable instrument.

Regardless of whether the United States actively participated in the Taliban's creation or merely tolerated it, America came to see it as a useful tool of U.S. regional policy, especially containing Iran and Russia as well as helping U.S. energy companies interested in Central Asia. Statements by some mid-level U.S. officials support this analysis. For instance, the assistant secretary of state for South Asian affairs, Robin Raphel, reportedly said that the Taliban was "an indigenous movement that had demonstrated staying power"[81] and therefore had to be acknowledged as such. After the Taliban captured Kabul, the acting state department spokesman, Glyn Davies, said that America could see "nothing objectionable" to their [Taliban's] version of Islamic law.[82] It was much later in 1998 that, after the Taliban-affiliated *Al Qaeda* attacked U.S. embassies in Tanzania and Kenya, the United States changed its view of and attitude toward the Taliban. In short, even if the United States did not create the Taliban, once it was created Washington saw its usefulness as an instrument of American regional policies. Meanwhile, some American companies lobbied the government to support the Taliban or at least not to object to its creation.

In sum, the Taliban were not a spontaneous religious movement. On the contrary, they were the result of strategic and geopolitical planning by some international and regional actors. Some non-state actors, especially important MNCs such as UNOCAL, were also instrumental. Religion was used as an instrument of mobilization and legitimization.

Even those who joined the Taliban did so for motives beyond religion, including harshness of life in refugee camps, ethnic animosities, and even simple boredom. These motives have grown in importance in the last two decades. Meanwhile, Pakistan continues to support the Taliban in order to influence Afghanistan's political destiny, even though the Taliban's Pakistani branch has become a headache for the government in Islamabad.

LESSER TERRORIST GROUPS

States have also been instrumental in the creation of smaller terrorist groups and constitute their main support base. For instance, while *Al Qaeda* was not originally a state creation, its ability to function depended on the complicity of the Pakistani government and the Taliban-ruled government in Kabul.

Even after the U.S. invasion of Afghanistan in 2001, the Pakistani government gave Osama bin Laden a safe haven in Abbottabad, a city close to its capital, although it continued to claim that it was fighting *Al Qaeda* and the Taliban.[83]

Many non-state actors in the form of militias or terrorist groups, which mushroomed in Iraq after the U.S. invasion of 2003, also had foreign governments as sponsors. Saudi Arabia, and later Qatar and even Turkey, funded Sunni groups while Iran supported Shia organizations. A similar situation developed in Syria after the outbreak of civil war in 2011 and the involvement of various international and regional players. The countries opposed to the government of Bashar Al Assad, especially Saudi Arabia, Qatar, and Turkey, helped create, finance, and arm different Sunni groups. Turkey also allowed foreign nationals to join these groups in Syria by allowing them transit routes through its territory. The most formidable of these groups is the IS. Inter-state rivalries and competing power interests have played critical roles in the creation of these groups in Iraq and Syria. Without state support they would not have emerged and if they did they could not have long survived.

Clearly, both Iraq's and Syria's sectarian and ethnic divisions as well as political rivalries among their diverse people greatly contributed to the emergence of these actors. Nevertheless, without external intervention many of these types of actors could not emerge and, if they did, they could not survive long. In short, most violent non-state actors are, in fact, creatures of states and cannot function without their support. At times, when they outgrow their usefulness, they complicate the work of states but they certainly do not supplant them. Moreover, it is only when the state is weak and fragile that these actors become powerful.

CONCLUSIONS

In the last several decades, the nation-state has been under stress and its powers and freedom of action in many areas has been eroded by the encroaching influence of a variety of non-state actors and the forces of globalization. Nevertheless, the nation-state still remains the main actor within the international system. International and regional organizations, multi- and transnational corporations, violent non-state actors, and a variety of NGOs have not been able to supplant it. On the contrary, states constitute the main units of various international organizations. They are also often behind the creation of most violent non-state actors as well as many types of NGOs.

What has been diagnosed as the irrelevance of states applies only to weak and the so-called failed states and thus, in reality, is about the inequality of states. The weaker a state the more irrelevant it becomes. Strong states often can and do resist pressures emanating from non-state actors of all types and categories. This means that any assessment of religion's role in international affairs should focus mainly on its impact on state actors' behavior. This does not mean that the influence that some non-state actors could bring to bear on states should not be adequately factored in. However, because non-state actors either are creatures of states or largely depend on support from states, their impact is clearly less significant. In short, analysis of religion's role should focus on, first, identifying the main determinants of states' behavior and religion's place within them; and, second, identifying the principal channels through which religious influences are brought to bear on states.

NOTES

1. Adam Watson, *The Evolution of International Society* (New York, NY: Routledge, 2009).
2. On the expansion and thus globalization of the European state system, see Watson, *The Evolution of International Society*.
3. For the types of non-state actors, see Bob Reinalda, *Non-State Actors* (Surrey, England: Ashgate Publishing Limited, 2011).
4. On the history of the evolution of international organizations, see David Clark Mackenzie, *A World Beyond Borders: An Introduction to the History of International Organizations* (Tonawanda, NY: University of Toronto Press, 2010).
5. The Mau Mau in Kenya was one of these groups. On the movement, see David Anderson, *Histories of the Hanged: The Dirty War in Kenya and the End of Empire* (London: Weidenfeld & Nicholson, 2005).
6. Stanley Hoffmann, "Obstinate or Obsolete? The Fate of the Nation-State and the Case of Western Europe," *Daedalus*, 95, 3 (Summer 1966).
7. Among the early works on the challenges of transnational organizations and relations on the state-centric system were those by Joseph Nye and Robert Keohane. See Robert Keohane & Joseph S. Nye, *Transnational Relations and World Politics* (Cambridge, MA: Harvard University Press, 1971).
8. L. H. Miller, *Global Order: Values and Power in International Politics* (Boulder, CO: Westview Press, 1994), 2.
9. Miller, *Global Order*, 2.
10. The organization was initially called the Islamic State of Iraq and the Levant (ISIL). For the history of ISIS, its evolution, ideology, and structure, see Christopher Reuter, "Secret Files Reveal the Structure of Islamic State." *Spiegel Online*, 18 April 2015, at: http://www.spiegel.de/international/world/islamic-state-files-show-str.
11. Among these scholars is James N. Rosenau, *Turbulences in World Politics: A Theory of Change and Continuity* (Princeton: Princeton University Press, 1990). However, Rosenau does not argue for total irrelevance of states or state-centered systems. Rather he talks about the emergence of a parallel "multicentric world" or system, each pursuing different goals.
12. Martin Wolf, "Will the Nation State Survive Globalization?" *Foreign Affairs*, 80, 1 (January/February 2001).
13. Hoffmann, "Obstinate or Obsolete? The Fate of the Nation State and the Case of Western Europe."
14. Wolf, "Will the Nation State Survive Globalization?", 190.
15. On the function of IGOs, see A. L. Bennett, *International Organizations: Principles and Issues* (Englewood Cliffs, NJ: Prentice Hall, 1991).
16. The EU has a character different from the other institutions listed in this sentence, based on nation-states that retain the full panoply of their sovereignty, in that there are functional

areas in which national sovereignty has been devolved on EU institutions and political processes.

17. NATO has always taken the position that, while the North Atlantic Treaty (Treaty of Washington) of 4 April 1949 specifically references both the United Nations Charter (Article 1 of the North Atlantic Treaty) and its Article 51 (North Atlantic Treaty Article 5), NATO is not a "regional organization," as such. This argument is made primarily in order for NATO to retain the option of acting, including militarily, without a formal UN mandate if it chooses to do so as, indeed, it did in Kosovo in 1999. See text at: http://avalon.law.yale.edu/20th_century/nato.asp.

18. See Seyom Brown, *New Forces, Old Forces, and the Future of World Politics* (New York: HarperCollins, 1995).

19. On the impact of IGOs on great powers, see M. Karns & K. Mingst, *The United States and Multilateral Institutions: Patterns of Changing Instrumentality and Influence* (Boston: Unwin Hyman, 1990).

20. Again, the nature of the EU makes it a partial exception to this rule.

21. Article 47 of the Charter did provide that "There shall be established a Military Staff Committee to advise and assist the Security Council on all questions relating to the Security Council's military requirements for the maintenance of international peace and security, the employment and command of forces placed at its disposal, the regulation of armaments, and possible disarmament." It proved to be moribund because of disagreements among the permanent members of the UN Security Council during the Cold War.

22. Marrak Goulding, "The Evolution of United Nations Peacekeeping," *International Affairs* 69, 3 July 1993, also Lise Marje Howard, *UN Peacekeeping in Civil Wars* (Cambridge: Cambridge University Press, 2008).

23. On the list of UN Security Council resolutions ignored by Israel, see: Jeremy Hammond, Rogue State: Israeli Violation of U.N. Security Council Resolutions," *Foreign Policy Journal*, 27 January 2010, at: http://www.foreignpolicyjournal.com2010/1/7/rogue-state-israeli-violations-of-un-security-council-resolutions.

24. On the inequality of states, see David Vital, *The Inequality of States: A Study of Small Power in International Relations* (London: Clarendon Press, 1972). However, mere size is not at the root of states' inequality. Rather it is their economic and military power. However, in general smaller states also tend to lack adequate resources to develop large militaries and powerful economies.

25. On the origins of the EU, see Martin Dedman, *The Origins and Development of the European Union, 1945–2008* (London/New York: Routledge, 2010).

26. This has always been the practice at NATO within its governing body, the North Atlantic Council. It never takes a vote, but any member state can in effect veto any decision. Some critics of this arrangement argue that it limits NATO's effectiveness, even though the larger powers (principally the United States) generally are able to sway opinion within the Council in order for it to make decisions. Others argue that the very fact of the Council's unanimity rule gives greater strength to its decisions, once taken, than would be true if they were taken by majority rule, in that unanimity means that every member has "signed on" to a decision and thus has at least political responsibility for its implementation. There is also the latent pressure to agree imposed by the possibility that a potentially dissenting state might want, on another occasion, to be supported by its allies. In fact, once NATO has taken a decision through this process, it has never defaulted, even when some of the members have elected not to take part, for example, in a military operation.

27. On Brexit see "A Background to 'Brexit' from the European Union," *The Economist*, 24 February 2016, at: http://www.economist.com/blogs/graphicaldetails/2016/02/graphics.

28. In the 1957 Treaty of Rome, the European Economic Community (now the European Union) was deliberately organized to divide power between a state-based institution, the European Council, and a supranational institution, the European Commission. However, given that Commission members are effectively appointed by member states, some members may at times tend to favor positions advanced by their country of nationality rather than to cleave to the supranational identity they are sworn to serve. This Council/Commission arrangement, with a division of powers, thus built in an inherent tension between nation-state and supranational

powers. The European Parliament is also state-based in terms of the way that members are elected, but groups of members from different states do work together in cross-border political-party-like configurations. Some of the more functional EU institutions, like the European Court of Justice, are truly supranational in character.

29. On the formation of European identity, see Michael Kryzanowsky, *The Discursive Construction of European Identities* (Frankfurt am Main: Peter Lang, 2010), and Senem Aydin Dugzit, *Construction of European Identity* (New York: Palgrave MacMillan, 2012).

30. Lenka Bastikova, "The Revenge of the Radical Right," *Comparative Political Studies*, February 2014.

31. This is particularly true with rules and regulations promulgated by the European Commission that affect aspects of internal life within the member states—e.g., governing standards for commerce. However, powers in this case have been consciously ceded by the member states to the Commission.

32. On the origins and evolution of multinational corporations and transnational corporations, see Paz Estrella Tolentino, *Multi-national Corporations: Emergence and Evolution* (London: Routledge, 2000).

33. On the Guatemalan case and the role of the United Fruit Company, see R. H. Immerman, *The CIA in Guatemala: The Foreign Policy of Intervention* (Austin: University of Texas Press, 1982), and Peter Chapman, *Bananas: How the United Fruit Company Shaped the World* (Edinburgh/New York: Canongate, 2008), and on ITT's in Chili see Paul Montgomery, "ITT Office Damaged by Bomb," *New York Times*, 29 September 1973.

34. E. R. Peterson, "Looming Collision of Capitalisms?" in eds. W. Kegley Jr. and Eugene R. Wittkopf, *The Global Agenda: Issues and Perspectives* (New York: McGraw-Hill, 1995), 259–69.

35. On the ways MNCs impact the decisions of state and in general the economic and political lives of the countries in which they operate, see Alfred Chandler and Bruce Mazlish, *Leviathans: Multinational Corporations and the New Global History* (Cambridge: Cambridge University Press, 2005).

36. Elizabeth Dickinson, "Shell Oil Infiltrates Nigeria's Government Ministries," *Foreign Policy.com*, 8 December 2010, at: http://foreignpolicy.com/2010/12/09/shell-oil-infiltrates-nigerias-government-ministries/, also, Tom Bawden, "Power in Nigeria," *The Independent*, 3 April 2012.

37. Opinion on the impact of the MNCs is divided. Some commentators consider the MNCs the main engine of global growth through their ability to invest freely across national borders. J. S. Goldstein, *International Relations* (Third Edition), (New York: Longman, 1999), 415. Some even welcome the replacement of states as the main economic unit by MNCs. Richard Barnet, *Global Dreams: Imperial Corporations and the New World Order* (New York: Simon and Schuster, 1994), 19–20. Others, by contrast, believe that they are instruments of exploitation of great capitalist powers. K. Mingst, *Essential of International Relations* (New York: W.W. Norton, 1999), 224. Yet others argue that their activities cause uneven development and create inequality in the international division of labor. S. Brown, *New Forces, Old Forces, and the Future of World Politics*, 213.

38. "International Business: Malaysia Imposes Controls on Trading in Its Currency," *New York Times*, 2 September 1998.

39. David Lewis, *Nongovernmental Organizations, Definition and History*, 2009, at: http://link.springer.com/referenceworkentry/10.1007%2F978-0-387-93996-4_3.

40. Lewis, *Nongovernmental Organizations.*

41. Lewis, *Nongovernmental Organizations.*

42. The National Endowment for Democracy, along with its four subsidiaries, one each for the two main U.S. political parties, one for labor (connected to the AFL-CIO), and one for business (connected to the U.S. Chamber of Commerce), was consciously patterned after the German *Stiftungen.*

43. During the Cold War, the U.S. Central Intelligence Agency funded a number of NGOs. Prominent among these was a blanket organization called the Congress for Cultural Freedom. It provided financial support to a number of organizations and publications, especially in Western Europe, of a liberal or leftist bent, in order to counter Soviet and other communist efforts. The

role of the Congress became public in 1966. The Soviet Union and the satellite countries also engaged in this practice in a major way.

44. Lewis, *Nongovernmental Organizations, Definition and History*.

45. Technically, Solidarity was a labor union, but its activities in some regards resembled those of an NGO.

46. Sami Cohen, *The Resilience of the State: Democracy and the Challenges of Globalization* (translated from French by Jonathan Derrick), (Boulder/ London: Lynne Rienner, 2006), 65–67.

47. See Josh Lev, "Which Mideast Power Brokers Support HAMAS," *CNN.com*., 6 August 2014, available at: http://www.cnn.com/2014/o8/06/world/mideast-hamas-support.

48. See Adnan Abu Amer, "Iran Resumes Monetary Aid to HAMAS," *Al Monitor*, 24 March 2014 at: http://www.al-monitor.com/pulse/originals/2014/03/iran-hams-finance-economy-resistance. Also see Jack Moore, "Iran Ceases Financial Aid to HAMAS in Gaza, Official Says," *Newsweek Europe*, June 28, 2015 at: http://europe.newsweek.com/iran-ceases-financial-aid-hamas-gaza-official-claims-330889.

49. For the shifting dynamics of HAMAS' relations with Iran and Saudi Arabia, see Samuel Ramani, "HAMAS's Pivot to Saudi Arabia," *Carnegie Endowment for International Peace, Sada*, 17 September 2015 at: http://carnegieendowment.org/sada/?fa=61315.

50. For more details on the origins of the Hizbullah, see, among others, Hala Jaber, *Hizbollah: Born with a Vengeance* (New York: Columbia University Press, 1996).

51. On Musa Sadr's activities and personality, see Fuad Ajami, *The Vanished Imam* (Ithaca: Cornell University Press, 1996).

52. On the history of Iran's relations with Lebanon, see H. B. Shahabi, *Distant Relations: Iran and Lebanon in the Last 500 Years* (London: I. B. Tauris, 2006).

53. On AMAL see Augustus R. Norton, *AMAL and the Shia: Struggle for the Soul of Lebanon* (Austin: University of Texas Press, 1987).

54. AMAL-Hizbullah rivalry in the 1980s also reflected the competition between Syria and Iran for influence in Lebanon. See Benedetta Berti, *Armed Political Organizations: From Conflict to Integration* (Baltimore: Johns Hopkins University Press, 2013), 34.

55. See Rudy Jaafar and Maria J. Stephan, "Lebanon's Independence Intifada: How an Unarmed Insurrection Expelled Syrian Forces," in Maria J. Stephan, *Civilian Jihad, Nonviolent Struggle, Democratization and Governance in the Middle East* (New York Palgrave Macmillan, 2009).

56. For a list of Sunni violent actors in Lebanon, see Patrick Hoover, "The Evolution of Sunni Jihadism in Lebanon Since 2011," *Terrorism Monitor*, vol. 13, Issue 21, 30 October 2015, at: http://jamestown.org/programs/tn/single/?tx_ttnews%5Btt.

57. On the evolution of Hizbullah ideology, see Joseph Elie Alagha, *The Shifts in Hizbullah Ideology: Religious Ideology, Political Ideology and Political Action*, ISIM (Institute for the Study of the Islamic World), (Amsterdam: The University of Amsterdam Press, 2005). Also Helena Cobban, "Hizbullah's New Face," *Boston Review*, April 2005.

58. After Hizbullah's strong resistance to Israeli forces in the 2006 Israel-Lebanon war, its leader, Seyyed Hassan Nasrallah, for a time became the most popular Arab personality. "Survey: Nasrallah Is the Most Admired Leader in the Arab World." *Haaretz Service*, 17 April 2008, at: http://www.haaretz.com/news/survey-nasrallah-is-the-most-admired-leader-in-the-arab-world.html.

59. Amin Saikal, *Modern Afghanistan: A History of Struggle and Survival* (London: I. B. Tauris, 2004). 221.

60. Saikal, *Modern Afghanistan*, 221.

61. Saikal, *Modern Afghanistan*, 221.

62. Ahmed Rashid, "Pakistan and the Taliban," in ed. William Maley, *Fundamentalism Reborn: Afghanistan and the Taliban* (New York: New York University Press, 2001), 87.

63. Rashid, "Pakistan and the Taliban," 87.

64. Anthony Davies, "How the Taliban Became a Military Force," in *Fundamentalism Reborn*, 55.

65. Saikal, *Modern Afghanistan*, 225.

66. Saikal, *Modern Afghanistan*, 225.

67. Rashid, "Pakistan and the Taliban," in *Fundamentalism Reborn*, 74.
68. Rashid, "Pakistan and the Taliban," 74.
69. Olivier Roy, *Islam and Resistance in Afghanistan* (Cambridge: Cambridge University Press, 1990). The book chronicles the process of the closure of Hanafi schools and their replacement by Wahhabi schools.
70. Other Pashtun groups included *Harakat e Inqilabi e Islami* (Islamic Revolutionary Movement) of Maulavi Muhammad Nabi Muhammad, *Mahaz e Melli Afghanistan* (National Islamic Front of Afghanistan) of Seyyed Ahmad Geilani, a pro-royalty group, and *Jebheh e Nejat e Melli Afghanistan* (Afghan National Liberation Front) of Sebgatullah Mojadedi, and *Itihad e Islami* (Islamic Union) of Adul Rasul Sayyaf.
71. These so-called Arab Afghans, battle-hardened in the fight against USSR, later would become involved in conflicts in the former USSR, notably Chechnya during the Russian-Chechen wars, 1994–2001, and also to a lesser extent in the Yugoslav conflict.
72. On America's unipolar moment, see Charles Krauthammer, "A Unipolar Moment," *Foreign Affairs*, 70. 1 (Winter 1990/91).
73. See Thomas Friedman, "U.S. to Counter Iran in Central Asia," *New York Times*, 6 February 1992.
74. On Dual Containment, see Martin Indyk, "Watershed in the Middle East," *Foreign Affairs*, 71.1, 1992.
75. For details, see, Shireen T. Hunter, *Iran's Foreign Policy in the Post-Soviet Era: Resisting the New International Order* (Santa Barbara: Praeger/ABC-CLIO, 2010), 143–49.
76. Cited in Saikal, *Modern Afghanistan*, 223.
77. *Ahmed Rashid, Taliban, Militant Islam, Oil and Fundamentalism in Central Asia* (New Haven: Yale University Press, 2000), 159.
78. On the role of UNOCAL on U.S. Afghan policy, including the role of the Taliban, see Tom Turnipseed, "Bush, Enron, Unocal and the Taliban," *Counterpunch*, 10 January 2002, at: http://www.counterpunch.org/2002/01/10/bush-enron-unocal-and-the-taliban/print.
79. Quoted in Saikal, *Modern Afghanistan*, 222.
80. Ejaz Haider, "Pakistan's Afghan Policy and Its Fallout," *Central Asia Monitor*, 5, 1998.
81. Richard Mackenzie, "The United States and the Taliban," in *Fundamentalism Reborn*, 97.
82. Mackenzie, "The United States and the Taliban," 97.
83. See Seymour Hersh, "The Killing of Osama bin Laden," *The London Review of Books*, 37, 10, 21 May 2015, at: http://www.irb.co.uk/v37/seymourhersh/the-killing-of-osama-bin-laden.

Chapter Two

Determinants of Behavior of International Actors

To assess the relative impact of religion on the behavior of international actors, it is necessary first to identify the principal factors that determine their actions. The behavior of both state and non-state actors is influenced by a wide range of factors and a complex mixture of motives. The factors which determine the behavior of non-state actors are easier to identify because they are reflected in the purposes for which they are established and in the objectives that they pursue. The only exceptions are large semi-statal and violent non-state actors like Hizbullah, the Taliban, and the more recently emerged Islamic State (IS).

Goals and objectives of the largest inter-governmental non-state actor, the United Nations, are spelled out in its Charter, which clearly indicates the motivations behind the UN's creation and operations. The purposes of its specialized agencies and hence motivations for their establishment and operations are likewise set out in their founding documents and are reflected in their names. The International Labor Organization (ILO) was established to ensure fair labor practices, and the object of the World Health Organization (WHO) is to promote global health.

The same is true of regional organizations. The Organization of African Unity (OAU), the Organization of American States (OAS), and the League of the Arab States were created by the desire to mitigate conflictual aspects of regional relations, foster cooperation among regional states, help resolve disputes, and ultimately contribute to the establishment and maintenance of peace and stability. The principal motivations for creating the most ambitious regional organization, what is now the European Union (EU), were to make impossible the reemergence of conditions that produced the two world wars and possibly in time even to build a United States of Europe. If realized, such a union would not only prevent future conflicts among European states and contribute to the Continent's economic welfare, but it would also enable Europe (at least in theory) to exert more influence globally by acting in a unified fashion.

The objectives of multi/transnational corporations and the primary motivation for their creation are equally easy to discern. Like any other commercial enterprise, they seek economic or financial gain. This does not necessarily mean they are indifferent to the impact their activities have on countries within which they operate. In all likelihood, most prefer that their activities, while lucrative, also benefit the countries where their activities are centered. Ultimately, however, everything else is subordinated to economic and monetary gain.

The same principle applies to most non-governmental organizations (NGOs). Often, their names reflect their goals and reasons for their creation. Thus Human Rights Watch (HRW) seeks to encourage respect for human rights globally, to bring human rights violations to the world's attention, and to seek remedies. Similar motives led to the creation of Amnesty International. Meanwhile, motivations for creating NGOs engaged in developmental activities, either independently or in cooperation with governments and international organizations, are reflected in the functions they perform. The same is true of religious NGOs, although they are often involved in developmental and charity activities in addition to evangelical work.

The case of violent non-state actors is more complex, and goals and motivations behind their creation are more varied. There is no uncertainty regarding ethnic separatist groups; but for others, such as those which claim to be motivated by religion, goals and motivations are not as easy to discern. In particular, it can be difficult to accurately determine to what extent religion acts as primary motivation and to what degree as a means to justify and legitimize groups' actions and mobilize support. A further complicating factor is that, as discussed in chapter 1, some violent non-state actors are supported either by their own governments or by foreign state actors. For example, the government of Pakistan allows the operation of home-grown militant Sunni groups, such as the *Lashkar e Taiba* and *Sepah e Sahaba*, because it often uses them as instruments of its regional policy.[1] The same is true of some militant Sunni groups which have sprung up in Iraq after the 2003 U.S.-led invasion and in Syria after the popular uprising in 2011 and the civil war that ensued. They all have received assistance from outside countries, such as Turkey, Saudi Arabia, and Qatar, which use them to advance their respective policy goals.[2] Meanwhile, some Shia groups have received help from Iran.

The following question thus arises: How autonomous are these groups? Or are they doing the bidding of either their own government or foreign sponsors, such as Saudi Arabia, some Gulf states, and Turkey in the case of the Sunnis, and Iran in the case of some Shia groups? In the case of larger semi-statal groups, such as the Taliban and Hizbullah, the situation is even more complicated. To what extent are these groups motivated by religion and to what extent by an urge to gain power or improve the economic and social conditions of their ethnic or sectarian communities? Can their power ambitions be separated from their sectarian/ethnic loyalties and beliefs? Nevertheless, even in these cases it is possible to establish the relative weight of various factors as the principal driving forces behind their activities, by applying some of the same analytical tools used to identify the forces which motivate the actions of state actors.

DETERMINANTS AND MOTIVATIONS OF STATE BEHAVIOR

As explained in chapter 1, despite considerable erosion in the autonomy and sovereignty of nation-states, especially smaller and weaker ones, they still remain the principal actors within the international system. At least thus far no viable alternative to nation-state has emerged. Therefore, the priority should be to identify the factors which shape the behavior of state actors and to discover the complex motivations behind their specific actions. These factors fall into two main categories: 1) underlying forces which help shape states' long-term patterns of behavior and are referred to as determinants; and 2) the complex motivations behind their approaches to specific cases. Because of the semi-statal character of some non-state actors, such as the Taliban and Hizbullah, the main factors determining their behavior and their motivations will also be addressed.

"Determinants" of states' behavior are either unchangeable or change very slowly. They shape long-term patterns of states' behavior by presenting them with certain options while excluding others, by forming their national identities, and by shaping their self-perceptions and world-views. "Motivations" refer to those factors which determine states' policies regarding specific cases. They fall into two main categories: internal and external. It is the interaction between the determinants and motivations on the one hand, and between the internal and external motivators on the other which shape the pattern of states' long-term behavior and the underlying character of their foreign policies. Some scholars, including, Frederick Northedge, see foreign policy as the outcome of a constant "dialogue between the inside and the outside"[3]; Margot Light sees foreign policy emerging from the interaction between "the micro level of [domestic] politics with the macro level of the international system."[4]

Internal determinants of state behavior include geographic location, relative size (although this can change in case of loss of territory or partition), material and human resource base, historical experience, self-perception, world-view, system of values/ideas/ideals/cultural traits, the character of political system and of government, character of leadership, and economic and military power. External determinants relate to the nature of regional and international environments or systems within which states operate. The character of these systems and states' relative weight and role within them primarily determine the range of choices available to them. Some internal factors, such as the nature of states' political regimes and that of their value systems, are subject to alteration, while others, like geography, are constant, except in rare instances, such as a shift in political borders resulting from the addition of territory or its loss.

The Impact of Geography

It is often said that geography is destiny. This may be an exaggeration, but no doubt states' geographical location significantly affects their choices. A small or weak country located in the proximity of a large and powerful country has fewer choices than a country whose neighbors are of more-or-less equal size and power or are much smaller and weaker. A large country like the United States, shielded by two large oceans and bordered by smaller or less powerful neighbors, is far less susceptible to military attack than a small or weak country surrounded by large and strong states. According to Aaron David Miller, because of its geography the United States remains "uniquely secure from foreign threats."[5] Historically, Russia's vast geography has confounded foreign conquerors from Sweden's Charles XII and France's Napoleon to Germany's Hitler. Similarly, a land-locked country usually has fewer choices than a country with access to the open seas.

Geographical characteristics also partly shape states' goals and ambitions. Russia's lack of year-round access to warm waters has often been cited as a major cause of its southward imperial expansion in the eighteenth and nineteenth centuries. Geography also helps determine states' defensive strategies and the pattern of their alliances. Britain's historic insistence on maintaining naval supremacy in the open seas as part of its defense strategy can be largely explained in light of its being an island nation dependent on trade. Spain's unsuccessful attempt to invade Britain in the sixteenth century further contributed to this British mindset.

Geography also influences the pattern of states' alliances. Generally, small countries neighboring large and powerful states seek to form alliances with more distant powers, in order to counterbalance their stronger neighbor or neighbors. Technological changes in aerospace and other fields, plus the greater ease of movement of peoples across national boundaries, have reduced the importance of geography, especially as a security blanket. Nevertheless, as explained by Aaron David Miller, geography still matters.[6] It also largely determines the quality of states' resource base and hence their chances of economic development and growth. Ricardo Haussmann has traced the causes of the underdevelopment of twenty-five countries to "their distinguishing geographical characteristics": they all "tend to be located in tropical regions, or because of their location face large transportation costs in accessing world markets or both."[7]

Geography also partly determines states' historical experience and even their ethnic and cultural characteristics. States which historically have been in the path of major migratory movements or imperial expansion tend to have a less homogenous ethnic and cultural make-up. Some of this type of states can undergo total cultural transformation as a result of migratory movements or imperial expansion. Good examples are those countries conquered by Arab/Islamic armies or subjected to Mongol/Turkic invasions. Ethnic and cultural composition of states has security dimensions, because often ethnically and culturally diverse countries tend to be more vulnerable to external pressures.

By partly determining states' historical experiences, geography also helps shape their self- and world-views as well as some of their ideas, values, and cultural characteristics. According to Aaron David Miller, "because American geographic position is so unique in the world, it has led to a world-view that is often unrealistic and riddled with contradictions."[8] He ascribes what he considers to be principal characteristics of American political culture, namely pragmatism, idealism, arrogance, and ambivalence, to its geography.[9] Russia's sense of its own cultural uniqueness can be explained partly in terms of its vast geography, as part of both Europe and Asia. By contrast, countries whose geography renders them vulnerable to frequent invasions or those that have been the victims of great power rivalries tend to have a pessimistic world-view. Good examples are Poland in Europe and Iran in West Asia. Thus, while Napoleon's belief that "the politics of all powers is determined by their geography" is excessive, its impact in determining states' political destinies by virtue of limits it imposes and opportunities it offers or withholds and by influencing their self and world views and even values and cultural traits cannot be denied.[10]

Historical Experience: Impact on States' Self- and World-views

States' historical experience greatly influences their self- and world-views and hence it also partly shapes their policy goals and the pattern of their external behavior. Often countries with a distinguished past but which are experiencing a period of relative decline seek to restore past glories, even if in a different guise. They also tend to demand the kind of treatment from other states that they believe befits their more glorious past, more than their present conditions. A recent example is Russia. Despite the loss of its empire and its declining power, post-Soviet Russia has been obsessively concerned about being treated as a great power. Still-dominant powers such as the United States can find it difficult to cope with relative decline and with the rise of new powerful actors, as illustrated by the United States' reaction to the rise of Japan in the 1980s and to an increasingly powerful China in more recent times. Likewise, countries dominated in the past or subjected to foreign manipulation can become obsessed with independence or unreasonably resentful of those countries which had dominated them. They often develop a victimhood complex and even engage in self-damaging behavior. Many aspects of the ex-colonialized and semi-colonialized countries' worldviews can be attributed to their experience of domination. They often view the world as hostile and unfair and divided between those who have power and dominate others and those which don't and are dominated. They also see the international political and economic systems as fundamentally unjust and working against their interests and to the benefit of more powerful states.

Many policies of the Third World countries in the 1960s and 1970s were influenced by this particular world-view. These policies included creation of the Non-Aligned Movement (NAM) in 1961, efforts to establish a New International Economic Order (NIEO) in the 1970s, and to promote more economic and political cooperation among Third World countries in the context of South-South relations. In the last four decades in the Muslim world, the traditional Third Worldist world-view has been expressed through religious vocabulary. The Islamic Republic of Iran's world-view and its foreign policy discourse best exemplify this phenomenon.[11]

Partly because of their historical experience, many states view themselves as exceptional and superior to others and hence destined to play a special role in world affairs because of their power but more so because of their virtue. Even powerful states justify their sense of exceptionalism and superiority mainly on the basis of their superior values and virtues rather than their material power. The United States is a good example of such a powerful state. In the 1980s, despite its limited economic and military power, the Islamic Republic of Iran claimed to be a spiritual superpower by virtue of its Islamic values and revolutionary ideology and the fact that it championed the rights of the world's dispossessed and oppressed peoples.[12] This moral/ethical/ideological component of states' self-view and their claims of superiority are where the impact of religion on their behavior can best be observed, although often in a changed or mutated form.

Religion and States' Views of Their Exceptionality

Until the last three hundred years, religion formed the foundation of most societies' values. Many of today's secular values are rooted in religion and are often the reworked and reinterpreted versions of religious principles. It is thus not surprising that the self-view of states that consider themselves to be exceptional and thus entitled to global leadership is at least partly rooted in their religious beliefs. Historically, often states' religion-based self-perceptions as exceptional justified their imperial policies. Some Western states rationalized and justified interventionist policies in other parts of the world in terms of higher values of both a religious and secular nature. By contrast, countries subjected to such interventions see them as reflecting the perpetrators' power ambitions and imperialistic impulses.

In the eighteenth and nineteenth centuries, Russia's view of itself as the Third Rome, the bastion of true Christianity (Russian Orthodoxy), and its defender served as justification for its southward expansion in the direction of the Black Sea and the Caucasus. Russia believed that as the defender of Christianity and the successor to the Eastern Christianity it had a duty to liberate Constantinople from Ottoman domination. Despite its declared atheism, the USSR's millenarian and utopian aspirations for a classless society contained a hint of this religion-based sense of Russia's moral superiority which bestowed on it special responsibility toward others. The Russian communists' attacks on the West as decadent and materialistic had a hint of traditional Russian views of Western Christianity as somehow less pure and worldlier than Orthodox Christianity practiced in Russia.[13] Vladimir Putin's characterization of the West as decadent also partly reflects these traditional Russian views.[14]

According to many scholars, the United States' belief in its special role in the world and its sense that it has a duty to guide world affairs in the right direction and to fight for the spread of democracy and human rights is rooted in religion. These scholars see America's commitment to foster these goals throughout the world as a secularized version of the country's religious origins and its self-view as the implementer of God's will. They trace the origins of this belief to the first Puritan communities in New England, with the Puritans' belief that they had been chosen by God to build in America an ideal community, "a city on the hill."[15] This ideal community then would be a model for the rest of the world to emulate.

Even before coming to America, some Puritans believed that the very discovery of America was the fulfillment of divine will and that God had chosen America for a special destiny. This early and largely religious belief was then transformed into the idea of America's Manifest Destiny and its exceptionalism. According to John Judis, in the late eighteenth century America's founders transformed this biblical millennialism into a "civilian millennialism," as: "They [America's founders] transformed Protestant millennialism into the language of American nationalism and exceptionalism. The chosen people—whom [Jonathan] Edwards identified with the visible Saints of New England's Congregational Churches—became the citizens of the United States; the millennium became a thousand-year reign of religious and civil liberty; and the adversary became English tyranny and Old World

Catholicism. In this way, Protestant millennialism ordered and gave meaning to Americans' intentions, but the intentions were now often expressed in language of politics rather than of pulpit."[16] What remained constant was the idea of America as the Chosen Nation, or in the words of Abraham Lincoln "the last best hope of earth" or, according to Madeleine Albright, the "indispensable nation." This millennialism also led to belief in America's role as guardian and promoter of global good against world evil. The nature of evil in America's perception has changed from Nazism in the 1940s to Communism during the Cold War years (1946–1989), to Islamic extremism from the 1990s onward, but belief in America's role as the upholder of good has remained constant.

Despite its religious origins, the idea of American exceptionalism and global role has become secularized. Some of the values that America is now promoting go against traditional religious beliefs and are opposed by America's own religious-minded people. Ironically, perhaps, a considerable segment of the American people is not aware of the religious foundations of its sense of exceptionalism and even nationalism. This means that the purely religious aspects of America's self-view have little influence on its external behavior, even though, at times, the words in which it is presented draw upon this religious heritage.

A sense of mission has not been unique to America. Russian and the European powers' imperial expansion was also justified on the basis of concepts such as "Civilizing Mission" (the French Mission Civilisatrice) or the White Man's Burden.[17] Although not clearly stated, this civilizing mission included bringing the benefits of Christianity to other peoples. The difference, however, was that none of the European powers claimed, at least not openly, to be God's chosen instrument. For some European countries, their championing of the ideals of democracy and human rights today can be seen as the continuation of their sense of mission to civilize the world.

Resource Base

A state's resource base—material, human, and increasingly technological—influences its behavior. Regardless of its self-perception as exceptional and destined to a leadership role, without adequate resources a state cannot fulfill its ambitions. The character of states' resource base influences their behavior by determining the range of options available to them. A resource-rich country can opt for a more self-reliant economy and for military and political neutrality than can a resource-poor country. If technologically and economically advanced, a resource-poor country will be interested in obtaining or at least safeguarding sources of supply. If not advanced, it will be interested in obtaining financial and technological assistance. Both will inevitably have to adjust their behavior to these requirements. A resource-rich country, meanwhile, will be more interested in export markets, although generally countries pursue both goals.

Historically and after its industrialization, Britain's policy of dominating the sea lanes had much to do with its need for sources of supply and export markets. The policies of other colonial/imperial powers were also partly determined by the same needs. The excessive interest of Western and increasingly Asian powers such as China, Japan, and India in the Persian Gulf has much to do with their lack of sufficient energy resources and the Persian Gulf's vast oil and gas reserves. China's recent interest and activities in Africa have had to do with its need for various raw materials as well as potential export markets.[18] Japan's expansionist policies toward its neighbors in the 1930s and 1940s, in the context of its so-called Greater East Asia Co-Prosperity Sphere, were partly determined by the limited base of its natural resources and hence its need to gain access to sources of supply.

Changing Internal Determinants

Those internal determinants of state behavior that are more subject to change include the character of their political system—for example, democratic, authoritarian or totalitarian, monarchical republican; the ideology or value system of their ruling elites; their public opinion regarding their role in the world; and the character and peculiarities of their key leaders.

In advanced and stable countries with a high degree of popular consensus regarding social and political values and ideals, changes in leadership produced periodically through elections do not generally lead to dramatic shifts in the main patterns of their external behavior. Changes occur only in some aspects of their external policies. Without external stimuli (e.g., invasion and more recently massive migration) with rare exceptions changes in French, German, or British governments do not produce massive shifts in their foreign policies. Such exceptions include the coming to power of a government whose ideology drastically departs from the existing consensus. This is what happened in Germany after the Nazis' electoral victory in 1933. Nevertheless, even smaller shifts in the policy orientations of the more powerful states whose behavior strongly affects the dynamics of international affairs can have significant consequences for all international actors. A change in U.S. policy toward a particular region, such as the Middle East, can have far-reaching ramifications for regional states, the region's balance of power, and the character of regional politics. To a lesser extent, the same also applies to the case of Russia, China, and the EU.

By contrast, in the more newly established states with fractured societies and underdeveloped political institutions, changes in governments often tend to occur as a result of non-constitutional means such as coups d'état, revolts, and revolutions. This type of change often dramatically alters a state's political system, the nature of its political elites and leadership, and even its ideology and value system—hence inevitably changing the pattern of its external behavior. This kind of change also influences the dynamics of regional and in some cases international relations. In the 1950s and 1960s, changes triggered by revolutionary movements in the political systems and leaderships of key Middle Eastern countries such as Egypt, Iraq, Libya, and Syria drastically shifted the pattern of regional politics and alliances, as well as the pattern of Middle Eastern countries' relations with major global powers. The political changes resulting from revolutions in the above-noted Arab states enhanced the Soviet Union's position in the Middle East and undermined that of the West. In the 1980s, Iran's foreign policy underwent a fundamental change following the victory of the 1979 Islamic Revolution, the fall of the monarchy, the establishment of an Islamic Republic, and the replacement of the essentially nationalist ideology of Iranian state with an ideology based on a mixture of Islam and Marxism. Cuba's socialist revolution in 1960 triggered far-reaching changes in Latin America's regional and international relations. In more newly established states, long-established but undemocratic states, or governments with narrow political bases, the imperatives of regime-survival often exert a tremendous influence on the nature and character of their external behavior. This is also true of ideological states. There, boundaries between political regimes and states become blurred and security and other interests of regime and state become indistinguishable. In this type of state, requirements of regime survival, as perceived by their leaders, often trump other considerations in guiding states' external behavior.

The Impact of Leaders' Personalities

To a greater or lesser extent, beliefs, proclivities, and characteristics of political leaders of all states affect their external behavior. According to Daniel L. Byman and Kenneth J. Pollack, leaders' "goals, abilities and foibles are crucial to the intentions, capabilities, and strategies of states."[19] Moreover, leaders' proclivities determine how they receive and interpret information. According to Hermann, Hermann, and Hagan, when leaders have a well-defined world-view, they "tend to look for cues that confirm [their] beliefs when making foreign policy. As a result, [they] will be insensitive to discrepant advice and data. In effect, leaders selectively use incoming information to support [their] predispositions."[20] Nevertheless, the impact of leaders' proclivities and ideas tends to be stronger in those states which lack democratic institutions and are ruled by authoritarian leaders. Leaders such as Ayatullah Rouhullah Khomeini, Saddam Hussein, Muamar Gadhafi, and Kim Il Sung exerted inordinate influence on the behavior of their respective countries of Iran, Iraq, Libya, and North Korea. In Iran, today, according to the statements of its government officials, Ayatullah Ali Khamenei, the country's

Supreme Leader, decides the goals of the country's foreign policy and its basic directions.[21]

Even in democratic countries, key leaders' personalities, beliefs, and ideational preferences influence the conduct of states' external relations. A recent example is the impact that the personalities of the U.S. president, George W. Bush, and the British prime minister, Tony Blair, and their ideational beliefs and preferences had on their decision to attack Iraq in 2003. According to a number of sources, both leaders tended to view the world through a binary lens and saw it as being made up of forces of good and evil which were in a constant battle. They also believed that their respective countries had a duty to support the forces of good and to vanquish the forces of evil. President George W. Bush's speech on January 2002 about the existence of an Axis of Evil consisting of Iran, Iraq, and North Korea clearly illustrates this particular mindset.[22] In addition, both men were fairly religious and thus saw combating evil as a moral and religious duty. The religious aspect of the characters of president George W. Bush and Tony Blair points to another channel through which religion's influence can be felt on states' external behavior and hence the character of international affairs.

Furthermore, President George W. Bush's beliefs and his behavior reflected the impact of that strain of America's self-view that saw it as being destined to do God's work and combat evil, both of which, as noted earlier, are rooted in religion. Earlier, other U.S. presidents had shown similar tendencies. President Ronald Reagan (1981–1989) characterized the Soviet Union as the "evil empire." Before him, President Franklin Roosevelt saw Nazi Germany as the manifestation of evil (with more existential justification). The United States viewed the USSR as evil partly because of its atheistic ideology. In other words, the American view of the USSR as evil was at least partly shaped by religious factors.

Thus the question arises whether America would have invaded Iraq if a different president, less influenced by this aspect of America's self-view and without strong religious tendencies, had been in power. Similarly, would Britain have eagerly supported invading Iraq if Tony Blair with his Manichean view of the world and his religious beliefs had not headed the British government in 2003? The answer to both these questions would be "Yes" because in the final analysis American and British policy to invade Iraq was determined by strategic, political, and economic considerations—whether or not accurately judged—and by a belief that the war would be an easy and quick affair. In reaching this conclusion they were influenced by the opinions of key figures in the American foreign policy community, including senior officials of the George W. Bush administration, including Vice President Richard Cheney. Kenneth Adelman, a former official in the Reagan administration, and Richard Perle, a member of the Pentagon's Defense Policy Board, in an article in the *Washington Post*, argued that the Iraq War would be a "cakewalk."[23] Both leaders, especially Tony Blair, also seem to have had a strong belief in their ability to control and direct the course of events.[24] In the absence of more tangible reasons and the perception that their goal could be easily achieved, George Bush's and Tony Blair's judgments about the Saddam regime's evil nature, their religious values, and their binary world-views would not have been sufficient to prompt them to attack Iraq.

Value Systems/Ideology/Ideas

The question of the relative role that ideologies and value systems, which are rooted in countries' cultures and of which religion is an important component, play in their external behavior has long been hotly debated among scholars of international relations and foreign policy making process. On this issue, among the international relations scholars, the main division is between the realists and those who subscribe to the liberal and in more recent times the constructivist schools of international relations theory.

According to the realist school, states are motivated by a desire for power, which is necessary to protect and advance their interests. Paramount among these interests is security which, in turn, is the function of the international system's "anarchical" nature, in the sense that there is no supra-national legal authority capable of adjudicating disputes and enforcing its decrees and thus preserving states' rights and preventing abuses by stronger states.[25] The only guarantor of states' rights is either their inherent power or a balance of international power which can provide a degree of protection to weaker states against the predatory ambitions of more powerful actors. The realists also believe that values/ideologies are largely at the service of power. Thus Hans Morgenthau, father of the modern realist school, believed that, without an ideological cover, states would be in an unfavorable position vis-à-vis their rivals. In his view, states need to appeal to principles and not merely power in order to garner popular support and a willingness to sacrifice on the part of their people without which "no foreign policy can pass the ultimate test of strength."[26]

Those belonging to the liberal and constructivist schools challenge this view. They point out that even if states' main goal is to preserve their interests and therefore pursue power in order to be able to do so, some fundamental questions remain unanswered. Most important are how and on what basis states determine their interests, especially those beyond the requirements of security? How do they redefine these interests in light of changing circumstances or of their own experiences? According to Joseph Nye, "how states define their interests and how their interests change has always been a weak area in realist theory."[27] The liberals and constructivists then argue that states' values or ideologies help shape their perceptions of their interests. In this way, ideology or a set of fundamental ideas and values determines the ends to which power should be used. Moreover, states' ideologies or values and ideals shape their reaction to different challenges and developments. They also largely determine the means states employ to attain their policy objectives. These systems, especially political ideologies, serve as a road map partly because, as put by Zbigniew Brzezinski, ideology is essentially "an action program."[28]

To acknowledge the role of values, ideas, and ideologies in shaping states' behavior does not mean that they are the determining influence either in broad terms or in specific cases. On the contrary, when overwhelming security and other interests are involved, values, ideas, and ideologies exert less influence on states' behavior, even though to some degree they shape states' perceptions of where their security and other interests lie, as well as their perceptions of threats posed to these interests. In particular, by shaping actors' world-view or what Max Weber has called "world images," they determine patterns of behavior through which interests are pursued.[29] Moreover, ideas and ideologies can act as blinders and thus "reduce the number of conceivable alternative [actions]."[30] Ideas/ideologies and value and belief systems become even more influential when they become embedded in institutions and linked to questions of power.[31] The significance of values in determining states' perceptions of where their interests lie is reflected in the fact that, when states' or their political elites' value systems/ideas or ideologies change, or when a whole new political elite with value and ideational system different from their predecessors comes to power, frequently their countries' perceptions of their interests and hence their behavior is also altered.

Moreover, security has never been solely about the safety of borders or preventing aggression. On the contrary, it has always had an identity dimension, to a considerable degree determined by states' values, ideas, or ideologies. Protecting states' identities and hence their values/ideologies has therefore always been an important security concern.[32] The Cold War was not merely about containing Soviet power but was also about protecting Western liberal countries' values and identities based upon them. Because of the recent explosion of communications in the last few decades, in a number of non-European, especially Muslim, countries the defense of traditional values has become a security concern. Thus in many Muslim countries, notably the Islamic Republic of Iran, increasingly there has been talk of cultural aggression and the need to defend indigenous values against foreign influences.[33]

This situation to some degree also prevailed in the distant past. For example, Europe of the Middle Ages was not just defending its frontiers against the Arabs/Muslims' advances but it was also protecting its Christian values and its Christian identity against Islam. Similarly, the resistance of non-European countries to colonial and imperial powers had a cultural/value dimension and was aimed as much at protecting territory as at defending national cultural and ideational heritage.

Over time, however, even the most ideological states feel the impact of more lasting determinants of behavior, such as geography, demography, resource base, historical experience, and deep-rooted cultural factors. Furthermore, when the physical survival of states is threatened, ideology/values exert a less powerful influence on their policy decisions and behavior.

RELIGION AS IDEOLOGY

Historically, religion has formed a significant, if not the most important, part of various states' value systems and identities and it still does, including in the highly secularized Western states. Thus religion influences how states and some non-state actors define their interests. Moreover, as noted in the introduction, in the last fifty years, under the impact of secular ideologies, new interpretations of religion have emerged that in effect are more akin to secular political ideologies than religion as traditionally defined and understood as a divine or spiritual belief system. When an ideologized version of religion prevails within a country or within its leadership, its impact in shaping national identities and state behavior becomes more direct and strong. For example, in the Islamic Republic of Iran where an ideologized version of religion prevails, the leadership has tried to recast Iran's national identity solely in religious terms and has waged a war against traditional components of this identity, albeit with very mixed results.[34]

Ideologized religion's impact is greater because in this version it becomes closely linked to political power and legitimacy and to the issue of who exercises leadership. Therefore, it performs the same role that ideology has often played as the legitimizer of political power and the justifier of political action. However, the characterization of such religion-based ideologies as religion is problematic. Moreover, it raises a basic question: If religion becomes ideology and acts as such, should not its impact on international actors' behavior be judged in the context of the dialectics of interests versus values/ideas and ideology?

EXTERNAL DETERMINANTS

States' external behavior is determined by an interaction between the internal and external contexts within which policy is formed, although there is no agreement among scholars of international relations as to their relative impact. Realists tend to emphasize the significance of external factors, especially the characteristics of the prevailing international system, especially the configuration of power among the key players.[35] The external setting related to the character of the international system affects all states, but its influence is greatest on smaller and weaker actors. The reason for this situation, as noted before, is the system's anarchical nature. Such a system renders weaker actors vulnerable to the predatory impulses of larger and more powerful members of the international system. In view of this reality, therefore, an international system characterized by a multiplicity of competing power centers, which tend to balance one another and thus inhibit powerful states from acting unilaterally in matters of war and peace, is more favorable to weaker states. Such a system offers them more policy choices and enables them better to retain their independence and protect their security. By contrast, an international system dominated by a single great power or a consort of great powers is less congenial to weaker states. For example, during the Cold War era the international system was bipolar and two competing alliances tended to balance each other. Consequently, during this epoch the great powers were less prone to engage unilaterally in military intervention in other countries, lest they would risk triggering a violent reaction from the other side. There were exceptions, such as the U.S. involvement in Vietnam and the Soviet invasion of Afghanistan in 1979, and, before that, Soviet military interventions in Hungary in 1956 and Czechoslovakia in 1968. The two blocs also engaged in proxy wars in different parts of the world. Nevertheless, both sides avoided situations which carried the risk of direct confrontation. By contrast, after the end of the Cold War and the elimination of the Soviet counterweight to American power, the United States has shown greater propensity to engage in military interventions and embark on the so-called "wars of choice," such as invading Iraq in 2003.[36]

The same logic applies to regional political systems. A regional system characterized by a balanced distribution of power among its principal actors tends to be more stable. Any significant disruption of power equilibrium at the regional level often causes conflict or increases its potential risk. A good example was Iraq's decision in 1980 to invade Iran. That decision was prompted by the disruption of the regional balance of power following the 1979 Islamic Revolution in Iran and the ensuing turmoil in the country and the subsequent weakening of the Iranian state. The disruption of the regional balance of power in the Persian Gulf and the Middle East following the 2003 U.S.-led invasion of Iraq had similar results. It led to intensified regional rivalries and conflicts, as well as to the emergence of new violent non-state actors, such as the Islamic State.[37] In sum, the disruption of power equilibria at either regional or international levels generally sets in motion new dynamics, thus compelling various actors to adjust to the new circumstances ensuing from these new dynamics; actors either try to take advantage of the new conditions or counter their real or perceived negative consequences.

Such disruption of equilibria in regional systems could occur as a result of internal changes within either key regional states or major international actors. For instance, as noted above, the change in Iran's political system from monarchy to Islamic regime dramatically altered the dynamics of the Middle East regional system and led to war and regional realignments. The fall of Iraq's Saddam Hussein had a similar impact. When such changes occur in the status of a key international actor, the consequences are even greater. Thus the 1945 defeat of Germany changed the trajectory of European politics, as it happened in a more positive direction, at least in the West (though that proposition is more questionable regarding the East). It opened the way for a new West European security, political, and economic system based on cooperation rather than conflict.[38] By contrast, the Chinese Communists' 1949 victory had more negative consequences and contributed to regional conflicts in East Asia. In more recent times, the USSR's disintegration has had a far-reaching impact on the character and dynamics of regional and international systems.

MOTIVATIONS AND GOALS BEHIND STATE BEHAVIOR

All states also pursue certain basic goals or national interests which constitute the principal motives behind their actions. As noted earlier, because of variations in states' inherent abilities, resources, ideology, and value systems, different states use different means to achieve their goals. But the significance of these goals for all states is beyond dispute.

Self-Preservation

Self-preservation is the most vital of states' interests, and everything else is subordinated to it. According to some scholars, even the most cherished values and ideologies must be sacrificed for this purpose because, as noted by Frederick Northedge, "States must survive and somehow prosper . . . (and) in the final resort the nation's will to survive is irresistible."[39] A recent case was the Islamic Republic of Iran's decision to sign a cease-fire agreement with Iraq in August 1988 after eight years of war. Because it could no longer carry on the fight without facing potential risk of collapse, Iran compromised on its revolutionary ideals and accepted the cease-fire. Although he likened it to drinking a cup of poison, Ayatullah Khomeini sanctioned the signing of the agreement; the urge to survive overcame the Islamic regime's and Khomeini's ideological proclivity to continue the war.

Territorial Integrity and Preventing Aggression

Closely linked with self-preservation are defense of a country against external aggression and maintenance of its territorial integrity, even though threats to the latter might have domestic sources, such as separatist movements.

Economic Well-Being/Prosperity

The achievement or safeguarding of economic prosperity rank next in the order of priority for states and thus are major motivators of state behavior, such as efforts to gain access to sources of supply and export markets. But even this motive has a security dimension. Without a sufficient economic base, states would be incapable of having adequate defensive forces. The lack of economic prosperity could also affect the states' internal security because less prosperous communities are often more vulnerable to dissent and conflict. Internal strife, in turn, could make states more vulnerable to external threats. Thus part of the states' tendency to maximize their power is explained in light of their desire for prosperity; more power tends to enable them to get the sources of supply and markets they want. At times, however, for ideological reasons or for regime survival, states forego economic prosperity, as exemplified by the cases of North Korea and to some degree the Islamic Republic of Iran. Despite costly economic sanctions, both countries have refused to alter aspects of their external behavior which have been largely responsible for most of their difficulties. However, the worsening of Iran's economic conditions, as a result of severe international sanctions, forced it to reach an agreement with the five permanent members of the United Nations' Security Council, plus Germany, regarding its nuclear program in July 2015, despite significant ideological and practical opposition from influential military and political personalities. In the context of this agreement known as the Joint Comprehensive Plan of Action (JCPOA), Iran accepted severe limitations on its program in exchange for sanctions relief. The Iranian action shows that even economic necessity, if serious enough, could trump ideological considerations.

Prestige

Desire for prestige and standing is another motivator of state action, albeit to a lesser degree than security and prosperity. Historically, a country's material power has largely determined the degree of its international prestige. In more recent decades, states' values and ideals and those of their actions motivated by these values have become important sources of national prestige. By becoming engaged in humanitarian activities or by helping less fortunate countries, some states have gained prestige which they could not have achieved by virtue of their material power. Desire for prestige on the part of either a state or its leadership could also lead it to engage in costly or unprofitable activities which ultimately could detract from its security and prosperity. Many non-European countries have engaged in such activities after becoming independent.

Autonomy and Independence

Some scholars have also cited the desire for autonomy and independence, namely the ability to decide on internal and external policies without undue interference by outsiders, as an important interest of states.[40]

POWER/INTEREST VERSUS VALUES/IDEALS: REAL OR FALSE DICHOTOMY?

The question of the relative roles of power and interest versus ideals/values and ideology in determining international actors' behavior has long been debated by scholars of international relations. In the distant past, this debate was mostly framed in terms of the tension between principle and expediency.[41] Yet the question remains unresolved as to what extent this dichotomy is real, or to what degree states are forced to choose between their interests and their values. A related question is whether a combination of interests and ideas/ideals does in fact determine international actors' actions. After all, is it not the case that interests are often defined under the influence of states' ideology/values? Moreover, is it not the case that various actors' ability to spread their values contributes to their power and prestige? The spread of their values also renders their external environment less threatening because generally like-minded states (at least democracies) tend not to attack one another and mostly are in good terms. By the same token, powerful countries have a better chance of spreading their ideals, although not always successfully. Empirical evidence shows that the dichotomy between interests and ideals is often false.

Without its enormous economic and military power, the United States could not have tried to "make the world safe for democracy"[42] or to defend freedom against Fascist or communist totalitarianism. But it is equally true that, without commitment to liberal and democratic ideals, the United States could have chosen other strategies to defend itself, safeguard its security, and protect its values, such as opting for Fortress America. In other words, America's values to a considerable degree have determined its views of where its interests lie, including its security interests, but values are not the be-all and end-all.[43] Nevertheless, their influence on states' and some non-state actors' behavior is strongest when advancing them also serves their interests and enhances their security and power or at least is perceived to do so.

MOTIVATION IN SPECIFIC CASES

Assessing the relative impact of values and interests on international actors' behavior, is best done by examining specific cases. It is better to ask whether the United States entered World War I in order to make the world safe for democracy or whether a stronger motivation was to prevent disruption of the European balance of power which a German victory would have produced and which could have proved detrimental to U.S. security and other interests. The same question could also be raised regarding World War II, although in view of the particularly distasteful character of Nazism, the impact of value-related motives was highly significant.[44]

In more recent times, the March 2003 American-led invasion of Iraq provides a good case for assessing the relative roles of values and interests. The U.S. decision was determined by a combination of factors, and the influence of all the determinants of state behavior discussed earlier can be detected in the decision. America's view of itself as the upholder of good against evil and as the promoter of democracy and human rights made it receptive to calls to fight against Saddam Hussein's cruel and dictatorial regime. President George W. Bush's own proclivities to see the world through the prism of an unending struggle between good and evil made him more susceptible to the urgings of those advisors recommending war. Idealistic arguments were used to convince the American public of the necessity of war against Iraq. It was said that the fall of Saddam's regime could usher in a so-called positive domino effect by spreading democracy in the Middle East and in this way contribute to regional peace.[45] Such a peace, it was argued, was in the U.S. national interest. Saddam Hussein was likened to Adolf Hitler in order to show that, by invading Iraq, the United States was fighting evil. These arguments clearly showed the role of ideals in garnering popular support for actions undertaken, at least partly, for other reasons. The intermingling of these diverse arguments illustrated what Morgenthau has called the symbiotic relationship between power and ideals.

However, the most convincing arguments were mostly security-related. It was argued (erroneously, as it turned out) that Iraq possessed weapons of mass destruction and also was in league with Muslim extremist and terrorist groups, such as *Al Qaeda*. The inevitable conclusion was that Iraq posed a security threat to the United States and its regional allies. Economic arguments were also used. It was claimed that Saddam could threaten the world's oil supply and hence the health of American and global economy.

Underlying all these arguments was the notion that in the post-Soviet era, through the exercise of its power, the United States should reshape the regional and international orders and in this way ensure its global supremacy and leadership. Writing in 2000, Condoleezza Rice, the one-time national security advisor and later secretary of state in the G. W. Bush administration, said, "Power matters, both the exercise of power by the United States and the ability of others to exercise it. Yet many in the United States are (and have always been) uncomfortable with notions of power politics, great powers and power balances." She added that this attitude leads to a situation where "the 'national interest' is replaced with 'humanitarian interest' or the interests of the 'international community.'" She then argued against this approach and maintained that "America's pursuit of [its] national interests will create conditions that promote peace, freedom and markets."[46]

The view that America should use the opportunities offered by systemic changes following the Soviet Union's collapse also prevailed within the Clinton administration, although motivations there might have been somewhat more idealistic. Anthony Lake, President Clinton's national security advisor, in 1995 wrote that "The end of the Cold War and the emergence of newly independent states in Eastern Europe have the potential to enlarge the family of nations now committed to the pursuit of democratic institutions, the expansion of free markets, the peaceful settlement of conflicts and the promotion of collective security."[47] Then turning to those states which he called the backlash states, meaning countries like Iran, Iraq of the Saddam era, North Korea, and Libya, he added: "As the sole superpower, the United States has a special responsibility for developing a strategy to neutralize, contain and through selective pressure to transform backlash states."[48] He believed this is possible because the United States has *"no longer to fear Soviet efforts to gain a foothold in the Persian Gulf by taking advantage of our support for one of these states (Iran and Iraq) to build relations with the other . . . the strategic importance of both Iraq and Iran has been reduced dramatically and their ability to play the superpowers off each other has been eliminated"*[emphasis added].[49]

What the above means is that, regardless of whether it was framed in idealistic or power politics terminology, the principal driver of U.S. policy vis-à-vis Iraq and the entire Middle East was America's determination to establish its hegemony over the region and enhance its global leadership. This was made possible by elimination of the Soviet counterweight to American power. It had been enhanced by the systemic changes ensuing from the USSR's collapse, thus making it easier for the United States to engage in military action of such magnitude as the invasion of Iraq. This option would not have been available to the United States during the Cold War era because it could have triggered a Soviet response and thus increased risks to America's security. This systemic situation was in sharp contrast with the 1980s. Then, during the American hostage crisis in Iran—November 1979–January 1981—the United States had a strong case for military intervention in Iran, in order to secure the release of its diplomats held hostage or simply to punish Iran. U.S. hesitation to use force, except for an ill-fated, small-scale rescue attempt, was largely because of concern over Soviet reaction, although some believe that the fear that such action would strengthen and consolidate the revolution was the main reason for the American inaction.[50] Nevertheless, the Soviet counterweight acted as a brake on U.S. ability for large-scale military intervention.

Regarding the 2003 U.S.-led invasion of Iraq, the security threat argument was the most convincing, including for the American public, followed by a general desire to produce positive political change in Iraq and possibly in the rest of the Middle East.

ENDS, MEANS/INSTRUMENTS, INTENTIONS, CAPABILITIES

As explained above, state behavior is determined by a combination of power/interest and value and ideology-related factors. However, it is not sufficient to know what motivates states' behavior. The means or instruments used to achieve objectives are equally, perhaps even more important. All states want power and prestige, but there are great differences in how they go about acquiring them and what means and instruments they employ. It is in the choice of the means and instruments that values and ideals play more important roles.

In Iraq's case, both the Clinton and Bush administrations wanted to bring down Saddam Hussein's government. Because of its greater commitment to multilateralism and greater aversion to the use of military force, the Clinton administration chose means other than military power. The article by Anthony Lake, noted earlier, clearly states how the Clinton administration intended to achieve its goals. Lake wrote: "We [the US] seek to contain the influence of these states, sometimes by isolation, sometimes through pressures, sometimes by diplomatic and economic measures. We encourage the rest of the international community to join us in a concerted effort. In the case of Iraq and Libya, for example, we have already achieved a strong international consensus backed by U.N. resolutions."[51] The Clinton administration did not rule out America's unilateral action, including military, and did engage in a limited use of airpower against Iraq for limited objectives.

By contrast, as gleaned from the article by Condoleezza Rice, the George W. Bush administration was more prone to both unilateral action and to the use of military force. In short, both administrations had the same goal, namely the strengthening of America's power and leadership and promoting its values, but the means they used to achieve them were different. As the consequences of the Bush administration's approach to Iraq have demonstrated, in terms of outcome, at times ultimately the means states use to achieve their goals could be more important than the goals they pursue.

Intentions and Capabilities

Regardless of their motivations and intentions, states can only hope to realize their goals if they have the requisite capabilities. Certainly, the ability of states to act unilaterally or in disregard of other states' concerns depends entirely on whether they have the means to do so without fear of retaliation or of other undesirable outcomes. If America decided to act in Iraq in defiance of a fair degree of international opposition and even more skepticism, it was because it had the military and economic power to do so, without fearing any serious retaliation by other countries or threats to its own security and interests.

Internal conditions in America after 9/11 were also strongly conducive to popular support for unilateral military action. The American public had been traumatized by the 9/11 attacks and was concerned about the perceived threats posed by terrorists to U.S. security. It is quite unlikely that without 9/11 those favoring more military intervention in pursuit of America's power-related and idealistic goals could have prevailed. In short, both the internal and external contexts of U.S. foreign policy enabled the United States to act the way it did. Ultimately, however, it could not have acted if it did not possess the requisite means.

MOTIVATIONS OF VIOLENT NON-STATE ACTORS

The factors that determine violent non-state actors' goals and their motivations in some cases are reflected in their very nature. Ethnic and sectarian separatist groups are essentially motivated by a desire for independence from the political entity to which they belong. The *PKK (Partyia Karkeran e Kurdistan*—Kurdish Workers Party) was formed to achieve independence for Turkey's Kurds, and, failing that, to gain a better deal for the Kurds within the existing structures of the Turkish Republic. *PEJAK (Party Zhian Nazadi Kurdistan*—Party of Free Life for Kurdistan) wants to gain independence for Iran's Kurdish population. Various Chechen movements, including the so-called Islamist movements and some movements in Kashmir, also fall into this category. Groups identified as national liberation movements historically have sought to gain independence from colonial/imperial powers. Today, such groups want to regain what they consider their land from what they see as an occupying power. The best example of this case is the Palestine Liberation Organization (PLO) during its early years of operation and before it recognized Israel's right to exist in the 1993 Oslo Accords.[52] The Islamist Palestinian movement, HAMAS, also falls into this category. Its motivation is to free all or parts of the lands it believes belong to the Palestinians and which now form part of the State of Israel or are under its occupation, such as the West Bank.

Motivations of some of the larger violent non-state actors are more complex and difficult to ascertain. Both the Taliban's and Hizbullah's actions are influenced by a variety of motives, ranging from the desire to obtain a dominant, or at least more significant political role within their respective societies' power structures, to realizing their ideological aspirations. Hizbullah is said to intend to establish an Islamic government in Lebanon. The Taliban claim that they want to create a pure Islamic state in Afghanistan as a spearhead to a revived global Muslim Caliphate. The relative impact of these motivations often fluctuates depending on circumstances, including changes in the leadership and structures of this type of actors and in external realities. Among the latter, changes in the policy priorities of states supporting this type of non-state actors are particularly important. Such changes could even lead to their dismantling, unless in the course of their development they manage to find other sources of financial and other support and alternative means to sustain their operations.

The Taliban

The Taliban's creation and the driving force behind their actions has generally been explained in terms of commitment to a particular interpretation of Islam and determination to create a government based on its principles, first in Afghanistan and then in the rest of the Muslim world. The Taliban's creation and their actions have also often been interpreted as evidence of religion's increasing influence on the international actors' behavior and on the dynamics of international affairs.

The Taliban's adherence to a highly conservative version of Islam and declared determination to create a state and society based on it have significantly contributed to their emergence and to a considerable extent motivated their actions and also indicate religion's greater role in international affairs. However, as explained in chapter 1, religion was not the only or the most important factor behind the Taliban's emergence. Other factors, such as ethnicity, desire for power, economic gain, and, more significant, the policies of regional states, especially Pakistan, played determining roles in their creation. Subsequently, in addition to religion, the same factors have shaped their behavior.

Despite their rhetoric of equality among all of Afghanistan's ethnic groups, the Taliban's actions have betrayed the influence of ethnicity. Consisting overwhelmingly of Pashtun ethnic elements, the Taliban's behavior has reflected the traditional Pashtun tendency to believe that, because of their numerical superiority, they are entitled to dominate Afghanistan's political structures. The ethnic factor also partly explains the Taliban's animosity toward the country's Hazara minority. Their dislike of the Hazaras, in addition to sectarian factors—Hazaras are Shia—has ethnic dimensions. The Hazaras are of Turkic origin and Persian speakers, characteristics the Pashtun dislike. According to one author, "The Taliban's campaigns at times have had overtones of ethnic cleansing, targeting either non-Pashtun ethnic groups of Afghanistan or Afghanistan's Shia minority, in particular in a series of well-documented massacres in Mazar-Sharif in 1998, in Shomali region in

1999, around Toleqan in 2000, and in Bamyian in early 2001."[53] This also explains why the Taliban have not been able to make significant inroads in the non-Pashtun areas of Afghanistan.

In addition to religion, ethnic factors have shaped the Taliban's regional likes and dislikes and the character of their relations with regional actors. Their anti-Iran tendencies are partly caused by Iran's Shia character and by the Taliban's view of the Shias as at best heretical and at worst unbelieving. However, their anti-Iran sentiments also partly derive from Tajik-Pashtun rivalry and the fact that the Tajiks and Iranians are ethnically and linguistically close. Moreover, because of these ethnic and sectarian links, during the Afghan wars (Soviet and civil) Iran supported the Persian-speaking Tajiks and the Shia Hazaras, which has contributed to the Taliban's negative view of and animosity toward Iran. By contrast, the Taliban is on good terms with Saudi Arabia and Persian Gulf Arab states, and even with Turkey; all these countries are majority Sunni.[54]

More important, the Taliban's anti-Iran positions reflect Pakistan's foreign policy priorities and those of its regional and international allies, especially Saudi Arabia and the United States. All three have wanted to contain Iran's influence in Afghanistan. Being to a great extent a creation of Pakistan and a beneficiary of Pakistan's and Saudi Arabia's help, the Taliban have followed the regional priorities of their patrons. However, since the appearance of IS in Afghanistan and its competition with the Taliban, they seem to have somewhat moderated their anti-Iran positions. There has even been talk of potential cooperation between Iran and the Taliban against IS, which they both see as a threat.[55] If true, this would prove that when common political and security interests are at stake religious and other ideological differences can be played down or even ignored.

Because the Taliban, despite having a leadership council, are not structurally very cohesive, their individual commanders and different networks have often acted independently of one another. Therefore, individual commanders' specific goals and ambitions should also be taken into account when determining what most motivates the Taliban's actions. Some commanders might be motivated by religion and the desire to reestablish the Islamic Caliphate, while other commanders might be moved by the desire for economic gain, including through illegal activities, or the pursuit of power and the quest for complete control over Afghanistan.

Motivations could also change because of changed circumstances. According to some reports, the Taliban's inability to regain political power following the U.S. intervention in 2001 has made financial gain a more significant motivation for behavior than religious impulses. An article quoting the United Nations' sanctions monitors in Afghanistan noted that "The Taliban's reliance on extortion and kidnapping, along with narcotics and illegal mining, is transforming it from a group driven by religious ideology to a criminal enterprise hungry for profit."[56] As noted in chapter 1, the profit motive also played a role in the movement's formation, at least on the part of some of its key leaders, while recruits might have been driven more by religious zeal. However, in view of the impoverished state of most Afghan refugees in Pakistan who formed the nucleus of the Taliban, economic factors might also have been important inducements.

In short, in addition to religious tendencies, ethnic issues and the desire to establish traditional Pashtun political superiority in Afghanistan as well as the desire for material gain have helped shape the Taliban's behavior. Because they have been dependent on Pakistan's support, Pakistan's foreign policy goals have also influenced, and some observers would argue have determined, their behavior.[57] As the Taliban became entrenched in certain areas and developed economic stakes and interests, maintaining these interests acquired more importance than mere religious beliefs and goals. But because any power needs some legitimizing value, the Taliban have continued to use their religious discourse in order to justify their actions and to legitimize their claim to power.

In light of the above, it is not justified to attribute either the Taliban's emergence or their actions solely to religion. Nor is it warranted to see them as proof of religion's increasing role in international affairs. A mix of factors has led to their creation and has shaped their behavior. These factors include Afghanistan's ethnic, religious, and political divisions; the policy priorities of regional countries, especially Pakistan; and the priorities of such key state actors as the United States. But because the Taliban and their supporters have used religion as an instrument of legitimization and justification and as a tool for mobilization, their actions have contributed to enhancing religion's profile in international affairs.

Hizbullah

Since its creation and certainly since the 1990s, Hizbullah has had close ties to Iran, which has also been its main financial and military backer. Because of this close connection to the Islamic Republic of Iran (IRI), both Hizbullah's ideology and its behavior in Lebanon and in the region have largely reflected the IRI's political ideology and regional priorities. As Iran's own policies and behavior have evolved over time, partly as a result of periodic shifts in the makeup of its political leadership and partly in response to external developments, so have Hizbullah's views and behavior. If the account given by Fred Halliday is accepted, Sheikh Qasim Naim, deputy secretary-general of Hizbullah, told him that "Hizbollah regards the Iranian spiritual leader, in this case Khamenei, as its ultimate authority: all major political decisions are referred to—when actually not taken in—Iran."[58] As an example, he noted that the decision in favor of Hizbullah's participation in Lebanese politics after 1992 was taken by Ayatullah Khamenei himself.[59] This is not surprising because at the time Iran had toned down its revolutionary rhetoric and had adopted a more pragmatic approach to foreign policy and therefore also wanted to play down the Hizbullah's revolutionary dimension and to emphasize its role as a normal player in Lebanese politics.

Therefore, in order to understand Hizbullah's ideology and religion's role in it, plus the causes of the periodic shifts in its behavior, it is necessary to comprehend the ideology of the Islamic Republic, its various ingredients, and the periodic shifts in Iran's domestic and foreign policies.

Iran's 1979 revolution has been characterized as Islamic, and certainly many of the ideas underpinning its ideology have Islamic/Shia roots. Many of the social, political, and cultural changes that took place after the revolution also have significant religious dimensions. However, in its various forms, the Iranian Left played an even more important role in bringing about the revolution. In particular, the Left's ideologization of religion and its particular reinterpretation of Shia Islam in light of Marxism, as exemplified by the works of Ali Shariati, along with the very popularization of the concept of revolution, were crucial factors in the advent of the revolution. Therefore, it is legitimate to ask whether the Iranian revolution was caused by religion or by secular leftist ideology and whether religion was only used as a means, at least by some elements.[60]

Regardless, the fact is that the Islamic Republic's world and regional views were mostly shaped by leftist concepts and ideas, which were popular in the Middle East and Iran in the 1960s and 1970s. The insistence of the IRI on combating the so-called global arrogance (*Istikbar Setizi*) is an Islamicized version of the Left's anti-imperialist credo. The same is true of the Iranian regime's animosity toward Israel and the conservative Arab regimes. This attitude is reminiscent of the leftist credo of anti-imperialism, anti-Zionism, and the struggle against Arab reaction. This ethos was particularly prevalent within the Arab Left in the 1960s and 1970s. Because Iran's leftists, including Islamic leftists, had close connections with Arab leftists and radicals, the latter's views became part of the Iranian revolutionaries' worldview and political vocabulary.[61]

Iran's anti-great-power policies were also influenced by views common among Third World countries, plus Iran's own historical experience of being used and manipulated by the great powers in their regional and global rivalries. Lebanon, too, had a similar experience of being subjected to colonial rule and great-power meddling. Consequently, the Iranian revolutionaries' rhetoric resonated with many Lebanese, especially the Shia. Their disadvantaged position within Lebanon made them especially receptive to the Iranian discourse of justice and support for the downtrodden. Islam's impact on Iran's world-view and foreign policy is best reflected in its preoccupation with the question of Palestine and its desire to foster Muslim unity, of course under its own leadership. However, it must be remembered that the Left both in Iran and in the Arab world has also traditionally championed the Palestinian cause. By contrast, many ostensibly Muslim countries, such as Saudi Arabia, have never been staunch supporters of the Palestinian cause, although at times they have voiced very moderate support for the Palestinians.

Hizbullah's 2009 manifesto clearly demonstrates the impact of this particular Iranian world-view. For example, the part of the manifesto dealing with the history of the post–World War II period accuses America of planning to dominate the world and blames it for supporting Israel and the Arab reactionaries. It identifies Israel as the main threat to the region and insists on continued resistance to it instead of seeking compromise and accommodation. Beyond these specific points, in this manifesto the general analysis of the global political system is imbued with leftist ideas, which are also common to the Iranian world-view. These characteristics prompted one analyst to comment that "the terminology and the analysis look more *like the product of a leftist movement than an Islamic one*" [emphasis added].[62]

The above implies that certain Hizbullah policies reflect Iran's priorities and are not necessarily in Hizbullah's own best interests. For instance, as a minority, the Lebanese Shias would be better served by having at least non-hostile relations with Israel, while their current stance has made them subject to regional and international pressure. However, Hizbullah's championing of the Palestinian cause has also been a way for the Shias to seek acceptance by Sunni Muslims who surround them, albeit so far with not much success.

In more recent times, Hizbullah's position on the Syrian Civil War has reflected Iran's policy toward the conflict; both have supported the regime of Bashar Al Assad against the largely Sunni opposition.

In short, like the Taliban, Hizbullah's policies and actions have not been solely or even primarily determined by religion. However, its creation reflects the impact of religion because the identity of the Lebanese Shias is mostly based on religion. Therefore, their desire for enfranchisement required strengthening their collective identity along religious lines.

CONCLUSIONS

The behavior of states and large non-state violent actors is determined by a mix of factors and through a dynamic and continuous interaction between their internal and external circumstances, as well as between their values/ideas/ideologies and interests. The impact of some of these factors, such as geography and historical experience, is lasting and even permanent. The impact of other factors tends to be more transient or at least subject to change. The significance of individual factors often differs in specific cases. Sometimes an actor's behavior is driven by security concerns, at other times by a desire for gain, and at still other times by ideological or idealistic impulses. Therefore, it is difficult accurately to measure the impact on their behavior of each and every factor.

Religion is clearly part of all societies' value systems, either directly or through its influence in shaping them. It is also an important foundation of states' national identities, their self-perceptions and world-views. By being part of actors' values and identities, religion is certainly among the factors that shape their behavior. However, its direct impact on behavior in specific cases as distinct from the influence of values/ideals or ideologies in general is hard to measure. This means that to treat religion as a separate factor outside the framework of values/ideologies is not justified and its influence would be best measured by analyzing its role in the formation of actors' value systems, identities, and self- and world-views. Finally, examples provided here show that, when more important material interests are at stake, and especially if actors' security is at stake, religion's impact on their behavior, like that of secular values and ideals, diminishes.

NOTES

1. In the past, Pakistan has used such groups against India in Kashmir and in Afghanistan. On 9 June 2014, it was reported that, according to Afghan authorities, the Pakistani intelligence service was behind an assassination attempt against Abdullah Abdullah, the front runner in the Afghan presidential race, which was carried out by the *Lashkar-e Taiba*. Since Abdullah is Sunni, a religious motive behind this operation is not very likely. See Ahmed Qureshi, "LT behind Kabul Assassination Attempt," *Pajhwok Election Site*, 9 June 2014, at: http://www.elections.pajhwok.com/en/2014/06/09/let-behind-kabul-assasination-attempt. Pakistan also uses similar groups against Iran.

2. See among others: Regan Doherty & Amena Bakr, "Exclusive: Turkish Nerve Center Leads Aid to Syria Rebels," *Reuters*, 27 July 2012, David Kirkpatrick, "Qatar's Support for Islamists Alienate Allies Near and Far," *New York Times*, 7 September 2014, Ian Black, "Syria Crisis: Saudi Arabia to Train New Rebel Force," *Guardian*, 7 November 2013.

3. F. S. Northedge, "The Nature of Foreign Policy," in ed. F. S. Northedge, *The Foreign Policies of the Powers* (London: Faber & Faber, 1968), 10.

4. Margot Light, "Foreign Policy Analysis," in eds. A. J. R. Groom and Margot Light, *Contemporary International Relations: A Guide to Theory* (London: Pinter Publishers, 1994), 94.

5. Aaron David Miller, "How Geography Explains the United States," *ForeignPolicy.com*, 16 April 2013, at: http://www.foreignpolicy.com/articles/2013/04/16/how_geography_explains_united_states.

6. Miller, "How Geography Explains."

7. Ricardo Haussmann, "Prisoners of Geography," January 2001, at: http://www.hks.harvard.edu/fs/rhausma/editorial/pf))1_prisoners_geog.htm.

8. Miller, "How Geography Explains."

9. Miller, "How Geography Explains."

10. "*La politiques de toutes puissance est dans leur geographie*." Quoted in Nicholas J. Spykman, "Geography and Foreign Policy, part 1," *American Political Science Review*, 32.1 (February 1938), 28.

11. For example, Ayatullah Khomeini's concept of global arrogance is an Islamicized version of imperialism of the Left as is his division of the world into Oppressors (*Mustakberin*) and the Oppressed (*Mustazafin*). On the IRI's world-view, see Shireen T. Hunter, *Iran and the*

World: Continuity in a Revolutionary Decade (Bloomington, Indiana: Indiana University Press, 1989), 36–39.

12. Hunter, *Iran and the World: Continuity in a Revolutionary Decade*, 41.

13. For a discussion of these issues see Shireen T. Hunter, *Islam in Russia: The Politics of Identity and Security* (Armonk, NY: M. E. Sharpe, 2004). Also, Alicja Curanovic, *The Religious Factor in Russia's Foreign Policy* (London: Routledge, 2012), 13–42.

14. "Bearded Drag Queen Symbolizes Western Decadence, Putin Ally Declares," *Globe and Mail*, 15 May 2014. Also, Elias Groll, "Why This Austrian Drag Queen Is the New *Bête Noir* of Putin Cronies," *ForeignPolicy.com*, 12 May 2014 at: http://foreignpolicy.com/2014/05/12/why-this-austrian-drag-queen-is-the-new-bete-noire-of-putin-cronies/.

15. The origin of the concept is found in *Matthew 5:14* (King James Version): "Ye are the light of the world. A city that is set on a hill cannot be hid." It was adopted by John Winthrop, Governor of the Massachusetts Bay Colony, and has been reprised by many American political leaders.

16. John B. Judis, "The Chosen Nation: The Influence of Religion on U.S. Foreign Policy," Carnegie Endowment for International Peace, *Policy Brief*, 37 (March 2005).

17. "Take up the White Man's burden—Send forth the best ye breed—Go send your sons to exile to serve your captives' need . . . (etc.)." This poem, by Rudyard Kipling in 1899, was an exhortation to the United States.

18. Yun Sun, "Africa in China's Foreign Policy," Washington D.C.: Brookings Institution, Research Paper, 10 April 2014. Also Zhang Wingmen and Sang Wei, *International Institute of Asian Studies, Newsletter No. 6* (Summer 2012). Also, Narayani Basu, "China and Africa: Is Honeymoon Over?" *Foreign Policy Journal.com*, 3 April 2013.

19. Daniel L. Byman, and Kenneth J. Pollack, "Let Us Praise Great Men: Bringing the Statesman Back," *International Security*, 25.4. 2001, 109.

20. Margaret G. Hermann, Charles F. Hermann, and Joe D. Hagan, "How Decision Units Shape Foreign Policy Behavior" in eds. Charles F. Hermann, Charles W, Kegley Jr., and James N. Roseneau, *New Directions in the Study of Foreign Policy* (Boston: Allen and Unwin, 1987), 314.

21. For example, Ali Akbar Velayati, advisor to the Supreme Leader on international affairs has said that "in foreign policy the government acts within the framework set out by the leader." *IRNA*, 22 July 20014, at: http://www.irna.ir/fa/NewsPrint.aspx?ID=81246429.

22. On the impact of these leaders' personal preferences and beliefs on the policies of the United States and the United Kingdom, see Stephen Benedict Dyson, "Personality and Foreign Policy: Blair's Iraq Decisions," *Foreign Policy Analysis*, 2, 2006.

23. For a discussion of this question, see Hendrik Hertzberg, "Cakewalk," *New Yorker*, 14 April 2003, at: http://www.newyorker.com/magazine/2003/04/14/cakewalk.

24. Dyson, "Personality and Foreign Policy: Blair's Iraq Decisions." According to the author, such a personality type favors a proactive foreign policy and is more willing to take risks.

25. Hedley Bull first used the concept of anarchy as the defining character of international system. See Hedley Bull, *The Anarchical Society, A Study of Order in World Politics* (New York: Columbia University Press, 2012), (4th edition).

26. Hans Morgenthau, *Politics among Nations: The Struggle for Power and Peace*, New York: Alfred A. Knopf, 1985, 29.

27. Joseph S. Nye, Jr., "Neorealism and Neoliberalism," *World Politics*, 40. 2 (January 1988), 238.

28. Zbigniew Brzezinski, *Ideology and Power in Soviet Politics* (Westport, CT: Greenwood Press, 1976), 4–5.

29. See Judith Goldstein and Robert Keohane, "Ideas and Foreign Policy: An Analytical Framework," in eds. Judith Goldstein and Robert Keohane, *Ideas and Foreign Policy: Beliefs, Institutions, and Political Change* (Ithaca: Cornell University Press, 1993), 12.

30. Goldstein and Keohane, "Ideas and Foreign Policy," 12.

31. Goldstein and Keohane, "Ideas and Foreign Policy," 22–24.

32. On the connection between identity and security, see Michael C. Williams, *Culture and Security: Symbolic Power and the Politics of International Security* (London: Routledge, 2007).

33. See "Iran Paper Says Cultural NATO More Dangerous Than Military One," *BIYOKU-LULE Online*, 21 August 2007, at: http://www.biyokulule.com/view_content.php?articleid=402.

34. See Shireen T. Hunter, "Iran, Islam and the Struggle for Identity and Power in the Islamic Republic of Iran, *ACMCU OCCASIONAL PAPER*, July 2014, at: https://issuu.com/georgetownsfs/docs/shireen_hunter_iran__islam__and__th.

35. Kenneth Waltz is among those scholars who believe that systemic pressures determine states' foreign policy behavior. Kenneth N. Waltz, *Theories of International Politics* (New York: Random House, 1979).

36. Richard N. Haass, *War of Necessity, War of Choice: A Memoir of Two Iraq Wars* (New York: Simon & Schuster, 2009).

37. This group was initially known as ISIS or ISIL standing for the Islamic State of Iraq and the Levant and al-Sham.

38. While Central and East European countries suffered under Soviet and communist domination, an *imposed* form of stability, the "stability" that the Cold War provided, with instruments that included NATO, did help the West Europeans, with U.S. engagement, to have sufficient "stability" to get on with creating a post-balance-of-power system internal to Western Europe.

39. F. S. Northedge (ed.), *The Foreign Policies of the Powers* (London: Faber & Faber, 1968), 31.

40. K. J. Holsti, *International Politics* (Englewood Cliffs, NJ: Prentice Hall, 1995), 98.

41. Ada Bozeman, *Politics and Culture in International History: From the Ancient Near East to the Opening of the Modern World* (New Brunswick, NJ: Transaction Publishers, 1994), 238–98.

42. The actual quotation is "The world must be made safe for democracy." President Woodrow Wilson in asking Congress for a declaration of war against Germany, 2 April 1917, at http://www.historymatters.gmu.edu/d/4943/.

43. See Robert Endicott Osgood, *Ideals and Self-Interest in America's Foreign Policy* (Chicago: The University of Chicago Press, 1953).

44. Osgood, *Ideals and Self-Interest*, 154–264. Also see Robert E. Hunter, "Perspectives: 'Europe Whole and Free: Ukraine Should Impel a Return to First Principles,'" *European Affairs*, May 2014, at: http://www.europeaninstitute.org/index.php/ei-blog/196-european-affairs/ea-may-2014/1903-perspectives-europe-whole-and-free-ukraine-should-impel-a-return-to-first-principles.

45. For a discussion of the theory of positive domino effect see Sam Tanenhaus, "The World: From Vietnam to Iraq: The Rise and Fall and Rise of the Domino Theory," *New York Times*, 22 March 2003, at: http://www.nytimes.com/2003/03/23/weekinreview/the-world-from-vietnam-to-iraq-the-rise-and-fall-and-rise-of-the-domino-theory.html.

46. Condoleezza Rice, "Promoting National Interest," *Foreign Affairs*, 79.1 (January 2000), 1–2.

47. Anthony Lake, "Confronting Backlash States," *Foreign Affairs*, 73.2 (March 2003), 45.

48. Lake, "Confronting Backlash States," 45–46.

49. Lake, "Confronting Backlash States," 48.

50. Based on conversations with official involved with the management of the crisis.

51. Lake, "Confronting Backlash States," 46. President Clinton did sign the Iraq Liberation Act of 1998, which set the objective of overthrowing Saddam. He chose not to use military force to promote this objective, however. See H.R.4655—Iraq Liberation Act of 1998, at http://www.thomas.loc.gov/cgi-bin/query/z?c105:H.R.4655.ENR.

52. On the Oslo Accords, see "The Oslo Accords and the Arab-Israeli Peace Process, 1993–2000," *Office of the Historian, US Department of State* at: http://www.history.state.gov/milestones/199302000/oslo.

53. Julie Sirrs, "The Taliban's International Ambitions," *Middle East Quarterly* (Summer 2001), at: http://www.meforum.org/486/the-talibans-international-ambitions.

54. The only countries which recognized the Taliban headed government in Afghanistan after their victory in 1996 were: Pakistan, Saudi Arabia, and the United Arab Emirates.

55. "Why Did the Taliban Go to Tehran," *Guardian*, 22 May 2015.

56. Louis Charbonneau, "Taliban Changing from Religious Group to Criminal Enterprise: U.N.," *Reuters,* 13 June 2014.
57. For example, the Afghan-origin scholar Amin Saikal subscribes to this view.
58. Fred Halliday, "A Lebanese Fragment: Two Days with Hizbullah," *Open Democracy,* 20 July 2006.
59. Halliday, "A Lebanese Fragment."
60. For a discussion of these issues, see Shireen T. Hunter, *Iran Divided: The Historical Roots of Iranian Debates on Identity, Culture, and Governance in the Twenty-First Century* (Lanham, MD: Rowman & Littlefield, 2014).
61. Some of the members of Iran's opposition during the reign of the Shah had been trained in the PLO camps in Jordan and Lebanon.
62. Rafid Fadhil Ali, "New Hizbollah Manifesto Emphasizes Political Role in a United Lebanon," *Terrorism Monitor,* 7, 38, 15 December 2009.

Chapter Three

Russia's Policy toward the Yugoslav Crisis

The Role of Religion

The Yugoslav Federal Republic's breakup began as early as 1988, and this process soon degenerated into several armed conflicts. The worst and the longest-lasting of these conflicts was the war in Bosnia-Herzegovina,[1] which lasted from April 1992 to September 1995. During Yugoslavia's long crisis, Russia, too, underwent drastic political changes. At the beginning, the Soviet Union was still in existence, but when in 1992 the Bosnian War started it had disappeared from the world's political map. Inevitably, such dramatic changes influenced Russia's approach to and handling of the Yugoslav crisis as it unfolded. What remained constant, both under the Soviet system and after its demise, was Russia's interest in Yugoslavia's fate.

This interest, especially in the Bosnian conflict, partly derived from ethnic, religious, and long-standing historical ties between the Russians and the Serbs, the largest ethnic group in the former Yugoslavia. In particular, the Russian public was concerned about the potential impact of the various conflicts on the Serbs' fate. That interest thus made the Yugoslav crisis a domestic political concern for Russian leaders. Further, because Yugoslavia's crisis coincided with the USSR's own period of transformation and because the factors which had triggered Yugoslavia's descent into dissolution were also present in the USSR, the course and outcome of the crisis acquired considerable importance for the USSR and later for the Russian Federation in both domestic and foreign policy terms. Soviet leaders feared that the outcome of the Yugoslav crisis could presage the USSR's own fate. These fears, in turn, further deepened the linkage between the Yugoslav crisis and the Soviet

Union's and later Russia's own domestic politics and, in particular, it was used in Soviet and then Russian domestic political rivalries.

While the USSR was still in existence, both supporters and opponents of Mikhail Gorbachev's reforms, which had already begun by 1987, used events in Yugoslavia in their power struggles. In the post-Soviet period, the opponents of Boris Yeltsin and his policies manipulated the Yugoslav crisis in their competition with him and his supporters. In fact, the linkage between Russia's domestic politics and its approach toward the Yugoslav crisis intensified in the post-Soviet period. The only difference was that during the Soviet period the main concern was whether it was possible to prevent Yugoslavia's disintegration, while in the post-Soviet period, the issue became how far and in what ways Russia should help the Serbs. The outcome was that Russian policy toward Yugoslavia was to a great degree shaped by its own domestic concerns and by the ebb and flow of its domestic politics, including the shifting balance of influence among various political groups that held diverging views both in regard to the overall direction of Russia's foreign policy and toward the Yugoslav crisis in particular.

When the Bosnian War began in 1992, the Russian Federation was in the early stages of transition to a post-Soviet era and to a different political and economic system and values. The country was gripped by intense debate about its future direction, both domestically and internationally, and regarding the principles which should underpin its domestic and foreign policies. The proponents of different views on Russia's future path were, meanwhile, engaged in a fierce power struggle. The country was also gripped by an intense debate about the character of its post-Soviet national identity and its principal foundations, triggered by the disappearance or at least severe erosion of Russia's union-based identity.

The question of Russia's approach to the Bosnian War thus became entangled with all these political, ideological, and identity debates and power struggles among its old and new economic and political elites. Consequently, differences over Russia's policy toward the Bosnian War partly reflected deeper schisms within Russian society.

THE USSR AND THE YUGOSLAV CRISIS: GORBACHEV'S APPROACH

When the Yugoslav crisis began, Gorbachev's reform program was already underway. In addition to economic, social, and cultural aspects, his reforms included the initiation of a new foreign policy framework known as the New Thinking (*Novoe Mishlenie*). The main impetus behind Gorbachev's reforms, including his New Thinking in foreign policy, was the USSR's economic crisis and its mounting social problems, in part caused by its decade-long (1979–1989) and costly war in Afghanistan.[2]

The New Thinking evolved over time and its interpretations varied. It is thus difficult to offer a clear and detailed definition of the New Thinking, and only its main underlying principles can be identified. These continued to influence Russia's foreign policy thinking in the post-Soviet era and as late as the early 2000s. The underlying principles were the following: Russia's economic revitalization should be a principal goal of its foreign policy; and Russia's foreign policy should become non-ideological.

According to some scholars, giving priority to Russia's economic revitalization as a main goal of its foreign policy was the outcome of the USSR's realization that "economic strength was proving more decisive than military strength in resolving many global issues. . . . [Thus] only by reversing its precipitous economic slide and especially establishing linkages to the international economy could the USSR qualify as a true super power."[3] The de-ideologization of foreign policy was also necessitated for economic reasons. Because of its economic problems, the USSR could no longer afford a costly and ideologically determined foreign policy, based on the principle of an existential struggle with the West in the context of a zero-sum game.

Instead, Gorbachev believed that the USSR should adopt a more realistic and less ideological foreign policy outlook, and at the same time should try to eliminate or at least to diminish tensions with the West. Such a foreign policy, he believed, would allow the USSR to focus on economic, political, and social reforms and on controlling the disintegrative forces that already by 1988 had appeared in the Soviet Union. Because of his domestic focus, Gorbachev was anxious that developments in Russia's neighborhoods not negatively impact his reform program or distract it from its domestic priorities.

Therefore, Gorbachev's principal objective during the early stages of the Yugoslav crisis was, first, if possible to prevent the Yugoslav Federation's disintegration and, if this were not feasible, to prevent the extension of its potentially disruptive impact to the rest of Eastern Europe and closer to Russia's neighborhood.

FEAR OF THE CONTAGIOUS IMPACT OF THE YUGOSLAV CRISIS

Gorbachev's goal had always been to preserve the USSR, albeit in a more democratic and modernized form. He had never imagined that his liberalizing policies could lead to an upsurge of ethnic and nationalist claims and to the emergence of separatist movements, which ultimately tore the Soviet Union apart. His lapse of judgment indicates his inadequate grasp of the nationality issues in the USSR and his underestimation of the power of nationalism.[4] He has admitted that he gravely underestimated the force of nationalist impulses, and this appears to have been partly due to his view of nationalism as a reactionary and *passé* phenomenon.[5]

In view of his concerns and priorities, especially his desire to preserve the USSR, when Yugoslavia's crisis broke out Gorbachev's first instinct was to help preserve its territorial and political integrity, albeit with appropriate reforms. He believed that within a reformed Yugoslav Federation "the success or failure of managing interethnic conflicts might have important consequences for the USSR."[6] He acknowledged that the outcome of Yugoslavia's political crisis would have implications for the Soviet Union's own transformation. After meeting with the Spanish prime minister, Felipe Gonzales, he said: "To say that it [Yugoslav events] affects the Soviet Union is saying nothing—it affects all of us."[7] Therefore, Gorbachev openly defended maintaining Yugoslavia's integrity and joined the U.S. president, George H. W. Bush, on 19 July 1991, in calling for Yugoslavia's territorial integrity to be preserved. For the same reasons, Gorbachev earlier had opposed Slovenia and Croatia's declaration of independence.[8] In short, because he was faced with the surge of nationalist and separatist movements in the USSR, Gorbachev was also concerned about the rise of nationalism and separatism in Yugoslavia, fearing that they could intensify the USSR's own similar challenges. He was particularly suspicious of the ultra-nationalist tendencies of the Serbian leader Slobodan Milošević.

Gorbachev's other priority was to prevent internationalization of the Yugoslav question, fearing that could lead to the introduction of foreign troops into the Balkans.[9] Given the USSR's own inter-ethnic and nationalist conflicts, he feared that any international interference in Yugoslavia, especially the introduction of foreign troops, could set a precedent that might be repeated in the USSR. Meanwhile, commitment to Yugoslavia's survival as a single country required that the USSR retain a neutral position vis-à-vis its various ethnic and religious groups and to avoid being seen as excessively pro-Serb. Nevertheless, because of the Russian public's pro-Serb sentiments, Gorbachev felt the need to refer to Russia's special ties with the Serbs. During his 1988 visit to Yugoslavia, he recalled these ties by saying that "Russia's best representatives always viewed the Southern Slavs' liberation struggle with profound sympathy and came to their assistance at crucial points . . . in the heart of every Russian and Serb, in their genetic memory, so to speak, is mutual benevolence and a propensity to friendship."[10]

THE IMPACT OF DOMESTIC POLITICS

The ebb and flow of Russia's own developments, its increasingly complicated domestic politics, and rivalries within the Soviet leadership thus significantly influenced Gorbachev's handling of the Yugoslav crisis.

Gorbachev's reformist policies had serious opponents within the Soviet Union's leadership and beyond, including conservatives and liberals. His conservative opponents, made up mostly of new nationalists and of hard-core Communists initially led by Igor Ligachev, opposed any kind of reform, believing that Gorbachev's reforms would end in the USSR's dissolution. His liberal opponents, consisting mostly of disgruntled minorities, those attracted to Western ideas, and those anxious for rapid improvement in their lives and clustered around Boris Yeltsin, considered Gorbachev's reforms insufficient and excessively timid. These competing factions had vastly different views both on the causes of the Yugoslav conflict and on the appropriate Soviet policy.

According to Gorbachev's conservative opponents, especially the Communists, imperialist plots were behind Yugoslavia's problems. They believed that imperialists had similar designs on the USSR and desired its dissolution. The nationalists believed that the cause of Yugoslavia's crisis was an anti-Orthodox, anti-Slav, and anti-Russian conspiracy by Muslims and Catholics.[11] These competing groups ran their own parallel Yugoslav diplomacies which differed from Gorbachev's official policy.

Conservative Russian groups had their counterparts in Yugoslavia. The common dislike of liberal political and economic reforms and the desire to retain the existing political structures brought Russian and Yugoslav communists together, while common Slavic and Orthodox Christian roots constituted the main bonds between Russian and Yugoslav nationalists. Russian and Yugoslav conservatives soon established contacts. Reportedly, in March 1991, high ranking members of the Yugoslav military, consisting mostly of Serbs and Montenegrins, along with those supporting the maintenance of the Yugoslav Federation, met in Moscow with Soviet military officers. Their goal was to obtain Soviet arms for the Yugoslav military.[12] Apparently, the meeting took place without Gorbachev's blessing.

By contrast, Gorbachev's liberal opponents saw the Yugoslav crisis as potentially encouraging faster and deeper reforms in the Soviet Union. They already had encouraged centrifugal tendencies in the USSR, as illustrated by Boris Yeltsin's call on the Soviet Union's constituent republics to take as much sovereignty as they could. Eventually, Yeltsin declared the Russian Federation's independence from the USSR, thus bringing it effectively to an end. Russian liberals and Yeltsin were therefore more sympathetic toward Yugoslavia's separatists. Yeltsin, who was not religious and did not identify with the Orthodox Serbs, strongly disliked the Serb nationalist leader, Slobodan Milošević. His dislike was caused by Milošević's silence during the aborted August 1991 coup in Moscow, or possibly even his sympathizing with its perpetrators.

By 1991, the process of Soviet dissolution accelerated and further undermined Gorbachev's Yugoslavia policy based on the principle of retaining the Yugoslav Federation. By 1991 and before the USSR's official dissolution, several of its constituent republics had slipped away from Moscow's control and were conducting their own independent diplomacy toward Yugoslavia. In the summer of 1991, leaders of various break-away Yugoslav republics, notably Slovenia and Croatia, visited Ukraine and the Baltic republics. In short, because of the USSR's own multi-dimensional problems and its gradual descent into dissolution, Gorbachev could not do much to stop Yugoslavia's disintegration. The Western countries' inability or unwillingness to act forcefully in order to prevent Yugoslavia's fragmentation further limited Gorbachev's ability to save it from dissolution and descent into war.

POST-SOVIET PERIOD: THE RUSSIAN FEDERATION AND THE WAR IN BOSNIA

In the course of Russian debates about the principles which should guide the country in the post-Soviet period and regarding a new Russian national identity, many new ideas, including Western-style liberalism, were advanced. At the same time, some old ideas, including nationalism and Pan-Slavism, re-emerged, and interest in Orthodox Christianity, as a foundation of Russian national identity and as a value system, was revived. Debates on Russia's post-Soviet identity and value system were closely connected to debates regarding Russia's future global role and the direction of its post-Soviet foreign policy.[13] Russia's approach toward the war in Bosnia was greatly influenced by the evolution of these debates.

FORGING A POST-SOVIET RUSSIAN IDENTITY: IMPACT ON RUSSIAN FOREIGN POLICY

In 1996, President Boris Yeltsin declared that what Russia needed most was a new national idea (*natsionalyana ideia*) or a new national identity. After his reelection in June 1996, he set up a commission of philosophers, historians, linguists, and other experts to develop such an idea and identity.[14] However, the issues that it considered had become evident much earlier. In fact, the establishment of the commission was a response to Russia's identity debate. The basic question asked was what is or should be Russia's post-Soviet identity and its principal components. Because many of the foundations of Russia's Soviet-era identity had disappeared or had been severely undermined, old visions of Russian identity and its key components reemerged and so did old disagreements and controversies surrounding them.

HISTORICAL FOUNDATIONS OF RUSSIAN NATIONHOOD AND STATEHOOD

The concept of national identity is nebulous and hard to define, largely because the concept of nation itself, especially in a political sense, is relatively new and eludes clear definition.[15] Reduced to its essentials, national identity can be defined as the way the majority of members of a political community view themselves and their understanding of specific characteristics that set them apart from other peoples and political communities. In fact, nations' identities often develop through their interaction with other communities or "the other" or others.[16] The concept of national identity is based on some real foundations, such as ethnicity, language, religion, and common history and traditions. National identities also partly stem from cultural and political engineering by various countries' dominant political and cultural elites. Therefore, to some extent, they are socially and politically constructed phenomena.[17] This is one reason that dramatic change in the character of a country's political elites and in their value system often leads to redefinition of its national identity or at the very least to the shift in the relative weight of its principal components.[18] Because of these characteristics, national identities are not static but evolving.

Until the late seventeenth century, religious, local, and even imperial, rather than national, affiliations determined the character of collective identities in Europe.[19] Modern European identities, largely based on ethnic and linguistic characteristics, are in part the product of cultural and political engineering, including the linguistic and cultural assimilation of minority groups. In the rest of the world, with few exceptions, this situation has lasted even longer. In many places, tribal and sectarian identities still remain strong, while national identities are fairly weak.

For most of its history Russia has been an empire—Tsarist or Soviet—and the concept of nation-state has a shorter history in Russia than in the rest of Europe. Because of this history, the notion of national identity, as opposed to other forms of collective identity such as belonging to an empire or to a multi-national union, is not well entrenched in Russia's political culture. Therefore, the question of the nature of national identity becomes more problematic when applied to Russia.

Viewed in historical perspective, it is difficult to speak of a single Russian national identity, a Russian nation, or even a single definition of what constitutes a Russian. Definitions of who can be characterized as Russian, what are the hallmarks of Russianness, whether there has been a historical Russian nation, and if so, what has been its underlying identity have changed and evolved throughout Russia's history. Russian intellectuals, as well as Western scholars of Russia, have had diverging views regarding the nature of Russian identity.[20] Some Western scholars have maintained that terms such as nation, nationalism, and nationalist, and therefore national identity do not apply to Russia and cannot explain the nature of the Russian consciousness. David Rowley believes that terms such as "imperialism and imperialist" can better explain Russia. The reason is that Russians historically have "expressed their national consciousness through the discourse of imperialism rather than the discourse of nationalism." Rowley also believes that the concept of Russia has always had a universalist dimension.[21] Both Imperial Russia and the USSR were different manifestations of this phenomenon. In addition, Russian culture, during both the imperial and Soviet periods, had a messianic streak, rooted in its Orthodox faith and its view of itself as the Third Rome and the bastion and defender of true Christianity.

Some past and current Russian intellectuals also subscribe to the view that, because of its imperial and Soviet pasts, Russia has failed to become a nation-state and to develop a purely Russian sense of national identity, as opposed to imperial or Soviet identities.[22] Russian and other scholars, however, disagree on whether this failure has been a source of weakness or strength for Russia. Some Russian intellectuals believe that this has been a source of weakness.[23] Others see this as a source of strength, maintaining that Russia has been able to develop a unique cultural and even anthropological sphere in Eurasia. This achievement, they believe, is far greater than the creation of Europe's nation-states.

Historians also hold different views regarding the beginnings of Russian statehood. They disagree on the question as to whether the emergence of Russian statehood coincided with the emergence of a separate sense of collective identity among Russians after their conversion to Christianity or whether it developed later. Some historians trace the beginnings of a Russian state to the Kievan Rus. Other, especially non-Russian, historians date its beginnings to the establishment of the Moscow principality and its expansion and eventual transformation into the Russian Empire. Proponents of the latter view believe that, in constructing their history, the Russians have unjustly appropriated to themselves the legacy of the Kievan Rus.[24] Regardless of the respective merits of these views, the Russians see their state as the continuation of the Kievan Rus.

Despite differences about the origins and characteristics of the Russian nation and state, scholars agree that historically cultural, and especially religious, bonds have been important in determining who qualifies as a Russian and in shaping the Russians' identity, at both individual and collective, including state, levels. Rowley identifies the Tsarist Empire as being religious, in addition to being universalist and multi-national.[25] Religion in Russia's case has been Orthodox Christianity, which has played a central role in the formation of its national identity or the Russian equivalent of such an identity. As Orthodox Christians, Russians have often defined themselves in respect both to a Muslim/Tatar and a Western Christian "Other."[26] In other words, Orthodox Christianity has been what has partly set apart Russia from other peoples. Orthodox Christianity has also shaped Russia's self-perception, its vision of its role and place in the world, its views regarding who are its natural friends and enemies, its traditional views of state and its relations to religion and religious establishment, and the basic characteristics of its political organizations and culture. In short, Orthodox Christianity has constituted the foundation of Russian national consciousness and statehood, its values, and its sense of being uniquely moral and special.

Orthodox Christianity and the Birth of the Russian State

Notwithstanding scholarly disagreements regarding whether Russians are justified in dating the birth of their nation and state to the Kievan Rus, in reality the legacy of the Kievan state has greatly influenced Russia's cultural and political development. Therefore, for the purposes of analysis, it is reasonable to assume the existence of a connection between the Kievan State and today's Russia.

The establishment of the first Russian state with its center in Kiev around the tenth century C.E., coincided with the advent of Orthodox Christianity among the Rus. Christianity arrived in the lands of the Rus when, in 998 C.E., Prince Vladimir converted to Orthodox Christianity. The Christianization of the Rus and especially their identification with Orthodoxy also marked the beginnings of the emergence of a distinctly Russian collective consciousness. According to a scholar of Russia, it was their conversion to Orthodox Christianity that became the "source of their separateness from the neighboring pagan people."[27] Some Russian scholars believe that conversion to Christianity formed the foundation of Russian unity. According to Victor Aksiuchits, it was "after baptism into Christianity that the Russian people became unified."[28] Religion, together with language, became "the most important determinant of identity for the Kievan Rus."[29] Some scholars have even viewed the Kievan Rus as principally a religious rather than ethnic community. In more recent times, other scholars, including Alexander Bennigsen and Marie Broxup, have characterized the Russian state before its imperial expansion in the eighteenth and nineteenth centuries as "religion state," implying that religion was the state's foundation and source of its legitimacy, rather than ethnicity or concepts of citizenship.[30] Thus, historically, being Russian has meant being Orthodox.

The traditions of Orthodox Christianity closely intermingled politics and religion in the context of what it defined as a perfect harmony between the secular state authority and the religious Church authority (*Symphony*). These traditions shaped the characteristics of state and governance in Russia.[31] To these were added Byzantine traditions of politics and statecraft, also partly based on Orthodoxy.

The state of Kievan Rus was dismantled by the Mongol/Tatar invasions in the thirteenth century, and the Tatars ruled Russia for nearly three hundred years. In the Russians' historical memory, this period is known as that of the Tatar Yoke. By the fourteenth century, the Princes of Moscow were challenging the Tatars, although they could not dislodge them until the sixteenth century. Finally, in October 1552, Ivan the Terrible, the Grand Duke of Moscow and later Russia's first Tsar, conquered Kazan, the Tatar capital, and the rest of the Kazan Khanate. This victory heralded the beginning of the transformation of the princedom of Moscow (Muscovite State) into the Russian Empire.

The Muscovite State saw itself as the continuation of the Kievan Rus and the inheritor of its traditions. It modeled its institutions after those of the Kievan state and, in the process, it underwent a degree of Byzantination of its government and politics.[32] One aspect of this process was the establishment of close connections between the Church and the State. However, beginning with Ivan's rule, within the relationship between the Church and the State, the State exerted more control over the Church. In the course of the following centuries, including even during the Soviet period, many aspects of this heritage of close church-state relations survived, albeit under different guises.

After the fall of Constantinople to the Ottoman Turks in 1453, Russia came to regard itself as the successor to the Eastern Church/the Second Rome. As such, Russia viewed itself as the Third Rome or, in the words of Fyodor Dostoevsky, as "the only God-fearing nation." This self-perception has had considerable implications for Russia's views of its international role and duties. Russia has often seen itself as the defender of true Christianity—Orthodoxy—against its enemies. Although this belief was not the most important motivation behind Russia's imperial expansion, it has been used to justify Russia's imperial expansion in Crimea, the Caucasus, and the Black Sea and its competition with the Ottoman Empire. For example, Dostoevsky saw the Crimean War of 1856 as aimed at liberating Constantinople from Turkish/Muslim domination. This aspect of Russia's self-perception is relevant even today. For example, President Vladimir Putin at one point stated that, by fighting Muslim extremists in Chechnya, Russia was defending Christianity and Europe against the threat of radical Islam.

Slavism and the Russian Identity

Despite the view that sees Russia as a universalist and multinational empire and that plays down the role of ethnicity in the formation of Russian identity and consciousness, the Slavic ethnic element has always had a central role in forming Russia's national identity. Before there was a Russian empire, there was a Slavic and Orthodox community that considered itself to be Russian. The pre-empire Russia, in addition to being a religion-based state, was also a nation-state because its population consisted overwhelmingly of Slavs.[33] After Ivan's conquest of the Kazan Khanate in the sixteenth century, it took another two centuries before Russia's imperial expansion gathered steam and gradually transformed Russia into a multi-ethnic and multi-confessional empire.

Following its imperial expansion, together with the introduction of other Europeans into the country, Russia became multiethnic and multi-confessional. Nevertheless, the Slavs remained the dominant ethnic element in the empire. More important, it was the Slavs who were overwhelmingly Orthodox. If one admits that Orthodoxy constituted the foundation of Russian consciousness, then the Slavs were its representatives. Aksiuchits clearly states that the ethnic Russians are "the subjects or agents" of Russian national consciousness.[34] Moreover, as a result of Russia's imperial expansion, many non-Russian peoples of the empire or at least their elites were linguistically and culturally Russified. Thus instead of the Slavs changing under the influence of the empire's non-Slavs, non-Slav peoples became partially Russified. Throughout the imperial period and the Soviet era, there was an understanding of Russianness which was built on the basis of Russian language and culture with its deep Slavic roots, notwithstanding other, including Asiatic, influences.

During the Soviet era, there was an effort to create a new identity through a process of ethnic blending of the USSR's various peoples. This was to be done first by bringing ethnically different people closer (*sblizhnie*), including through encouraging inter-ethnic marriages, and ultimately by merging them within a socialist family (*sliyanie*). Even today in Russia, some believe that this goal was achieved. An article published in *Pravda* in 1992 claimed that the peoples of the former USSR have "a single genetic code discovered by scientists at the Institute of General Genetics of the Russian Academy of Sciences."[35] Such claims are highly exaggerated, and although there has been some inter-ethnic mingling, ethnic differences and identities have remained strong among both the Slavs and non-Slavs. The persistence of separate ethnic identities is partly due to the fact that, during the Soviet period, despite efforts to create a new Soviet man transcending ethnic and religious divisions, the Slavs were the dominant group within the Union, culturally and politically. Instead of the Sovietization of Slavs in the sense described earlier, the USSR's cultural and political policies, including the spread of the Russian language, led to a degree of Slavization of other ethnic elements. Russia's cultural policies vis-à-vis other peoples, during both the imperial era and in Soviet times, shows that the essence of Russian universalism has always been to turn others into Russians, and ideally also into Orthodox Christians or fervent Communists, and not to create a new mixed race and culture. For example, the Eurasianists of the nineteenth and twentieth centuries believed that even Muslims of Russia were potentially Orthodox.

Russia as the Leader of Slavs

Historically, the Slavic element's central role in the formation of Russian national identity has helped shape another aspect of its self-perception: its role as the Slavic peoples' natural leader or at least that of Orthodox Slavs. Ideologies such as Slavophilism and Pan-Slavism reflect this aspect of Russia's self-perception. The first ideology glorified the Slavs', especially Russians', ethical and other virtues and their traditional ways of life and advocated the promotion of these virtues. According to them, because of challenges posed by encroaching West-European cultural and ideological influences, such as liberalism and secularism, and by Russia's Westernization, this task had become more urgent. The promotion of indigenous Slavic values they believed was needed to counteract Western influences.

Pan-Slavism advocated the unity of all Slavs under Russian leadership. Because of religious differences between Russia and some Slavic peoples, such as the mostly Catholic Poles, the sense of Slavic solidarity was strong only in the case of Orthodox Slavs. Non-Orthodox Slavs resented Russia's claims to leadership of the Slavic world. As a result, Russia's relations with non-Orthodox Slavs were often marked by competition and conflict. Because of the close connection between nations' understanding of their identity and their external behavior and because of the significance of the Slavic element in Russia's identity and self-view, pan-Slavist ideas did affect aspects of Russia's external behavior. Pan-Slavic solidarity in part can explain Russia's support for the independence movements of the Ottoman Empire's Slavic subjects which emerged in the 1800s. These movements led to a series of Balkan wars, during which Russia supported the Serbs' and the Bulgarians' revolts against the Ottomans. However, even in regard to the Orthodox Slavs, Russian policy was first and foremost determined by its own security considerations and by its other interests. Ideas of Slavic solidarity and Pan-Slavism served more as cover and justification for Russian policies, rather than being the main motive behind them. This preponderance of more tangible interests, rather than feelings of ethnic and religious solidarity and the pull of a common sense of identity, as principal motivations of Russia's behavior vis-à-vis other Slavs is clearly reflected in the history of Russo-Serbian relations.

The Western Challenge, Russian Reforms, and Debates on Identity and Values

Despite their importance, Orthodox Christianity and Slavic ethnicity were not the only influences felt by Russia. Since the time of Peter the Great (1677–1725), Russia's identity debate has been affected by its effort to modernize and by its subjection to intellectual influences emanating from Western Europe. Since that time, an important aspect of Russia's identity debate has been the question of the extent to which Russia should emulate the West and to what degree it should remain loyal to its own indigenous traditions and unique culture largely based on Orthodox Christianity.

Peter's Reforms and Their Consequences

Peter the Great was the first Russian monarch to realize that Russia's scientific and industrial underdevelopment in comparison to West European states had serious implications for its security. Because of its scientific and industrial backwardness, Russia could not develop the sophisticated military and naval power it needed to defend itself effectively against more powerful countries, let alone to compete with them. Realization of Russia's vulnerability was the principal impetus behind Peter's reforms. They were undertaken to bring Russia closer to West European standards. Peter's wide-ranging, including educational, reforms opened the way for the introduction to Russia of Western ideas and philosophies. The efforts of Empress Catherine to Europeanize and modernize Russia further accelerated the flow of ideational influences from the West to Russia. Among these Western ideas were those of the Enlightenment. Under the impact of Western ideas, some Russian intellectuals questioned the value of Russia's intellectual and spiritual heritage and hence also those values and concepts which had shaped its national identity. In particular, they believed that Orthodox Christianity and Byzantine influences had negatively affected Russia's cultural development and were largely responsible for its backwardness compared to West European countries.

One of the harshest critics of Orthodoxy and of Byzantine influences on Russia was Pyotr Yakovlevich Chaadaev. Chaadaev, who converted to Catholicism, viewed Orthodoxy as the main cause of what he characterized as Russia's cultural barrenness. He wrote "what were we doing while the edifice of modern civilization was arising out of the struggle between the energetic barbarism of the northern peoples and the high idea of Christianity? Obedient to our fatal destiny, we turned to miserable Byzantium, the subject of profound contempt among those peoples, for a moral code on which to base our education."[36] The remedy for Chaadaev and his like-minded intellectuals for Russia's ills was its Westernization. Because of their embrace of

Western civilization, Chaadaev and his like-minded intellectuals were labeled as the "Westernizers."

Their ideas were challenged by those who believed in the superiority of Russia's native values and culture, of which Orthodoxy formed a big part, over Western culture. Early representatives of this trend were known as the "Slavophiles." They were critical of Peter and Catherine's policies. An early Slavophile, Prince Mikhail Shcherbatov, believed that by eliminating all the old privileges of the nobility and the Church, Peter's policies had encouraged the growth of autocracy and servility. He maintained that ancient Russia was superior to post-Petrine Russia. According to him, in contrast to the new Russia, ancient Russia was based on mutual obligations and responsibilities and was tempered by Christian mercy.[37] Others, notably Nicholas Berdyaev, writing later, acknowledged the necessity of Peter's reforms, but he also believed that they were badly carried out and thus "did terrible violence to the soul of the people."[38] This violence was inflicted on the people because the Westernizers "denied any original distinctive character of the Russian people and Russian history . . . and clung to naively simple ideas of enlightenment and civilization and saw no mission of any sort for Russia except the necessity of catching up with the West."[39]

Partly as a reaction to the Westernizers' near contempt for Russia's values and traditions, the Slavophile philosophy, as articulated by Yuri Samarin, stressed that Russia must find its own model of social, economic, and political evolution. He argued that Western formulas were not applicable to Russia. Moreover, he maintained that the way of a nation "is an expression of specific principles unknown to other nations; our [Russia's] evolution is subject to its own laws."[40]

Therefore, in contrast to Westernizers, Slavophiles emphasized religiosity and spiritualism instead of rationalism and materialism; national self-consciousness (*norodnost*), meaning both Russia's spirit and belief in its spirit, as well as in both the cult and the essence of Russian national identity; belief in Russia as "a historical nation" and hence in its historic mission.[41] On economic and social issues, they were populist and communalist. According to Nicholas Berdyaev, they opposed Roman law on property and were defenders of the commune which they saw as the original Russian structure of economic life. The second idea, Pan-Slavism, as noted earlier, advocated the unity of all Slavs under the Russian leadership.

This ideological debate between what could be called the Russian authenticists, those who believed in the uniqueness and superiority of Russian ideas and ideals, and those who believed that Russia needed to emulate the West, has ebbed and flowed throughout Russia's modern history. The Soviet Union's hegemonistic discourse of socialism and scientific materialism buried this debate. But it was resumed with great vigor and intensity after the USSR's collapse.

POST-SOVIET RUSSIAN IDENTITY AND FOREIGN POLICY: THE RETURN OF OLD DEBATES

The Soviet project of developing an individual in whom commitment to socialist ideals would dominate over all other ethnic and sectarian values and identities and would create a new individual, a *Homo Sovieticus,* failed. Ethnic, religious, and regional identities remained strong in the USSR and came forcefully to the fore in the more politically open atmosphere created by Gorbachev's reforms. Nevertheless, the Soviet system and ideology dominated the lives of the USSR's various peoples and arrested the natural evolution of their national identities. Meanwhile, despite the USSR's failure to create a Soviet Man, a union-based identity emerged among considerable portions of its population, including ethnic Russians. In an interview in 1990, Boris Yeltsin said that "I recognized myself to be a citizen of the country [i.e., the USSR] and not of Russia"[42] Moreover, for many Russians, Russia and the Soviet Union were one and the same. This view is reflected in the following comment by Gorbachev. He asked "What is Russia? It is the Union. What is the Union? It is mostly Russia."[43] The outcome of the weakness of local identities together with the disappearance of the union-based identity generated an identity crisis in all Soviet successor states, including Russia.

Shortly after the fall of the USSR, the need to define Russia's post-Soviet identity was felt and, as noted earlier, in 1996 the Russian president, Boris Yeltsin, called for the development of a new national identity for Russia.[44]

In the course of the debate on Russian identity, many old and new ideas emerged regarding what should be the foundations of Russia's post-Soviet identity. Vera Tolz has identified five types of ideas for the 1990s, including a union identity, which defined the Russians "as an imperial people or through their missions to create a supranational state."[45] Another idea was that of Russians as a nation of all East Slavs. Thus some intellectuals and politicians argued that the definition of Russia and hence its national identity should extend to all east Slavic nations, namely the inhabitants of the Russian Federation, Belarus (formerly called Belorussia), and Ukraine. A prominent advocate of this idea was Alexander Solzhenitsyn,[46] along with politicians associated with the National Salvation Front. They believed that the new Russian national identity could be only crystalized through a union with Ukraine and Belarus. In addition to the ethnic element, they saw the common bond of Orthodoxy and a common past as the foundation of such a union and identity. Others saw Russia as consisting of all Russian speakers regardless of ethnicity, while some groups offered a racial definition of Russianness. Some saw Russia as "a spirit, a consciousness" and concluded that whoever shared this spirit and consciousness should be characterized as Russian.[47] Finally, there were those who believed that Russians should be defined as those who are citizens of the Russian Federation. The last-named group had a civic notion of Russianness and hence of Russian national identity.[48]

The debate on Russia's national identity and its core components has not yet ended. Nevertheless, in the last two decades, it has become clear that traditional components of Russian national identity will form a significant part of its post-Soviet national identity.

Reassertion of Orthodoxy

Despite years of atheistic propaganda during the Soviet era, today at least 75 percent to 80 percent of Russia's population identifies with Orthodoxy. This identification does not always imply religiosity, being observant, or belonging to the Russian Orthodox Church. Rather, it means being culturally part of the Orthodox community. This fact is even recognized by the Church itself. For instance, the Patriarch Alexy II reportedly has said that the Russian people "through the tradition and national culture feel an affinity with the Church."[49] In other words, their Orthodox identity is more cultural. By contrast, the identity of the believing Christians is religious, and is formed "through personal experience of communion with God and religious outlook on the world."[50] It short, it is the cultural, rather than theological, dimension of religion which is most important. Orthodoxy is important because it has become part of Russians' culture.

Whether interpreted in cultural or religious terms, as early as the late 1980s views had emerged which regard Orthodox Christianity as one of the foundations of a new Russian identity and value system, as well as a religion-based concept of Russian nationalism,[51] and this trend has continued in the following decades. The unfulfilled promises of rapid improvement in the lives of the Russians after the fall of Communism, the consequent loss of attraction of Western liberal ideas, and the generation of a degree of resentment toward the West among many Russians contributed to the increased attraction of Russia's own cultural traditions.[52]

However, because Russia's post-Soviet conditions have been very different from the past, this emerging Orthodox identity has in many ways been different from Russia's traditional Orthodox identity. The following observation by S. V. Kortunov illustrates both the significance of Orthodoxy in the context of Russia's identity debate and its limitations: "Russia's revival as a national and cultural unit is impossible without the restoration of Orthodox Christianity in it, without returning it [Russia] to Christianity as the foundation of its spiritual world."[53] But he also acknowledges that, because Russia is a multi-religious state, the new Orthodoxy cannot be hegemonic. Nor does he believe that Russia could become an Orthodox state similar to that of the Tsars or, as he puts, it to become "an imperial link." But he maintains that

Orthodoxy can form the foundation and moral paradigm of Russia's development.[54]

Such a shift has already occurred to some degree, and many Russians have increasingly looked to Orthodox Christianity to provide part of their post-Soviet value system and to form a key component of their new national identity. Meanwhile, the Orthodox Church's public and political profile has risen in post-Soviet Russia. According to some polls, the Orthodox Church is the institution most trusted by the Russians.[55] State-church relations have also grown closer.[56]

One outcome has been an increase in the Church's influence on the formulation of Russian foreign policy. However, there is no agreement among scholars and observers of church-state relations in Russia about the extent of the Church's influence.[57] Its influence on Russian politics and foreign policy has fluctuated, although there is no evidence that the Church has actually determined Russia's policy toward different issues. Yet it does appear that in many policy areas and in places where there are considerable numbers of Orthodox Christians, the Church has become an instrument for advancing Russia's foreign policy objectives. However, the Church has not always been a passive executor of government policies. Rather, the Church and the Russian state have worked best in those areas where the interests of the Church and Russian State have coincided.[58]

Because of the close connection between Orthodox Christianity and Byzantium, renewed interest in Orthodoxy in Russia has also revived interest in Byzantium and its traditions. In particular, Byzantine traditions have been mined in order to find guidelines and lessons for Russia as it struggles to define its new role in the world. This interest has intensified in the last decade, and Byzantium and its symbols have been "discussed on talk shows, their imperial grandeur cited as an example for Russia's future glory; Orthodox priests with distinguished beards [have] read sermons on how Russia, if it is to achieve greatness, must look into its Christian predecessors."[59] Russia is not on the way to become a new Byzantium. Nevertheless, for those who yearn to resurrect Russia's great-power status, Byzantium has served as an inspiration.

Reassertion of Ethnic Identities: Impact on Russian Slavism

Developments in the last years of the USSR and in post-Soviet Russia have strengthened the linkage in most Russians' minds between Slavness and Russianness. The tenacity of separate ethnic identities in the USSR was dramatically demonstrated when, profiting from Gorbachev's policy of openness (*Glasnost*), ethnic separatist movements proliferated in the USSR. The rise of ethno-centric nationalism and separatism among Russia's non-Slav populations contributed to the emergence of similar sentiments even among ethnic Russians, although Russians mostly controlled the USSR's highest state structures and Russian culture and language dominated its social and cultural spheres. It was this revived sense of Russian nationalism and the Russian Federation's declaration of independence that most contributed to the USSR's demise.

Afterward, ethnic and religious tensions continued to bedevil the Russian Federation, even leading to long and bloody wars, as in Chechnya. The rise of ethno-centrism and separatism among Russia's non-Slav peoples and the ensuing conflicts intensified ethno-centric tendencies among Russia's Slavic people, who rightly or wrongly had long felt that they had borne the burden of providing for the rest of the USSR. These feelings had existed since the 1960s and 1970s.

In addition, by then a belief was developing that too much Soviet cosmopolitanism was threatening Russian culture and even the survival of ethnic Russians. Some extremists even suggested that Muslims' higher birthrate would eventually make Slavs a minority in the USSR.[60] As an expression of this fear, pictures by dissident Alexander Zinoviev depicted Moscow with minarets and the Russian leaders with Central Asian features.[61] When various separatist movements developed in the late 1980s and 1990s, the feeling that Russians had done too much for other peoples of the Union without receiving any gratitude was sharpened. Based on historical evidence, this feeling of betrayal is not warranted; but its impact is undeniable.

Several developments in the post-Soviet period intensified many ethnic Russians' feelings that they were threatened by the Russian Federation's non-Russian citizens. Most important were the Chechen war and the rise of terrorism, partly motivated by religion—Islam in the North Caucasus, which at times reached Moscow; Russia's economic difficulties in the immediate post-Soviet period; the decline in the Slavic Russian birth rate together with the still-rising Muslim birth rate; and a sharp increase in the number of Caucasian and Central Asian immigrants to large Russian cities, such as Moscow and St. Petersburg.

These developments further eroded the attraction of multiethnic conceptions of Russia and sharpened the traditional distinction between those who are merely citizens of the Russian Federation or before that those of the empire (*Rossiski*) and the ethnic/Slav Russians (*Russki*). Moreover, as some scholars have pointed out, in Russia there has always been "a strong tradition of ethnic perception of nation,"[62] and therefore the more ethno-centric vision of Russianness, which has become stronger in recent times, also reflects this tradition.[63] Officially, too, there has been a degree of ambivalence about defining the Russian nation: should it be done in a civic or an ethnic sense? However, Russian leaders still mean Russian citizens when they use the term "Russian." But at the popular level, the ethnic definition is the point of reference.

The reassertion of the Slavic dimension of Russia's national identity has also had foreign policy implications. Russia's desire to forge closer relations with Belarus and its concerns with the fate of ethnic Russian inhabitants of states which emerged after the fall of the Soviet Union reflect the increasingly ethno-centric aspects of Russia's post-Soviet identity. However, other reasons, such as a desire to recreate at least part of what was the Soviet Union under Russian influence have also contributed to this aspect of Russia's foreign policy. The feelings of solidarity with the Serbs can at least to some degree be traced to such developments.[64]

Russia as a Great Power/Russia as Civilization Creating and Civilizer

After the USSR's fall, the traditional notions of Russia's global role and its place in the world reasserted themselves. These include the view of Russia as a great power (*Derzhava*) with a recognized and legitimate place within the councils of major global powers and as a civilizational and cultural construct. According to the latter view, the boundaries of civilizational Russia go beyond the territorial confines of the Russian state and encompass those of the greater "Russian World" (*Russky Mir*).[65] Another favorite view sees Russia as a creator of civilization, a civilizer, and a force connecting the East and the West.

The reemergence of these broad views of Russian identity was inevitable because, as noted before, since the consolidation and expansion of the Moscow state, Russian history has been one of empire.[66] Similarly, Russia has always seen itself as a civilizer and as a connector of the East and the West. For example, Russia, too, saw its imperial expansion, especially in the nineteenth century, as a civilizing mission.

These traditional beliefs and patterns, however, did not become dominant during the early years of the post-Soviet period. Until 1994–1995, they were eclipsed and challenged by new ideas, especially those advanced by Russia's new breed of Westernizing elite, which advocated its greater liberalization, and its joining the West as an equal partner in the post-Soviet international order. The Westernizers subscribed to a more civic definition of Russia's national identity. By the mid-1990s, however, more traditional ideas about Russia had gained greater currency, including the notion that it has its own unique civilization and thus must find its own voice based on its indigenous culture, values, and historical experience.

These ideas became more popular in the 2000s. The greater popularity of the idea of Russia's uniqueness is reflected in the statements of Russian officials and analysts. For example, in 2006, Vladislav Surkov, President Dmitry Medvedev's chief of staff, said that "we [Russians] should have our own voice . . . we should have our own political language." He justified his view on the basis that "if a people cannot develop their own images and thoughts . . . then they will have, in general, no political or cultural thought of their own."[67] He later said that Russia needed to develop its own version of democratic order because, although "the new democratic order arises from European civilization . . . but within it there is a specifically Russian version."[68] His words bring to mind Berdyaev's criticism of Peter the Great's reforms, especially their disconnectedness from authentic Russian traditions.

The shifting of the balance of influence between these two perspectives has also influenced Russia's foreign policy thinking and hence its approach to different foreign policy challenges, including the Bosnian crisis.

SERBIA IN THE CONTEXT OF RUSSIA'S SELF-IMAGE

The Yugoslav crisis and especially the war in Bosnia coincided with the rising influence of Orthodox Christianity and Slavic identity in Russia and thus influenced Russia's approach to the war.

Compared to some other Slavs living closer to Russian lands, such as the Belarusians and the Russian-speaking parts of Ukraine, the Serbs are quite distant from Russia and do not trigger the same intense feelings of kinship and closeness as do the former. Historically, too, until the mid-seventeenth century, Russia had much closer relations in terms of religious contacts and cultural exchanges with Bulgaria than with Serbia. However, shortly after this time, Serbia acquired greater importance for Russia than Bulgaria, and eventually cultural and religious exchanges with Serbia surpassed those with Bulgaria.[69] Today, the Serbs are considered as close kin of the Russians, just after the Belarusians and the Russian-speaking Orthodox Ukrainians. For example, Serbia is included in the triumvirate of Russia, Belarus, and Serbia, which supposedly are bound together by the ties of "a mystical brotherhood."[70]

These feelings of connectedness between Russians and Serbs have generally come to the fore at times of crisis, especially when the latter faced threats of either a physical or a civilizational nature or when there was a perception of such threats.[71] This was clearly the case during the crisis of 1992–1996 triggered by the war in Bosnia, even if the Serbs were not justified in feeling threatened. Consequently, the war brought to the fore feelings of solidarity with the Serbs on the part of many Russians, including a number of politicians. This sentiment might have also been intensified by the fact that many Russians felt confused and threatened following the Soviet Union's fall. Therefore, many were more receptive to arguments that the Orthodox community as a whole was facing a civilizational and even existential threat. Nevertheless, the position of various politicians and even the general public, especially regarding the extent to which Russia should help the Serbs, was influenced more by their views on issues such as the nature of Russia's post-Soviet identity, its place in the world, and the character of its relations with the West, than by a sense of Slavic/Orthodox solidarity. Additionally, the cost-benefit calculations of a Russian policy of assisting the Serbs greatly impacted the positions of both Russia's political class and public on this issue.

In general, those who believed in Russia's cultural/civilizational uniqueness, opposed its excessive Westernization, and believed in its special role in the world and its right to be a great power supported a policy of assisting the Serbs. By contrast, Russia's new generation of Westernizers, who wanted to link Russia closely to the Atlantic community, believed that Russia's new relations with the West should not be compromised because of excessive support for the Serbs. As the relative influence of these views and their proponents shifted during the Yugoslav crisis, so did the approach of the Russian government. Some of the shift was caused by Russia's domestic evolution, especially the public's reaction to the consequences of Western-devised economic and political reforms. The rapid privatization of Russian economy (the so-called shock therapy) led to the excessive enrichment of a few and the impoverishment of most Russians, and it worked against the Westernizers. Certain Western policies, especially the inclusion of Central European countries in NATO, also contributed to this trend. With the expansion of NATO to the Baltic States, the position of the Westernizers further eroded. This shift was reflected in Moscow's policy toward the Kosovo crisis in 1998–1999, which was more out of step with the West's approach than had been the case during the 1992–1995 Bosnian War and represented a dramatic shift in Russian orientation that was inadequately understood in the West as deriving in significant part from other things that NATO was doing that affected Russia's perceptions of its interests.

In both cases, however, Russia's policies were determined more by its security calculations, consideration of its other interests, and by a cost-benefit analysis. They also reflected its changing domestic political dynamics. Feelings of religious and ethnic kinship with the Serbs, although important, were never decisive. This is not surprising and, instead of being an aberration, reflects the historic pattern of Serbian-Russian relations. In reality, despite the Serbs' and the Russians' view of each other as the protected and the protector, historically their relationship has always been more nuanced. Russia has always treated Serbia in light of its own broader strategic and security interests, it has taken a manipulative approach toward Serbia, and it has been willing to trade Serbia's interests for its own. In the past, Serbia has also shown that, if it could find other supporters, it could forgo close ties with Russia, at one time using France as an alternative.[72] Nevertheless, for most of Russian and Serbian history, the two countries and peoples have found each other to be useful allies and partners.

RUSSIAN FOREIGN POLICY DEBATES AND THE BOSNIAN WAR

As noted earlier, the shift in Russia's foreign policy thinking had already occurred under Mikhail Gorbachev in the context of his New Thinking. A principal aspect of this theory was its emphasis on Russia's national interests as opposed to ideologically determined objectives. However, this theory did not actually determine the basis on which Russia's national interests should be defined, although it emphasized that a major goal of Russian foreign policy should be revitalization of its economy and reduction of tensions with the West.

The New Thinking was progressive for its time. However, it was the outcome of the era of the Cold War and of bloc politics. It also represented the Soviet Union as a multinational entity. As such, it could not provide adequate guidelines for Russia's post-Soviet foreign policy. Consequently, soon after the USSR's demise, in parallel with talk of developing a new Russian national identity, debate also began on what should be Russia's new foreign policy concept or framework. Some politicians and intellectuals, including Russia's first post-Soviet foreign minister, Andrei Kozyrev, questioned the need for an overarching framework. He criticized the Russians' habit of "thinking in terms of blueprints."[73] He added that the Russians seem to "need *Das Capital* or a *CPSU* program that gives a schematic answer to all questions. But there can be no blueprint. What exist are reactions to specific situations and those reactions display Russia's national interests. No country has an official description of its national interests."[74]

The problem, however, was to determine the basis on which Russia's national interests should be defined and who should define them. Divergences that soon developed on this issue were directly linked to debates about Russia's national identity and its foundations. As had been the case at the time of Peter's and Catherine's reforms, a major dividing line was between those who favored Russia's Westernization and its turning toward the Atlantic community and those who believed in Russia's *sui generis* nature and the Eurasian and universal dimensions of its culture and identity. The latter's views were in part shaped by Russia's geographical, demographic, and cultural realities. Geographically, it spans Asia and Europe. Demographically, it is ethnically mixed. It has also been subjected to cultural influences emanating from both East and West.

During the early 1990s, the Westernizers were known as the Euro-Atlanticists. Those who believed in Russia's uniqueness and recommended a Russian-centered foreign policy were known as the Eurasianists. Within each group there were subtle differences, and each had its more pragmatic and more radical tendencies. Nevertheless, both groups shared the goals of restoring Russia's role as a great power and preserving its role as agent of civilization in Central Asia and the Caucasus.

The Characteristics of the Westernizers/Euro-Atlanticist School

The underlying principles of the Euro-Atlanticist School were the following:

1. *The primacy of domestic issues and the need to create a favorable external environment for Russia to pursue its economic and political reform agenda.* The principal objective of Russia's foreign policy should be to enable it to become "a democratic, market-oriented and civilized nation." The primary test whether Russia had become a civilized nation was the level of its peoples' living standard.[75] To Euro-Atlanticists "civilized" meant "Westernized."
2. *Russia's full integration in the international system.* This meant that Russia should subscribe to universal values embodied in the United Nations Charter, the Charter of the CSCE (later OSCE), and the Paris Charter on Human Rights; it should abandon ideological and other vestiges of its communist and tsarist pasts; and it should overcome its messianism and "excessive Russianness." In this way, Russia could become part of what Andrei Kozyrev called "a special civilized club."[76] In other words, the Euro-Atlanticists believed that Russia must embrace Western culture in its entirety.
3. *Russia must become a normal power but also retain its great-power status.* Russia's possession of nuclear power and having a permanent seat on the United Nations Security Council justified this status.
4. *Russia should remain a civilizer of its traditional spheres of influence in Central Asia and the Caucasus and serve as a bridge between these regions and the West.* Kozyrev opined that, through its dynamism and persistence, Russia would transform these regions. This indicates that even the Euro-Atlanticists wanted to be the West's partners and not its mere followers and that they were not completely immune from traditional views of Russia and its global role.

According to the Euro-Atlanticists, the major security threats to Russia emanated from its Muslim-inhabited south and not from the West or East. They believed that since the West also faced similar threats, Russia and the West, through confidence-building measures and disarmament, could form a partnership and alliance which eventually could develop into a global security system. This vision was reflected in the Charter of Russian-American Partnership signed on 17 July 1992.[77] In addition, Russia saw the consolidation of its former sphere of influence into the Commonwealth of Independent States (CIS) as part of this global system of security.

Eurasianist School/Advocates of a Multipolar International System

The main alternative to the Euro-Atlanticists vision was offered by the Eurasianists.[78] Over time, the more moderate and modernized version of this school evolved into that of multipolarism and was identified with Russia's then-foreign minister, Yevgeny Primakov. This concept rejected the notion of a unipolar world under U.S. hegemony and believed that an international system based on it would be unstable. Principal characteristics of the Eurasianist School are the following: 1) belief in Russia's unique and *sui generis* nature, which combines both European and Asiatic elements, belief in Russian civilization's superiority to that of the West, and belief in Russia's mission; and 2) emphasis on geographical factors, including climate, in shaping various states' and nations' character and outlook and hence their priorities.[79] The Eurasianists believed that the Euro-Atlanticists had unrealistic expectations of how joining the West quickly would help them achieve their ambitions for Russia. They also misjudged the extent of the West's willingness to treat Russia as an equal partner. When their expectations were not realized, they became subject to scathing criticism by their opponents, notably the Eurasianists. Their main criticisms of the Euro-Atlanticists were

1. *Naïveté and Idealism.* The end of the Cold War had not meant that Russia and the West now had identical national interests. On the contrary, the West would continue to act according to its own national interests and not those of Russia. The Euro-Atlanticists were turning their romantic vision of Russian-Western relations into a dogmatic ideology.[80]
2. *Inequality.* The Russian-Western partnership had been unequal and that Russia had made all the concessions.[81]
3. *Neglect of a mission for Russia.* Sergei Stankevich first articulated this criticism. He wrote that "pragmatism not balanced by healthy idealism would with us [Russians] alas, most likely develop into cynicism." Therefore, Russia must have a mission. Stankevich identified this mission as: "to initiate and support a multilateral dialogue of cultures, civilizations and states. . . . Russia as conciliator, Russia connecting, Russia combining; . . . a country imbibing the West and East, North and South, unique and exclusively capable, perhaps of the harmonious combination of many different principles of a symphonic harmony."[82]
4. *Inadequate attention to the South and the East.* Because of its proximity to China and the Muslim south, Russia is vulnerable to the impact of developments in those regions and therefore should not relegate them to second place, focusing only on relations with the West.

By contrast, the Eurasianists offered the following underpinning principles of an effective Russian foreign policy:

1. *Foreign policy as a support for Russian statehood.* Reform is needed, but its success depends on reassertion of Russia's statehood. Its foreign policy should help it shape its post-Soviet statehood. To perform this task, Russian foreign policy should be assertive and realist.
2. *Interest over ideals.* Even in the post–Cold War world, states will act according to their own national interests rather than in pursuit of ideals. Therefore, Russia, too, should act according to its national interests.
3. *Adequate attention to Russia's geographical realities,* which requires a multi-dimensional rather than solely West-centered approach. For some extreme Eurasianists, initially this meant that the entire post-Soviet space should be Russia's exclusive sphere of influence. Yevgenii Ambartsumov even said that Russia should develop its own version of a Monroe Doctrine in the post-Soviet space.[83] Also, Russia should not follow America's lead in relations with the Muslim world because it risked wasting its long accumulated capital in these countries, especially since, for the foreseeable future [1990s], Russia was "doomed to the role of a loved but bankrupt 'distant relative to the West.'"[84]

However, the more moderate and sensible Eurasianists were not anti-West per se. They only wanted a more nationalist and assertive Russian foreign policy and insisted on Russia's treatment as a great power. Beginning by 1993 and increasingly so after 1995, Eurasianists exerted more influence in shaping Russia's foreign policy, including to some extent its approach to the Bosnian War.

YELTSIN AND THE BOSNIAN WAR

The last year of Gorbachev's tenure as the USSR's leader had demonstrated Russia's limited ability to have a decisive impact on the evolution of events in Yugoslavia. This ability was further eroded during Yeltsin's tenure. However, the same fundamental factors which had shaped Gorbachev's policy toward the Yugoslav crisis determined the basic outlines of Russian policy toward the Bosnian War under Yeltsin. The dominant discourse on Russia's foreign policy and the dynamics of domestic politics, including the consequences of Russia's post-Soviet economic meltdown and the ebb and flow of Russo-Western relations, shaped Russia's policy.

Increased Importance of Domestic Context of Foreign Policy

After the USSR's demise, the importance of domestic factors in determining Russia's post-Soviet foreign policy grew significantly. The main contributors to this trend were the disappearance of the hegemonic discourse of the Soviet era, which as discussed earlier led to the appearance of new discourses and the reemergence of old ones.[85]

Meanwhile, the introduction of parliamentary and more-or-less democratic politics in post-Soviet Russia created an environment conducive to debate and rivalry among the proponents of competing discourses on foreign policy. It also established closer linkages between foreign policy and domestic politics. In short, as put by one analyst, Russia's post-Soviet foreign policy became "democratized."[86] As a result, officials engaged in policy-making, including the president himself, had to consider the impact of their foreign policy decisions on their political and electoral fortunes. Meanwhile, issues related to foreign policy were increasingly used by politicians in their quest for power and thus became part of the overall political power game. The result was that Russia's foreign policy, including regarding the Bosnian War, became less consistent.

The Dominant Foreign Policy Thinking of the Yeltsin Era: Impact on Bosnia Policy

During the first years of Boris Yeltsin's presidency, the Euro-Atlanticist School was in the ascendant within Russia's foreign policy-making community. As noted earlier, the adherents of this school desired to Westernize Russia and to integrate it in the West or in the words of Andrei Kozyrev, the "civilized world."

This paramount Euro-Atlanticist objective required that Russia should not allow the war in Bosnia and issues surrounding it to derail its goal of becoming integrated in the Atlantic community. Russia was also eager to prove that it could play a positive role in providing for European security and for resolving regional disputes and that it was "a good international citizen."[87] In practical terms, this basic objective meant that regarding the Bosnian War Russia should essentially follow the Western and international consensus and avoid taking positions significantly at odds with it. This was the principal reason that, despite some domestic opposition, and notwithstanding Serbo-Russian religious and ethnic ties, Russia supported international sanctions against the Serbs. Failing to do so would have endangered Russia's relations with the United States and other Western powers.

Russia's other important objective was to show that it was still a great power and should be treated as such. To achieve this goal was important for Yeltsin and his foreign minister for domestic reasons as well as for safeguarding Russia's international prestige. This was important domestically because many Russians were unhappy about the USSR's dissolution and they blamed Yeltsin for the Soviet Union's demise. In fact, while the West viewed Yeltsin as a hero, many Russians saw the entire Yeltsin era as a time of "national shame."

To regain Russia's international prestige and particularly to avoid its further humiliation were also main priorities of Russian leaders. They fully realized that their country had effectively lost its superpower status. Yet they were also "painfully anxious to avoid being treated as inferior."[88] This concern was reflected in a statement by Vitaly Churkin, special representative of the Russian president to the international talks on Bosnia.[89] He said that his main concern during the time he was involved in the Bosnian problem was to prevent "a national humiliation for Russia."[90] It was thus important that Russia should not appear as blindly following the West's orders. Foreign Minister Kozyrev tried hard to explain Russia's behavior as that of a responsible great power and at the service of the broader international community. He said that Russia was "discharging its responsibility as a great power for the maintenance of international law and order."[91]

Therefore, Russia agreed to United Nations sanctions on the Serbs and went along with other decisions adopted by Western powers and the United Nations.[92] These included providing military forces for the United Nations Protection Force (UNPROFOR), which was set up in January 1992 to ensure the ceasefire between Croatia and the Serbs in Croatia's Serb-occupied region of Krajina. According to some observers, this was "the high point of Moscow's pro-Western foreign policy."[93] Even afterward, Russia's policy essentially followed the West's lead on Bosnia, despite reservations regarding some of these policies, such as the NATO air strikes on the Serbs when Russia believed they went beyond the United Nation's resolutions. What most riled Russia was the Western tendency to take decisions without prior consultation with Moscow. At times, the West did not even inform Russia of its decisions. This Western neglect was a pointed reminder to the Russians of their diminished international status. A particularly embarrassing case was when NATO forces bombed Serb positions near Gorazde in April 1994.

In the following years the West's disregarding of Russian concerns and ignoring it during its decision-making process caused Russia to harden its positions on a whole range of foreign policy issues. This shift was reflected in Russia's less accommodating, albeit still ineffective, policy toward the Kosovo crisis of 1998–1999. But the full impact of these changes was to be felt only after Yeltsin's departure from Russia's political scene.

The Impact of Domestic Politics

Under Yeltsin, too, the evolution of Russia's domestic conditions and politics affected its approach toward the Bosnian War. In particular, Russia's economic problems during the immediate post-Soviet years had significant implications for the conduct of its foreign policy.

A particularly important economic factor behind Russia's diplomacy was its need for external help to carry out economic reforms and revitalize its shattered economy. This help had to come from Western sources and institutions such as the IMF and World Bank. Russia also needed foreign investment; this, too, had to come from Western sources. Russia's economic and financial woes and its need for external assistance severely diminished its ability to pursue a more activist and independent foreign policy. In particular, Russia could not adopt policies on sensitive issues which were seriously at odds with Western preferences. The war in Bosnia was such an issue. The consequence of its not following this line could be the dashing of its hopes one day to join the West. Eric Shiraev has succinctly put Russia's dilemma in the following terms: Russia could not pursue an anti-West policy in Yugoslavia while also having its hand out for aid and investment.[94]

Russia also faced security challenges, which largely emanated from separatist movements, especially in Chechnya. The Chechen quest for independence eventually resulted in a long and bloody war. When Gorbachev was in power, Yeltsin encouraged Russia's minorities to seek sovereignty as a means to undermine Gorbachev's position. But when he gained power, he wanted to rein in the separatist forces. Eventually, he went to war in Chechnya in 1994 in order to stop its separation from the Russian Federation. A Russian policy vis-à-vis the Bosnian War which significantly departed from that of the West potentially could have prompted some Western powers to pressure Russia by supporting its separatist movements.

Even more significant were consequences of the democratization of Russia's foreign policy-making process, especially the multiplication of actors. Following this process, the Russian legislature became more vocal on foreign policy issues as did civil society organizations. Another contributing factor was manipulation of foreign policy issues in political power struggles to a greater degree than during Gorbachev's tenure. Consequently, in order to undermine his position, Yeltsin's opponents frequently criticized his foreign policies and in particular his handling of the war in Bosnia. This manipulation of foreign policy for domestic purposes made Russia's policy toward the Bosnian War a pawn in struggles among its political elites. As noted by Suzanne Crow, disagreements over Russia's Bosnia policy reflected a bigger battle over deeper conflicts in Russia's political life.[95] A number of Russian analysts also support this analysis. Sergei Romanenko believed that the Yugoslav crisis had turned into "an element of political struggle in Russia."[96]

In this context, the Russian legislature became an important player, and various deputies criticized Moscow's Yugoslav policies, especially what they labeled as Russia's blind acceptance of Western decisions. Their sharpest criticism was directed at Andrei Kozyrev. A particularly harsh critic was the chairman of the International and Foreign Economic Committee of the Russian legislature, Yevgeneii Ambartsumov. He accused Kozyrev of abandoning Russia's "historic" approach toward the Balkans and its traditional pro-Serb policy.[97] Another critic was Vladimir Lukin, chairman of the Committee on Foreign Affairs of the State Duma. At one point, he complained that Russia did not have a policy on Yugoslavia and that its impact on the Yugoslav situation had been "extremely weak, minimal."[98] He then attributed this situation to Russia's economic and military weakness in the post-Soviet period.

In these criticisms, the theme that Russia had betrayed its fellow Slav and Orthodox Serbs figured prominently. But they reflected even more the pain of Russia's apparent loss of great power status than a sense of betrayal of the Serbs. They were also prompted by feelings of humiliation generated by what people like Ambartsumov and Lukin perceived as the West's ignoring of Russia, despite Russian cooperation and even submission to Western decisions.

Obstruction by the Russian legislature finally forced Yeltsin militarily to occupy the Supreme Soviet, to evict the troublesome deputies, and to establish a new legislature, the *Duma*. However, changing the legislature's name did not solve Yeltsin's problems because in the new parliamentary elections held in 1994 nationalists and communists made considerable gains. In particular, the election of Vladimir Zhirinovsky, leader of the liberal democrats and an ardent nationalist and pro-Serb figure, complicated Yeltsin's Bosnia policies.

The rise of Russian nationalists was partly a reaction to Russia's conditions in the Yeltsin era and partly a response to the West's ignoring of Russia. Showing support for nationalists was one way for Russians to show their frustration with their country's predicament. The nationalists' rise also indicated the erosion of the appeal of the Euro-Atlanticists' vision of Russia's foreign policy.

With the presence of nationalists in the parliament, criticism of Yeltsin's policy toward the Bosnian War intensified. Zhirinovsky was particularly outspoken. In addition to criticizing Yeltsin-Kozyrev policy toward the war, he offered his own policy prescriptions, suggesting that Russian troops be placed on the Serb side while NATO troops would be stationed on the Croat, Muslim, and Slovenian sides. Once this objective was reached, the new situation should be frozen.[99] The Communists also joined in the criticism of Yeltsin's policies.

The growing influence of nationalists and other opponents of Russia's Euro-Atlanticists' foreign policy forced Yeltsin to adopt some of their rhetoric and to use tough language toward the West. According to one observer, "official Russian rhetoric reached heights seldom achieved even during the Cold War."[100] For instance, Yeltsin said that NATO's activities regarding the Bosnian War, together with its eastern expansion, could light the fires of war in Europe.[101] Meanwhile, as noted by W. Abarinov, "in the changed political conditions incessant reminders that Russia is a great power seemed to be the order of the day."[102] In short, the weaker Russia became, references to its great power status increased.

The weakening of the Euroatlanticists' position and the hardening of Russian rhetoric toward the West was also affected by the West's ignoring of Russia. By indicating Russia's increasing irrelevance in global and European affairs, this Western attitude undermined Kozyrev and other Euro-Atlanticists' claim that Russia would be an equal partner of the West in managing global affairs. Even Mikhail Gorbachev in 1994 commented that the West had treated Russia as a junior partner who was expected only "to nod his head and support the choices of [the Western powers]."[103] In order to counter the nationalists' and other opposition groups' propaganda that Russia lacked an independent foreign policy and was blindly following the West's lead, in addition to hardening its rhetoric Russia became more active within the United Nations and various other groups. One such was the EU-sponsored Contact Group on Bosnia. Moreover, in discussions with Western powers Russia tried to moderate the anti-Serb aspects of some decisions made by the United Nations and other institutions and players.

Nevertheless, the basics of Russia's policy toward the Bosnian War remained constant, and Russia's parliament was unable to produce significant change in its approach toward the Bosnian War, beyond the hardening of rhetoric. Some Russian commentators have attributed parliament's failure in producing change in Russia's Bosnia policy to its limited role in the formulation of the country's foreign policy in general. According to Abarinov, the "parliament, just as before does not have a great influence on the decisions of the cabinet."[104] Other analysts share this view. They maintain that, although the number of officials involved in the policy-making process had increased in the post-Soviet period, Yeltsin decided Russia's foreign policy by primarily playing different people off against each other. They believe that Kozyrev did not have much independent influence on policy. Whatever influence he had derived from the fact that Yeltsin shared his vision of what Russia's foreign policy should be. It was Yeltsin who, despite mounting criticism against Kozyrev, kept him afloat until he finally left his post in January 1996.[105] But even more important was the limited range of Russia's options because of its serious domestic difficulties.

Serb Intransigence: Limits on Russian Influence

Russia's ability to influence the course of the Bosnian War and to play a more important role in international decision-making regarding the conflict was also undermined by the intransigence of both Serb and Bosnian Serb leaders. Both sets of leaders often rejected Russian proposals and thus severely weakened Russia's hand in dealing with Western countries. The Western powers reasoned that if Russia could not deliver the Serbs and in this way contribute to resolving the crisis, why should they be concerned about Russian sensitivities? Russian inability to influence the Serbs was due to Moscow's lack of any serious levers of influence either on the Serbs or on the Bosnian Serbs. The Serbs' intransigence showed the limits of religio-cultural factors in shaping international actors' behavior. Despite their ethnic and religious affinity with Russians, the Serbs were not willing to sacrifice what they saw as their national interests for the sake of shielding Russia from embarrassment. The following statement by the Russian commentator, Konstantin Eggert, shows how little influence Moscow had on the Serbs: because they lacked any means of pressure on the Serbs, Moscow and Andrei Kozyrev "have literally to beg Milošević and Karadzic for concessions."[106]

The Serbian attitude was used by the opponents in Moscow of a policy of helping the Serbs to argue that the policy, which at times meant defying international consensus and striking a more independent posture, had undermined Russia's international position. Consequently, some commentators, including Konstantin Eggert, dismissed the view of "the proponents of the so-called 'enlightened great-power status' for Russia, who believed that Russia lost influence over Yugoslavia's developments when it agreed to UN sanctions on Yugoslavia." Instead, he argued that Russia's ability "to influence Balkan events disappeared when, under pressure from the nationalist lobby, it decided to sacrifice solidarity with the world community for the sake of an artificially constructed 'independent foreign policy.'"[107]

RUSSIAN CIVIL SOCIETY AND PUBLIC OPINION: ATTITUDES ON THE BOSNIAN WAR

By all accounts, at the time of the Yugoslavia crisis and the war in Bosnia, the Russian public's primary preoccupation was with Russia's own deteriorating conditions. In general, foreign policy matters held little interest for the average Russian. In particular, in view of Russia's own internal problems of separatism, the public was not well-disposed toward the use of Russian military forces abroad. But there were exceptions. For example, most Russians agreed to the use of military force to protect ethnic Russians in other countries. According to one survey, 67 percent of Russians felt that, if the lives of ethnic Russians were in danger, Russia should use military force to protect them.[108] However, because there were no ethnic Russians in Yugoslavia whose lives were in danger, most Russians did not support the use of Russian military forces in defense of the Serbs.

Nevertheless, while, according to available evidence, there was no groundswell of popular pressure on Russian officials to support the Serbs effectively, especially by the use of military means, pro-Serb sentiments did exist among Russians. At the very least, a majority opposed such actions as the NATO air strikes on the Bosnian Serbs. In 1994, as reported in the *Daily Telegraph*, 77 percent of Russians opposed NATO air strikes and two-thirds shared the view expressed by Vladimir Zhirinovsky that an attack on Serbia would amount to an attack on Russia.[109] However, popular opposition to NATO actions did not translate into support for active prevention of its actions, especially if this implied the use of military force. Furthermore, it appears that, even at the public level, opposition to NATO strikes primarily stemmed from Russia's not being consulted beforehand. It appears that it was the feelings of hurt pride, rather than a sense of Slavic and Orthodox solidarity with the Serbs, that mostly shaped the Russian public's attitudes. Nevertheless, religious and ethnic factors were also important. Because of such feelings and despite Russia's own economic difficulties, a substantial minority of around 32 percent supported supplying humanitarian and economic aid to the Serbs. A smaller percentage even supported the provision of Russian arms and military advisors to the Serbs. A main reason for the lack of public support for the provision of arms and military personnel to Serbs was the belief that Russia would need all of its human, military, and other resources to respond to challenges posed by separatist movements on the home front. This belief was proved correct in 1994 when the war in Chechnya started.

Russian Volunteers in the Yugoslav Conflict

This belief helps explain why, despite considerable popular sympathy for the Serbs, only a relatively small number of Russian volunteers, variously estimated between 500 and 700, went to fight alongside the Serbs. Reportedly, most of these volunteers had belonged to the Russian military forces, and some of them were veterans of the Soviet-Afghan War.

Mikhail Polikarpov, a historian of the Bosnian War who also took part in it, told *Pravda* that "Russian military men volunteered to serve in Bosnia in 1992–1995, and several hundreds of Russian soldiers took part in the Balkan War."[110] Russian fighters also included a unit of Cossacks, whose commander, Alexander Zagrebov, was a veteran of the Soviet-Afghan War.[111] Another group of volunteers was called the Tsarist Wolves and was commanded by Alexander Mukharev. It is hard accurately to determine the motivation of these volunteers. A sense of Orthodox and Slavic solidarity certainly was a factor in their decision to fight on the Serb side. But a taste for adventure might have also been an attraction. According to a report published in the *Los Angeles Times,* money was another important inducement for some volunteers.[112] According to this article, every volunteer was paid $155 a month, not a negligible sum in view of Russia's economic difficulties at the time. Others, meanwhile, seem to have looked at the Yugoslav conflict as a training ground for similar wars of nationalities in Russia itself.[113] Some volunteers have expressed the view that Slavic-Orthodox solidarity had played very little role in organizing the volunteers. They claim that volunteers were mainly organized by opposition groups made up of those who had been "members of the state machine [and] who were dissatisfied with the collapse of the Soviet Union." They considered "Yugoslavia as one of the fronts for the USSR's restoration."[114]

THE ROLE OF THE ORTHODOX CHURCH

Despite its reemergence on the national scene, during the Yeltsin era the Church had not yet become an important political player and did not exert much influence in shaping the country's foreign policy. According to some scholars, the Church's negligible role in foreign policy in this period was due in part because it had not yet clearly defined and articulated its role in international affairs. Only in 2000 was the Church's "Social Concept" developed, identifying specific areas of international relations and foreign policy where the Russian Orthodox Church could make a contribution.[115]

According to this document, the Church's primary role in international affairs is to contribute to peace "at international, interethnic and domestic levels."[116] Although only officially formulated later, these ideas must have been prevalent within the Church during the Bosnian crisis, an assumption validated by the Church's activities during the crisis. It tried to strike a balance between appearing as impartial as possible, by sounding an ecumenical note and voicing sympathy for all those who had suffered as a result of the conflict, including the Serbs, and expressing support for the Serbs. Thus in a message in August 1995, Patriarch Alexy II said that "I grieve for the victims and deprivation suffered by the Serb, Croatian and the Bosnian Muslim nations." He then called on the Serbian, Croatian, and Bosnian Muslim religious leaders to return their people to the path of peace.[117] Meanwhile, the Church made a number of statements and through sermons and other ceremonies expressed support for the Serbs. For example, services were held for the Serbs, and people prayed in public places to St. Sava, Serbia's Patron Saint.[118] The Church also organized marches in support of the Serbs and condemned what it considered to be the Western powers' anti-Serb policies. Church leaders condemned NATO actions, and Metropolitan Kirill characterized NATO strikes as the next Crusade against Orthodox believers. Alexi

II, meanwhile, called these operations a "sin and a crime against international law."[119] The Church also organized humanitarian aid for the Serbs.

The Church's activities and approaches toward the conflict strengthened the position of Russian nationalists and, in general, that of the opponents of Yeltsin's seemingly pro-Western policies, conferring greater legitimacy. What the Church did might have helped the nationalists in their opposition to Yeltsin's policies by helping them gain more public acceptance and thus contributed to their electoral victory. However, rather than reflecting the Church's support for the nationalists per se, its statements showed that its position on many issues was more in line with those of the nationalists than the Westernizers. For example, the Church opposed the spread of Western-style liberalism in Russia, with its secular dimensions. It believed that such a development would inevitably undermine Orthodoxy's influence and hence that of the Church. It also believed in Russia's unique character and thought that excessive Westernization would undermine Russia's indigenous character and culture.

In short, the Church's activities, together with shifts in the composition of the Russian Parliament and activities of nationalists and other opponents of Yeltsin's policies, forced the Russian government to try at least to appear more pro-Serb and to help the Serbs through diplomatic and international channels. The Church was also the principal channel through which religious influences operated on the Russian government, in addition to religion's role as a component of Russian national identity. However, it is difficult to identify any specific cases where the Church influenced the formulation of the government's policy toward the war in Bosnia. Indeed, it is clear that the Church's influence on Russia's Bosnia policy was quite limited. Yeltsin's personality and the fact that he was not particularly religious contributed to the Church's limited influence on Russia's Bosnia policy.

CONCLUSIONS

The Yugoslav crisis began at a time when the USSR itself was undergoing profound changes and faced significant internal challenges. The pace of change accelerated in the post-Soviet era, when Russia's many challenges became more formidable. Consequently, throughout the Yugoslav crisis and the Bosnian War, both the USSR and then Russia were preoccupied with their own domestic problems. Their main concern regarding external developments, including the Yugoslav crisis and the Bosnian War, was their potential impact on Russia's own domestic evolution. In fashioning their approach toward these events, Soviet and then Russian leaders were mainly concerned about preventing the crisis and war from negatively affecting Russia's domestic evolution and delaying or hindering its internal reforms.[120]

In other words, the dominant view both during the last days of the USSR and in the early days of post-Soviet Russia was that foreign policy should help advance domestic reform agendas and not complicate them.

The state of the Soviet Union's and later Russia's relations with the West, along with the question of how the Yugoslav crisis could affect these relations, was Russia's other important preoccupation. Under Gorbachev, the belief was that resolving the USSR's economic and social problems required a non-confrontational Soviet approach toward the West. Therefore, he was not willing to risk causing problems with the West through Soviet policy toward the Yugoslav crisis. He wanted to prevent Yugoslavia's disintegration because he accurately perceived that it could presage the USSR's own dismantling. But he certainly was not prepared to take drastic actions in order to ensure Yugoslavia's survival, especially if such a policy caused tensions in Soviet-Western and especially Soviet-American relations.

The importance of the Western factor in the context of Russian foreign policy was enhanced under Boris Yeltsin, as the Euro-Atlanticist vision of Russia's foreign policy became ascendant within the Russian foreign policy elite. If Gorbachev wanted to ease tensions with the West, the Euro-Atlanticists wanted to integrate Russia into the Atlantic community. Any display of too strong a sense of Orthodox-Slavic identity and solidarity and the adoption of excessively pro-Serb policies which went against Western positions would have jeopardized the Euro-Atlanticists' objective of integrating Russia into the Atlantic community.

However, even Russia's Euro-Atlanticists could not ignore the importance of religious, ethnic, cultural, and identity-related factors. They had to account for these factors, if not in formulating the essentials of their policy, at least in their less-significant dimensions. Because the Russian public felt a sense of kinship toward the Serbs, both under Gorbachev and later under Yeltsin, Russia expressed sympathy for the Serbs and extended some support. However, expressions of sympathy and support remained tepid, especially under Gorbachev.

During Yeltsin's presidency, several factors contributed to more pronounced Russian support for the Serbs, although even then this support remained mostly rhetorical. The first factor was the reassertion of a more national rather than union-based Russian identity. In this identity, both Orthodoxy and Slavism are more pronounced. This shift contributed to the strengthening of the Russians' sense of solidarity with the Serbs. The second factor was that the Bosnian War enhanced the perception of threats to the Serbs and even to the entire global Orthodox community, thereby increasing pro-Serb feelings in Russia. Moreover, because historically Russia has had a perception of itself as the protector of the Orthodox community, many Russians felt that they had a duty to support the Serbs. Russia's view of itself as the leader of the Slavic people further contributed to its desire at least to appear active in helping the Serbs.

By 1993, a large fraction of Russians had become disillusioned by their country's pro-West policies, including its following the West's lead on the Bosnian War. This shift in the public's view was translated into electoral changes. The outcome was a more pro-Serb policy, although Russian support for the Serbs continued to remain largely at the rhetorical and diplomatic levels. Despite their sympathy for the Serbs, the Russians were not willing to sacrifice their country's own security and other interests for the sake of religious and ethnic solidarity. This reluctance could be partly explained by the fact that the Serbs, being Southern Slavs, were not viewed as being as close to the Russians as the East Slavs, such as the Russian-speaking Orthodox Ukrainians and the Belarusians. However, even if they were, it is unlikely that Russia would have sacrificed its state interests for the sake of ethnic and religious solidarity.

Geographical factors also influenced Russia's approach. For example, because of Yugoslavia's geographic distance from Russia, neither the Yugoslav crisis nor the Bosnian War posed a direct security threat to Russia. These realities enabled Russia not to become too deeply involved in the crisis and essentially to follow the international consensus. If Yugoslavia had had common borders with Russia, Russian attitudes toward its crisis and the war in Bosnia would have been different. For example, it is unlikely that Russia would have acquiesced in NATO's bombings of the Serbs out of fear that they might extend to Russia proper. In that case, Russia would have tried to prevent a UN resolution authorizing such strikes by using its veto power in the Security Council. Similarly, had there been an ethnic Russian population in Yugoslavia, Russia's approach would in all likelihood have been different. However, Russia's cautious posture on Yugoslavia and the Bosnian War reflected its limited ability to act because of its economic and other problems and needs and thus the restricted range of its options. As a result, the cost of an aggressively pro-Serb policy for Russia would have been prohibitive.

In the final analysis, both the Russian public's attitudes and the Russian government's policies toward the Yugoslav crisis and the Bosnian War were determined by Russia's own national and state interests. Neither the Russian public nor the Russian government were willing to pursue policies which could endanger Russia's interests or damage its security and economy.

Religion did influence Russian attitudes toward the Yugoslav crisis and especially the war in Bosnia. It did so by being a key component of Russia's national identity and of its self-view. Without the bonds of Orthodoxy, the Russians would not have been as concerned with the Serbs' fate as they were. Because of religious, ethnic, cultural, and identity-related factors, Russia tried to help the Serbs within the limits imposed by its conditions and its own interests. However, rather than religion, the requirements of Russian security, economic, and political interests, plus its desire to safeguard its national pride, decided the nature of its policies.

Still, ethnic and religious factors became significant tools both in the context of Russia's domestic politics and in its bargaining with the West. Opponents of reform during the Soviet era, along with the opponents of Yeltsin's pro-Western vision of Russia's future, effectively used these factors to challenge policies they opposed mostly for other reasons and to weaken their rivals.

At certain junctures, by exaggerating pro-Serb feelings at home, Russian officials tried to get the West to adopt a less anti-Serb posture or to pay more attention to Russian pride. For example, Kozyrev argued that taking sides in the Bosnian conflict should be avoided and that the West should not side with the Muslims. He justified his position by saying that the "Russian public believes that we [the Russians] should be protectors of the Serbs."[121] As the Russians became disappointed with the West and felt that their pride had been hurt, increasingly religious and ethnic factors were used to explain its shifting attitude toward the Bosnian War. This theory is supported by Wolf Oschlies, who argued, "The idea of Slavic, Orthodox integration, which had been considered merely as a historical joke, has suddenly become an instrument of policy."[122]

In sum, the analysis of Russia's policy toward the Yugoslav crisis and the Bosnian War indicates the predominant role of national and state interests over religious and identity-related factors in determining states' external behavior. The latter factors are used more as instruments in internal political debates, in struggles for power, and as tools of states' diplomacy. Nevertheless, in cases where external events do not pose a direct threat to national or state interests, religious and identity-related factors are often behind states' interests in such developments. The case of Russia and the Yugoslav crisis and the Bosnian War is a good example. In the absence of ethnic, religious, historical, and identity-related factors, neither the Russian public nor the Russian government would have been as interested in the Bosnian War as they were.

NOTES

1. For details see Appendix.
2. Some authors have also contributed the emergence of the New Thinking to the greater acquaintance of the new generation of Soviet foreign policy experts with Western thinking. Alexander Dallin, "New Thing on Foreign Policy," in ed. Archie Brown, *New Thinking in Soviet Politics* (New York: St. Martin's Press, 1992), 72. Others also noted the learning process that the Soviet leaders underwent, particularly during the Soviet-Afghan War. Sarah E. Mendelson, *Changing Course: Ideas, Politics and the Soviet Withdrawal from Afghanistan* (Princeton, NJ: Princeton University Press, 1998), 23–25.
3. Robert Donaldson and Joseph Nogee, *The Foreign Policy of Russia: Changing Systems, Enduring Interests* (Armonk and NY: M. E. Sharpe, 1998), 94.

4. Mike Bowker, "The Wars in Yugoslavia: Russia and the International Community," *Europe-Asia Studies*, 50. 7. 1988, 1247.

5. On Gorbachev's views on nationalism, see Mikhail Gorbachev, *Perestroika: New Thinking for Our Country and the World* (London: Fontana, 1988), 137–38.

6. Lenard J. Cohen, "Russia and the Balkans: Pan-Slavism, Partnership and Power," *International Journal*, 49. 4. (Autumn 1994), 817.

7. Michael Parks, "Gorbachev Sees Major Peril in Yugoslav Crisis," *Los Angeles Times*, 10 July 1991.

8. Parks, "Gorbachev Sees Major Peril."

9. Cohen, "Russia and the Balkans: Pan-Slavism, Partnership and Power," 820.

10. See Foreign Broadcasting Information Service (*FBIS*) *Sov*, 88-052, 17 March 1988, 21.

11. Sergei Romanenko, "What Is in a Name: Independent Russia and the Disintegration of Yugoslavia," *Institute of Economic, Russian Academy of Sciences, International Economics and Political Branch*, 2005.

12. As reported in *Politika: The International Weekly* (published in Belgrade), No. 80, 28 September–4 October 1991, 7.

13. For more details, see James Richter, "Russian Foreign Policy and the Politics of National Identity," in ed. Celeste Wallander, *The Sources of Russian Foreign Policy after the Cold War* (Boulder, CO: Westview Press, 1996).

14. The commission failed to come up with a concrete concept and instead it stressed the necessity of finding a new unifying idea. See Bronwyn McLaren, "Big Brains Bog Down in Hunt for the Russian Idea," *St. Petersburg Times*, 18–24 August 1997.

15. Anthony D. Smith, *Ethnic Origins of States* (Oxford: Basil Blackwell, 1986).

16. See for example, Iver Neumann, "Russia as Central Europe's Constituting Other" *East European Politics and Society*, 7. 2, 1993.

17. Anthony D. Smith, *National Identity* (Reno: University of Nevada Press, 1991).

18. For example, Turkish national identity underwent a dramatic change under Atatürk, and that of Iran after the Islamic Revolution of 1979.

19. On the question of religion as the foundation of national identity, see Anthony D. Smith, *The Cultural Foundations of Nations* (Oxford: Blackwell, 2008).

20. For a detailed analysis of these issues, see Nicholas V. Riasanovsky, *Russian Identities: A Historical Survey* (Oxford: Oxford University Press, 2005). However, all identities emerge through a process of change. Current European identities have also gone through various stages. Also see Vera Tolz, "Forging the Nation: National Identity and Nation Building in Post-Communist Russia," *Europe-Asia Studies*, 50. 6. 1998.

21. David G. Rowley, "Imperial versus National Discourse in the Case of Russia," *Nations and Nationalism*, 6. 1. 2000, 23.

22. In the nineteenth century, V. O. Kliuchevskii believed in this theory. For his ideas, see R. F. Byrnes, *V. O. Kliuchevskii, Historian of Russia* (Bloomington: Indiana University Press, 1995).

23. For details see Tolz, "Forging the Nation: National Identity and Nation Building in Post-Communist Russia," 996–98.

24. Taras Kuzio, "Historiography and National Identity among the Eastern Slavs: toward a new Framework," *National Identities*, 3. 2. 2001, 115.

25. Rowley, "Imperial versus National Discourse in the Case of Russia," 23.

26. For more detailed study of these issues, see Shireen T. Hunter, *Islam in Russia: The Politics of Identity and Security* (Armonk, NY: M. E. Sharpe, 2004), 148–68.

27. Alicja Curanovic, *The Religious Factor in Russia's Foreign Policy* (London: Routledge, 2012), 15.

28. Based on author's talks with Aksiuchits in Moscow in 2000.

29. Curanovic, *The Religious Factor in Russia's Foreign Policy*, 15.

30. Alexander Bennigsen and Marie Broxup, *The Islamic Threat to the Soviet State* (NY: St. Martin's Press, 1983), 9.

31. For more detailed discussion of the concept of *symphony*, see Curanovic, *The Religious Factor in Russia's Foreign Policy*, 14.

32. However, Tatar rule also left its mark on the Russian state, although its traditions were later Christianized. Some Tatar scholars, notably Raphael Hakimov, have claimed that Tatar rule actually helped Russia to survive and not succumb to pressures from the West and enabled the Russians to unite. Raphael Hakimov, "Russia and Tatarstan at a Crossroads of History," *Anthropology and Archeology of Eurasia*, 37. 1 (Summer 1998).

33. Bennigsen and Broxup, *The Islamic Threat to the Soviet State*, 9.

34. Based on author's conversations.

35. *Pravda*, 9 September, 1992.

36. Pyotr Yakovlevich Chaadaev, "Letters on the Philosophy of History: Letter 1," in eds. & trans., W. J. Leatherborrow & D. S. Offord, A *Documentary History of Russian Thought* (Ann Arbor, MI: Ardis Publishers, 1987), 73.

37. Andrzej Walicki, *The Slavophile Controversy*. Trans, Hilda Andrews Rusiecka (Oxford: Clarendon Press, 1975), 32–44.

38. Nicolas Berdyaev, *The Origins of Russian Communism* (London: Geoffrey Bless, 1995), 12–13.

39. Berdyaev, *Origins of Russian Communism*.

40. Quoted in *The Slavophile Controversy*, 32–44.

41. Stephen Lukashevich, *Ivan Aksakov, 1832–1886: A Study in Russian Thought and Politics* (Cambridge, MA: Harvard University Press, 1965), 3–5.

42. Quoted in John Dunlop, *The Rise of Russia and the Fall of the Soviet Empire* (Princeton, NJ: Princeton University Press, 1993), 55.

43. Dunlop, *Rise of Russia*, 3.

44. On the question of Russia's search for identity over the centuries and in the post-Soviet era, see Timothy McDaniel, *The Agony of the Russian Idea* (Princeton, NJ: Princeton University Press, 1996).

45. Tolz, "Forging the Nation: National Identity and Nation Building in Post-Communist Russia," 995–96.

46. See his articles in *Pravda*, 1 & 2 November 1994, and in *Novyi Mir* (The New World), 1994.

47. Dina Moulikova, "Dialectic Relation between Foreign Policy and Russian National Identity," University of Miami, *European Union-Miami Analysis (EUMA) Special Series*, 11 June 2011, 6.

48. Tolz, "Forging the Nation: National Identity and Nation Building in Post-Communist Russia," 996.

49. S. V. Rijova, "Formation of the Russian Orthodox Identity: Traditional, Cultural and Civil Dimensions," *Sociologiskei Issledovoniya*, No. 12, 2010, available at: http://www.ecsoman.hse.ru/data/2011/03/11/1214896884/Ryzhova_6.pdf.

50. Rijova, "Formation of the Russian Orthodox Identity."

51. The advocates of this view were known as Christian Democrats. For details see Shireen T. Hunter, *Islam in Russia: The Politics of Identity and Security* (Armonk, NY: M. E. Sharpe, 2004), 178–80.

52. O. E. Kazmina, "Russian Orthodox Church and the Problems of Identity, Religious Legislation, and Human Rights in Modern Russia," *Ethnographia Religii*, 1, 2009, at: http://joutnal.iea.ras.ru/archive/2000s/2009/kaz'mina_2009_1.pdf.%20.

53. S. V. Kortunov, *National Identity: Understanding the Meaning* (Moscow: Aspect Press, 2009), available at: http://www.ino-center.ru/doc/national-identity.pdf.

54. Kortunov, *National Identity*.

55. See Kimmo Kaariainen and Dmitri Furman, "Orthodoxy as a Component of Russian Identity," *East-West Church & Ministry Report*, 10 (Winter 2002), 12–13.

56. On Church-State relations in post-Soviet Russia, see, among others: Nicholas K. Gvosdev, "The New Emperors? Post-Soviet Presidents and Church-State Relations in Ukraine and Russia," *Sophia Institute, Columbia University, Studies on Orthodox Theology*, 2010, at http://www.academiacommons.columbia.edu/catalog/ac/%3A156386.

57. See Blair Ruble, "The Orthodox Church and Russian Politics," Kennan Institute, Woodrow Wilson Center for International Scholars, 2011, at: http://www.wilsoncenter.org/publications/the-orthodox-church-and-russian-politics.

58. For how the State uses the Church to advance its foreign policy objective, see: Curanovic, *The Religious Factor in Russia's Foreign Policy*.
59. Nina L. Khrushcheva, "Lost in Byzantium," *Los Angeles Times*, 1 June 2008, at: http://www.articles.latimes.com/2008/jun1/01/opinion/op-khrushcheva.
60. For details see Tolz, "Forging the Nation: National Identity and Nation Building in Post-Communist Russia," 1003.
61. Tolz, "Forging the Nation: National Identity and Nation Building in Post-Communist Russia," 1003.
62. E. M. Pain, "Dynamics of Russian National Identity," *Ethnopanorama*, 1. 2002, available at: http://demoscope.ru/weekly/2002/085/analit01.php.
63. See Astrid Tuminez, "Russia in Research of Itself: Nationalism and the Future of the Russian State" *PONARS* Memo, 20. October 1997, at: http://www.gwu.edu/~ieresgwu/assets/docs/ponars/pm_0020pdf.
64. See Nuray Aridici, "How Vladimir Putin Has Changed the Meaning of 'Russian,'" *The Conversation*, 9 April 2014, at: http://theconversation.com/how-vladimir-putin-has-changed-the-meaning-of-russian-24928.
65. See Igor Zevelev, "The Russian World Boundaries," *Russia in Global Affairs*, 7 June 2014, at: http://www.eng.globalaffairs.ru/print/number/The-Russian-World-Boundaries-16707.
66. Some scholars have pointed out one of the problems Russia has faced in defining its post-Soviet national identity is that it has never existed as a nation-state.
67. Vladislav Surkov, "Russian Political Culture: A View from Utopia," in Konstantin Remchukov (ed.), *Russian Political Culture: A View from Utopia*, Moscow: Nezavisimaia Gazeta, 2007
68. Surkov, "Russian Political Culture."
69. David Mackenzie, *Serbs and Russians* (New York: Columbia University Press, 1996), 3.
70. Quoted in Curanovic, *The Religious Factor in Russia's Foreign Policy*, 151.
71. Curanovic, *The Religious Factor in Russia's Foreign Policy*.
72. See Mackenzie, *Serbs and Russians*, 3–19. On Serbs views of Russia see Chloe Kay, "Contemporary Russian-Serbian Relations: Interviews with Youth from Political Parties in Belgrade and Vojvodina" Spring 2014, available at: http://www.sras.org/russia_serbia_relations_youth.
73. Quoted in Suzanne Crow, "Competing Blueprints for Russian Foreign Policy," *RFE/RL Research Report*, 1.50., 18 December 1992, 45.
74. Crow, "Competing Blueprints," 45.
75. See Kozyrev's interview with *Le Monde*, *Le Monde*, 8 June 1992.
76. Yevgeniy Gurasow, "toward a Europe of Democracy and Unity," *Rossiskaya Gazeta*, 5 March 1992.
77. For the text of the Charter see *FBIS Daily Report*, FBIS-SOV-92-118, 18 June 1992.
78. Some also refer to them as Civilizationalist. See Zevelev, "The Russian World Boundaries."
79. For more detailed discussion, see Hunter, *Islam in Russia: The Politics of Identity and Security*, 289–310.
80. Andranik Migranyan, "Russia and the Near Abroad" [in Russian], *Nezavisimaya Gazeta*, 12 January 1994, reproduced in English in the *Current Digest of Post-Soviet Affairs*, 46. 6, 9 March 1994.
81. Migranyan, "Russia and the Near Abroad" 46.
82. Sergei Stankevich, "Russia in Search of Itself," *National Interest* (Summer 1992), 47.
83. Suzanne Crow, "Ambartsumov's Influence on Russian Foreign Policy," *RFE/RL Research Report*, 2.19., 7 May 1993, 32–90.
84. Alexei Malashenko, "Rossiia I Islam (Russia and Islam)," *Nezavisimaya Gazeta*, 22 February 1992.
85. For a discussion of these issues, see Wayne Allensworth, *The Russian Question: Nationalism, Modernization, and Post-Soviet Russia* (Lanham, MD: Rowman & Littlefield, 1998).
86. See Allensworth, *The Russian Question*.

87. Paul Goble, "Dangerous Liaisons: Moscow, The Former Yugoslavia and the West," in ed. Richard H. Ullman, *The World and Yugoslavia's Wars*, New York: Council on Foreign Relations, 1996, 187.
88. Eric Shiraev and Deone Terrio, "Russian Decision-making Regarding Bosnia: Indifferent Public and Feuding Elites" in eds. Richard Sobel & Eric Shiraev, *International Public Opinion and the Bosnian Crisis* (Lanham, MD: Lexington Books, 2006), 137.
89. Churkin also represented Russia at NATO.
90. Quoted in Shiraev and Terrio, "Russian Decision-making Regarding Bosnia," 135.
91. Cohen, "Russia and the Balkans: Pan-Slavism, Partnership and Power," 822.
92. Bowker, "The Wars in Yugoslavia," 1248.
93. Bowker, "The Wars in Yugoslavia," 1248.
94. Shiraev and Terrio, "Russian Decision-Making in Bosnia," 3.
95. Suzanne Crow, "Reading Moscow's Policies toward the Rump Yugoslavia," *RFE/RL Research Report*, 6, November 1992, 13–19.
96. Romanenko, "What Is in a Name: Independent Russia and the Disintegration of Yugoslavia."
97. On Ambartsumov's influence on Russian foreign policy, see Suzanne Crow, "Ambartsumov's Influence on Russian Foreign Policy," *Radio Free Europe-Radio Liberty, RFE/RL, Research Report*, 22, 1993.
98. See "Chronicle of the Meeting of the State Duma," 9 September 1995, at: http://www.api.duma.gov.ru/api/transcriptFull/1995-09-09.
99. "Chronicle of the Meeting."
100. Allen C. Lynch, "The Realism of Russian Foreign Policy," *Europe-Asia Studies*, 53.1., 2001, 16.
101. Lynch, "Realism of Russian Foreign Policy," 16.
102. W. Abarinov, "Rosja na Balkanach, Wyscig Meditiarow," *Eurazja* 5. 6. 1994, 49.
103. Quoted in Shiraev and Terrio, "Russian Decision Making Regarding Bosnia," 153.
104. Abarinov, "Rosja na Balkanach Wyscig Meditiarow," 49.
105. Shiraev and Terrio, "Russian Decision Making Regarding Bosnia," 137–38.
106. Konstantin Eggert, "Yugoslav Watershed between Russia and the West," *Izvestia*, 3 August 1994.
107. Eggert, "Yugoslav Watershed."
108. Shiraev and Terrio, "Russian Decision Making Regarding Bosnia," 9–10.
109. *The Daily Telegraph*, 18 February 1994.
110. Stanislav Varikhanov, "The Fate of Russian Volunteers in Bosnia," *Pravda.ru*, 13 October 2003.
111. Varikhanov, "The Fate of Russian Volunteers in Bosnia," 13.
112. Carol J. Williams, "Cold Cash Fuels Russian Fighting Spirit in Bosnia," *Los Angeles Times*, 12 April 1993, at: http://www.articles.latimes.com/print/1993-04-12-news/mn-22063_1_russian.
113. Williams, "Cold Cash Fuels Russian Fighting."
114. Oleg Valetsky, "About the Wars in the Balkans, Their Causes and Russian Volunteers," *Sozidatel*.
115. Andrew Evans, "Forced Miracles: The Russian Orthodox Church and Post-Soviet International Relations," *Religion, State & Society*, 30. 1. 2002, 35.
116. Evans, "Forced Miracles," 35.
117. Published in *Kommersant Daily*, 10 August 1995, at: http://www.kommersant.ru/doc/114817?isSearch=True.
118. J. Sherr & J. S. Main, "Russian & Ukrainian Perceptions of Events in Yugoslavia, *Conflict Studies Research Center*, May 1994.
119. Evans, "Forced Miracles," 33–34.
120. Of course, the Bosnian War began after the dissolution of the Soviet Union, but the USSR did witness the initial stages of the Yugoslav crisis.
121. Quoted in Lynch, "The Realism of Russian Foreign Policy," 16.
122. Wolf Oschlies, "*Russische Balkanpolitik: Mythos in Realpolitischer Bewahrung*, Vol. 1, *Panslavische Illusionen Und Balkan Realitaten*, Köln: Bohlau, 2000, 12.

Chapter Four

Turkey's Policy toward the Bosnian War

The Yugoslav crisis and the Bosnian War occurred at a time when Turkey was engaged in two interrelated debates. The first was about the character and foundations of the country's national identity. The second concerned the direction of Turkey's foreign policy in changed international conditions. In the course of both these debates the continued relevance of Kemalist orthodoxy, which had guided the Turkish Republic since its establishment in 1923, was questioned.

This debate was triggered by a series of dramatic regional and international developments and by the social and political shifts which had taken place in Turkey during the 1980s. The most consequential of regional and international developments in terms of their impact on Turkey were the Persian Gulf War of March 1991 and the subsequent collapse of the Soviet Union that December. Among the internal developments, the erosion of the social and political hegemony of the Kemalist ethos, the reassertion of pre-republican traditions and values, the rise of Islam's social and political profile, and the emergence of a new generation of political and economic elites influenced by Islam were largely responsible for generating these twin debates.

The emerging new elites that were strongly influenced by Islam did not subscribe to all or even most of the Kemalist ethos. They challenged the republican understanding of Turkey's national identity and its foundations, in particular its playing down of the Islamic component. Largely because of their Islamic inclinations, they hold different views about the appropriate direction Turkey's foreign policy should take in the post-Soviet world, as well as Turkey's place and role within the post-Soviet international system.

A major question was whether Turkey should continue its West-centered foreign policy or pursue new opportunities in the Muslim world and in the post-Soviet newly independent Turkic republics of Central Asia and the Caucasus. Differences of opinion partly reflected the country's emerging Secular-Islamic divide. Turkey's secular elite continued to support an essentially Western-oriented foreign policy, while the emerging Islamic elites preferred a Turkish foreign policy directed more toward the Islamic and Turkic worlds.[1]

By the 1980s, the emerging Islamic elite had become more influential in Turkish politics and governments. For example, Turgut Özal, Turkey's prime minister from 1983 to 1989 and its president from 1989 to 1993, sympathized with this new elite and shared some of their views. Like the new Islamic elite, he believed that many Kemalist-era restrictions on social manifestations of Islam should be eliminated. By this time, Turkey's Islamist party, *Refah* (Welfare) had also become more influential. Therefore, although Turkey's secular elite was still in power at the start of the Bosnian War, they had to be mindful of competition from the emerging Islamic elite. This relative shift in the balance of power between the old Kemalist elite and the new Islamic elite meant that the Turkish government in devising policy toward the Bosnian War had to be mindful of its potential impact on Turkey's domestic politics. This caution was necessitated because of the Islamist party's and the new Islamic elite's tendency to manipulate the Bosnia conflict's religious aspects to advance their own political interests and agenda. In short, as was the case with Russia, the Bosnian War became entangled with Turkish debates on identity and foreign policy. Thus various political parties' positions on how to handle the crisis and the appropriate Turkish policy toward the war in part reflected their views regarding ongoing Turkish debates on identity and foreign policy. In general, the Islamic elite and political parties identified more with Bosnian Muslims and advocated active Turkish support.

Nevertheless, more Islamically oriented Turks were not the only supporters of Bosnian Muslims. On the contrary, most Turks, both secular and Islamic, plus even the Turkish government identified with Bosnia's Muslims and their trials and tribulations. Principally, the Turks felt a sense of kinship (*Qarabat*), the result of the long history of Ottoman rule over the Balkans. This rule had created extensive religious and cultural ties between the Turks and some Balkan peoples, including Bosnians, as some of the Balkan peoples had become Islamicized and culturally Turkified under the Ottomans. Additionally, after the collapse of the Ottoman Empire, large numbers of Balkan Muslims, including Bosnians, had migrated to Turkey, further strengthening the Turks' sense of kinship with Bosnian Muslims. This sense of a cultural-religious kinship with the Bosnian Muslims affected the Turks' perceptions of the causes of the Bosnian War and the relative guilt of parties involved for its instigation and prolongation. As with Orthodox Russians, who attributed responsibility for the war to Muslims and Catholics, Muslim Turks saw Orthodox Serbs as the main culprits.[2] The Turkish public's sense of kinship for Bosnian Muslims made it imperative that the Turkish government at least appear to be doing all it could for them.

The foundation of this sense of kinship was the Turks' and most Bosnians' common adherence to Islam, although other cultural ties contributed to it. However, Islam's role was central because it was the Islamization of segments of Yugoslavia's population under Ottoman rule that had facilitated the spread of other forms of Turkish culture. Because of its role in generating this sense of kinship between the Turks and the Bosnian Muslims, as a factor in Turkish domestic politics and as a component of Turkey's national identity, religion influenced the formation of Turkish policies toward the war. More than any event before that time, the Bosnian crisis highlighted Islam's growing influence in Turkish society and politics. It also showed the potential impact that religion and identity-related factors could have on the process of foreign policymaking. However, ultimately more tangible interests and concerns determined Turkey's Bosnia policies. These concerns related to Turkey's own security, the potential impact of policies regarding Bosnia on Turkey's ties with its traditional allies, their impact on Turkey's economic and political interests, and their impact on its regional and international prestige and aspirations. In addition, Turkey's geography and resource base influenced its policy toward the war. The policy that emerged was the result of the Turkish governments' efforts to reconcile the competing demands of security and other interest-related factors with those of religious, cultural, and identity-related pressures.

TURKISH NATIONAL IDENTITY: FOUNDATIONS AND EVOLUTION

As noted in chapter 3, the concept of national identity is fairly nebulous, partly because the concept of nation itself is hard to define. Furthermore, because for most of its history Turkey was the center of the Ottoman Empire, the idea of a Turkish nation is of recent origin. During the Ottoman era, Turkey's collective identity was based first on Islam and second on a sense of belonging to an empire.[3] Ethnicity and a pronounced sense of Turkicness had a far less important impact in shaping Turkey's Ottoman-era identity. According to David Kushner, the Ottomans had buried their Turkic ethnic roots in Islam[4]: "An Ottoman gentleman well into the nineteenth century would therefore identify himself as a Muslim and an Ottoman, never as a Turk."[5] The term "Turk" was "used to differentiate between Turks and non-Turks or as a derogatory reference to the ignorant peasant or nomad of

Anatolia."[6] In short, pre-republican-era Turkish identity was religious and imperial and not national.

By the mid- to late nineteenth century, this situation began to change, as the Ottoman Turks became more conscious of the Turks' central role in the foundation of the empire and of their status as its most loyal subjects. They also grew more interested in their Central Asian origins. These developments resulted in the emergence of a new concept and spirit known as Turkism (*Turkçuluk*), thus presaging the beginnings of a more ethno-centric sense of Turkish identity and the burgeoning of Turkish nationalism. Several factors contributed to this development:

1. The rise of ethno-centric nationalism in Europe and among the non-European peoples, some of whom, such as the Arabs, were under Ottoman rule. The rise of such sentiments among other peoples influenced the Turks and made them more conscious of their own ethnic and linguistic characteristics and enhanced their sense of separateness from other peoples, including fellow Muslims such as the Arabs.
2. The loss of most of the empire's European possessions. These losses were triggered by the growth of independence-seeking movements in the Balkans beginning in the early nineteenth century and the ensuing wars between the Ottomans and their Balkan subjects. These wars often involved Russia, which supported the Slavs of the Balkans in their struggle with the Ottomans. Some West European powers also supported Balkan independence movements, such as that of Greece.
3. The erosion of the empire's influence in its Muslim-inhabited possessions in the Middle East and North Africa, consequent to European expansion. This development strengthened the belief that only ethnic Turks were truly loyal subjects of the empire, which helped to strengthen an ethno-centric sense of Turkish identity.
4. Growing contacts between the Ottomans and the Central Asian Turks and the Ural Turks, such as the Tatars. These contacts acquainted the Ottomans with the literary and other achievements of the Tatars and Central Asian Turks. The Ottomans realized that there was a vast and relatively sophisticated Turkic world, and that not all Turks were peasants and nomads.[7]

By the beginning of the twentieth century, and although Islam and a sense of being part of a larger empire remained as the main foundations of Ottoman identity, a Turkic ethnic element was added to it, as reflected in a commentary published in the daily *Ikdam*: "We [the Ottomans] by our social order are Ottoman, by our religion Muslims, and by our ethnic nationality (*Kawmiyet*) we are Turk."[8] In short, by the dawn of the new century, Ottoman-era Turkish identity was not just religious and imperial but also ethno-nationalist.

Some authors, however, believe that even this sense of a burgeoning Turkish nationalism had an Islamic flavor. They suggest that Ottoman-era nationalism was in effect an "Islamic nationalism."[9] Be that as it may, by this time religious and imperial belonging were no longer the only foundations of Turkish-Ottoman identity.

Religion, Ethnicity, Political Legitimacy, and Foreign Policy

Like in most late medieval and early modern societies, religion formed the principal foundation of political legitimacy and law in the Ottoman Empire. Although the Ottoman rulers were not related to the family of the prophet of Islam and were not even Arab, they considered themselves as the successors to the earlier Islamic Caliphates, notably that of the Abbasids.[10] This claim was also the primary source of their political legitimacy. Had the Ottoman sultans acted as mere Turkic rulers rather than Muslim Caliphs, their rule over non-Turkic peoples would have been more precarious. Thus the Ottoman sultans were keen to demonstrate their Islamic credentials and to use the language of Islam to legitimate their policies and activities.[11]

Ottoman foreign policy, meanwhile, was imperial, statist, and, when required by circumstances, pragmatic. Religion colored the Ottomans' worldviews and their conceptions of their interests. But religion was rarely the determining impulse behind their behavior, except when religious differences became entangled with imperial power struggles, as was the case with Ottoman-Safavid and Russo-Ottoman relations.[12]

By the late nineteenth century, the dwindling of the empire's European domains and the rise of a new Turko-Islamic identity had led to the articulation of new foreign policy concepts, such as Pan-Islamism[13] and Pan-Turkism.[14] In order to retain their remaining influence and, if possible, expand it, the Ottomans increasingly resorted to the conscious use of Islam and Turkism as instruments of foreign policy. Islam and Turkism were put at the service of the Ottoman state rather than being the motivator of their policies.

END OF EMPIRE, ESTABLISHMENT OF THE TURKISH REPUBLIC, AND ISLAM'S ECLIPSE

After the establishment of the Turkish Republic in 1923, the formulation of a new and essentially ethno-centric notion of Turkey's national identity and a new conception of Turkey's foreign policy undermined Islam's role as a component of Turkish national identity and as a guiding principle and instrument of its foreign policy.

The vision of Turkey held by the founder of the Turkish Republic, Mustafa Kemal, known as *Atatürk* (Father of the Turks), was fundamentally different from that which had existed during the Ottoman era. In Atatürk's vision for a post-Ottoman Turkey, Islam did not figure prominently. He wanted to modernize and Europeanize Turkey. He believed that to accomplish these tasks, Turkey's legal and political foundations should be secularized and Islam-based Ottoman cultural vestiges should be eliminated. It appears that Atatürk, like a number of other intellectuals and reformers in other Muslim-inhabited lands at the time, saw Islam as a reactionary force and a significant barrier to modernization and Europeanization. According to some scholars, Mustafa Kemal had said that he wished that Turkey was a Christian country.[15] Other scholars and observers, however, maintain that Atatürk was not against religion or Islam per se. What he wanted was an enlightened Islam that he could harness at the service of his secularizing and modernizing project. Some scholars claim that the republican elite, in fact, used Islam to this end. According to Hakan Yavuz, the "Kemalist elite opportunistically employed Islam for the realization of a modern and secular Turkey."[16]

Nevertheless, because of his view of Islam as an essentially reactionary force, Atatürk systematically reduced its role in Turkey's social, cultural, and political life. He brought religious institutions more firmly under state control, abolished the Caliphate in 1924, closed the Sharia courts, banned the wearing of the *Fez* for men, banned the veil for women, and expanded secular judicial and educational systems. He also changed Turkish script from Arabic to Latin and developed a new Turkish vernacular by eliminating Persian and Arabic words and replacing them with either authentic Turkic or Western words. These measures to a great extent delinked future Turkish generations from their Ottoman past and were part of Atatürk's cultural de-Ottomanization and de-Islamization of Turkey.

Atatürk also forged a new republican national identity for Turkey. It was based on ethnic and linguistic Turkishness, stressed the country's Turkic roots, glorified the Turks' virtues, and pursued an assimilationist policy toward the republic's ethnic and linguistic minorities, largely by means of a widespread and aggressive policy of their linguistic Turkification. Andrew Mango, a Turkey specialist, has noted that Atatürk's dictum "Citizen Speak Turkish" had a distinctly "coercive ring."[17] The result of Atatürk's policies was a significant but short-lived erosion of Islam's social and political role in Turkey and its eclipse as a major basis of the country's national identity.

LIMITS TO ATATÜRK'S PROJECT, ISLAM'S RESILIENCE, AND ITS REAPPEARANCE IN IDENTITY DEBATES

Atatürk's policies aimed at undermining Islam's influence in Turkish identity, society, and politics only succeeded partially and only after significant protest and resistance by significant numbers of Turkey's population, especially its Kurdish inhabitants.[18] As a result of his policies, a significant number of Turks became secular, although often without abandoning their Islamic beliefs. Others merely went underground, waiting for opportunities to reappear. The countryside, in general, the Anatolian heartland, and small cities were barely touched by Atatürk's secularizing policies and remained solidly Islamic.

Meanwhile, new Islamic movements emerged. Some of them, such as that of Bediuzzaman Said Nursî, concentrated on inner purification and adopted a kind of passive resistance to the state's secularizing policies.[19] However, years after Atatürk's passing these movements, mostly inspired by Nursî's teachings, became politicized and were transformed into new politically motivated Islamic movements. Currently in Turkey, the most prominent is that of Fethullah Gülen, espousing a more modernist version of Nursî's teachings.[20]

In short, Islam proved far more resilient and with greater staying power than Turkey's secularizing leaders had initially expected, and it retained a strong hold over a large segment of the Turkish population. Islam's resilience and strength meant that the new ethno-centric and secular identity forged by the state was not embraced by all or even a majority of Turks. One reason for this failure was that, in addition to ignoring Islam's significance in most Turks' individual and collective identities, the people's contribution to the formulation of Turkey's republican identity was insignificant. According to some Turkish scholars, the new Turkish identity was developed by the modernizing elites without any input from the people. Caglar Keder maintains that the people "remained silent partners. . . . The masses in Turkey generally remained passive recipients of the nationalist message pounded by the elites."[21] Hakan Yavuz points out that "The determination of the national identity, in particular after 1925, was made strictly at the level of the statist Republican elite and pointedly excluded the mass of society."[22]

Consequently, soon after Atatürk's death many of his most stringent anti-Islam policies were canceled or ignored. The mosques were reopened, the Sufi brotherhoods were once more allowed to operate, religious schools were reestablished, and the call to prayers was again said in Arabic. Overall, a more flexible approach toward the expression of religious feelings in public was adopted. However, there was no rollback of secularizing decisions regarding the judiciary or the educational system. The principle of the strict separation of religion and politics was also upheld.

Over time, however, the Kemalist elite could not ignore Islam's deep roots in society and hence its potential usefulness as an instrument of state policy. Thus according to Tamer Balci, the state used Islam as a tool "to promote Turkish culture and interests."[23] In this way, Islam was to some degree nationalized and nationalism was Islamicized, and those of its aspects which served the interests of the Republic were incorporated in its nationalist ideology.

The continued importance of Islam as a key part of being a Turk in the republican era is reflected in the fact that, during the early life of the republic, being Muslim was often more important than Turkic ethnicity in qualifying non-Turks as Turk. For instance, ethnically Slavic Balkan Muslims were viewed as culturally Turk, whereas ethnically Turkic Christians were not.[24] This interaction between Islam and the state further contributed to Islam's retaining its role as an important identity-marker in Turkey and its place as part of its social, cultural, and political landscape. In the following decades, this role grew even more important.

TURKEY'S POLITICAL DEVELOPMENTS: IMPACT ON ISLAM'S POSITION

Turkey's internal political developments after World War II further contributed to Islam's revival and enhanced its place in Turkish national identity and in Turkey's social, cultural, and eventually political landscape.

Parliamentary Politics

An important aspect of Turkey's internal developments in the aftermath of World War II was its pursuit of parliamentary politics largely but not exclusively because of U.S. insistence. The United States encouraged Turkey on this path partly because of its own democratic ideals and its belief in their universal application. When Turkey joined the North Atlantic Treaty Organization (NATO) in 1952, its democratization became more imperative in order to bring its institutions and practices closer to those of its American and European allies. Paradoxically, the logic of parliamentary politics required that politicians pay more attention to religious segments of the population, address their religious concerns, and promise to meet their religious demands. Consequently, in response to their religious constituencies, many post-World War II Turkish governments diluted the most stringent of Kemalist principles and relaxed many of the Kemalist-era restrictions on religion. These measures further lifted Islam's profile in society and eventually enhanced its political role as well.

This Islamic rebirth in Turkey was reflected in the emergence of Islamically oriented political parties. The first was the National Order Party (*Milli Nizam Partisi*). It was founded in 1970 by Necmettin Erbakan, but shortly after its establishment it was banned by the government. In 1972, Erbakan reestablished the party under a new name, the National Salvation Party (*Milli Salamet Partisi*).[25] This party, too, was promptly banned. In 1983 it reappeared under the name of Welfare Party (*Refah Partisi*). Eventually Refah was also banned and splintered after the 1997 military coup d'état known as coup by ultimatum. The coup forced Erbakan, who had become Turkey's prime minister in coalition with the True Path Party (*Dogru Yol Partisi*), to resign. The present Justice and Development Party (AKP) has its roots in this party and its later incarnations.[26]

Anti-Leftist Struggle

Another contributing factor to the rise in Islam's profile in Turkey was the country's struggle against leftist forces in the post–World War II era. By the 1960s, the Left's influence in Turkey had risen sharply and had thus prompted the Turkish government and military to engage in a search for ways to counteract leftist influence. Turkey's military and political elites considered the Left as the most serious threat to Turkish security, a view also shared by Turkey's Western partners. Consequently, they were willing to use all available means, including Islam, to combat the Left. The result was the further relaxation of restrictions on public manifestations of Islam, including in the political arena. Consequently, partly because of this government policy, by the mid-1970s the Islamists and their main political party had emerged as the principal counterweight to leftist forces. An early manifestation of the Islamist party's rising influence was the involvement in 1978 of the NSP and its leader, Necmettin Erbakan, in a coalition government formed by the extremely secular Republican Peoples Party (*Cumhuriat Halk Partisi*) and its leader, Bülent Ecevit.

The instrumental use of Islam and Islamist groups and political parties as counterweights to the Left intensified in the 1980s and further enhanced Islam's social and political profile and influence. According to the Turkish scholar, Fatih Yasli, after the 1980 military coup d'état, the Turkish government set about "to mercilessly crushing the left" while "the doors of the state were flung open to religious fraternities—which from then on started to get entrenched in the state bureaucracy."[27]

Other Causes of Islam's Rise in the 1980s

The following developments also contributed to Islam's rise of influence in Turkish society and politics:

1. *The 1979 Islamic Revolution in Iran.* In order to prevent a repeat of the Iranian experience in Turkey, the Turkish government under Turgut Özal further eased restrictions on Islam and granted it a more prominent social and political presence. It also moved from simply tolerating Islamically oriented people and groups to actually promoting them.
2. *Özal's premiership.* Özal had a totally different interpretation of secularism than the Kemalist elite. He rejected the anti-religion secularism

which he claimed the Kemalists had borrowed from France and embraced a type of secularism more akin to that of the United States. This version of secularism is less strict than the French *laïcité* and allows a role for religion in the public sphere while upholding the principle of the separation of religion and politics. Özal also subscribed to a liberal interpretation of Islam, which he defined as Turkish Islam. He claimed that Turkish Islam, unlike the varieties practiced by the Arabs and the Iranians, was progressive, moderate, and tolerant. He thus concluded that a secularism which was not anti-religion and a liberal Islam were not only compatible but mutually reinforcing.[28]

3. *The emergence of new and Islamically oriented economic and political elites.*[29] They were the product of Turkey's remarkable economic development in the 1980s under Özal's leadership and his policy of encouraging private enterprise. Their emergence reflected the advancement of Turkey's modernization process and its extension to the Anatolian heartland beyond Istanbul and other European parts of the country. Their appearance was also partly due to the steady easing of restrictions on Islam in Turkey after World War II, notably the relaxation of rules regarding Islamic education. The easing of these restrictions led to an explosion in the number of religious schools called *Imam Hatip* that many of Turkey's new Muslim elites attended. These new elites were committed to secularism in the sense of the separation of religion and politics, or at least they were reconciled to it; but they opposed what they saw as the anti-religion dimensions of Kemalist style secularism. Some observers have claimed that the emerging Muslim economic elites, which became strong during the 1990s and were often referred to as Anatolian Tigers, benefited from active government support.[30]

Ultimately, however, the rise of Islam's profile in Turkey was due mainly to its deep roots in Turkish society and culture and the inadequacies of Turkism and Westernism as total replacements.

The rise in Islam's social and political profile enhanced its position as a key component of Turkey's national identity, but it also caused a more open divergence on this issue between the extreme secular Kemalists and various shades of Islamists.[31] Nevertheless, for a considerable number of Turks, today, including many Islamists, Islam and Turkish nationalism both form part of their identity.[32] Indeed, Islamists such as Erbakan, Gülen, and Erdoğan are also ardent Turkish nationalists. Moreover, many Turks see Islam and Turkish nationalism as mutually reinforcing, especially in terms of dealing with Turkey's competitors. Some believe that most Turks do not see any contradiction between their commitments to Islam and to Kemalism.

ATATÜRK'S VISION FOR TURKEY'S FOREIGN POLICY

Atatürk also had a new vision for Turkey's external relations and the direction of its foreign policy, which was largely determined by his domestic priorities, with his first priority the consolidation of the young republic. Turkey required a period of peace and stability in relations with its neighbors and with other countries. Atatürk's famous dictum "Peace at Home, Peace Abroad" was coined for this purpose. It was also to this end that he tried to regularize Turkey's relations with its immediate neighbors by demarcating their common borders and by resolving outstanding disputes. His second priority was to continue unimpeded his project of Turkey's modernization and Europeanization. "Consequently, in foreign as well as in domestic policy, Atatürk pursued an essentially Western-oriented approach and, except for Turkey's immediate neighbors, he did not want to become embroiled in the politics of Muslim, including Middle Eastern, countries."[33]

Nevertheless, the republic was not immune to the pull of Pan-Turkism, although the Turkish government did not pursue this strategy in any organized manner. Pan-Turkism remained mostly an aspiration rather than a concrete policy. One reason was that the new Bolshevik government in Russia incorporated the Tsars' imperial possessions, including the largely Turkic-inhabited parts of Central Asia and the Caucasus, in the new Union of the Soviet Socialist Republics, despite having promised them independence. Atatürk wanted to establish peace between the young Turkish Republic and the USSR. The pursuit of a Pan-Turkist policy would have jeopardized obtaining this goal.

For several reasons, in the context of Atatürk's vision for Turkish foreign policy, the Balkans remained of high importance for the young republic:

1. Atatürk was born in Thessalonica (Thessaloniki) and thus had a Balkan background;
2. Turkey shared common land and sea borders with such Balkan countries as Bulgaria and Greece, and therefore its security was impacted by developments in this region;
3. Turkey had historic ties with the Balkans; and
4. Atatürk wanted to orient Turkey toward Europe and make it a European power. As one gateway to Europe, the Balkan region was a natural area for Turkey's involvement.

Unlike many of his domestic policies, especially those related to Islam's role in Turkish society and national identity, Atatürk's basic vision for Turkey's foreign policy, especially its orientation toward the West, survived his passing. The rise of the USSR on Turkey's borders led Turkey to adopt a pro-West posture in the Cold War. This partnership was formalized in 1952 when

Turkey joined NATO, and it also joined other Western-led security alliances.[34] For fifty years, all other aspects of Turkey's foreign policy were influenced by the Cold War's overarching paradigm and by the imperatives of membership in the Western alliance. Because Balkan states, with the exception of Greece and later Yugoslavia under Tito, which struck an independent posture, were part of the Soviet-dominated Eastern Bloc, Turkey's relations with them remained limited. As part of its West-centered policy, Turkey also took part in European institutions, such as the Council of Europe and the Organization for Development and Cooperation (OECD). After the creation of the European institutions, intended gradually to unify Europe and which led to the emergence of the European Union (EU), Turkey decided to join them. This drive to join European institutions became the second overarching paradigm guiding the basic outlines of Turkish foreign policy, even after the end of the Cold War and the Soviet Union's collapse.

UNRAVELING OF THE USSR: IMPACT ON TURKISH DEBATES

The Soviet Union's disintegration fundamentally altered the international and regional contexts of Turkey's external relations, created new uncertainties, and posed potential new threats to its security. At the same time, the Soviet Union's demise offered Turkish diplomacy new opportunities in regions outside of the traditional purview of Turkey's foreign policy. The combination of potential threats and opportunities generated intense debate regarding the guiding principles and primary objectives of Turkey's post-Soviet foreign policy.

Consequences of the USSR's dissolution also intensified Turkey's identity debate, in particular sharpening the dichotomy between the Kemalist secularists and the Islamists on these issues. These twin debates, in turn, produced new alternative frameworks for Turkish foreign policy, such as neo-Ottomanism, a Turkey-centered version of Eurasianism, and a new interpretation of Pan-Turkism.

Because there is a close and according to some scholars "a dialectic"[35] connection between national identity and a state's foreign policy, Turkish debates on foreign policy and national identity closely interacted and exerted mutual influence. For example, those who believed Turkey should have a more Islamically influenced national identity and closer ties with other Muslim states favored ideas such as neo-Ottomanism as the basic framework for Turkey's post-Soviet foreign policy. They believed that a more Islam-centric concept of national identity and foreign policy would enable Turkey to extend its influence beyond Turkic and Muslim-inhabited lands to a geographic area extending from the Balkans to China.

Turkey's Identity Debate: Renewed Interest in Islam

By the time of the USSR's collapse, Islam's social and political profile in Turkey had risen sharply, and a revisionist trend regarding Turkey's Ottoman past and legacy had begun. Like many other changes that he had introduced in Turkey which challenged Kemalist orthodoxy, Turgut Özal significantly contributed to this trend. According to the British journalist Edward Mortimer, Özal "debunked the orthodox Kemalist vision of history with its near deification of Atatürk and the denigration of the Ottoman regime."[36] Further, in adjusting to new post-Soviet international and regional realities, Turkey soon discovered Islam's usefulness as an instrument of policy and means to advance its ambitions, especially in the newly independent Muslim republics which had formed part of the Soviet Union.

Mikhail Gorbachev's reforms and the USSR's collapse had generated greater interest on the part of former Soviet Muslims in their Islamic faith, traditions, and heritage. These Muslims expressed their new-found interest by displaying greater religiosity and by looking to Islam as a foundation of their post-Soviet national identities, value systems, and guide for the organization of social and political life. One outcome was the emergence of Islamist political parties in former Soviet Muslim republics. Turkey wanted to assume a leadership role in these republics, to increase its economic, political, and cultural presence, and also to prevent other Muslim states from gaining too much influence. Therefore, it had to prove to these republics that it could satisfy their religious as well as their economic and cultural needs. This meant a more systematic use of Islam as an instrument of Turkish policy in the former Soviet Muslims republics. Thus in Central Asia and the Caucasus, Turkish governments often supported the activities of schools run by the Islamist Gülen movement, and Turkey's Religious Affairs Directorate *(Diyanat)* organized various Eurasian Islamic meetings and conferences.

As a result, Islam's socio-political profile rose even more and Islam's role as a key component of Turkish national identity was enhanced. This cycle of interaction between identity and foreign policy continued in the following years. In the context of the dialectic interaction between identity and foreign policy, Islam's rising profile resulted in a foreign policy more interested in ties with the Muslim world, and, in turn, expanding ties with Muslim states, enhanced Islam's profile in Turkey. The outcome was that identity-related issues—both Turkic and Islamic—became more important in Turkey's domestic politics and in shaping its foreign policy.

INTERNATIONAL REPERCUSSIONS OF SOVIET COLLAPSE AND TURKEY'S FOREIGN POLICY DEBATES

By 1988, Mikhail Gorbachev's reforms, especially his policy of reducing tensions between the Soviet Union and the West, had significantly altered the dynamics of international and regional politics. In particular, the easing of East-West tensions had caused the major powers to alter and reassess their security calculations and recalibrate their relations with regional allies. Countries geographically closest to the USSR, including Turkey, were most susceptible to the effects of these systemic changes, largely because in the past their value to their great-power allies had been a function of their role in the Cold War. Thus even before the Soviet Union's unraveling and soon after Gorbachev's easing of tensions with the West, some prominent American politicians, such as Senator Robert Dole (R-Kansas), indicated that in the post–Cold War era the United States should rethink its economic and military assistance to a number of countries. He added that Turkey could be one of these countries.

Ramifications of the Soviet Union's demise for the dynamics of international and regional politics and hence for the security and other interests of various countries, including their relative weight and importance regionally and internationally, were greater than Gorbachev's reforms. Countries located in the USSR's proximity again were more strongly affected by these changes. At the international level, the United States became the undisputed dominant global power, thus altering the bi-polar character of the international system, ushering in what some commentators have characterized as the unipolar moment in the history of international relations, even if it proved short-lived.[37]

This new configuration of international power diminished American and Western need for regional allies, including Turkey—or so it appeared. This development exacerbated Turkey's anxieties about its future relations with the West, its regional role, its importance for its Western allies, and the prospects of continued Western military and economic aid. To ward off any negative consequences of these changes, Turkey focused on finding new ways to prove its continued value to its traditional allies and its regional importance.

During the Cold War, the common threat of communism and the Soviet Union had tended to keep in check regional animosities and rivalries. But after the USSR's fall, these rivalries emerged with greater force, and new elements of competition were added to the traditional sources of discord, especially as follows:

1. the emergence of the former USSR's Muslim republics as new players in regional power equations;

2. the establishment of contacts between these republics and neighboring countries; and
3. the unleashing of a race among regional states to establish contacts with these republics and to expand their influence.

These newly independent states faced serious problems of ethnic and territorial disputes both within their own countries and with other former Soviet republics. Thus the Soviet Union's dissolution created new security dilemmas for neighboring regional states. For Turkey, security challenges originated in the South Caucasus, where Armenia and Azerbaijan were waging a war over the district of Nagorno-Karabakh, thus posing a serious dilemma for Turkey: how to balance its European aspirations against its aspirations for greater Turkic/Islamic unity and cooperation under its own leadership. Turkey's aspirations for a greater role in the Muslim and Turkic worlds seemed to require it to give total support to Azerbaijan, while its European ambitions argued in favor of a more even-handed attitude toward the conflict and to show some concern for the Christian Armenians. This more sensitive approach was made more necessary because of Turkey's checkered past regarding the Armenians and also because there was considerable public sympathy for the Armenians in Europe and in America. More seriously, Turkey risked being dragged into the dispute, which could then turn into a larger regional conflict. Meanwhile, the opening up of these regions created new opportunities for Turkey to expand its economic, political, and cultural influence.[38] This was also true of the Balkan countries, especially those with significant Muslim or Turkish minorities. However, in the Balkans, too, inter-ethnic conflicts posed dilemmas for Turkey similar to those it faced in the Caucasus. In short, the Soviet Union's fall presented Turkey with both risks and opportunities and thus made imperative that Turkey develop a new framework and fresh guidelines for its foreign policy.

A NEW FOREIGN POLICY FRAMEWORK

Even before the USSR collapsed, a series of regional developments, especially the 1991 Persian Gulf War, had raised questions about the continued validity of Atatürk's dictum of "Peace at Home and Peace Abroad," along with his admonition that Turkey should stay out of regional conflicts, as sufficient guidelines for Turkey's foreign policy.

The 1991 Persian Gulf War: Reassertion of Turkey's Strategic Importance

The January–February 1991 Persian Gulf War was triggered by Saddam Hussein's attack on Kuwait in August 1990 and served as another catalyst for redefining Turkey's regional and international roles. More important, the war enabled Turkey to demonstrate its continued value to its Western allies. Its Incerlik military base proved invaluable for the anti-Saddam coalition, as did Turkey's closure of the Iraqi oil pipeline passing through its territory. Turkey's contributions to Saddam's defeat demonstrated that even in a post–Cold War world Turkey was of high strategic value to its allies. The Gulf War also turned Turkey into a potentially pivotal player in the Middle East, further enhancing its strategic importance. According to Peter Rodman, the war showed why the West should continue to support Turkey by military, economic, and other forms of assistance.[39]

The Persian Gulf War also ended Turkey's self-imposed isolation from the Middle East and ushered in a more activist Turkish policy there and in the Persian Gulf. The conceptual framework for this activist Turkish Middle East policy was the Özal Doctrine, named for Turkey's president.

The Özal Doctrine indicated Turkey's eagerness to play a major role in post–Gulf War security arrangements and within any potential regional security structures which might be established in the Persian Gulf and possibly even in the broader Middle East. But no such structures were set up in the Persian Gulf, and the United States continued to dominate regional politics through various policy decisions. A key U.S. act was enunciation in 1993 of its dual-containment policy. The objective was to undermine the governments of both Iran and Iraq through various economic and other pressures, with the ultimate goal of bringing about a change in these states' political regimes.

With the U.S. assumption of direct responsibility for Persian Gulf security, Turkey's engagement remained limited. However, it became more involved in Arab-Israeli issues and by 1994 had forged a close relationship with Israel.[40] In the following decades, Turkey's involvement in the politics of the Middle East and South Asia grew even further. In short, at least this aspect of the Kemalist legacy of Turkish foreign policy was totally abandoned.

New Horizons beyond Europe

Despite its forays into the Middle East and the former Soviet space, throughout the 1990s[41] Turkey's foreign policy's priorities were to safeguard its Western connections and alliances and to enhance its chances of joining Europe. In part, this West-centric approach reflected Turkey's domestic political dynamics, which were still dominated by secular elites faithful to the country's Western orientation. For them, the main virtues of Turkey's Middle East forays were to prove to its Western allies that it remained a valuable and useful partner. Turkey was also aware that it needed Western economic and military help and diplomatic support to play a major role in the Middle East and in the former Soviet space.

However, many Turkish leaders and observers did not subscribe to the idea of the priority of Turkey-West relations as the guiding paradigm of its post-Soviet foreign policy; as noted earlier, they advanced new concepts such as neo-Ottomanism and Pan-Turkism as more appropriate frameworks. Cengiz Çandar, a prominent Turkish journalist, wrote that "Turkey must develop an imperial vision," although he hastened to add that this vision did not imply territorial expansionism or adventurism. Aydin Yalçin argued that that Pan-Turkism was an ideology whose time had arrived and that the USSR's collapse and the discrediting of communism "had finally given a public expression and support for Pan-Turkism."[42] This version was not irredentist and territorially expansionist, but merely meant that Turkey should serve as the leader of a union of Turkic states. Turkey's prime minister and later president, Turgut Özal, subscribed both to this new interpretation of Pan-Turkism and to neo-Ottomanism. In fact, he had a rather idealized vision of the Ottoman Empire as a commonwealth of different peoples living in peace and harmony.[43]

The European Community's (EC) rejection of Turkey's 1987 application for membership accelerated Turkey's search for new partners outside Europe. The rejection also increased the appeal of alternative foreign policy frameworks like neo-Ottomanism and Pan-Turkism. Meanwhile, Turkish Islamists were developing their own alternative framework to Turkey's West-centric foreign policy. The underlying principle of the Islamist alternative was Muslim cooperation and unity under Turkish leadership and resembled the earlier Ottoman conceptions of Pan-Islamism. For example, Necmettin Erbakan, leader of the Islamist *Refah* Party, advocated the establishment of Islamic alternatives to Western institutions such as NATO and the EC, and he believed that Turkey should focus on expanding its relations with Muslim states.[44]

RECONCILING WESTERN AND TURKO-ISLAMIC VISIONS

As Turkey tried both to convince its allies and the newly independent countries of the post-Soviet space that it still remained a strategically and culturally pivotal country and to reconcile its Western/European and Turko-Islamic aspirations, it developed a vision of itself as the center of a new concept of Eurasia and representative of an enlightened Islam.

According to the Turkish version of Eurasianism, first advanced by Prime Minister Özal, Turkey and not Russia was the real center of Eurasia, both geographically and civilizationally. The Turkish version of Eurasia, according to Prime Minister Suleiman Demirel, extended "from the wall of China to the Adriatic Sea." This view has considerable merit. Geographically, Turkey is inherently Eurasian because it is located both in Europe and in Asia and can serve as a bridge between the two, especially with the Muslims of the post-Soviet space. Turkey is ethnically, linguistically, and religiously closer than Russia to the peoples of Central Asia and other Turkic peoples of the post-Soviet space. Civilizationally, too, Turkey shares their Islamic and Turko-Iranian culture. Turkey thus argued that these ties, coupled with its European inclination, would enable it to mediate between the West and the Muslim peoples of the ex-USSR and indeed other Muslims, by transmitting Western culture, values, and ways of doing business.

Turkey succeeded in this goal. Despite Russia's expectation that it would be the West's preferred partner in the former Soviet space, the Western countries chose Turkey as their main intermediary with the ex-USSR's Muslims and as the principal route for the supply of Central Asian and South Caucasian energy to Europe. They also channeled a good part of economic and technical aid to the Central Asian countries through Turkey and gave Turkish embassies in these countries the lead for contacts with NATO. Western powers, especially the United States, actively prevented Turkey's potential rivals, particularly Iran, from gaining any foothold in these areas; among other measures, they excluded Iran as a potential export conduit for Central Asian energy to Europe and beyond, although it was the cheapest and shortest route.

Turkey actively promoted itself as the representative of a modern, democratic, and secular Islam and as an antidote to Iran's revolutionary Islam. Turkey argued that it could direct Central Asians' newfound interest in Islam in a modern and liberal direction, or what Özal had described as Turkish Islam. Therefore, it would prevent the spread of both Iranian-style Islam and Sunni Arab extremist ideas, which had become popular because of the Afghan wars, to both these regions and beyond and thus also protect Europe against the threat of Islamic extremism. A favorite slogan of the Turkish prime minister, Tansu Çiller (1993–1996), was that the West must either choose modern and liberal Turkish Islam or be faced with the danger of Iranian-style Islam. This slogan encapsulated the Turkish strategy of marketing itself to the West, especially Europe, as both a bridge and a frontier buffer.[45] Turkey also used the Iran factor to gain concessions from Europe. During the negotiations for the signing of a customs union between Turkey and the European Union, Tansu Çiller, in a speech to the annual meeting of the World Economic Forum in Davos, said that "Turkey and Iran are two models for one billion Muslims. We are the only model that is open, democratic, and secular."[46] Nevertheless, some scholars maintain that it was the West that encouraged Turkey to have a more activist policy in the former USSR and to offer itself as the model of a secular Muslim state to Muslim countries, especially those of Central Asia, and thus bar or counter Iran's potential influence.[47]

Turkey's European Ambitions

Despite embracing new roles and expanding its foreign policy horizons, the cornerstone of Turkish foreign policy remained its eventual integration into the emerging European Union and maintenance of its American and NATO connections. In addition to traditional arguments in favoring this approach, Turkey realized that its European and NATO ties would enhance its ability to function as a multi-dimensional actor in multiple regional and international contexts, including the post-Soviet space. It could even be argued that Turkey developed new roles for itself in order to demonstrate its value for Europe. This view is supported by Tansu Çiller's comment that as much as Turkey needed a secular Europe, implying that Turkey's being overwhelmingly Muslim should not hinder its membership in what is now the EU, Europe, too, needed a secular Turkey. She implied that the EU's rebuff of Turkey's membership bid could increase the Islamists' power and appeal not only in the region but also in Turkey itself, thus endangering Europe's interests and security. Europe's significance for Turkey further increased as early euphoria about the economic and other potential of the new Turkic republics dissipated in the face of less-pleasant realities. Turkey soon realized that its cultural and other differences with these states were more than it had anticipated and that their economic and other problems were far greater than it had expected and were beyond Turkey's ability to solve. Moreover, Central Asian Turks were not willing to accept Turkey's leadership and mentorship pretentions. They resented the fact that Turkey saw itself as a big brother to its little Central Asian relatives.

Islam's Growing Role: Dilemmas for Turkish Foreign Policy

Islam's rising social and political profile both in Turkey and in the Muslim-inhabited and newly independent republics of the former USSR helped Turkey in its efforts to expand its economic, political, and cultural presence. However, it also presented Turkey with some dilemmas in formulating foreign policy. Most serious was how Turkey could use Islam as an instrument to extend its influence in Central Asia and potentially the Middle East without antagonizing its European allies and possibly harming its prospects of joining Europe. Turkey had also to be careful that its instrumental use of Islam in its foreign relations did not antagonize such Christian partners as Russia, with whom it had significant economic and energy relations.

Turkey faced this dilemma more acutely in South Eastern Europe, especially the Balkans, where there were significant numbers of Turkish and

Muslim minorities. In the Balkan context, dissolution of the Yugoslav Federation posed the greatest challenge for Turkey in terms of reconciling its European ambitions, the requirements of its membership in the most prominent Western security alliance (NATO), and its newly developed ambitions of being a leader of Turkic and Islamic worlds. It also showed the growing distance between the old secular elite and the emerging Islamist elite, as the Islamists argued for a more robust Turkish support for the Bosnian Muslims. Such a policy, however, especially if it included military assistance, would have jeopardized Turkey's relations with its Western allies.

TURKEY'S OTTOMAN LEGACY IN THE BALKANS: ADVANTAGES AND LIABILITIES

In dealing with the Balkan region and the Bosnia crisis, Turkey felt the heavy weight of its Ottoman legacy in the region. The Ottomans had reached the Balkans soon after establishing their power in the fourteenth century and long before the conquest of Constantinople in 1453 by Sultan Mehmet Fatih or the Conqueror.

The Ottomans first entered the Balkans by capturing the Greek city of Thessalonica. Then in 1389 they defeated the Serbs in Kosovo. After the capture of Constantinople, the expansion of Ottoman power into the Balkans and other parts of Eastern Europe accelerated, and by the early sixteenth century all of the Balkans was under Turkish rule, which lasted for nearly four hundred years. By the early nineteenth century, however, the Ottomans' Balkan possessions were growing increasingly restive and independence movements were multiplying, eventually leading to the gradual dwindling of the Ottomans' Balkan possessions.

Despite its long duration, Ottoman rule did not produce a massive change in the Balkans' ethno-linguistic or religious map. It only resulted in introduction of pockets of Turkish and Muslim elements to the region and the Islamization of some Slavs. Present Turkish communities in Bulgaria and Greece and Muslims in Bosnia, Kosovo, and Albania, as well as ethnic Slav Bulgarian converts to Islam known as Pomaks, are reminders of this Ottoman past.[48]

The Ottoman presence in the Balkan region created both friends and enemies for Turkey. The Islamization of some Balkan peoples and to some extent their cultural Turkification has resulted in the existence of pro-Turkey constituencies which could be potential conduits for its influence. By contrast, Ottoman rule has left a largely negative legacy for Turkey in terms of its relations with the region's Christian populations. Balkan Christians viewed the Ottoman presence as a period of foreign occupation which resulted in the spread of a foreign religion, Islam, and which undermined their

Christian faith and traditions. Thus the region's Christians resent Turkey and they remain suspicious of its regional intentions. The Serbs, in particular, were bitter about their loss at the battle of Kosovo on June 28, 1389.[49]

These conflicting legacies of the Ottoman era came into play during the 1992–1995 Bosnian War. Bosnian Muslims looked to Turkey for support, although some commentators have noted that Turkey's cultural and religious influence on the Bosnians should not be exaggerated. They point out that Bosnia's Prime Minister (December 1990–October 1996) Alija Izetbegovic's brand of Islamism was closer to that of Iran and that he shared many of the ideals of the Islamic Revolution.[50] He finally chose Turkey largely because of the West's policy of containing Iran; he feared that ties to Iran could prompt the West to side completely with the Serbs.[51] Meanwhile, the Serbs used to their advantage the Ottoman legacy, especially the Kosovo War. Turkish scholars Meliha Altunişik and Özlem Tür explain that "the Ottoman legacy had played negatively in the case of the Serbs, who invoked and reinterpreted it negatively in their quest for dominance."[52]

Another legacy of Ottoman rule was that segments of the Turkish public felt a sense of moral responsibility toward the Balkan Muslims. With the enhancement of Islam's role in Turkish identity, society, and politics, together with the rehabilitation of its Ottoman past and the emergence of neo-Ottomanism as a potential framework for a new Turkish foreign policy, this feeling of responsibility was intensified.[53] It appears, however, that this sense of responsibility was less strong in the case of Turkey's ruling elites, which is in sharp contrast with their attitude toward Turkish minorities in Bulgaria and Greece. The Turkish scholar Sabri Sayari has attributed this attitude partly to the lack of linguistic affinity with the Bosnians and also to the fact that Bosnian Muslims' religious traditions, dating back to the Ottoman era, did not resonate with the Turkish political elites.[54]

Meanwhile, Turkish Islamists used the Turks' sense of responsibility toward the Bosnians to their own political advantage and criticized the government's tepid reaction to the crisis. For example, Necmettin Erbakan ridiculed Suleiman Demirel by saying that he was not a true Suleiman, meaning the Ottoman Sultan known as the Magnificent. He said if Demirel were a true Suleiman, he would have done much more for the Bosnians.[55]

But the real cause of Turkey's cautious approach was its desire to not overly antagonize the region's Christian populations. An excessively anti-Christian Turkish policy would have intensified anti-Turkey sentiments throughout Europe, thus severely undermining its chances of joining European institutions. Consequently, according to some scholars, Turkish decision makers were anxious that the Bosnian conflict not morph into "a war between Christianity and Islam."[56] If this had happened and if Turkey were seen as siding with Muslims, it could have given a further excuse to those who claimed that Turkey is not part of Europe, especially since at the time of the Yugoslav crisis anti-Turkish sentiments were still strong in a number of Balkan countries.[57] These sentiments were on display in various publications in Greece, Serbia, and Bulgaria in the 1990s.

Some of these publications expressed anxiety about Turkey's real intentions and suspected Turkish activism of having irredentist dimensions.[58] Thus Turkey had to be careful that its actions in the Balkans did not create a perception that it might have wanted "to lay any claim on former Ottoman territories."[59] In particular, Turkey had to be mindful of Greek anxieties about increased Turkish influence in regions of concern to Greece, anxieties which had been exacerbated following Balkan events. The Greeks saw the Balkan Muslims not only as Turkish assets in terms of Turkey's regional influence, but also as a barrier that "separated Greece from her Slavic Christian neighbors."[60] The Greeks thus developed a deep sense of anxiety about what they called "an Islamic arc," which would have cut off Greece from its Slavic neighbors.[61]

Turkish Citizens of Balkan Origins: Impact on Turkey's Approach to the Yugoslav Crisis

Another legacy of Ottoman rule in the Balkans was the presence within the Turkish citizenry of a considerable number of people who traced their origins to the Balkans, including a large number of Turks of Bosnian descent.[62] In theory, the existence of this group of Turkish citizens would have constituted a source of pressure on the Turkish government to adopt a strong posture in defense of the Bosnians. However, it appears that their influence was relatively limited. Certainly, there was no strong pressure on the government by this group to act in support of the Bosnians, especially if that meant defying Turkey's Western allies or the United Nations. According to some scholars, the reason for this lack of pressure on the part of Turks of Bosnian origin was their long presence in Turkey and the fact they had become "Turkicized and therefore no longer had very close links to their country of origin."[63] Moreover, it seems that some Turks of Bosnian origin were radically secular, left-leaning, anti-West, and anti-NATO. Not only did they not support Turkish help for Bosnians, they were defenders of Serbia's president, Slobodan Milošević, because they saw him as fighting Western imperialists.[64] Not all scholars of Turkey agree with this interpretation. Stephen Larrabee and Ian O. Lesser have noted that, by the early 1990s, there was a growing interest among Turkish citizens about their ethnic roots, and various ethnic lobbies had been created, including one by Bosnian-origin Turkish citizens.[65] On balance, however, it seems that the Turks of Bosnian origin did not have an undue influence on Turkey's Bosnia policy, and they were mostly active in providing help for Bosnian refugees in Turkey.[66]

TURKISH DOMESTIC POLITICS AND PUBLIC OPINION

The Bosnian crisis occurred when the Turkish political scene had become less stable and governments, often formed through coalitions, followed one another in rather quick succession. The secular elites were faced with serious problems of corruption, loss of public trust, and the weakening of the traditional parties. These problems were exacerbated by the fact that, after Özal's departure from the political scene (he died in office in April 1993), there were no charismatic personalities capable of forming political parties that could harness commanding majorities in the parliament. The weakness of traditional political parties had contributed to the Islamists' greater acceptance by the public, thus increasing their hopes of one day forming the government. The Islamists' greater public acceptance had made Turkish governments more sensitive to the potential domestic ramifications of foreign policy decisions. In handling the Bosnia crisis, the Turkish government was keenly aware of this new reality of Turkish politics.

Meanwhile, Turkish public opinion had become more interested in foreign policy debates. Some scholars have marked the beginning of this greater public interest to the 1989 EC rejection of Turkey's application for membership and to the 1991 Persian Gulf War.[67] Both events seem to have intensified Turks' Islamist and nationalist feelings. This new dynamic, too, meant that, in its decisions regarding Bosnia, the Turkish government had to pay attention to the impact on public opinion and hence on the ruling coalition's electoral prospects, especially given that the Islamists were using the war to score political points.

Diverging positions on the appropriate Turkish policy on Bosnia also reflected Turkey's identity debates. In view of the dialectical interaction between identity and foreign policy, it is not surprising that the Islamists used the Bosnia policy debate to promote their own vision of Turkey's national identity. Thus some of the government's statements and actions regarding Bosnia can be explained in the context of competition over the content and direction of the identity debate and in terms of the governing coalition's ability to retain its electoral edge.

The most pro-Bosnia statements calling for a more robust Turkish response to the crisis came from the Islamists. They used the crisis and, in particular, the large-scale massacre of Bosnian Muslims, to undermine the Westernizing secular Turks by attacking the West's double standards. For example, during a protest march largely attended by Islamists, the slogan of "Muslims are here, where are the secularists?" was used.[68] The Islamists were intimating that secularists were not interested in the Bosnian Muslims' fate. They also promoted their own vision of an appropriate Turkish foreign policy and argued that there were Islamic alternatives to joining Europe, especially in the new post-Soviet geopolitical context.

There were also fundamental differences in the Islamists' and the more secular Turks' understanding of the causes of the Bosnian War, reflecting their respective self-perceptions and world-views. The Islamists, including the leader of the *Refah* party, Necmettin Erbakan, saw the war in essentially religious terms and as a manifestation of the Europeans' determination to eliminate Islam from the Continent. More secular Turks and political parties had a more nuanced understanding of the causes of the war. However, because of political competition with the Islamists, even these parties were tempted to attribute the conflict to religio-cultural and identity-related causes. For example, Turkey's president, Turgut Özal, who had been leader of the Motherland Party, at a public gathering stated that "Turkey will not allow Bosnia to become another Andalucía." He meant that Turkey would not allow Bosnian Muslims to be expelled from Europe as Spain's Muslims were expelled after the Spanish *Reconquista* in the fifteenth century. This statement indicates that he, too, saw strong civilizational elements involved in the Bosnian conflict. Even the leftist and very secular politician, Bülent Ecevit, once remarked that the war in Bosnia had turned into "a crusade against the Muslims."[69]

Because of this understanding, Islamists advocated an activist Turkish approach to the conflict and direct support for the Bosnian Muslims. They also called on the Turks to join the fighting on the side of the Bosnian Muslims, formed the largest percentage of people in demonstrations organized in support of the Bosnians, and raised the most funds for them through public donations. The Islamists, however, did not insist on unilateral Turkish action. They endorsed the general consensus that Turkey's efforts should be conducted through multilateral organizations. Their attitude shows that even those who emphasize identity and value-related issues in their approach to the outside world are greatly influenced by more tangible factors such as security. They are also subject to the same restraints imposed by a country's actual capabilities as are the more realist practitioners. Nevertheless, the Islamists and some other secular parties claimed that the government could have done a more effective job within multilateral organizations to help the Muslims.[70] It is difficult, however, to determine whether they really believed in this view or rather such statements were part of their function as the opposition.

The Islamists' credibility as staunch supporters of Bosnians suffered when in 1994 it was alleged that the main Islamist political party, *Refah*, had used the substantial funds it had gathered for the Bosnians to finance its own electoral campaign. This revelation generated serious doubts about the sincerity of *Refah* in its professions of Islamic solidarity.[71]

Turkey's secular leaders, however, were not silent on the question of the Bosnian Muslims' plight. They bemoaned what was happening and criticized the lack of adequate international response to the Bosnian crisis. But it seems that their actions, too, were essentially motivated by political considerations rather than by religious sympathies or by any sense of kinship with the Bosnians. Tansu Çiller, the Turkish prime minister, went twice to Sarajevo, once in February 1994 and then in November 1995, ostensibly to express support for the Bosnian Muslims. However, both these trips coincided with Turkish election campaigns and were essentially used to counteract *Refah*'s pro-Bosnian propaganda and to burnish Çiller's tarnished image. As noted by Sylvie Gangloff, *"it was well thought important not to leave Necmettin Erbakan, the president of the Refah, with the 'monopoly of indignation.'* In short, "the *government had to compete with the Refah in terms of condemnations of the massacres, criticism of the United Nations and so on*" [emphasis added].[72]

Moreover, Turkish leaders were aware that their actions were being watched by other Muslim states, including in Central Asia. Some wanted to see what weight Turkey had within Western and international organizations. Others in the Muslim world wanted to find out how sincere Turkey was in its proclamations of support for Muslims. Thus, *"Turkey could not look unconcerned—and especially less concerned than Iran—and so multiplied the condemnation of double standards etc."* [emphasis added].[73] Further complicating the government's task was the fact that public opinion was as divided as the elites on the broader directions of Turkey's post–Cold War foreign policy. Some still favored a European-focused policy, others favored policy directed toward the Turkic world and some toward the Muslim world. Some meanwhile wanted an activist Turkish foreign policy on all fronts.

More fundamentally, Turkey's dilemma was that if it did not act forcefully it would be accused of betraying the Bosnian Muslims. But if it did, it would be accused of imperial ambitions and neo-Ottomanist designs. In other words, Turkey did not have any really good policy options on Bosnia.

THE YUGOSLAV CRISIS: BALANCING CONFLICTING INTERESTS AND PRESSURES

When the Yugoslav crisis began, in addition to undergoing heightened debate on its identity and direction of foreign policy, Turkey was experiencing anxious times because of increasing ethnic and religious tensions in its neighborhood, largely ensuing from the USSR's gradual disintegration. Because of Turkey's ethnic, linguistic, and religious links with some of the peoples involved in these tensions, it faced a risk of becoming embroiled in some of them, such as those brewing in the Caucasus. Therefore, Turkey was concerned about similar developments in its Balkan neighborhood. Such developments would have added to Turkey's geopolitical challenges. Moreover, with its own disgruntled ethnic minorities, in particular the Kurds with whom it was still waging a war, Turkey was extremely wary of any developments which could end in the ethnic fragmentation of existing political entities, including those in the Balkans. Meanwhile, prolonged instability in the Balkans would have led to large migration of Turks and Muslims to Turkey from this region.[74] According to one author, slowing Balkan migration to Turkey was at the time a major goal of the Turkish government.[75]

Moreover, Turkey had excellent relations and significant economic and trade connections with Yugoslavia. The Turkish state minister, Cemil Çiçek, went to Belgrade shortly before the outbreak of the civil war in order to attend the 8th meeting of the Joint Commission of Turkish-Yugoslav Economic Cooperation.[76] These contacts continued in 1990.[77] In the long term, too, Turkey needed to have reasonable relations with the Yugoslav Federations' successor states, including Serbia, if it wanted to retain and enhance its presence in the Balkans. Turkey might have also calculated that it was important not to leave the field in Serbia totally open to Greece and Russia. Consequently, even at the height of the Bosnian conflict, Turkey did not cut diplomatic relations with Belgrade, leading members of the Democratic Left Party to complain that the government was indifferent to Bosnia's predicament. As proof of this indifference, they noted that not a single minister had visited Sarajevo, while high-ranking bureaucrats had gone to Belgrade.[78]

Consequently, as long as there was any possibility that the Yugoslav Federation could be saved, Turkey declared its support for its survival and called for a diplomatic solution to the problems between the Federal authorities and Slovenia and Croatia. The Turkish foreign minister, Hikmet Çetin, said that Turkey considered Yugoslavia as one country and did not desire its division.[79] In view of this basic approach to the Yugoslav crisis, Turkey was unhappy with Germany's decision to recognize Croatia, although later it itself recognized both Slovenia and Croatia. This is why the Serbs expressed their satisfaction with Turkey's position.[80]

Turkey's early cautious approach to Yugoslav events could also be explained in light of the fact that they did not pose any immediate security threat to Turkey, especially of the "hard security" variety. These events did not pose the threat of military incursions into Turkish territory or any other kind of potential military entanglement. However, Turkey did face what some have called a "soft security" threat, by potentially increasing the rate of Balkan migration to Turkey and by impacting identity-related debates.[81] In short, Turkey could afford to wait and watch how events and regional and international politics of the conflict evolved.

OLD ALLIANCES, NEW AMBITIONS

The Bosnian crisis in many ways crystallized the dilemmas of Turkish foreign policy in the post-Soviet era: how to retain its old alliances and use them to its own advantage while carving out a new role for itself internationally, especially in the Muslim and Turkic worlds. In this context, Turkey's NATO membership was of vital importance. It provided Turkey with a security umbrella and conferred special prestige among Central Asian and Middle Eastern countries where Ankara was seeking to expand its influence. Thus Turkey had to be careful that its policies in the Balkans, including Bosnia, did not depart from the basic positions of NATO. Moreover, Turkey had to demonstrate that it could be a useful ally in promoting security in post-Soviet Europe. This was important because after the collapse of the USSR many in the West had come to see Turkey more as a consumer rather than a producer of security.

Turkey had also to be mindful of the potential impact of its Bosnia policy on its European aspirations. An excessively Islam-driven approach would not have helped. Within this general framework, Turkey's policy evolved in light of developments in the former Yugoslavia. As long as the conflict in Bosnia remained limited, Turkey's concerns were threefold:

1. to bring an end to the war in Bosnia-Herzegovina and help it to retain its independence;
2. to prevent the spill-over of the conflict to Kosovo, Albania, Macedonia, Sandjak, and Vojvodina; and
3. to draw attention of the international community to the crisis through all possible diplomatic means.[82]

After the fighting intensified, Turkey's focus shifted more to the diplomatic front, and it tried to achieve its goals through the following means.

COMPONENTS OF TURKEY'S BOSNIA POLICY

Given the many conflicting interests it had and the various domestic and international pressures it was subjected to, Turkey decided on an essentially multilateral approach to handling the Bosnian crisis and avoiding any unilateral undertaking, especially of a military nature.[83] It tried to help the Bosnians by acting through various multilateral organizations and by using its influence and powers of persuasion. In following this logic, Turkey decided to act as:

1. *Faithful NATO Ally.* To prove its loyalty, Turkey followed the strategy adopted by NATO, and whatever military contributions it made to the war were as part of NATO operations. However, Turkey did try to convince NATO to act more forcefully in defense of the Bosnian Muslims and was the first member of the alliance to suggest the use of military power and backed all U.S. calls for NATO's military engagement. It thus strongly supported NATO air strikes, and the Turkish military took part in NATO operations by sending eighteen F-16s to Italy. According to some sources, Turkey's main objective in this exercise, as with its other efforts to appear as a leader in managing the conflict, was to revive its value for its traditional allies and "retain its Western identity."[84] Yet Turkey's role was not as vital as it has claimed.[85] In fact, it could be argued that NATO invited Turkey to take part as a way of enhancing Turkey's prestige and influence in the Muslim world. Some scholars have noted that the Turkish press interpreted the NATO invitation to Turkey as "a great success of Ankara" and a "great source of prestige."[86]
2. *Intermediary between Western Partners and Bosnian Muslims.* Turkey at times played the role of intermediary between the Western powers and the Bosnian Muslim leaders and it facilitated meetings between them in Istanbul. For example, Turkey arranged for a meeting in Istanbul between the U.S. negotiator, Richard Holbrooke, and the Bosnian leader, Alija Izetbegovic.[87]
3. *Activist UN member.* Turkey endeavored to help the Bosnian Muslims by pursuing an active diplomacy at the United Nations. It worked hard toward lifting the arms embargo on the combatants in the conflict, since the embargo largely penalized the Bosnian Muslims. It insisted that UN decisions be implemented, even if this required the use of military force as eventually happened. As part of this diplomatic activism, in August 1992 Turkey presented an action plan on Bosnia to the permanent representatives of the UNSC, consisting of proposals on both diplomatic and military levels. Turkey also contributed personnel to the United Nations Protection Force (UNPROFOR).
4. *Supportive of EU Diplomatic Actions.* Early on in Balkan tensions and hostilities, Turkey tried to draw attention to the fact that inaction on the part of the international community could lead to a wider Balkan war. Therefore, it supported all activities which could prevent such an outcome. Because of this activism, Turkey was invited to take part in a conference convened by the EC in London on 26–27 August 1992. Again, Ankara interpreted this invitation as a success and a sign of Turkey's growing regional importance and international profile.
5. *Acting as a Balkan Leader.* Turkey further highlighted its role as a Balkan leader. To this end, it organized a meeting of the Balkans on

25 November 1992 in which eight other countries took part: Macedonia, Croatia, Slovenia, Bulgaria, Austria, Italy, Hungary, and Romania. Turkey maintained that it had taken this initiative because of the inaction of the international community. In this conference, too, Turkey emphasized the risks of the spread of the conflict and the need for military action. A side benefit was the highlighting of Turkey's pivotal place in the Balkan region.[88]

6. *Activism within the Organization of Islamic Cooperation (OIC).* Turkey used the Bosnian crisis to showcase itself as the moderate and progressive voice of Islam and to enhance its role in the Islamic world. Taking advantage of its chairmanship of the OIC in 1992, it convened a conference in Istanbul on 17–18 June 1992 to highlight the Bosnian Muslims' plight, in which foreign ministers from fifteen Muslim states participated.

7. *Efforts by Turkish Political Leaders.* Additionally, Turkish political leaders, most notably Prime Minister Tansu Çiller, visited Bosnia in order to bring more global attention to Bosnian Muslims' sufferings. On one of these visits, she was accompanied by the Pakistani prime minister, Benazir Bhutto.[89] President Özal, too, personally contacted a number of world leaders, including the U.S. president, George H. W. Bush; the French president, François Mitterrand; King Fahd of Saudi Arabia; and Hosni Mubarak of Egypt.[90] Along with Prime Minister Çiller's activities, President Özal's efforts to acquaint world leaders with the Bosnian Muslims' dire circumstances had a strong domestic political dimension: they were intended to show the more religious Turks that their political leaders were not indifferent to the fate of other Muslims, especially the Bosnians, and in this way undermine their Islamists rivals. The Turkish foreign minister at the time, Hikmet Çetin, has summed up Turkey's efforts by stating that *"no one can argue that we have not done enough for Bosnia"* [emphasis added].[91]

Be that as it may, beyond efforts noted above at the governmental level, Turkey did not do much more in support of Bosnians. Even in terms of financial assistance, its contribution was minimal. After the end of hostilities and following the signing of the Dayton Agreement, Turkey did not particularly favor Bosnia. Rather, it moved swiftly to establish relations with all of former Yugoslavia's component parts, including Serbia. In fact, in terms of economic relations and investments, Turkish businessmen, including members of the Muslim Federation of Turkish Industries (MUSAID), were more interested in the more industrially advanced republics of Croatia and Slovenia than Bosnia. For example, in 1997 Turkey extended a line of credit of $100 million to Croatia and Romania whereas only $80 million was promised to Bosnia.[92]

Non-Governmental Assistance and Activism

Turkish involvement in the Bosnian conflict was not limited to the government. Private individuals and various groups were active in garnering financial and other support for the Bosnian Muslims, as well as joining them in their fight against the Serbs and Croats.

The greatest help came from Islamic groups, organizations, and individuals. The involvement of the *Refah* Party in raising funds, which eventually led to a scandal following allegations that the funds were used to finance electoral campaigns, was noted earlier. But other groups also raised funds, and some were established with the specific goal of helping the Bosnians. One of the most significant was the *Insan Hak ve Hurriyetleri Insani Yardim, Vakfi*—IHH (the Foundation for Humanitarian Aid and for Human Rights and Liberties). According to the foundation's director, Bulent Yildrim, in 2009, the foundation was created in 1992 "to help oppressed people who were victimized by the massacres going on in Bosnia-Herzegovina in late 1992."[93] According to Yildrim, the foundation first started with three people who went to Bosnia. Their number was subsequently increased with new volunteers from Turkey.

Some Turks joined the Bosnian Muslims in battle. The exact numbers are not clear, although all agree that they did not exceed a few hundred at best. Six Turks were killed in the war or, according to the Turks, martyred, including Salaheddin Diran. His death inspired many poems which celebrated his sacrifice. According to an interview with the father of a Turkish volunteer who died—martyred—in Bosnia, Ilhan Atli, "when the war started approximately 400 people left Turkey for Bosnia and among them some 40 fell *Shehid* (martyr)."[94] Interestingly, there was also a socialist Turkish volunteer, Refik Erduran, who went to Serbia ostensibly to fight the imperialists. On his return, he wrote a book called *Bosnian Samurais: The Memoirs of a Turkish Socialist*. This indicates that, as was the case with Russian volunteers, some Turks went to Bosnia for reasons other than mere sense of religious solidarity.

However, most Turkish groups and individuals who helped Bosnia were motivated not by worldly ambition but essentially by feelings of religious solidarity and by the belief that Islam enjoins Muslims to help their fellow Muslims. The sense of Turkish-Bosnian kinship referred to earlier was also an important inducement. However, political parties, including the Islamist *Refah*, as evidenced by the scandal of using of funds collected for Bosnians to help finance a political campaign, were mostly motivated by political calculations.

THE IMPACT OF PUBLIC OPINION

There was significant sympathy for the Bosnian Muslims among the Turks regardless of the level of their religiosity, although more religious Muslims felt greater sympathy for them. Therefore, most Turks favored a policy supportive of Bosnian Muslims. However, there is no evidence to suggest that at any time the government felt undue pressure from the public to take measures in support of Bosnian Muslims beyond what it was already doing. In particular, most Turks disapproved of any action on the Bosnia front which could jeopardize Turkey's own vital national interests, such as its NATO membership and its European aspirations, or embroil it in military confrontation. However, some sources have claimed that the Turks of Bosnian origin pressured the government for more active support for the Muslims. According to Şerif Turgut, Suleiman Demirel reportedly had said at a NATO meeting that "you must do something; I cannot control my army anymore," implying that officers of Bosnian heritage were pressuring him.[95]

CONCLUSIONS

The Bosnian crisis erupted at a time when dramatic international and regional changes triggered by the Soviet Union's collapse had seriously undermined the foundations of Turkey's traditional foreign policy. By creating new challenges and opportunities for Turkey, these changes had generated a significant debate about what should be the guiding principles of a post-Soviet Turkish foreign policy. They had also sharpened Turkey's identity debate which had been going on since at least the mid-1980s, when the Kemalist definition of Turkish identity was challenged by new and more religious elites. They resented the Kemalists' denial of Turkey's Ottoman past and its Islamic traditions, and they looked to Turkey's Islamic and Ottoman heritages to fashion a new Turkish identity. Moreover, issues of identity and foreign policy had become more closely linked with domestic politics than had been true before.

The coincidence of the identity and foreign policy debates created a greater linkage between identity politics and the making of foreign policy. Thus when the Bosnian War erupted, it became entangled with Turkey's identity and foreign policy debates and became an issue in Turkish domestic politics and power struggles. The result was that the Bosnian War was not just a challenge for Turkey's foreign policy and its security and other interests and aspirations, but also became a domestic political as well as identity-related challenge.

Through its various policies, the Turkish government tried to address the conflicting demands of identity on the one hand, and security and other traditional foreign policy challenges, on the other. It tried to handle the crisis in a way that would safeguard Turkey's existing security and political ties and alliances without preventing it from exploring new opportunities for forming new partnerships and relations. Moreover, with an eye to the domestic context of its policies, the government tried to ensure that its handling of the crisis did not undermine the ruling parties' position vis-à-vis their rivals. Especially, the government tried to make sure that it did not appear unconcerned or insufficiently concerned with the fate of Bosnian Muslims and thus hand the Islamists an advantage in domestic politics.

Despite these political considerations, Turkish policies regarding the Bosnian crisis demonstrated:

1. *The primacy of concrete and tangible state interests.* In devising their policy toward the crisis, Turkish leaders were primarily influenced by what they saw as Turkey's national interest rather than by any sense of religious solidarity with the Bosnian Muslims. In this context, protecting Turkey's internal and external security, safeguarding its traditional alliances such as those with NATO, securing its European connections and aspirations, promoting a Turkish leadership role on several fronts—such as the Balkans, the Turkic world and the Islamic world—had the highest priority for Turkish leaders. This does not mean that religious sympathy and a sense of kinship with the Bosnians did not play a role. They did, and some of Turkey's diplomatic and other actions in support of Bosnian Muslims can be attributed to these sympathies, although they also helped promote Turkey's other interests. It simply means that, in order to safeguard Turkey's national interests, more hard-headed security, political, and national interest considerations and calculations were given priority. Assistance was rendered to the Bosnians only to the extent that it did not jeopardize Turkey's fundamental interests.
2. *The importance of domestic political considerations.* The positions of the governing political parties on Bosnia were partly determined by their calculations regarding the potential impact of their handling of the crisis on their positions vis-à-vis their competitors, including in future parliamentary elections.
3. *The prevalence of interest over identity-related issues and religious affinity even within the Islamist groups.* Thus the Islamist leaders and party manipulated the Bosnian War to undermine the secular governments. They even used the money gathered for Bosnian Muslims to finance their electoral campaign. They, too, gave priority to safeguarding Turkey's interests and favored helping the Bosnians to the extent that this help did not jeopardize peculiarly Turkish interests. In particular, they were as shy as were the secular elites of entangling Turkey

in direct military conflict in the Balkans outside the protective umbrella of multilateral frameworks.
4. *The instrumental use of the religious factor.* The Turkish government used religion to advance other goals. For example, the Turkish government used its connection with the Bosnian Muslims to revive its value to its traditional allies, prove its importance in the context of European security, gain more stature in the Islamic world, and enhance Turkey's regional and international prestige.

In sum, Turkey's handling of the Bosnian crisis, as was the case with that of Russia, indicates that when substantial interests are at stake, considerations of religious and cultural affinity play a relatively small role in determining states' policies. In particular, in those cases where religious bonds are not complemented by ethnic or linguistic ties or where the country in question does not have a significant importance from a security perspective, religious motivations play a secondary role in determining policy. Turkey's experience in dealing with the Bosnian War showed that non-governmental and grass roots organizations' approach to crises involving their religious or ethnic kin is more affected by religious factors and feelings of ethnic and cultural solidarity than those of governments and political parties. However, Turkish experience also demonstrated that these organizations have a relatively limited impact on state policy, especially in the absence of significant pressure from the broader public.

Nevertheless, the case of Turkish policy toward the Bosnian crisis strongly indicates the importance of identity-related issues, including religious ties, in generating interest in a given foreign policy issue, especially when overwhelming security and other interests are not involved. Turkey's interest in the Bosnian crisis, the intensity of feelings that it generated, and its efforts to help Bosnian Muslims within the requirements of its own security and national interests, largely derived from its religious ties with Bosnian Muslims. Without these ties, it is unlikely that it would have spent so much time and effort to help them.

NOTES

1. After the fall of the Erbakan government in 1997 under pressure from the Turkish military, most Turkish Islamists, including its current president, Recep Tayyip Erdoğan, became champions of Turkish EU membership. They saw preparations for EU membership, which included democratization and reducing the military's influence in politics, as making it easier for them to achieve power.
2. For a discussion of these issues, see Esra Bulut, "The Role of Religion in Turkish Reactions to Balkan Conflicts," *Turkish Policy Quarterly* (Spring 2004).
3. In this regard, Turkey is quite similar to Russia, although Turkey has a longer history than Russia as a nation-state.

4. David Kushner, *The Rise of Turkish Nationalism, 1876–1908* (London: Frank Cass, 1977), 1.

5. David Kushner, "Self-Perception and Identity in Contemporary Turkey," *Journal of Contemporary History*, 32. 2. 1997, 219.

6. Kushner, "Self-Perception and Identity," 219.

7. Kushner, "Self-Perception and Identity," 220.

8. Kushner, "Self-Perception and Identity," 221.

9. Hakan Yavuz, *Islamic Political Identity in Turkey* (Oxford: Oxford University Press, 2003), 45.

10. For a short discussion of the topic, see Karen Barkey, "Political Legitimacy and Islam in the Ottoman Empire: Lessons Learned," *Philosophy and Social Criticism*, 40. 4–5. 2014. Also Ahmet Yaşar Ocak, "Islam in the Ottoman Empire: A Sociological Framework for a New Interpretation," *International Journal of Turkish Studies*, 9. 1–2. 2003.

11. Barkey, "Political Legitimacy," 472.

12. In the case of the Safavids, sectarian differences were a major factor as the Ottomans were Sunni and the Safavids were Shia. Russia, of course, as the defender of Orthodoxy, resented Ottoman control of Constantinople.

13. Jacob Landau, *The Politics of Pan-Islam: Ideology and Organization* (Oxford: Oxford University Press, 1990).

14. Jacob Landau, *Pan-Turkism in Turkey: A Study in Irredentism* (Hamden, CT: Archon Books 1981). Also by the same author, *Pan-Turkism: From Irredentism to Cooperation* (Bloomington: Indiana University Press, 1995).

15. Phillip Robbins, *Turkey and the Middle East* (London: Pinter Publishers for the Royal Institute of International Affairs, 1990), 7.

16. Yavuz, *Islamic Political Identity in Turkey*, 46.

17. Andrew Mango, *Turkey: The Challenge of a New Role*, Washington Paper 163 (Washington, DC: CSIS/Praeger, 1994), 33.

18. On Kurdish revolts, see among others: Robert W. Olson, "The Kurdish Rebellion of Sheikh Said," *Die Welt des Islams*, *New Series*, 40.1. March 2000. This rebellion initially was mostly of a religious character but later developed an ethnic and cultural dimension. See Robert W. Olson, *The Emergence of Kurdish Nationalism and the Sheikh Said Rebellion 1880–1925* (Austin: The University of Texas Press, 1989). It should be pointed out, however, that the Kurdish rebellions were triggered by ethnic and cultural as well as by religious causes. On the broader issue of reactions to reforms, see Mahmut Gologlu, *Devimrler ve Tepkiliri* (Reforms and Reactions to Them), (Ankara: n.p., 1972).

19. Said Nursî, known by the honorific Bediuzzaman, was an ethnic Kurd and a Sunni theologian. He believed in a synthesis of Islam and science and advocated the teaching of religious sciences at secular schools and sciences at religious schools. See Surkan Vahide, *Islam in Modern Turkey: An Intellectual Biography of Bediuzzaman Said Nursî* (Albany: SUNY Press, 2005). Also Şerif Mardin, *Religion and Social Change in Turkey: The Case of Bediuzzaman Nursî* (Albany: SUNY Press, 1989).

20. On the Gülen movement, see Hakan Yavuz, *Toward an Islamic Enlightenment: The Gülen Movement* (Oxford: Oxford University Press, 2013). The more purist followers of Nursî are called *Nurcu*.

21. Caglar Keder, "Whither the Process of Modernity: Turkey in the 1990s," in eds. Sibel Bozdoğan and Reşat Kasaba, *Rethinking Modernity and National Identity in Turkey* (Seattle: University of Washington Press, 1997), 43.

22. Hakan Yavuz, "Turkish Identity and Foreign Policy in Flux: The Rise of Neo-Ottomanism," *Critique* (Spring 1998), 25.

23. Tamer Balci, "From Nationalization of Islam to Privatization of Nationalism: Islam and Turkish National Identity," History Studies. *International Journal of History*, 1.1. 2009, 86.

24. Dov Waxman, "Islam and Turkish National Identity," *The Turkish Yearbook*, Vol. XXX, 2000, 9.

25. On the history of these parties, see Jacob M. Landau, *Radical Politics in Modern Turkey* (Leiden: E. J. Brill, 1974), 188–93. Also Turker Alkan, "The National Salvation Party," in eds.

Metin Heper and Raphael Israeli, *Islam and Politics in the Middle East* (London & Sidney: Croom Helm,1984), 79–102.

26. The present *Saadat* (Happiness) Party is the inheritor of Refah's legacy.

27. Fatih Yasli, "The Long Road that Led to the AKP's 'New Turkey,'" *The Turkey Analyst*, 28, 1. 14 January 2015, available at: http://turkeyanalyst.org/publications/turkey-analyst-articles/item/368-the-long-road-that-led-to-the-akp%E2%80%99s-E2%80%9Cnew-turkey%E80%9D.h.

28. Sedat Laciner "Turgut Özal Period in Turkish Foreign Policy: Özalism," The *Journal of Turkish Weekly*, 9 March 2009, at: http://www.turkishweekly.nrt/print.asp?type=2&id=333.

29. Nilüfer Göle, "Secularism and Islamism in Turkey: The Making of Elites and Counter-Elites," *The Middle East Journal*, 51. 1 (Winter 1997).

30. Yaşli, "The Long Road that Led to AKP's 'New Turkey.'"

31. See, for example Timur Muhidine, "Le Grand Debat en Turquie sur Islamisme et Laicité," *Le Monde Diplomatique*, October 1994.

32. Sami Zubeida, "Turkish Islam and National Identity," *Middle East Report*, April-June 1996.

33. On Atatürk's foreign policy, see William Hale, *Turkish Foreign Policy, 1774–2000* (London: Frank Cass, 2000), 44–109.

34. Turkey was also a member of the Baghdad Pact, later renamed the Central Treaty Organization following the Iraqi revolution of 1958. The alliance brought together Iran, Turkey, and Pakistan.

35. Ilya Prizel, *National Identity and Foreign Policy* (Cambridge: Cambridge University Press, 1998), 8.

36. Edward Mortimer, "A Tale of Two Funerals: Reviving Islam Challenges Atatürk's Legacy of Secularism," *Financial Times Surveys*, 7 May 1993.

37. Charles Krauthammer, "The Unipolar Moment," *Foreign Affairs*, America and the World Issue, 1990.

38. On the opening up of new opportunities for Turkey, see Sabri Sayari, "Turkish Foreign Policy in the Post-Cold War Era," *Journal of International Affairs*, 54. 1 (Fall 2002). Also Graham Fuller, *From Eastern Europe to Western China: The Growing Role of Turkey in World Affairs and its Implications for Western Interests*," Santa Monica, California: RAND, 1993.

39. Peter W. Rodman, "Middle East Diplomacy after the Gulf War," *Foreign Affairs* (Spring 1991), available at: https://www.foreignaffairs.com/articles/israel/1991-03-01/middle-east-diplomacy-after-gulf-war.

40. On Turkish-Israeli alliance, see Suha Bulakbashi, "Behind the Turkish-Israeli Alliance: A Turkish View," *Journal of Palestine Studies*, 29.1 (Autumn 1999). Also, Daniel Pipes, "A New Axis: The Emerging Turkish-Israeli Entente," *National Interest* (Winter 1997–1998), available at: http://www.danielpipes.org/293/a-new-axis-the-emerging-turkish-israeli-entente.

41. On the more activist Turkish foreign policy in the 1990s, see Alan Makowsky and Sabri Sayari, *Turkey's New World: Changing Dynamics of Turkish Foreign Policy*, Washington, D.C: Washington Institute for Near East Policy, 2000.

42. Sami Kohen, "Contacts with Central Asian States: A Foundation for Pan-Turkism," *The Washington Report on Middle East Affairs*, August/September 1992.

43. Laciner, "Turgut Özal Period in Turkish Foreign Policy: Özalism."

44. On Erbakan's foreign policy vision, see Alan Makowsky, "How to Deal with Erbakan," The *Middle East Quarterly*, 4. 1. March 1997. These ideas still remain influential. It was reported that Mustafa Kmalkak, leader of the Islamist party, *Saadat*, which is the last of the parties which traces its roots to parties established by Erbakan's under different names, during a trip to Morocco proposed the creation of an Islamic NATO and an Islamic peacekeeping force. "Turkish Party Saadat Proposes the Establishment of Islamic NATO" *STARTRISK*, 16 July 2012 at: http://www.startrisk.com/geostrat/6972.

45. See Shireen T. Hunter, "Bridge or Frontier: Turkey's Post-Cold War Geopolitical Posture," *International Spectator*, 34.1. 1999.

46. Terence Roth, "Turkey's Çiller Heightens Pleas for Closer Ties to EU," *International Herald Tribune*, 30 January 1995.

47. Sabri Sayari, "La Turquie et la Crise Yugoslave" (Turkey and the Yugoslav Crisis), *La Politique Étrangère*," 2. 1992, 314.
48. For more details, see Sylvie Gangloff, "The Impact of the Ottoman Legacy on Turkish Policy in the Balkans (1991–1999)," Paris, Centre Nationale De La Recherche Scientifique, November 2005, at: http://www.ceri-sciencepo.org.
49. On the 600th anniversary of this defeat, 28 June 1989, The Serbian president, Slobodan Milošević, staged a rally at Gazimestan that attracted more than 1,000,000 Serbs. See Gazimestan speech at https://en.wikipedia.org/wiki/Gazimestan_speech. Ironically, June 28th was the calendar date of the assassination of the Austro-Hungarian Archduke in Sarajevo in 1914, by a Bosnian Serb, Gavrilo Princip, thereby igniting World War I.
50. Gangloff, "The Impact of the Ottoman Legacy on Turkish Policy in the Balkans (1991–1999)."
51. Gangloff, "The Impact of the Ottoman Legacy."
52. Meliha Altunişik and Özlem Tür, *Turkey: Challenges of Continuity and Change* (London: Routledge, 2005), 128.
53. Gülnur Aybet, *Turkish Foreign Policy and Its Implications for the West* (London: Royal United Services Institute, 1994), 36. Also Alan Cowell, "Turkey Faces Moral Crisis Over Bosnia," *The New York Times*, 11 July 1992.
54. Sayari, "La Turquie et la Crise Yugoslave," 312.
55. Quoted in Mustafa Türkeş, "Turkish Foreign Policy toward the Balkans: Quest for Enduring Stability and Security," in ed. Edris Bal, *Turkish Foreign Policy in the Post-Cold War Era* (Boca Raton, FL: Brown Walker Press, 2004), 203.
56. Birgul Demirtaş-Coşkun, "Turkish Foreign Policy Toward the Bosnian War (1992–1995): A Constructivist Analysis," *Karadeniz Arastirnalari (Journal of Black Sea Research)* 28, (Winter), 6.
57. For details, see Gangloff, "The Impact of the Ottoman Legacy on Turkish Policy on the Balkans (1991–1999)."
58. For examples, see Gangloff, "Impact of the Ottoman Legacy."
59. Aybet, *Turkish Foreign Policy and Its Implications for the West*, 32.
60. Thanos Veremis, "Greek-Turkish Relations and the Balkans," *The South-Eastern European Yearbook*, Athens: *The Hellenic Foundation for Defence and Foreign Policy*, 1991, 240.
61. For examples of the Slavs' views of Turkey and its approach to the Balkans, see Zarco Petrovic and Dušan Areljić, "Turkish Interests and Involvement in the Western Balkans: A Score-Card," *Insight Turkey*, 13. 3. 2011, 168–70.
62. The number of these Bosnian-origin Turks is currently estimated at 4 million.
63. On the attitudes of Turkish citizens of Bosnian origin, see "The Weight of Islam in the Turkish Foreign Policy in the Balkans," *Turkish Review of Balkan Studies*, 2011.
64. They belong to the leftist political party *Iscilik* (Workers) Party.
65. Stephen F. Larrabee and Ian O. Lesser, *Turkish Foreign Policy in an Age of Uncertainty* (Santa Monica, CA: RAND, 2003), 35.
66. Gangloff, "The Weight of Islam."
67. Aybet, *Turkish Foreign Policy in an Age of Uncertainty*, 34.
68. Quoted in Bulut, "The Role of Religion in Turkish Reactions to Balkan Conflicts," 5.
69. Didem Ekinci, "The War in Bosnia-Herzegovina (1992–1995) and Turkish Parliamentary Debates," *Ulusrarasi Iliskiller*, 6.2 (Summer 2004), 56.
70. Ekinci, "The War in Bosnia-Herzegovina," 56.
71. Gangloff, "The Weight of Islam," 6.
72. Gangloff, "The Weight of Islam," 6.
73. Gangloff, "The Weight of Islam," 6.
74. Türkeş, "Turkish Foreign Policy toward the Balkans: Quest for Stability and Security," in *Turkish Foreign Policy in the Post-Cold War Era*, 203.
75. Türkeş, "Turkish Foreign Policy," 203.
76. Ekinci, "The War in Bosnia-Herzegovina," 40.
77. Ekinci, "The War in Bosnia-Herzegovina," 41.
78. Ekinci, "The War in Bosnia-Herzegovina," 42.

79. For Çetin's statement, see *Foreign Broadcasting Information Service (FBIS), Europe section-FBIS-WEU,* 12 January 1992.
80. Sayari, "La Turquie et La Crise Yugoslave," 310.
81. Demirtaş-Coşkun, "Turkish Foreign Policy toward the Bosnian War, 1992–95: A Constructivist Perspective," 6.
82. Duygu Bazoğlu Sezer, *Turkish Security in the Shifting Balkans* (New York: Columbia University Press, 1996), 102.
83. In general, during the early 1990s multilateralism was a major principle of Turkish foreign policy.
84. Muge Kinacioglu & Aylin G. Gürzel, "Turkey's Contribution to NATO's Role in Post-Cold War Security Governance: The Use of Force and Security Identity Formation," *Global Governance: A Review of Multilateralism and International Organizations,* 19. 4. October–December 2013, 598.
85. Based on interview with Turkish journalist.
86. Demirtaş-Coşkun, "Turkish Foreign Policy," 11.
87. Demirtaş-Coşkun, "Turkish Foreign Policy." 12.
88. Demirtaş-Coşkun, "Turkish Foreign Policy." 8.
89. On Çiller's visit, see "Islamic Leaders Visit Sarajevo to Support Bosnian Government," *New York Times,* 3 February 1993.
90. Ekinci, "The War in Bosnia-Herzegovina," 42.
91. See Barçin Yinanç, *Milliyet,* 30 July 1994, 17.
92. Demirtaş-Coşkun, "Turkish Foreign Policy."
93. For the text of the interview, see http://www.haber5.com/siviltoplum/bosnadan-basladik-120-ulkeye-ulastik. The organization currently is active in 120 countries.
94. Interview available at: http://dunyabizim.com/index.php?aType=haber&ArticleID= 685%3Dbosna%3Dsavasi.
95. Şerif Turgut interview, at: http://www.on5yirmi5.com/haber/guncel/olaylar/86297/serif-turgut-bosnaninin-hunzu-ve-buyusu.html.

Chapter Five

European Policy toward Turkish Membership in the EU

As of the summer of 2016, Turkey had failed in its quest to join the European Union. A large body of scholars, analysts, and observers of international affairs attribute Turkey's failure to join the EU to deep religious and cultural differences between the still largely religious Turkey and the predominantly secular EU member states. The Turks certainly subscribe to this view and have characterized the European Union as a "Christian Club." These scholars also cite the Turkish case as a good example of how religion affects decisions of international actors. Yet how correct is this judgment? Can religious differences alone explain the EU's refusal so far to admit Turkey? Have religious differences been the principal barrier to Turkey's accession to the EU, or have other factors been equally if not more important?

TURKEY'S LONG QUEST TO JOIN EUROPE

Turkey's efforts to join Europe began long before November 1, 1993, when the European Economic Community (EEC) and later the European Community (EC) were transformed into the European Union (EU). In the course of its long quest to join European institutions, Turkey has succeeded in establishing closer economic and other relations with them. In 1963, Turkey signed an Association Agreement with the EEC and later in 1995 a customs union with the EU.[1] In 1999, when the European Union at the Helsinki Summit of its Council accorded Turkey the status of a candidate country, it appeared that the goal of becoming a full EU member was finally within Turkey's reach. The EU's recognition of Turkey as a candidate country was a major achievement. Yet a still long and arduous road lay ahead of Turkey:

notably, when the EU Council granted Turkey the status of candidate country, it did not set a date for the start of accession talks. It only stated that Turkey needed to do more to comply with the EU's economic and political criteria, known as the *Acquis Communautaire*, before accession talks could begin.[2]

In February 2001, the EU formally adopted an "Accession Partnership with Turkey," spelling out the priorities that Turkey needed to address as part of the process of adopting and implementing EU standards and legislation. Despite Turkey's hopes for a firm date to commence negotiations, the EU left the date undecided (possibly because of the reservations of some members and as a way to maintain a degree of flexibility). Finally, in December 2002, at its meeting in Copenhagen, the European Council stated: "The EU would open negotiations with Turkey without delay, if the European Council on December 2004, on the basis of a report and a recommendation from the Commission, decides that Turkey fulfills the Copenhagen political criteria."[3] The Commission recommended that accession talks begin, and subsequently, the Council ratified the recommendation. The Council noted that Turkey had made sufficient progress in its legislative processes, economic stability, and judicial reform, as well as in meeting the EU criteria. This progress the Council declared justified the start of accession talks.

In October 2005, the EU Council agreed on a "Negotiating Framework" with Turkey. But the language indicated that the negotiating process was open-ended and that there was no guarantee that at the end Turkey would be admitted to the EU.[4] The accession talks eventually began in 2006 but almost immediately hit snags; for almost seven years they remained effectively, although not officially, frozen.[5] Principal culprits were Turkey's and the EU's diverging positions on Cyprus, plus unresolved issues in Greek-Turkish relations. In 2013, the talks eventually resumed in a relatively more sustained fashion, when Turkey tried to reinvigorate them through a number of steps, including the establishment of a new ministry to handle EU affairs.[6] Progress on Turkish accession talks has remained slow, however, and many barriers remain to Turkey's full admission to the EU.[7]

The slow rate of progress has raised doubts whether Turkey will ever become a full EU member. In particular, Turkey has come to believe that conditions placed on its membership have not been, as the Europeans have claimed, designed to encourage reforms, but to undermine its resolve to seek full membership and to settle for something less.[8] Regardless, it is generally agreed that a number of influential EU members, including Germany, France, and Austria, prefer a special kind of affiliation for Turkey short of full membership. In fact, the former French president, Nicolas Sarkozy, and the German federal chancellor, Angela Merkel, have openly expressed their opposition to Turkey's full EU membership. Thus far, however, Turkey has adamantly refused to accept any form of association short of full membership. Some long-time observers of Turkish affairs and its relations with the EU attribute Turkish insistence on full membership to "excessive national pride."[9]

This European tactic has succeeded in changing the attitude of the Turkish public. According to a poll conducted by the University of Bosphorus in 2012, while 73 percent of Turks favored EU membership in 2003, only 41 percent did so in 2012.[10] Even some Turkish officials have raised doubts about their country's eventual membership in the EU. Thus in 2014, the Turkish minister of European affairs and its chief negotiator with the EU, Egemen Bagis, confessed that "Turkey probably will never be an EU member."[11] Consequently, according to some accounts, Turkey has explored other options beyond the EU. For example, it was reported that President Recep Tayyip Erdoğan had told Russia's president, Vladimir Putin, that if Turkey were invited to join the Shanghai Cooperation Organization (SCO), it would no longer wait in the EU's admission room.[12]

The EU's delaying tactics have not been the only reasons for diminished Turkish desire to join the EU. Other factors have included Turkey's economic advances, the perception of the availability of other options to EU membership (such as new opportunities in the Middle East and Asia), plus the Turks' perception that the EU was facing many economic and political problems and could even unravel. These factors were largely responsible for the decline in the percentage of Turks favoring EU membership in 2012.[13] Equally important have been shifts in the ideational and civilizational foundations of Turkish foreign policy under the Justice and Development Party (AKP). As discussed in chapter 4, Turkey's shift away from a West-centered identity and foreign policy began in the late 1980s. By the 1990s, Islam had become a more prominent part of Turkish national identity, and Turkish foreign policy had become more multi-dimensional. This shift became more pronounced under the AKP's rule.

These shifts changed Turkey's vision of its foreign policy away from traditionally Western-centeredness to one that sees Turkey as a multi-regional actor and emphasizes the Islamic world as a natural area for a greater Turkish role. This vision also stresses Turkey's historical role in Islam's expansion, an emphasis partly reflecting the AKP's Islamic roots and the Islamic piety of its leaders, notably Recep Tayyip Erdoğan. It also reflects the AKP's neo-Ottomanist thinking.[14]

In this new vision of Turkey's role and place in the world, EU membership becomes only one of Turkey's foreign policy objectives.[15] Certain political developments in Europe, especially the rise in overall anti-EU sentiment among European populations, as reflected in demands in Britain that the country leave the Union (Brexit),[16] the rise of the right-wing political parties (which are among the most virulent opponents of Turkey's admission), the feeling of an overall expansion fatigue in the EU, and the election in 2014 of a new president of the European Commission who believes in a halt to the EU expansion have added to Turkish disenchantment with the accession process.

However, Turkey has not abandoned its quest for EU membership, and getting admitted to the EU is still a major Turkish foreign policy goal. There are significant economic reasons. Close to 80 percent of Foreign Direct Investment (FDI) in Turkey originates in EU countries and close to 90 percent of technology transfers to Turkey are also from Europe.[17] Most of Turkey's trade is with Europe, especially its exports. According to TurkStat, the EU's twenty-eight member countries account for 43 percent of Turkey's exports.

Moreover, between 2011 and 2016 Turkey suffered setbacks in its efforts to become a dominant player in the Middle East, including the fall of the Turkish-supported president of Egypt, Muhammad Morsi, who belonged to the Muslim Brotherhood; the Syrian governments' and Bashar Al Assad's unexpected show of resiliency and hence the thwarting of Turkey's goal of rapidly removing him; and the general turmoil in the Middle East. These setbacks enhanced the EU's importance for Turkey and rekindled its desire to join. This may be why in 2013 Turkey sought to revitalize talks with the EU.[18] The impact of these developments was also reflected in the Turkish public's view of the EU. Thus in 2014, the percentage of Turks favoring EU

Table 5.1. Total Goods: EU Trade Flows and Balance with Turkey, 2005–2015

Year	Imports Value Mil. €	Imports % Growth	Imports % Extra-EU	Exports Value Mil. €	Exports % Growth	Exports % Extra-EU	Ex-Im Value Mil. €	Total Value Mil. €
2005	36,230	–	3.1	44,620	–	4.3	8,390	80,850
2006	41,927	15.7	3.1	50,018	12.1	4.3	8,091	91,945
2007	47,378	13.0	3.3	52,830	5.6	4.3	5,451	100,208
2008	46,288	–2.3	2.9	54,476	3.1	4.2	8,188	100,764
2009	36,446	–21.3	3.0	44,486	–18.3	4.1	8,040	80,932
2010	43,062	18.2	2.8	61,831	39.0	4.6	18,769	104,894
2011	48,820	13.4	2.8	73,275	18.5	4.7	24,455	122,096
2012	48,822	0.0	2.7	75,410	2.9	4.5	56,587	124,232
2013	50,654	3.8	3.0	77,683	3.0	4.5	27,029	128,337
2014	54,395	7.4	3.2	74,725	–3.8	4.4	20,329	129,120
2015	61,607	13.3	3.6	79,107	5.9	4.4	17,499	140,714

% Growth: relative variation between current and previous period.

% Extra-EU: imports/exports as % of all EU partners—i.e. excluding Member State trade.

Source: Eurostat Comext—Statistical regime 4.

membership rose to 45 percent, registering a ten-percentage-point increase over 2013 figures.[19]

For its part, the EU has tried to keep the talks with Turkey alive. In 2012 it adopted a "Positive Agenda."[20] The EU Commissioner for expansion, Stefan Fule, stated that the Commission had no intention of giving up on Turkey's EU accession.[21]

In view of the long and tortuous history of Turkey's attempts to join Europe, questions have been raised about the real reasons behind the EU's refusal to admit it. These questions became more pressing after the several waves of expansion of the EC and the EU. Some of the new members such as Spain, Portugal, and Greece at the time of their accession did not meet the declared European political and economic standards. All three countries had just emerged from dictatorships and their democratic institutions were still fragile. They were also economically inferior to other EC members, which made their integration financially costly. The same was true of the EU's post-Soviet expansion and the admission of economically weak and politically and democratically underdeveloped countries, such as Bulgaria and Romania. Moreover, if the process of the EU's expansion were to resume, in all likelihood several Balkan countries, like Serbia, Montenegro, and even Kosovo and Albania, might be admitted to the EU before Turkey. Because of this history of EC/EU expansion, some observers have questioned the significance of economic and political arguments against Turkey's admission and have attributed the EU's rejection of Turkey to religious and cultural factors.

REASONS FOR THE EU'S REJECTION OF TURKEY

Because of the sheer length of time that has elapsed since Turkey first attempted to join Europe, many changes have occurred in Turkey, Europe, and internationally. These changes have affected the dynamics of EU-Turkey relations and shifted the relative weight of different arguments in favor or against Turkey's admission. Consequently, analysis of the real causes of the EU's refusal to admit Turkey should be done in a dynamic fashion.

Some of the changes which have occurred in the course of Turkey's drive for membership in Europe, such as its economic progress, success in enforcing political and judiciary reforms, and improving its human rights conditions and bringing them closer to the EU standards have at least in theory increased its chances of admission to the EU. These changes have reduced the significance of economic and political barriers to its membership, although not completely eliminating them. By contrast, some changes taking place in Turkey have exacerbated religio-cultural differences between it and the EU and negatively impacted Turkey's admission chances. They have notably included Islam's rising social and political profile in Turkey. Ironically, most of these changes have occurred because of Turkey's political and human rights reforms, largely undertaken in response to EU prodding. In Europe, meanwhile, the increased number of its Muslim population has enhanced Islam's socio-political profile, often leading to increased tensions between Muslim immigrants and the indigenous populations. At times, these tensions have resulted in violent, including terrorist, acts. The radicalization of a portion of second- and third-generation Muslim youths in Europe has also contributed to the further exacerbation of these tensions and has increased risks of violence and terrorism. These developments have intensified cultural and religious arguments against Turkey's membership.

During this long period, the dynamics of EU-Turkey talks and internal developments in Turkey, in the EU, and in Europe have been affected by international developments, particularly the Persian Gulf War of 1991, the fall of the USSR in December 1991, and the U.S. invasions of Afghanistan and Iraq in 2001 and 2003, respectively. In more recent years, the Arab Spring and its ramifications, including the civil wars in Syria and Iraq, have deeply affected the dynamics of Turkey-EU relations. A sharp and sudden increase in the influx of refugees to Europe in the fall of 2015 from Syria and some other countries, such as Iraq and Afghanistan, had a contradictory impact on Turkey's chances of eventual EU membership. On the one hand, the influx exacerbated fears in many European countries about a potentially excessive rise in their Muslim populations and thus further undermined their receptivity to Turkey's eventual membership. On the other hand, some European countries, notably Germany, said that they would be willing to make a number of concessions to Turkey and offered $2.2 billion in financial aid provided that it agreed to host a larger number of Syrian and other refugees headed to Europe or at least to halt refugee flows to Europe. Turkey reacted negatively to these suggestions.[22] Its president, Recep Tayyip Erdoğan, said that Turkey will not accept any offer short of complete acceptance by the EU.[23] In March 2016, however, the EU increased the amount of its financial aid to $6.6 billion.[24] It also indicated that the process of negotiations with Turkey would be accelerated. There were also talks of allowing Turkish citizens to travel to EU countries visa free.

There were strongly negative reactions to the suggestion of accelerating the process of Turkey's EU membership from the European Parliament. France's former president, Nicolas Sarkozy, said in an interview with the Russian television network *Russia Today* that "anyone who says that Turkey is a European country wants EU's death."[25] In the future, too, similar changes in the internal dynamics of EU member states and Turkey and in the pattern of regional and international relations will impact Turkey's prospects of EU membership and, at least as pertinent, Turkey's desire to join the Union.

Many reasons are cited for Turkey's exclusion from Europe. Some are related to very specific issues, such as reforming the economy and political and judicial systems and improving human rights standards. In theory, these could be easily overcome. Problems such as the Cyprus issue and some disputes in Greek-Turkish relations also could be resolved if there were enough will on both sides. But other reasons related to Turkey's geography, demography, history, and—above all—religion and culture (or in other words identity-related issues) are more difficult to overcome.

Political Issues: The Cyprus Problem

The long-standing dispute over Cyprus[26] and the status of the Turkish part of the island has been a major obstacle to Turkish EU membership. In theory, provided the willingness of the parties involved—Turkey, Greece, and the Greek and Turkish Cypriots—this obstacle could be overcome. In reality, however, a number of factors have made resolving the dispute extremely difficult (at least at time of writing). These include the history of the island, especially the Turkish military intervention of 1974; the ensuing change in the ethnic balance of the island; the creation of a Turkish republic in the north; the symbolic importance of the Cyprus issue in Turkish politics and the nationalist passions it raises; and the bitter history of Greek-Turkish relations. Meanwhile, at least two EU principles have kept the Cyprus issue as a barrier to Turkish admission:

1. *All EU member countries should recognize one another.* However, since the Greek Cypriots refused a unification plan negotiated by the United Nations in 2004, followed by a referendum, Turkey has refused to deal with the Greek Cypriots and has refused to honor in Cyprus' case the obligations undertaken under its customs union with the EU. For example, after Cyprus became an EU member in May 2004, Turkey refused to recognize it and to open Turkish ports to Cyprus, although it is obligated to do so under its EU Customs Union provisions. This refusal nearly doomed Turkey's EU admission negotiations before they had even started. In June 2006, the EU presidency warned Turkey that "its failure to implement its obligations fully will have an impact on the negotiations process."[27] This warning was followed by another by the EU enlargement commissioner, Ollie Rehn. He said that if Turkey did not implement its obligations under the Accession Agreement and the Additional Protocol, a "train crash" would be coming, implying that the entire process could collapse.[28] A train crash was avoided, but the Cyprus issue has remained a stumbling block to Turkey's membership.[29]

2. *EU members should not have any territorial disputes.* Turkey has refused to recognize Cyprus, and the Greek Cypriots declined the 2004 reunification plan. This situation in effect has involved Turkey in a territorial dispute with Cyprus, which is against EU rules. Thus the Cyprus problem has slowed progress on Turkish EU accession talks.[30] Since joining the European Union in 2004, the Republic of Cyprus has blocked many aspects of the EU-Turkey negotiations and has prevented even the opening of various chapters on economic, judicial, and other issues, which must be negotiated and resolved if Turkey is to join the EU.[31] Turkey has remained adamant, however, that as long as the status of the Turkish part of Cyprus is not clarified, it will not recognize the (Greek) Republic. In general, Turkey believes that the question of Cyprus is being used as another excuse to deny Turkey EU membership. It maintains that if there were a real desire to include Turkey in the EU, the Cyprus problem could have been resolved or at any rate the Republic of Cyprus could have been prevented from blocking or delaying the negotiating process. This mindset is reflected in a statement by a member of the Turkish parliament, Volkan Bozkir, that most obstacles to Turkish membership, including the issue of Cyprus, are politically motivated.[32] Regardless of whether the Cyprus dispute is a real obstacle or a political excuse, so long as it is not resolved (which is still true at the time of writing), it will prevent Turkish admission to the EU.

Greek-Turkish Territorial Disputes

Some unresolved disputes between Turkey and Greece regarding the delimitation of their continental shelf constitute another barrier in the path of Turkey's EU admission. These disputes became quite serious in 1995, when the Turkish parliament declared that Greece's extension of its territorial waters would be viewed as a *casus belli*. Tensions again rose in 2007 when, in response to Cyprus's launching of oil and gas exploration in the Eastern Mediterranean, Turkey launched its own plans.[33] The Turkish plans included part of the continental shelf off the Greek island of Castellorizo. In response, the EU Council reiterated its serious concern, and urged Turkey to abstain from making threats or taking any actions directed against a member state which could harm good-neighbor relations and peaceful settlement of disputes.[34]

Domestic Politics and Human Rights

Another barrier to Turkey's admission has been the state of Turkey's domestic politics and its human rights record. Until the Justice and Development

Party (AKP) came to power in 2003, the Turkish military's excessive role in the country's politics and the lack of adequate civilian control over the military was a key problem. Historically, the Turkish military has been prone to interfere in politics through coups d'état, either openly or by indirect pressure, as in 1997 against the Islamist prime minister, Necmettin Erbakan. Since coming to power, however, the AKP-dominated governments have drastically curtailed the military's role in politics. The reduction in the military's sway on Turkish politics and the AKP government's determination to impose civilian control on the military was reflected in its trial in 2013 of a former army chief involved in a 1997 coup attempt against the Erbakan government.[35] This development certainly was in line with the EU requirements, but it is still not clear to what extent the principle of civilian control over the military is an established fact in Turkey or whether the possibility of another military coup d'état still exists. However, those who favor Turkey's admission to the EU argue that EU membership would inoculate Turkey against such developments, as it has done in countries like Spain, Portugal, and Greece, which also have had histories of military coups and military rule.

The EU has also been concerned about the underdeveloped state of Turkish democracy, including the relative weakness of political parties and the excessive role of personalities in Turkish politics (itself partly the consequence of frequent military interventions and periodic banning of political parties). At a time when European democracies are being tested by the rise of extreme left- and right-wing political parties, the inclusion of another fragile democracy in the EU would be highly problematic.

Trends in Turkish politics since 2013 and up until the completion of this work have increased the EU's concerns that Turkey might return to the unstable politics of the 1970s, 1980s, and 1990s. These trends include President Recep Tayyip Erdoğan's desire to change the Turkish Constitution which would enable him to achieve his goal of turning Turkey's government into a presidential system from the current parliamentary form. This change would give the president much more extensive powers. Rifts also developed within the AKP, including Abdullah Gül, a cofounder of the AKP and Turkey's prime minister and later president, and President Erdoğan. The latter's display of authoritarian tendencies has also raised the specter of a potential rise of presidential dictatorship in Turkey.[36] Particularly disturbing was the 2013 dismissal of several hundred police officers over a corruption scandal case allegedly involving Erdoğan's son.[37] Tensions also developed between Erdoğan and the Turkish judiciary,[38] triggering a response from the European Commission. In an October 2014 statement, the Commission said that "the response of the government following allegations of corruption in December 2013 has given rise to serious concerns regarding the independence of the judiciary and the proper separation of executive and judicial powers."[39]

A further problem was the rivalry which developed between Erdoğan and the leader of an Islamist group, Fethullah Gülen. The movement and Gülen first supported Erdoğan and greatly contributed to the AKP's rise to power, but later they moved away from him.[40] By mid-2016, Erdoğan appeared the winner in this power struggle. However, this crisis also confirmed that corruption, even at high governmental levels, which is a main EU concern, still remains a big problem in Turkey.

The inconclusive results of Turkey's parliamentary election on 7 June 2015, further added to its political uncertainties. The AKP failed to garner sufficient votes to form a government on its own. It failed to form a coalition, and it called for early elections, which were held in November 2015 and produced an AKP victory. The election campaign was particularly intense and Erdoğan resorted to Islam and the Quran to undermine his rivals.

None of these developments were reassuring to the EU. By mid-2016, Turkish politics seemed to be poised between a growing threat of dictatorship or another period of volatility.[41] The resignation of Turkey's prime minister, Ahmet Davutoğlu, on 5 May 2016, further confirmed the volatility of Turkish politics. Anxieties over the future direction of Turkish politics reached a high level when a group of officers staged a coup on 15–16 July 2016. The coup plotters failed in their attempt and the government embarked on a large-scale purge of the military and judiciary. Erdoğan accused Gülen and his supporters within the Turkish military and judiciary for orchestrating the coup. However, there was no firm evidence to support this accusation.[42] The failed coup attempt demonstrated that European concerns over still unstable Turkish politics and the fact that they have fallen short of European standards are real and cannot be dismissed as mere excuses hiding other, especially religious and cultural, motives to deny Turkey admission to the EU. These problems, in turn, reflect the still-unfinished project of Turkey's modernization and democratization.

Turkey's human rights record, including its treatment of its ethnic minorities, especially the Kurds, as well as issues related to gender rights and to broader civil society, has constituted another obstacle to EU membership. Some observers have also noted that despite the secular character of the Turkish state, there are limitations on religious freedoms for non-Muslims, notably Christians.[43] Turkey's own Alevis also complain of unequal treatment by the government.[44] In this context, the raising of the issue of the Armenian Genocide by Pope Francis on the event's hundredth anniversary and Turkey's angry response highlighted the still-considerable gap between the EU states and Turkey on these issues.[45] The German Parliament's passing of a resolution on 2 June 2016 recognizing the 1915 Armenian genocide aggravated tensions between Turkey and the EU over the issue of minority rights.

For most of the 2000s, it seemed that Turkey was making progress in bringing its human rights record close to EU standards. For example, the AKP government tried to reach an accord with the PKK (*Partiye Karkeran Kurdistan*), which has been involved in a war with the government for over two decades.[46] However, the Syrian Civil War and Turkey's siding with opponents of the Assad government has led to a sharp deterioration of Turkey's relations with its Kurdish minority, leading to military confrontations. It has raised the specter of a return to the situation of the 1980s when the Government-Kurdish war raged.

Between 2013 and 2016 under the premiership and later the presidency of Recep Tayyip Erdoğan, Turkey has slipped in other areas of human rights. Growing restrictions have been imposed on journalists and electronic media and in general Erdoğan has displayed dictatorial behavior.[47] The restrictions imposed on journalists and the large number of jailed journalists, plus the government's attempt to control the Internet, has worried the EU Commission and led it to express its concerns in its above-noted statement. The Commission noted that these actions "reflected a restrictive approach to freedom of expression."[48] A more detailed assessment of Turkey's human rights record was provided in the EU Commission's October 2014 Turkey Progress Report. The human rights conditions worsened in 2016 as illustrated by the closing down of the *Zaman* newspaper in March.[49] European countries and the EU officials reacted very negatively, noting that this Turkish action at a time when the EU wants to start a new dialogue with Turkey was not very constructive.[50]

Yet some commentators have attributed the inadequate progress and even regression of Turkey's human rights reforms to the slow pace of accession negotiations and the ever-receding horizon of EU membership. According to this perspective, the AKP felt that EU membership was a distant and perhaps unreachable goal and therefore decided to slow the pace of reforms. Instead, freed from concern over the EU's reaction, it "adopted Turkey's authoritarian political culture and engaged in illiberal practices of its own."[51] Some Turkish scholars also share this perspective. According to one study, "with a decline in the EU's credibility as an anchor and viable target, [we] are able to see a reversal of political reform process correlating with the decreased probability of accession."[52] Others, however, see Turkish backsliding on reforms as evidence of the deep cultural differences between Europe and Turkey and the latter's still-immature democracy. Another viewpoint is that there were always segments of Turkish political and military elites which did not like the idea of Turkey's joining Europe. It was only the liberal elites which, in order to consolidate democratic practices, favored Turkish membership in Europe.[53]

Regardless, issues related to Turkey's political system and culture and the state of human rights remain serious barriers to its EU admission and are not merely excuses used to deny it accession. According to some scholars, issues of human rights, especially the question of minority rights, became more important for the EU after the admission of the Central and East European countries. The EU has rightly judged that unresolved minority issues could endanger peace and stability within the EU member states.[54] Moreover, the human rights discourse has become the cornerstone of the EU's value system and an important constituent of its emerging identity. Still, it could be argued that if other overwhelming reasons existed for accepting Turkey, the EU might be more indulgent regarding Turkey's violations of human rights. This is evidenced by Chancellor Angela Merkel's offer of speeding the process of Turkish membership if it halted the flow of refugees to Europe at a time of increased human rights restrictions in Turkey.[55]

Economic Barriers

Broadly speaking, economic barriers to Turkey's EU accession fall into two categories: 1) the state of Turkey's economy compared to other EU members; and 2) the economic impact of Turkey's admission on other EU member states.

When Turkey first applied for membership in the European Community, the gap between its economy and the living standards of its people and those of other EC members was large. This gap meant that bringing Turkey's economic conditions close to other EC countries would be costly. After having spent considerable sums to revitalize the economies of new members such as Spain, Portugal, Ireland, and Greece, EC members were not willing to take on another costly case. This reluctance became stronger after EC became EU and in the 2000s admitted several Central and East European countries at great financial cost to other member states.

In the last two decades, Turkey has made considerable economic progress. Therefore, the significance of barriers to its admission has diminished. Today, Turkey's economic conditions are better than some EU members, such as Bulgaria and Romania, although in terms of per capita GDP and PPP, it still lags behind most EU members.

Many observers still see structural weaknesses in the Turkish economy. For example, some have pointed out that a large part of Turkey's economic growth resulted from a construction boom, which could easily stall, and they see the overdependence of Turkish economic growth on the construction sector as a cause of concern. They also believe that, despite progress made toward creation of a functioning market economy capable of competing within the EU, compared to other EU members Turkey's market economy remains insufficiently developed. The overdependence of the Turkish economic growth on foreign investment because of its low savings rate is also cause for concern. A sharp drop in the level of foreign investment as a result of

Table 5.2. GDP Per Capita in Selected EU Countries, the EU, and Turkey (Thousands of Euros)

Country	2002	2012
Turkey	4,000	8,225
EU	20,700	25,549
Germany	26,000	32,406
Italy	23,300	26,136
Spain	18,600	23,039
Greece	15,600	18,024
Poland	5,000	9,600
Bulgaria	2,400	5,403
Romania	2,415	6,436

Source: Kemal Dervis, "Turkey and Europe, a New Perspective," Policy Brief 3, Global Turkey in Europe, November 2012.

political or other problems could slow Turkey's economic growth or even stall it. Others have also pointed out that the rate of Turkey's real unemployment and underemployment is much higher than stated in official statistics, reflecting a basic weakness in Turkey's economy.[56]

Nevertheless, because of Turkey's economic advances, economic arguments against its EU membership have lost some of their force, while still remaining valid. Turkish economic development is still fragile and its economy susceptible to shocks.[57] In 2014, the rate of Turkey's economic growth fell sharply to only 2.4 percent.[58] It recovered somewhat in 2015 and was at 3.5 percent. However, in 2015, Russian-Turkish relations seriously deteriorated following Turkey's downing of a Russian airplane over Syria and the killing of its pilot. This incident prompted Russia to ban travel by its citizens to Turkey for tourism and halting the import of Turkish goods. Both these measures negatively impacted Turkey's economy. By the summer of 2016, Turkish-Russian relations were on the mend. However, these kinds of incidents, plus the resumption of military actions against the Kurds and the occurrence of several terrorist attacks in major Turkish cities clouded Turkey's future. There were warning signs that Turkey could potentially face greater political instability. Inevitably, such political instability would negatively impact Turkey's economic prospects.

Concerns over the impact of Turkish membership on the economic prospects of existing EU members are still valid. In particular, those members that rely heavily on agriculture or produce the same goods in which Turkey has a comparative advantage are anxious about economic repercussions of Turkey's admission. These concerns are at times balanced by other perceived or actual benefits of Turkey's membership, as in the security realm.[59] In short, as with political considerations, Europe's worries about the economic impact of Turkey's admission are real and not mere excuses to keep it out.[60]

Those in favor of Turkey's membership, by contrast, argue that, with its big market, Turkey could stimulate economic growth in the EU. They also believe that membership in the EU would accelerate Turkish economic reforms as the signing of the Customs Union did in 1997.[61]

More Intractable Obstacles: Geography

A main issue in the debate over Turkey's admission is whether it can geographically be considered to be part of Europe. A segment of Turkey's territory is located in Europe, which gives it a certain claim to being a European country. This aspect of Turkey's geography might also explain why the European Communities did not reject out of hand its application for admission as it did for Morocco. However, the European part of Turkey constitutes only a small portion of its territory (3 percent), and most of its land mass is located in Asia. As put by one scholar, this makes Turkey "an Asian peninsula with a European appendage."[62] At best, Turkey is a Eurasian country with a preponderant Asian dimension. This aspect of Turkey's geography poses dilemmas for many EU members, especially because, despite considerable progress, the Asian part of Turkey is still economically less developed and culturally more religious and conservative. This ambivalent position is reflected in the comment by former French president Valéry Giscard d'Estaing that Turkey is not only Istanbul.

Turkey's geography is a physical fact that cannot be altered. Yet some scholars have pointed out that, unlike other continents such as Africa and Asia, Europe's boundaries have never been clearly demarcated. They maintain that Europe was first a mythological construct and was only later defined in geographical terms. Moreover, in its mythological version Europe was the outcome of an encounter between Greece, symbolized by Zeus, and a Phoenician princess, hence Europe's partly Asian origins.[63] They also note that the notion of Europe and its borders has evolved over many centuries and that, initially during the time of the ancient Greeks, Europe meant first Athens and Sparta and then the entire mainland Greece, thus implying that its borders can again expand by embracing Turkey.[64] Some go further and argue that neither the Greeks nor the Romans had a clear notion of Europe and it was only after Europe's Christianization that the territorial confines of Christendom came to be known as Europe. Even then, only the Western part of Christendom qualified as Europe, and Byzantium and the Eastern Christian world were excluded. In short, the concept of Europe was coextensive with Western Christendom.[65] They also note that, even in more recent history, Greece and some Balkan countries were not seen as belonging to Europe. But today Greece and several Balkan countries are EU members and others may join it in the future. In other words, as put by the Turkish scholar, Kemal Kirişci, historically Europe's borders have been subject to negotiation.[66]

Regardless, the reality is that the question of where EU's borders are and whether they completely correspond to those of Europe is still debated. At the moment, some European countries, notably Norway and Switzerland, are not EU members but they are clearly part of Europe, and so are those Balkan states that have not yet joined the EU. Then there is the question of Europe's natural borders. For example, are the Urals and the Mediterranean Europe's natural borders or does Europe end where Russia begins?[67] Other commentators, meanwhile, point out that the Ottoman Empire was part of the European state system. The very appellation of the Ottoman Empire as "the sick man of Europe" indicates its inclusion in the continent. Moreover, in the nineteenth century the Ottoman Empire was admitted to the European Council, partly as compensation for joining Britain in the Crimean War, a fact which attests to Turkey's inclusion in the concept of Europe.[68]

Nevertheless, the inescapable fact is that in thinking of, or as some scholars have put it, "imagining," Europe, Turkey has had no part in the constitution of this imagined Europe.[69] At best, Turkey has been what some have described as a "liminal" country much like Russia, meaning that Turkey both is and is not part of Europe. The concept of liminality also applies to other aspects of Turkey's relation to Europe, including politically, economically, and culturally. In all these respects, Turkey possesses some elements of Europeanism while lacking others.[70]

The question of the EU's geographical boundaries and hence whether Turkey can be included within it is also related to the perception of what EU is or should be. If the EU is viewed as representing Europe or, in other words, the EU is synonymous with Europe, then its boundaries should correspond to those of "Europe." The need to define the borders of Europe and hence the EU was expressed by one MEP in the following terms: "we have to say Europe stops here. . . . We have to answer the question, where does Europe end?"[71] He then added that "the boundary is not Islam. I think Albania, Bosnia can be integrated. . . . Turkey could be integrated but I am very skeptical whether this will happen." Another MEP noted that "if I say Bulgaria, Warsaw, Prague, they are Europe. . . . It is not a religious definition. . . . We also have Muslim states like Bosnia, it is clearly Europe in a geographical sense."[72] However, if the EU is defined more as a "project," whether in economic or value terms, then its geographical boundaries do not necessarily need to correspond to those of Europe.

Determining the boundaries of the EU would also depend on what kind of community is envisaged. This point was made clear by former French prime minister Michel Rocard. He said: "Necessity for boundary depends on the type of Europe you have and you wish. If the initial project of a federation with strong power at the top, if that had been realized boundaries would be absolutely necessary. . . . Some of the present members of the EU would not have been accepted . . . the six founding members had that in mind. That project is killed now."[73]

Others, especially those who see Europe more as a project, believe that the EU should not be defined in geographical terms, but rather on the basis of values and civilizational factors. They argue that if countries accept European values and civilization and adjust their behavior to them, or in other words Europeanize, then they can become members. But this approach, too, raises other questions about Turkey's inclusion, namely whether Turkey is part of Europe civilizationally and hence should be included in the EU, or whether Turkey even *wants* to Europeanize.

However, even if a more value-based notion of Europe and the EU and a looser association is envisaged, geography would still matter and some boundaries for the EU would have to be established. Otherwise, why not include all countries which commit themselves to adhere to European values in European institutions regardless of where they are located? This question becomes more relevant in the case of non-European countries such as those of the Maghreb, which are located in Europe's proximity and also have strategic significance for it, as does Turkey. Some of the arguments in favor of bringing Turkey in as a way of improving its economy, consolidating democratization, and preventing radicalization could also apply to them. Similarly, if Turkey is entitled to join Europe, why not the South Caucasian countries, two of which—Armenia and Georgia—are also Christian?[74] Or is Turkey to be Europe's last frontier? Turkey's geography poses other problems deriving from its proximity to the Middle East and the Caucasus with all that this implies in terms of actual and potential instability and conflict. Turkey's inclusion potentially could mean a far greater involvement of European countries in these local disputes and conflicts.[75]

Turkey's size is also of concern to some EU members, especially the smaller ones. Turkey would be the second largest member of the EU after Germany. This perspective worries some member states. In short, Turkey's geography poses questions for the EU, its outer limits, and ultimately its very nature that cannot be easily dismissed.

Turkey's large population is also a problematic issue. At 79,622,026 in 2015, Turkey's population is larger than those of all EU members except Germany, and because of Turkey's higher birthrate compared to the EU member states, in the following decades Turkey's population will exceed even the Federal Republic.

Many Europeans feel that the inclusion of such a populous country would disrupt the balance in Europe and in the European institutions, especially with regard to voting both in the European Parliament and in the European Commission. Because each member's voting rights depend on the size of its

Table 5.3. Population Trends in Turkey, Selected EU Members & EU (thousands)

Country	2003	2015	2025	2050
Turkey	71,325	82,150	88,995	97,759
Germany	82,467	82,497	81,959	79,145
France	60,144	62,481	64,165	64,230
UK	59,251	61,275	63,287	66,166
Italy	57,423	55,507	52,939	44,875
Spain	41,060	41,167	40,390	37,337
Romania	22,330	21,649	20,806	18,063
Netherlands	16,149	16,791	17,231	16,954
EU 28	454,187	456,876	454,422	431,241
EU 28 with Turkey	555,734	567,482	570,832	552,318
Turkey as % of EU 28	12%	14.4%	15.5%	17.7%

Source: European Commission Report, 2004.

population, this demographic imbalance, in turn, would limit the ability of the currently largest and most populous EU members to decide the direction of its policies. A Turkish member of parliament admitted that this imbalance poses a dilemma. In an interview with the *Daily Sabah*, Volkan Bozkir said: "In the EU decision making mechanism, the attributed number of votes is based on a country's population and area. For example, both Germany and France have 29 votes, Croatia has six. It is possible to block a decision with 91 votes. When Turkey becomes an EU member it will possess 29 votes and along with the other two largest countries will determine the agenda of the EU."[76]

This, of course, is not a prospect that the leaders of the big European countries would relish, especially given that Turkey could, with the cooperation of smaller countries, form a bloc to exert even more influence on EU decisions. The admission of the Central and East European countries with their special perspectives on certain issues has already complicated EU's decision-making process.[77] The same would also apply to the European Parliament. According to the same Turkish parliamentarian, "Turkey will have 100 parliamentarians in Brussels. *Many EU countries do not seem ready for this*" [emphasis added]. Moreover, those European countries (Germany, France, Netherlands, and Austria) which have the largest Turkish immigrant populations worry that they might get a disproportionate percentage of new arrivals from Turkey, should it become a member state.

Another aspect of Turkey's large population is its impact on EU labor markets, especially in light of high rates of unemployment in Turkey and better economic and social conditions in Europe. Some Europeans worry that Turkey's entry into the EU would lead to a large-scale influx of Turkish labor, a prospect which is particularly worrisome to those countries with serious unemployment problems. Some analysts, however, argue that as Turkey's economy expands its unemployment issues will ease and thus its accession would not lead to large migration to Europe. Others, meanwhile, argue that in view of its aging population, Europe will need to import labor, a need that Turkey can fill. The question is what kind of labor force EU will need and if its needs were to be for more skilled workers than unskilled laborers, could Turkey satisfy this need?

Cultural Differences as the Real Obstacle?

Despite the foregoing, many observers argue that these barriers could be overcome and that the real cause of the EU's rejection is that Turkey does not fit Europe's cultural map. Certainly, this is what Turks believe. This is reflected in the statement of Turgut Özal, Turkish prime minister and later president during the 1980s and the early 1990s. He said that Turkey has been excluded from the process of European integration because Europe is Christian and Turkey is Muslim.[78]

The burden of this argument is that the question of Turkish membership, more than its being about geography, politics, economics, human rights, or even security, has been about Europe's identity, the constituent components of this identity, and whether Turkey can ever be accommodated within the framework of European identity. In other words, Turkey's quest for membership in the EU has raised the questions of "Who is a European and what makes one European." It has also posed similar questions for Turkey. What are the core constituents of Turkish identity and is Turkey willing or able to give up aspects of its identity to qualify as European? It is also in this framework that the question of religion and its role in the formation of European and Turkish identities, and hence its role in deciding EU's approach to Turkish membership, comes into play.

In this context, the following questions have been asked: Is religion a core component of Turkish and European cultures and identities? And does Turkey's predominantly Muslim population pose an insurmountable barrier to its inclusion in the overwhelmingly Christian, albeit mainly secular, Europe? More fundamentally, Turkish quest for EU membership has raised the following question: Given Europe's declared secularism, what exactly is meant by religion in the European context? Does the term religion refer to theological beliefs about creation, life, and afterlife, or is it really concerned with specific Turkish and European patterns of social behavior, which in Turkey's case are influenced more by religious precepts than is true in nearly all European countries, and their mutual incompatibility? If the former, there should be no difficulty in accommodating a different religion—Islam—as Europe has done with other faiths. But if the latter, the question is more problematic because it involves matters of social peace and interaction, as well as the issue of acceptable patterns of social behavior.

This difference between religion as a set of theological beliefs and as culturally determined patterns of social behavior is evidenced by the fact that most of the tensions between Europeans and their Muslim populations do not derive from theological disputes. On the contrary, they are mostly caused by Muslims' social and cultural habits and practices. Examples of such practices include women's veiling, forced marriages, honor killings, and in general the unequal treatment of women. Muslims' conservative approach to issues of sexual orientation is another area of discord. Yet most of these issues have nothing or very little to do with Islam's theological precepts. For example, honor killing reflects tribal and patriarchal traditions and not Islamic law. As to the question of sexual orientation, all Abrahamic religions have the same approach, although some Christian denominations and some reformed branches of Judaism have altered their positions in this respect. In short, the dispute is not about the theological foundations of Christianity and Islam but rather the differing manners and mores of Muslims and Europeans, respectively. This is one reason why Westernized Muslims find it easier to integrate into European societies than those who have kept their local habits.

EUROPEAN IDENTITY AND EU IDENTITY: ARE THEY THE SAME?

In discussing the impact of cultural/identity-related factors in the EU's approach to the Turkish quest for membership, a distinction needs to be made between Europe as a geographical and cultural construct and the European institutions, including the most ambitious of these institutions, the European Union. This distinction is important because there is no agreement among EU members and their populations regarding what the EU is or should be. EU member states differ on the question of the EU's underlying character and its goals. Their opinions differ on whether the EU is essentially an economic, political, and security undertaking, with the objective of creating more prosperity, encouraging political cooperation, and contributing to the Continent's security, and thus is a performance-based institution, or is it something more? Likewise, member states disagree on whether the EU is a value- and norm-based institution with no specific geographic or cultural boundaries, or is first and foremost geographically and culturally a European institution.[79]

Security, political, and economic considerations (especially the desire to make another European-wide war impossible and help Europe's post-war reconstruction) were powerful motivations behind efforts to create European institutions. The founders of the European institutions thought that, by bringing European countries, especially France and Germany, together they could prevent another war in Europe. They also believed that a more united and prosperous Europe could cope better with the challenges posed by the USSR and also resist domination by the United States. Those members who were not among the founding states, were even more motivated to join the organization by the economic and security benefits that the EU membership entailed. Nevertheless, the fact that all EU members are located in Europe and their populations overwhelmingly adhere to Christianity, illustrates the importance of feelings of cultural kinship and the sense of belonging to the same geographic and cultural space, in both aspiring to membership and in obtaining it.

In particular, because of this feeling of cultural kinship and geographical belonging EU members have felt a sense of duty toward other European states wanting to join the organization. According to some scholars, this sense of duty played a particularly important role in the EU's decision to admit the East and Central European countries.[80] This sense of duty is reflected in the European Council's statement in its 1991 meeting in Rome: "The Community is aware of its special responsibility toward these [East European] countries."[81] Because of the feelings of kinship, the EU's Eastern enlargement was explained "in terms of Europe's other half coming home."[82]

In Turkey's case, such sentiments do not exist. Rather, both Turkey and Europe have seen the rationale for Turkey's membership in economic and security terms. For Turkey, the economic advantages of EU membership and the prestige that it would bestow on the country, rather than a deep sense of cultural kinship and belonging in Europe, have been the main motives behind its quest for membership. For Europe, meanwhile, security considerations have been particularly important. As noted before, the proponents of Turkey's membership in the EU have argued that this would stabilize Turkey and prevent its potential radicalization or fragmentation and in this way would contribute to European security. As a NATO member, Turkey is also viewed as a security asset for Europe. Turkey, too, has emphasized its importance to Europe and hence its desire for memberhip in the EU on security and foreign policy rather than cultural and value grounds. According to one Turkish scholar, since the 1990s Turkey has consistently argued that "if the EU were serious about becoming an important actor on the world stage, it needed to include Turkey."[83]

The performance dimensions of the EU are still important with peoples of most member states, including those in its founding countries, such as France. In the last few years, with low economic growth and financial problems, some people have begun to question the value of their EU membership. Some political groups, especially on the right, have even held EU membership responsible for their economic woes.[84] As alluded to earlier, in the spring of 2016 the United Kingdom was considering pulling out of the EU because it finds some of its regulations, notably those regarding the free movement of labor among member states, damaging to its national interest.[85] Following a referendum on 23 June 2016, the British people voted to leave the EU. In short, to some extent the EU is a performance-based organization.

However, if the EU is something more than just a security- and prosperity-generating instrument, as some of the reasons noted for its enlargement seem to indicate, such as representing a particular vision of Europe and of European identity, then the following question arises: What are or what should be the ingredients of this EU and European identity? Thus far, this question has not generated an agreed-upon response.

Universalism, Europeanism, Deepeners, Wideners

A major point of contention regarding the basis of an EU identity derives from conflicting visions of the EU as either a universalist or a more limited European entity.

According to Ingrid Kylstad, the main question is whether the EU is "the offspring of a tradition of cosmopolitanism as formulated by Immanuel Kant, or despite the oratory, it is a closed club for Christian states located between the Urals and the Atlantic.[86] Those preferring a limited conception of the EU are concerned that if it is defined in cosmopolitan and universalist terms, it could eventually turn into a watered-down free trade zone. They prefer an EU whose membership is highly unified at all levels and has the potential to become a United States of Europe. Historically, the group has preferred to keep the EU membership limited and has opposed its rapid enlargement. The members of this group are known as the "deepeners." Their counterparts are those who prefer a looser union with a large membership. They are known as the "wideners." Thus far, deepeners have lost to the wideners as the EU has expanded rapidly, although there has also been considerable deepening as reflected in the adoption of the common European currency, the Euro.[87]

For the deepeners, Turkey is a bridge too far, but the wideners, such as Great Britain, which has opposed the idea of European federalism, are better disposed toward Turkey's eventual admission. The final outcome of this debate will inevitably affect Turkey's membership chances. A more tightly knit Europe would find it harder to accommodate Turkey.

Foundations of EU Identity: Can It Be Different from Those of European Identity?

Another fundamental and often overlooked question is whether an EU identity can be created outside of Europe's historical and cultural experiences and memories. Even if the view is accepted that identities are merely social and political constructions engineered by the power elites and derive more from myths and lack any religious or ethnic foundations, they still cannot be built in a short time. Also identities must be constructed on the basis of some foundational notions.[88] Furthermore, constructed or not, they are formed and reformed over centuries and are the product of shared experiences, practices, memories, and values.[89] More important identities are generally formed in the context of interaction with one or several of the "other/s." If this be the case, can an EU identity be developed based solely on one aspect of European experience, such as the traditions of enlightenment and modernity which have given rise to Europe's current value system as the universalist and value/norm-based vision of the EU seems to suggest? Or does the entire European experience, of which the Enlightenment and modernity is only one aspect, have to be taken into account? Similarly, can an EU identity be formed outside its interactions with Europe's traditional "others"?

How these questions are answered will have serious implications for Turkey's chances of being admitted to the EU. The reason is that, as expressed by José Casanova, "If Europe is defined in terms of its traditional historical civilization as 'Christian' or 'Western,' then one could legitimately argue that there can be no room for Turkey, unless Turkey undergoes a drastic Westernization. By contrast, if Europe is defined in terms of the civilization of 'modernity,' then there should be no reason why a 'modern' Turkey which meets the usual economic, legal and political conditions required of all new states ought not to be admitted to the EU."[90] In short, if Turkey adopts all EU norms and values then it should be allowed to join. This is also the view of those who see the EU as an essentially norm- and value-based organization, rather than as an organization defined in geographic and civilizational terms.

There is a problem with this view because it sees modernity which developed in Europe and the norms and values and the civilization to which it gave rise as something separate from the broader European experience. Yet in reality, European modernity and its values have been the outcome of Europe's particular historical, political, economic, religious, and cultural evolution. Non-European countries' difficulty in successfully assimilating modernity to their indigenous cultures and their frequent backsliding show the importance of cultural and historical precedents to the onset of modernity.[91] In particular, as has happened in the Muslim world, it has become clear that state-sponsored modernization, without fundamental changes in the attitudes and belief systems of very large segments of society, is doomed, at least in its initial phases. This period can last for decades if not centuries. Furthermore, this type of modernization is often followed by cultural counter-reactions.[92] In the context of the Middle East, including Turkey, the rise of politically active Islamist movements is a good example of reactions to state-sponsored modernization projects. Even countries such as Russia have had problems in modernizing.

Some European and American scholars have challenged the view that modernity is particularly and uniquely European.[93] Instead, they maintain that different versions of modernity developed within all great religions during the Axial Age.[94] This approach stretches the concept of modernity too far. Its essence is the primacy of reason as the basis of knowledge. Modernity in this sense developed in Europe or, to be precise, in Northwestern Europe, although certainly the Renaissance was an important stage in its emergence. The manifestation and peculiarities of the modernization process, including the relative place of religion in a modern or modernizing society, have differed throughout the world, including in Europe. But this cannot be characterized as multiple modernities because the essence of modernity, namely the supremacy of reason and the denial of hegemony to religious discourse, remains the same. It is hard to argue against the view that modernity, as most broadly understood, developed in Northwestern Europe and then spread to the rest of the Continent and beyond.

A further question is: Can identities be formed outside of existing and widespread traditions and customs, since traditions are essentially the outcome of day-to-day practice of beliefs and ways of life over a very long period? Diverging national traditions within the EU have already been an obstacle to forging an EU identity. Thus the resentment felt at least initially by the citizens of some EU member states to changes in their traditional ways of doing things imposed by EU guidelines shows that changing traditions is not easy. For example, the British initially were unhappy about having to convert to the decimal system or to accept other EU guidelines.[95]

If the view is accepted that an EU identity inevitably will have to be built on the basis of the entirety of European experience, including that of modernity, two further questions regarding Turkey's membership arise: First, are Turkish historical experiences and traditions part of the European experience? Second, how deep has been Turkey's modernization?

Viewed realistically and impartially, it is hard to accept that Turkey's and Europe's historical experiences and traditions are one and the same or even similar. Yet some scholars have argued that Turkey shares in the European historical experience because Turkey is the inheritor of Byzantium. And since Byzantium is part of the European experience, so is Turkey.[96] These scholars further point out that the Ottomans closely interacted with Europe and greatly influenced the cultural landscape of certain parts of Europe, including that of some current EU members, such as Hungary, Bulgaria, and

Romania. They also note that the Turkish Republic has embraced Europe and has tried to Europeanize Turkey, a fact which creates another link in the European and Turkish historical experiences. The proponents of this view ignore the fact that European-Ottoman interaction was mostly negative. Those European countries which came under Ottoman rule were eager to free themselves from Turkish control. Similarly, the Europeans have generally seen the Ottomans/Turks as adversaries rather than as part of the European community.

Even if an EU identity were to be constructed only on the basis of Europe's Enlightenment legacy, it would be difficult to include Turkey because Turkey's modernization has been a top-down effort which has only partially succeeded. This point is made by Perry Anderson, who states that Kemalism was a "cultural revolution without a social revolution."[97] Others have even challenged the idea that Turkey was actually secularized, by arguing that even under the republican system, being Muslim was a requisite for being recognized as Turk.[98] If this view is correct, it raises the question of how far the Turks have internalized the notion of secularism and other European values. If Turkey's experience in the last fifty years is any guide, the answer is "not much." This reality is also reflected in the fact that Turkey has not justified its desire to join Europe in value terms. Nor has it explained its value for Europe in terms of spreading European values. Rather, it has argued that Turkish membership will enhance Europe's security and international role.

In short, an EU identity cannot be built on any other basis than Europe's entire experience of which Turkey has not been an integral part. Even if an EU identity were to be constructed in this way, it would not be an easy task, partly because national identities in Europe have proved stronger than was first believed.[99] Indeed, by the summer of 2016 it seemed that a new wave of nationalism could spread in Europe. But if an EU identity is to be built around Europe's entire historical experience, then the role of religion in this endeavor and in EU-Turkish relations becomes pivotal. The reason is that the role of religion in shaping respective historical experiences, Christianity in Europe's case and Islam in Turkey's case, has been very significant. Consequently, in the evolving dynamic of EU-Turkey relations, in Europe's case religion's influence will be felt in many subtle and not so subtle ways, despite Europe's secular ethos and its desire to foster civilizational dialogue with the Muslim world.[100] In Turkey's case, the role of religion as culture and not merely in its theological and other-worldly dimension will remain even more important.

RELIGION AS CULTURE: CHRISTIANITY AND EUROPEAN CULTURE

As discussed in earlier chapters, until a little over two hundred years ago, all societies, including Europe's, were principally organized on the basis of religious precepts. In fact, all world civilizations initially developed on religious foundations. Even after the rise of secularism in Europe and its gradual spread to other parts of the world, the influence of religion on societies' ethical and other norms remained strong. Only in the last hundred years or so has the influence of religion in secular societies of Europe and North America been sharply reduced, albeit not to the same degree in all countries. In particular, the culture of European societies defined as patterns of social interaction, forms of interaction which bind societies together, and values cherished by the majority of their peoples and the artistic and other forms of creativity that these values generate, is still influenced by religion. In short, even completely secular societies and those individuals who deny religion any social and political role cannot escape its cumulative impact and influence.

In Europe's case two elements form the foundations of its civilization as well as the basis of its various national cultures:

1. *The Intellectual and Political Legacy of Greece and Rome.* The impact of Greece has been extremely significant. Greece has formed the foundations of European rationalism and hence also that of its secularism, a great part of its esthetic and artistic sensibilities, and its political traditions of democracy. In short, Europe's current political culture is rooted in what some scholars have characterized as Greek humanism.[101] It is no wonder that both the Renaissance and Enlightenment coincided with a resurgence of interest in Greece and Rome. For its part, Rome provided Europe with its legal and political foundations, later complemented by Canon Law. It also gave Europe its view of itself as constituting the civilized world. As put by Helene Ahrweiler, "The Roman Empire, the first world empire, extended its administration over the whole of the civilized world."[102] Thus, even if the Greece and Rome of European imagination is not an exact representation of the realities of these two great civilizations, their heritage nevertheless creates a common bond among various European peoples, even those whose Europeanness is disputed, such as Russia's.

2. *Christianity.* If Greece and Rome have shaped the intellectual and many of the esthetic aspects of Europe, Christianity, along with those elements of Judaism included in it, has formed the basis of its values and fundamental aspects of its culture, both high and popular. Moreover, it was the spread of Christianity that led to the development of a

sense of belonging by various European ethnic groups to a shared community and civilization within the geographical confines of Europe. As put by one observer of EU affairs: "It was Christianity that forged the disparate tribes of Europe—Latin Spaniards, the Irish Celts, the Teutonic Scandinavians, and the Hungarian Magyar—into one community united by a common faith in Jesus Christ."[103] In the case of some European countries such as France, their conversion to Christianity marks the birth of the nation.[104] The very concept of Europe as a community and civilization resulted from Christianity and its melding with the political and legal legacy of Rome.

According to this view, for several centuries Europe and Christendom were one and the same. Later, Europe's various nation-states rose from the historical matrix of "the medieval unity of European Christendom." Others have gone further and argued that it was their common adherence to Christianity that first gave those inhabiting the European continent the awareness that they formed a distinct people. According to John Hale, "Although scholars throughout the Middle Ages had known that they lived in a continent called by classical geographers 'Europe,' to distinguish it from other land masses partially known to them, Africa and Asia, the word had little resonance. What men knew *from the stories of martyrs and missionaries and crusades and from harangues from the pulpit was that they had been chosen by the divine providence to be the home of Christian witness to the true faith*" [emphasis added].[105] Others note the fact that the adjective "European" was first used by Pope Pius II during the Renaissance in his book *De Europa*. In that book, he wrote that Europe is united in terms of religion and should express its identity in this respect. Yet it took several more centuries for the concept of Europe to replace that of Christendom, and it was only in the very late seventeenth century that reference to Europe begun to replace that of Christendom.[106]

In sum, Christianity gave spiritual content and cultural identity to geographical Europe and its various components. Moreover, Christianity affected Europe's esthetic sensibilities, for a while obscuring the influence of Greece and Rome, and its imagery and architecture largely shaped European artistic landscape and forms a great part of its cultural heritage. The best manifestation of this spiritual and political unity of Europe achieved under the influence of Christianity, at least in its Western part, was the empire of Charlemagne. Although short-lived, its ideal continued to inspire those who sought to bring about a united Europe, albeit through different means and, at times, by repudiating the Christian religion as the French revolutionaries did. Yet Charlemagne did not see his empire as representing Europe but as symbolizing Christendom. The early founders of the European movement toward unity, while clearly secular and committed to the secular and democratic principles of Europe, believed that the new Europe should be built on the basis of Christian values. This approach partly resulted from their view that the two world wars which devastated Europe in the twentieth century were caused by "a forgetfulness of Europe's Christian values."[107] Thus Robert Schuman, one of the founders of new Europe, stated that "We [the Europeans] are called to bethink of ourselves of the Christian basis of Europe by forming a democratic model of governance which through reconciliation develops into a 'community of peoples' in freedom, equality, solidarity and peace which is deeply rooted in Christian values."[108] This statement also supports the view expressed earlier that Europe's current values have their roots in its Christian past. Moreover, some scholars have traced the beginning of movement toward European unity in Catholic internationalism and in the activities of Europe's Christian Democrats.[109]

Those who do not subscribe to the notion of Europe as Christendom point out that even if Christianity at some point in history had given Europe a semblance of unity, the schism which developed within Christianity ended this unity. It divided Europe into three zones of Orthodoxy, Catholicism, and Protestantism and caused some of its most devastating wars, such as the Thirty-Years War. To some extent this criticism is valid. But it ignores the point that, despite their divisions, Christians have more in common with one another than with the followers of other faiths. They also share a number of historical memories, traditions, and practices.

In light of the increasing size of Europe's Muslim population as a result of immigration, especially in the last two decades, some commentators have argued that Islam, too, forms part of Europe's cultural heritage. They argue that through their works Muslim scholars contributed to the Renaissance and to Europe's cultural revitalization and thus ultimately to the arrival of the Age of Enlightenment.[110] Yet this argument misses the point that what Islamic scholars transmitted was essentially their interpretations of Greek philosophy. Some, such as Avicenna, expanded on this philosophy, and individual Muslim scientists, mostly non-Arab, made contributions which benefited Europe. But their contributions, although important, can hardly be considered Islamic since they were not inspired by any peculiarity of Islam. Indeed, in the Muslim world these philosophers and scientists were viewed with suspicion by religious purists and were even accused of being unbelievers.[111] Moreover, after the eleventh century scientific production in the Muslim world nearly stopped, largely because of the excessive role of juridical religion.

Those scholars who challenge Christianity's predominant role in the formation of European culture also point to the role of Judaism. They conclude that Europe and European culture has always been a multi-religious phenomenon. According to Delanty, Europe "must be seen as a constellation consisting of links rather than stable entities or enduring."[112] Yet even after taking into account the Judaic and Islamic influences on European culture, it must be acknowledged that Christianity's role in the formation of European culture and identity has been overwhelmingly superior to, and more significant than, those of other influences, including even those of Greece and Rome.

Christian Roots of Europe's Secular Values

Those who do not subscribe to the idea of Europe as Christendom and challenge the essentially Christian roots of its culture argue that, even if Christianity once was the foundation of the European culture and value system, after its widespread secularization it has lost its central place in this respect. It is quite true that by the early eighteenth century Europeans began to define the values which separated them from other peoples more in secular terms. For example, while until that time the European peoples saw the reason for their superiority over others mainly in religious terms and because of their Christian faith, by the early eighteenth century Europeans had found secular justifications for their sense of superiority. For example, Montesquieu[113] saw the reason for Europe's superiority to the Ottomans in Europe's democratic nature, as opposed to the Ottomans' despotic system of governance, plus some other natural and social characteristics. This trend continued in the following decades and centuries.

Those who insist on the essentially Christian roots of European values respond that European secularism and rationalism, its democratic values, and the values related to human rights grew from within its Christian traditions.[114] For instance, they maintain that the roots of the Enlightenment can be traced to the efforts of St. Thomas Aquinas to reconcile faith and reason and to the Protestant Reformation. The latter at first divided Europe and Christianity, but ultimately it led to the development of a form of Christian liberalism, which in its secular version formed an almost universal creed. Similarly, the very foundation of secularism, which is the separation of the domains of the sacred and the profane, is most openly recognized in Christianity. It is based on Christ's admonition to "render therefore unto Caesar the things which are Caesar's; and unto God the things that are God's,"[115] and his saying that his kingdom was not of this world, although for long periods in Europe his admonition was not heeded and this distinction was not always observed.

Nevertheless, the existence of this tradition made the emergence of secular governments easier in the Christian world than has been the case in the Muslim world, where this distinction has not been made, at least not unequivocally. In other words, certain characteristics of Christianity and especially that of Western Christianity as opposed to Eastern Orthodoxy have made the development of European secularism and democracy easier than has been the case in other cultures.

In sum, European secularism peculiarly reflects Europe's Christian experience. The same also applies to the area of human rights. With considerable justification, it can be argued that modern concepts of human rights and their universal application have their roots in the Christian theory of natural rights and in the ideas of figures like the sixteenth-century Dominican theologian Francisco de Vitoria of Salamanca. However, today European notions of the range of human rights exceed those recognized by religion and some of them are either rejected or challenged by religion, including by many Christians.

Christianity as the Foundation of the European Way of Life and Historical Memory

Communities are formed and develop a sense of common identity on the basis of many different criteria, including the bonds of kinship, ethnicity, and religion. Of equal importance, however, is the shared way of life, symbols, and common memories of the past, whether real or imagined. In Europe, for centuries Christianity and its rites formed the foundations of the European ways of life. They regulated the main stages of life such as birth, marriage, and death. The names of Christianity's saints are still associated with different European countries and many of them are still venerated by substantial numbers of people. Its festivals of the birth and resurrection of Christ are still the most important and widely observed occasions in Western countries, even if having somewhat lost their religious significance and, especially in the case of the celebrations related to the birth of Christ (Christmas), partly morphed into secular festivals. Because of this shared Christian heritage, it cannot be denied that, in the main, European peoples feel more at home in European states than in those belonging to different civilizational zones built upon different religions.

The importance of historical memory in the identity of peoples and communities cannot be overestimated, even though not easily quantifiable. What is certain is that this historical memory cannot be easily erased with all that it implies in terms of views of who constitutes a "friend" and who is the "enemy" or the "other." For instance, even a secular Frenchman will identify with Charles Martel in his defense of Europe against Arabs and Muslims. Or being secular does not necessarily mean not bemoaning the Turkish onslaught on Europe. (At the same time, for many Muslims, the Crusades are the comparable received memory.) This is especially true if there are no other compelling material reasons to try overcoming the negative aspects of these historical memories. Their impact is much more powerful because often it operates at the sub-conscious level. Clearly, individual European countries have their own separate and specific historical memories; these at times clash with those of other European states or at least are different from theirs.

Within the context of Europe's common Christian tradition, there are diverging historical memories such as those between the Protestants and the Catholics or between them and Eastern Christianity. Yet there is also a significant degree of commonality among them. There have also been differences in the more recent historical memories of European countries because of their political developments, diverging experiences of Nazism and Communism, and their differing positions during the Cold War. Nevertheless, what various European countries have in common in terms of their historical memories exceeds what they have in common with non-European peoples, including the Turks. Because Christianity is the preeminent foundation of Europeans' historical memory, its influence is still considerable. In fact, as put by François Foret, "European identity is more religious than is often suggested, although religion's influence is not active or conscious."[116]

THE ROLE OF THE "OTHER" IN EUROPEAN IDENTITY

Samuel Huntington wrote that "We know who we are only when we know who we are not and often only when we know who we are against."[117] This statement reflects the view referred to earlier that collective identities are formed and developed in relation to other peoples, groups, and religions. Often it is the realization of being different from other peoples, cultures, and collectivities that makes one conscious of one's own peculiarities and hence separate identity.

It is often noted that the Greeks became conscious of their Greekness only when they came into contact with the Persians. In other words, being Greek first and foremost meant not being Persian. It was in relation to the Persians that the Greeks developed their sense of being morally and politically superior to others. According to Helene Ahrweiler, "This [Greek] awareness found expression in the resistance of the free, democratic cities of ancient Greece to the Asiatic despotism of the Persian Empire."[118] Gradually, the concept of Greeks versus Persians morphed into the notion of the West versus the East, with Europe representing the West and the lands beyond it the East, initially symbolized by Persia.

After the spread of Christianity in Europe and later Islam in most of the Near and Middle East, the old Greek-Persian and east-west divide morphed into the Christian-Muslim divide. It is safe to say that the encounter between Islam and Christianity consolidated the emerging European-Christian identity. As the Muslim armies encroached on Europe's or Christendom's frontiers, Europe's Christians united to stop its advances. In the process, they consolidated their common identity as Christians and Europeans. In other words, Muslims served as the "other" against which the Europeans defined themselves, as the Persian "other" had helped the Greeks to forge their separate identity. They certainly had their own internal differences and disagreements but they had more in common with one another than with the Muslim "other." The Crusades further consolidated the Muslims' function as the "other" for Europeans.

In the same vein, Christendom/West served as the "other," albeit less effectively, for Muslims and helped them to develop a sense of Muslimness and belonging to an Islamic civilization, especially for the peoples of the Near and Middle East. When in the fifteenth century the Ottoman Turks conquered Constantinople, appropriated to themselves the legacy of the Islamic Caliphate, and later expanded their power in Europe, in the Europeans' eyes Muslim and Turkish "others" became one and the same.[119] And since the Europeans viewed Islam in a negative light and considered it to be inimical to both European values and interests, Turks also acquired a negative image in European eyes.

The predominance of negative views of Islam and Turks in the Europeans' historical memory does not mean that there were no positive interactions between Muslims and Christians and Europeans and Turks, both at individual and community levels. Similarly, despite the predominance of negative perceptions of Islam and the Turks among Europeans, more positive views of both also existed. Certain aspects of Islam were appreciated by some Europeans as were certain characteristics of the Turks and the Ottomans. For example, in his *La genealogie du Grand Turc,* written in 1520, Theodoro Spandugino offered a positive image of the Ottomans.[120] Nevertheless, the fact is that the respective collective memories that Muslims and Christians and Turks and Europeans have of each other have largely been negative. These negative sentiments and memories should be overcome. But denying their existence will not help the effort to transcend them.

East as the Inferior Other

Until the late eighteenth century, the notion of the East, here defined as the Muslim East, despite being negative, did not denote inferiority in a material sense. The East was seen as inferior to the West mostly in a moral and spiritual sense. This view changed after Europe's scientific and industrial advances resulted in the expansion of its military and political power to Muslim lands, beginning as early as the sixteenth century and greatly expanding by the beginning of the nineteenth century. Consequently, the East came to be viewed as inferior in all respects and not only morally and spiritually. In this new context, too, because of its proximity to Europe and its greater interaction with it, Turkey occupied a central place. As noted by the Turkish scholar Hakan Yilmaz, Turkey becomes Europe's "inferior other" as well.[121] The legacy of this experience of otherness is that many Europeans find Turkey's incorporation into Europe difficult to accept.

Yet if in the past identities were largely formed in opposition to real or imagined "others," it does not mean that they should continue to be so constructed. If this should be the case, the entire EU project would collapse because the fundamental basis of European integration is the elimination of pre-existing concepts of the "other," such as those between the French and the Germans, Catholics and Protestants, the English and the Irish, within Europe itself. The question, therefore, is whether Turkey can be transformed from Europe's traditional "other" into a member of the European family. This idea is not new. A number of authors in the eighteenth and nineteenth centuries argued that the Ottomans could develop as the Europeans had done and eventually could be integrated in Europe. Charles de Vergennes, Alexander Blacque, and David Urquhart were among these authors.[122] Some European political leaders, such as Lord Palmerstone, expressed similar ideas.[123] This divided European view of Turkey and its potential for progress and integration into Europe still persists. Some European scholars have even argued that Turkey's real objective in joining the EU is not Turkey's Europeanization but Europe's Islamization. The growing influence of Islam in Turkish social and political life in the last few decades, and an apparent erosion of Turkey's zeal for Europeanization has been partly responsible for these views. Yet the possibility that Turkey could one day attain European standards and join the European community still exists, assuming that the EU survives in its present shape. Thus far, however, partly because of changes both in Europe and in Turkey, neither Turkey's transformation nor its acceptance by Europe has happened.

EU EXPANSION, MUSLIM IMMIGRATION, AND RETURN OF RELIGION TO THE EUROPEAN POLITICAL SCENE

The founders of what has become the EU believed that Europe's Christian values should be part of its guiding principles. In the following decades, however, the vision of Europe that has evolved has been thoroughly and one could even say militantly secular. This European secularity is reflected in the aforementioned refusal of the drafters of the European Constitution to accept any reference to God or to Europe's Christian religious roots, despite calls from some religious leaders, and even the late pope, John Paul II.[124]

In the last two decades or so, five developments have somewhat changed this picture without, however, eroding Europe's secular orientation:

1. The USSR's collapse and the end of East-West ideological confrontation and hence the emergence of an ideological vacuum;

2. The incorporation into the EU of Central and Eastern European countries, some of whose populations are still more religious-minded than those in Western Europe, partly in reaction to the Soviet period when religion was suppressed by the state;
3. The increase in the size of Europe's Muslim population as a result of immigration;
4. The fact that considerable segments of Europe's Muslim immigrants and their descendants are highly religious and are unwilling to conform to European cultural norms; and
5. The impact on Europe of developments in Muslim states.

Of these developments, challenges posed by Islam's presence in Europe, including the linkages between some of Europe's Muslim population and radical movements in several Muslim countries, has had the greatest impact. European concerns over Islam's presence in the Continent have been exacerbated by terrorist attacks committed by radical Muslims in Europe, such as bombings in Spain in 2003 and in London in 2005 and hostage-taking operations and hijacking of airplanes which occurred in the 1980s, plus latest incidents involving the bombing of the offices of the French satirical journal *Charlie Hebdo* on 7 January 2015, the November 2015 bombings also in Paris, and the March 2016 bombings in Brussels.[125] Especially worrying in recent years has been the attraction of young European Muslims to radical Islam as reflected in their participation in so-called Jihad on the side of the Islamic State (IS).[126] In short, as put by one European expert, at least since 9/11 a linkage has been formed between Islam, terrorism, and extremism.[127] This is not quite fair and can be overdrawn, but it has a reality.

Meanwhile, the greater Muslim presence in Europe and what some European analysts have seen as the excesses of multiculturalism have generated anxiety on the part of some Europeans about the loss or at least the dilution of their specific identity. They believe that multiculturalism, by responding to all sorts of demands by various ethnic and religious minorities, forces the indigenous culture to withdraw into itself. This could eventually culminate in the loss of indigenous peoples' identity.[128] Even in secular Europe, religion is an aspect of this identity which many people believe is under threat. People may not be practicing or even religious believers but the sense of belonging to a religion-based civilization—primarily Christianity in Europe's case—is quite strong.

Meanwhile, Islam's greater visibility in Europe, including through efforts to establish institutional representations of their faith such as mosques and schools has made many non-observant European Christians more aware of their own faith. This awareness has not yet been translated into greater religiosity on the part of the Europeans. However, it has led to opposition to the growing symbolic presence of Islam in Europe, as manifested, for example, in the number of mosques with high minarets, something to which many Europeans object.[129] In sum, Europeans may not go to church any more, but many don't want minarets in their cities to be higher than church spires.

The inclusion of Central and East European countries in the EU has also enhanced popular awareness of Europe's Christian roots. Many East European religious leaders have urged that the EU pay greater attention to religion and to Europe's Christian values. Stanislav Zvolensky, the Roman Catholic archbishop of Bratislava, Slovakia, has complained that "there is a movement in the European Union that wants total religious neutrality and cannot accept our Christian traditions."[130] He has bemoaned this attitude, especially at a time when Europe is struggling to forge a common identity.[131] However, movement in this direction is unlikely to happen simply because religion's influence in Europe, especially in Western Europe, is still declining.[132]

Nevertheless, many Europeans have become more aware of Christianity's role as the primary foundation of European cultures and more sensitive to the possible erosion of its role under pressures emanating from the presence of other religions, most particularly Islam. Many secular Europeans and even some atheists now argue that Christianity should continue to be Europe's cultural foundation, in order to protect it against Islam's influence. One such individual was Italian journalist Oriana Fallaci. Reportedly, she characterized herself as "a Christian atheist" largely because she believed Christianity provided Europe with a cultural and intellectual bulwark against Islam.[133] Others see Christianity as a convenient protection against the impact of radical Islam. Niall Ferguson, who identifies himself as an "incurable atheist," champions the restoration of Christendom because he believes there is not enough "religious resistance to radical Islam in Europe."[134] Another figure is Italian philosopher and politician Marcello Pera. He is the author of a book entitled *Why We Must Call Ourselves Christians*. He argues that Europe needs to restore its Christian identity in order both to defend itself against Islam and to fight moral degeneration.[135]

In short, as religion has remained the main identity marker for Europe's Muslims, it has helped Europeans to rediscover their own religious roots, even if this discovery has not caused many of them to become more religious. It has also brought back the issue of religion to the European political landscape. For example, it has raised the question whether Europe should continue to remain neutral on the issue of religion, if this neutrality leads to the growing presence of Islam in its political and cultural landscape. At least some Europeans, especially on the right wing of European politics, believe that this should not be the case. For example, Monsignor Georg Ganswein warned in 2007 that "attempts at the Islamification of Europe cannot be denied."[136] Even David Cameron, Britain's prime minister, who belongs to the centrist right as a member of the Conservative Party, said that Britain is a Christian country and it should not shy away from calling itself so, a statement which was attacked primarily by commentators on the Left.[137] Meanwhile, political groups with the specific goal of preventing or at least halting what they see as Europe's Islamization have been formed. One such group is the German PEGIDA (*Patrotische Europeaer gegen die Islamisierung des Abendlandes/Patriotic Europeans against the Islamization of the West*). The group organized mass demonstrations in Germany in December 2014. Mainstream German politicians and political parties openly opposed its extremist views on the issue of Muslim immigration. However, they will inevitably take into account the existence of such sentiments in their future political decisions, including whether or not to include in their midst a large Muslim country such as Turkey.

The flow of refugees from Muslim countries in 2015 and some incidents involving Muslim youth and European women has intensified fears of Europe's being submerged by Muslims. This development, as noted before, has also caused tensions in European and Turkish relations, which could not fail negatively to impact Turkey's chances of admission.

In sum, the growing presence of Europe's historic Islamic "other" in its own territories has generated a defensive reflex on the part of at least some portions of its peoples and has triggered a renewed interest in the potential of Christianity as a unifying force in Europe, even without its religious dimensions. It has also raised the salience of religion as a factor in defining what it means to be European.

Impact on the Debate on Turkish Membership

These factors have intensified cultural and religious arguments against Turkey's admission to the EU. This is quite natural because Turkey's admission would dramatically increase the number of Muslims in Europe and might enable it to, as some Europeans claim, to try to Islamicize Europe instead of itself becoming Europeanized.[138] As evidence, among other factors, they point to Erdoğan's statement during a visit to Germany that the assimilation of Muslim Turks in Europe would be a crime against humanity.[139] Therefore, Turkish membership is not only about bringing Turkey up to Europe's economic and political standard. Rather, as put by François Foret, Turkey's quest for membership requires "*a reformulation of European belonging*" and "*throws into question the very nature of Europeanness*" [emphasis added].[140] A further reason is that Turkey's inclusion would impact the relationship between religion and politics and church and state within EU member states. Paradoxically, European secularists are also wary of Europe's rising Muslim population and of Turkish accession. They seem to believe that a Muslim presence would tend to strengthen Christian religious identity and thus undermine Europe's secular ethos.[141]

Yet the level of the salience of religion in various EU member states is not the only determinant of their position on Turkey's EU membership. Security, political, and economic considerations are equally important in deciding their stance. Thus individual EU member states' positions on the issue of Turkey's admission to the EU are determined by their perception of how Turkey's membership will affect their own political, strategic, and economic fortunes. For example, Poland is relatively more religious than many EU countries, but it has a more nuanced approach toward Turkish membership. In the past, Poland's unease about possible Turkish membership stemmed from its view that this could undermine Ukraine's chances of one day joining the EU. By contrast, France, arguably the most secular EU member state, opposes Turkish membership.[142]

In short, whether Turkish membership ultimately would be decided on the basis of cultural arguments is hard to predict. Thus far, their impact on the EU's decisions has been considerable, albeit unacknowledged, and they will continue to affect the EU's final decision on accepting or rejecting Turkey because Turkish membership touches the very issue of identity and what it means to be European.

ISLAM, TURKISH IDENTITY, HISTORICAL MEMORY, AND TURKEY'S VIEW OF ITS INTERNATIONAL ROLE

In the final analysis, whether or not Turkey joins Europe will not depend solely on the Europeans' decision. It will also depend on whether Turkey continues to see its own future in Europe and on how Turkey's national identity and its perception of its international role evolve.

Islam and Turkish Identity

As discussed in chapter 4, Islam has played a similar and perhaps even more important role in the formation of Turkish identity than Christianity has played in that of Europe. As noted earlier, until the establishment of the Turkish Republic in 1923, following the fall of the Ottoman Empire, Islam was the foundation of identity in what is now Turkey, and, as put by David Kushner, no people as much as the Ottoman Turks had submerged their ethnic identity in their religion. Moreover, as with Christianity in Europe, Islam formed the legal, moral, and spiritual foundations of life in the Ottoman Empire and, together with the hybrid Islamo-Persian culture, shaped its esthetic and artistic sensibilities.

Similarly, as Islam and later the Ottoman Turks constituted Europe's "other," Christian Europe performed the same function for the Turks. Changing the name of Constantinople to Istanbul and transforming the Church of Santa Sofia into the mosque of Hagia Sophia symbolized this relationship of adversaries. Later, European-Ottoman wars consolidated the Turks' and the Europeans' mutually antagonistic vision of each other. The Ottoman Empire might have been part of Europe's political system and even formed alliances with some of the European states against rival Muslim powers, but it never was part of Europe's spiritual and cultural landscape.

The republican project tried to recast Turkey's identity in a different context by locating it more firmly in ethnic and linguistic Turkism. But since Turkism outside of Islam lacked any elaborate and relevant spiritual and cultural context, the republican elites tried to replace Islam with the notions of modernization and Europeanization. However, as discussed in the previous chapter, their project of modernizing, secularizing, and Europeanizing Turkey only partially succeeded. Islam remained part of Turkey's national identity, to the extent that even today being Muslim largely defines who is a Turk.

Moreover, as noted in chapter 4, since the 1950s and especially in the last three decades, the Kemalist project has been steadily diluted and has led to a rise in Islam's profile in Turkey's cultural, social, and political landscape. Its outward manifestations have included the relaxation of the ban on Islamic cover (*hijab*). A symbolically significant manifestation of this trend was the wearing of Islamic *hijab* by the wives of both Gül and Erdoğan during official ceremonies, including during trips to European capitals. Because the Islamic *hijab* has become such a controversial issue in Europe and a symbol of cultural and value differences between Europe and the Muslim world, as well as between Europe's indigenous populations and their Muslim immigrants, the Turkish leaders' emphasis on their Muslim identity was also a political statement. If the trend toward Turkey's Islamization continues, it will inevitably affect its chances of admission to the EU by intensifying Europe's culture and religion-based reservations about Turkish membership. In fact, by doing so, Turkey might exclude itself from Europe, thus rendering moot the question of its acceptance by the EU.

Equally significant, greater Islamization of the Turkish society and polity could undermine the desire to join Europe and lead to the search for new areas of cooperation in the Islamic world, especially if the goal of incorporation into Europe remains unreachable or if it required too many changes and concessions. As mentioned before, a portion of Islamists do not favor Turkey's integration into Europe, fearing that this would dilute their Islamic culture and character.

Even those who still see a future for Turkey in Europe increasingly seem to believe that joining the EU cannot sum up the goal of Turkish foreign policy and determine the scope of its international role. On the contrary, increasingly Turkey is seeing EU membership as one aspect of a multidimensional Turkish international role.[143] But this Turkish desire potentially can cause problems in its relations with the EU. In recent years, Turkey's greater involvement in Middle East politics, which at times has been contrary to European and American preferences, has highlighted diverging perceptions and interests partly caused by cultural differences. A recent example has been disagreements on how to handle the Islamic State (IS). There have also been differences between Turkey and Europe over the treatment of Russia after its occupation of Crimea and its activities in Ukraine. For example, unlike the EU and the United States, Turkey, which has significant economic relations with Russia, has not imposed sanctions.[144] The rising tensions between Turkey and Russia between November 2015 and the summer of 2016 because of their disagreements regarding Syria, Russia's military involvement in support of the Assad regime, and finally the downing of a Russian aircraft by Turkey and the killing of the Russian pilot caused fresh dilemmas for Europe. These divergences in Turkish and European approaches to various regional and international issues also demonstrated that because of geographic factors total symmetry between Turkish and European security needs and policies, especially in the absence of an overarching paradigm such as that of the East-West conflict, would be difficult to achieve.

One area of EU-Turkey relations which remains vigorous is the economic realm and it could act as a force for closer EU-Turkey relations. By early 2015, it appeared that Turkey and the EU had decided to put the question of Turkey's membership aside and focus on strengthening their economic ties by strengthening the customs union.[145] However, tensions resulting from the failed July 2016 coup attempt could even undermine prospects for expanded economic relations.

POPULAR VIEWS ON TURKEY'S MEMBERSHIP: THE IMPACT OF CULTURAL/RELIGIOUS FACTORS

Even if for economic, political, and strategic reasons the EU governments decide to admit Turkey, selling it to the European publics will not be easy because opposition to Turkish membership is even higher among European publics than it is within European governments. According to surveys, economic, political, and human rights factors play roles in European publics' opposition to Turkish admission to the EU, albeit to varying degrees in different countries. These differences in the European publics' views on Turkish membership reflect different countries' particular economic conditions or their security and political concerns.[146] Popular views regarding Turkey are also affected by generational factors, with older Europeans more opposed to Turkish membership.

In general, most Europeans believe that Turkey does not meet the EU's economic, political, and human rights criteria, but most who oppose Turkey's admission do so on geographical, historical, and cultural grounds.

Moreover, cultural differences play an even more important role in the case of those Europeans who strongly oppose Turkish membership. European publics also are skeptical about the benefits of Turkey's admission for Europe's relations with the rest of the Muslim world. In sum, most Europeans "have trouble seeing Turkey as culturally compatible with the European Union . . . widely believe that Turkey is actually too incompatible with the EU culturally to become a member, [and] believe Turkey's history places it outside of Europe."[147] Moreover, according to some studies, opposition to Turkish membership has been on the rise among European publics, a trend that recent developments in Turkey and in the Middle East are unlikely to stop unless there is a change in these developments. The increase in the number of Muslim refugees in Europe has already intensified the European public's fear of the potential impact of Islam's presence on Europe's indigenous culture and identity.

As the EU is trying to shed its image as an organization detached from its members' populations, any decision on Turkey will certainly be affected by public opinion. It must be noted, however, that public opinion is not immutable and should circumstances change and new factors argue in favor of Turkish membership public opinion can also shift. Thus the real question will be how far Turkey can adopt European values and standards. But equally important would be how Turkish opinion on its own national identity and views of its interests evolve.

THE EVOLUTION OF THE EU AND ITS IDENTITY

Turkey's chances of one day joining the EU would also be influenced by how the societies of EU member states, their attitudes toward EU membership, and their views regarding the kind of EU that they want evolve. If the integration process in the EU moves toward deepening and religion acquires a greater salience as a key component of European and EU identity, the chances of Turkish membership would lessen. However, if the EU moves toward looser arrangements, becomes more like a free-trade area without

Table 5.4. EU Public Opinion on Turkey's Membership 2005–2010 (percent)

	2005	2006	2008	2010
For	31%	28%	31%	30%
Against	55%	59%	55%	59%
Don't Know	14%	13%	14%	11%

Source: Demetrios Dagdeverenis, "EU-Turkey Dialogue Initiative Working Paper, No. 2," August 2014, Bridging Europe: More Europe, More Democracy, and Based on EU Barometer Surveys at: http://www.bridgingeurope.net/eu-public-opinion-and-turkeys-eu-membership.html.

broader political ambitions, and the secular trend continues then the chances of Turkish membership could increase. This judgment is based on the fact that Turkey is already part of Europe's economic zone by virtue of its customs union with the EU and already plans are underway for greater economic rapprochement between the EU and Turkey. However, as noted earlier, the realization of these plans has become less certain.

CONCLUSIONS

The objections raised by the EU to Turkey's membership on economic, political, geographic, and demographic grounds have not been mere excuses. They have not been intended solely to obscure the real cause of EU's rejection of Turkey, namely deep religious and cultural differences between the two. These have been real obstacles. Similarly, the fact that the construction of European institutions and the development of an EU-wide identity have been a work in progress have impacted Europe's approach toward Turkish membership. Throughout this process, the evolution of the European project has been affected by dramatic international developments, especially the demise of the Soviet Union, and by the American-led wars in Afghanistan and Iraq and more recently the civil war in Syria which began in 2011 and their regional ramifications, including the large-scale flow of Muslim refugees to Europe.

Even today, there is no agreement among the EU's current members and their populations about the ultimate character of the EU, its foundational principles, and the basis of an EU-wide identity. In recent times, doubts have even been raised about the EU's benefits for its members. Yet as long as the EU and its populations are not clear about what kind of union they want and what values they most cherish, they cannot decide whether Turkey fits in their particular scheme for European unity. A tightly knit EU approaching a federation would find it more difficult to incorporate Turkey than would a more loosely structured union.

Nevertheless, it has become clear that the construction of a European union and a European-wide identity is nearly impossible outside of Europe's entire historical experience and not based solely on its traditions of liberalism and secularism. In this context, Europe's Christian past and the Christian roots of its culture, both high and popular, separate it from Turkey. However, it is not so much Christianity as a divinely revealed religion and its theological precepts that distinguish Europe from Turkey. Rather it is Christianity as culture, the foundation of many of Europe's secular values, a critical component of its historical memory, and a key part of its identity.

Viewed in this light, religion and the culture emanating from it have indeed been important barriers to Turkey's admission to the EU and principal causes of so much of the European population's reluctance to embrace Turkey as a member. According to François Foret, based on his study of the members of the European Parliament, "the influence attributed by MEPs to religion on the issue of Turkey is greater than on the general functioning of the EP." This is because religion acquires more salience "as soon as the issue is what it means to be European."[148]

EU-Turkey and more broadly Europe-Turkey relations have also been affected by the fact that Turkey's evolution into a modern and secular country whose values mirror those of Europe has not been yet completed. On the contrary, in the last three decades Turkey has been tempted by Islamist notions and options beyond Europe. The Turks, too, have not yet made up their minds where they belong and what values they cherish most. The project of Europeanizing Turkey has been only partially successful, and in today's Turkey there is still a conflict between the secular values of the republican era and Islam, which has proved far more resilient and persistent than had been thought before.

Turkey's national identity, too, is still in a state of flux and its different elements, such as Turkish nationalism, Islam, and Europeanism, are competing for supremacy. Recent developments have shown that Turkey, too, cannot escape the weight of its historical experience and its indigenous culture, no matter how strongly it wants to join Europe. Yet Turkey's historical experience and culture put it outside Europe.

In short, religion as cultural and civilizational phenomenon, rather than theological construct, has been influential in determining Europe's approach toward both Turkey and its admission to the EU, although other factors have also played key roles and have not been mere excuses to obscure the real cause of Turkey's rejection. The case of EU-Turkey relations has shown how religion's impact is felt on the actions of international actors and hence on the character of international relations, namely through their role as building blocks of collective identities. It has shown that the impact of identity-related factors, including religion, are strongest in the absence of compelling security and other material interests. Had Turkey been indispensable for the EU's Common Security and Defense Policy (CSDP) or if NATO did not exist as the principal Western alliance structure with Turkey as a member, some of the cultural reservations about Turkey's inclusion in the EU might have been overcome. EU-Turkey relations also illustrate the fact that no single factor can explain all of international actors' behavior. Rather their behavior, like that of state actors, is the outcome of interaction among diverse and often competing forces whose relative influence tends to ebb and flow depending on circumstances.

NOTES

1. For a brief history of Turkey's membership quest, see Edel Hughes, *Turkey's Accession to the European Union: The Politics of Exclusion?* (London/New York: Routledge, 2010).
2. All EU members must comply with the *Acquis*.
3. European Council: EU would open negotiations with Turkey, at: http://www.consilium.europa.eu/ueDocs/cms_data/docs/press/en/ec/73842.pdf.
4. For more details, see Vincent L. Morelli, "European Union Enlargement: A Status Report on Turkey's Accession Negotiations," *Congressional Research Service*, No. 7-5700, August 5, 2013, at: http://www.crs.gov.
5. Stephen Castle, "EU Freezes Talks on Turkey Membership," *The Independent*, 12, December 2006.
6. Şaban Kardaş, "Turkey's New Drive to Reenergize EU Accession: Moving beyond Suboptimal Equilibrium?" *German Marshall Fund of the Unites States, Analysis on Turkey*, 13 March 2013.
7. For a timeline on negotiations, see William Chislett, "Turkey's 10 Years of EU Accession Negotiations: No End in Sight—Analysis, Facts On Turkey," 8 October, 2015 at: http://factsonturkey.org/2186/turkey's-10-years-of-eu-accession-negotiation-no-end-in-sight-analysis.
8. Morelli, "The EU Enlargement: A Status Report on Turkish Accession Negotiations."
9. Based on conversation with Marc Pierini of Carnegie Endowment in Brussels and former French Ambassador to Turkey on 16 May 2015.
10. "Majority of Turkish People against EU membership Bid: Poll," *PRESS TV*, 24 January 2013.
11. Alex Spilius, "Turkey 'Will Probably Never be EU Member,'" *Daily Telegraph*, 21 September 2013, at: http://www.telegraph.co.uk/news/europe/turkey/10325218/Turkey-will-probably never-be-EU-member%2Chtml.
12. Quoted in Kardaş, "Turkey's New Drive to Reenergize EU Accession: Moving beyond the Suboptimal Equilibrium."
13. Erhan İçner and David Phinnemore, "Turkey and the EU: Looking Beyond Pessimisms," *Insight Turkey*, 16. 3 (Summer 2014), 41.
14. This new ideational influence is reflected in the statements of Turkish officials who frequently refer to the glorious episodes of Turkish history, notably what they call the "opening of the gates of Anatolia" by Muslim Turks, and the desire to recreate this lost space. See Ahmet Davutoğlu's speech at the Diyarbakir University on 12 October 2013.
15. For more details, see Jorge Baudner, "The Evolution of Turkey's Foreign Policy under the AK Party Government," *Insight Turkey*, 16. 3 (Summer 2014,) 91–95. Also, Nurullah Ardiç, "Civilizational Discourse, the 'Alliance of Civilizations' and Turkish Foreign Policy," *Insight Turkey*, 16. 3 (Summer 2014).
16. The "domino effect" is a reference to the war in Vietnam and the idea that if the West did not prevail there, other countries in Southeast Asia could fall to the communists "like dominoes." The term was coined by President Dwight Eisenhower in April 1954 at the time of the battle for Dien Bien Phu, which the French lost. See http://www.history.com/topics/cold-war/domino-theory.
17. Based on conversations in Brussels, May 2015.
18. See Kardaş, "Turkey's New Drive to Reenergize EU Accession: Moving beyond the Suboptimal Equilibrium."
19. For details see Transatlantic Trends Survey of 2014, German Marshall Fund, at: http://trends.gmfus.org/files/2012/09/Trends_2014_complete.pdf.
20. On the positive agenda, see Cengiz Aktar, "The Positive Agenda and Beyond: A New Beginning for the EU-Turkey Relations?" *Insight Turkey*, 14. 3 (Summer 2012).
21. Quoted in İçner and Phinnemore, "Turkey and the EU: Looking beyond the Pessimisms," 42–43.
22. Nick Tatterrel and Paul Carrel, "Merkel in Bind on Migrants Ready to Back Faster Turkish EU Bid," *Reuters*, 18 October 2015 at: http://uk.reuters.com/article/uk-europe-migrants-germany-turkey-idUKKCN0SC08020151018.

23. Mathew Holehouse, "Turkey Ridicules the Offer of EU Membership in Exchange for Halting Refugee Influx," The *Daily Telegraph*, 16 October, 2015, at: http://www.telegraph.co.uk/news/worldnews/Europe/turkey/11937537/EU-approves-Turkey-migrant-plan.html.

24. "EU, Turkey Strike Heralded Migrant Deal but Costs Are High," *Japan Times*, 19 March 2016, at: http://www.japantimes.co.jp/news/2016/03/19/world/eu-turkey-strike-heralded-migrant0d.e.

25. "Anyone Who Says Turkey Is a European Country Wants EU's Death," *RT QUESTION MORE*, 20 March, 2016, at: https://www.rt.com/news/336385-sarkozy-turkey-eu-death.

26. References in this section to Cyprus as an EU member refers to the government in Nicosia that is Greek-Cypriot-dominated, that is, the Republic of Cyprus. The Turkish-dominated part of Cyprus, the Turkish Republic of Northern Cyprus, is not included. See "Politics of Cyprus," at https://en.wikipedia.org/wiki/Politics_of_Cyprus.

27. "Presidency Conclusions," 15/16 June 2006, Council of the European Union, 15/16 June 2006, at: http://www.concilium.europa.eu.

28. Interview with Ollie Rehn, *Reuters*, 28 March 2006.

29. "Turkey Stumbles over Cyprus on Way to EU," *Deutsche Welle*, 5 November 2013. For a more in-depth analysis of this issue, see Samin Suvarierol, "The Cyprus Obstacle on Turkey's Road to Membership in the European Union," *Turkish Studies*, 4. 1. 2003.

30. By the spring of 2015, the election of a moderate president in the Turkish part of Cyprus had increased hopes for an eventual resolution of the dispute. See George Kyris, "Is Mustafa Akinci the Best Hope Yet for a Solution to the Cyprus Problem?" *The Guardian*, 28 April 2015.

31. "EU observer: Cyprus Threatens to Block EU Deal on Turkey Talks," *EU Observer*, 23 September 2008, at: http://euobserver.com/9/23008. Also, "Cyprus Won't Open EU Accession Chapters for Turkey," *PSEKA*, at: http://news.speska.net/index.php?module=article&id=12350.

32. "Deputy Bozkir: Cyprus Used as Excuse to Block Turkey's EU Accession," *Daily Sabah*, 30 September 2014.

33. "Turkey Set to Launch Tender for Offshore Exploration," *Hurriyet Daily News*, 16 March, 2007 at: http://www.hurriyetdailynews.com/turkey/set/to-launch-tender-for-offshore-exploration.aspx?pageID=438&n=turkey. Also "Eastern Mediterranean Oil Exploration Pits Turkey Against Cyprus," *IHS/ Global Insight Perspective*, 15 February 2007 at: https://www.ihs.com/country-industry-forecasting.html?ID=106598398.

34. For details, see *EU Turkey Progress Report*, 3 October 2014.

35. "Turkey Opens Trial over 1997 'Post-Modern' Coup," *BBC News, Europe*, 2 September 2013, at: http://www.bbc.com/news/world-europe-23925035?print=true.

36. Robert Fisk "Has Recep Tayyip Erdoğan Gone from Model Middle East Strongman to Tin Pot Dictator?" *The Independent*, 10 April 2014.

37. "Hundreds of Turkish Police Officers Dismissed," *BBC News/Europe*, 7 January 2014.

38. "Erdoğan Highlights Judicial Impartiality, While Top Judge Focuses on Judicial Independence," *Journal of Turkish Weekly*, 1 September, 2014, 18.

39. Robin Emmott, "EU Chastises Turkey Over Interference in Courts, Freedom of Speech," *Reuters*, October 8, 2014, at: http://www.reuters.com/assets/print?aid=USKCN0HX16820141008.

40. "Turkey: The Erdoğan-Gülen Showdown," *Turkish Digest*, 19 March 2014, at: http://www.turkishdigest.blogpost.com/2014/03/turkey-erdogan-gulen-showdown.ftcom.html.

41. Sonar Çağaptay, "What Turkey's Election Results Mean," The Washington Institute for Near East Policy, 9 June 2015, at: https://www.washingtoninstitute.org/policy-analysis/view/what-turkey. Also, Francesco Milan, "What Does Erdoğan's Setback at the Elections Mean for Turkey's Role on Global Stage," *The Telegraph*, 9 June 2015, at: http://www.telegraph.co.uk/news/worldnews/europe/turkey/11661812/What-does-Erdogans-setback-at-the-elections-mean-for-Turkeys-role-on-the-global-stage.html.

42. See "Turkish Crowds Rally to Democracy Calls After Coup Attempt," *BBC World News/Europe*, 16 July, 2016 at: http://www.bbc.com/news/world-europe-36817980. Also, "Turkey Coup: Who Was behind Turkey Coup Attempt," *BBC World News/Europe*, 16 July 2016 at: http://www.bbc.com/news/world-europe-36815476.

43. Roberto de Mattei (translator John Laughland), *Turkey in Europe: Benefit or Catastrophe* (UK: Gracewing, 2009), 34–37.

44. Renata Janka Toth, "Alevis Rights and the Freedom of Religion in Turkey: An Ignored Minority," at:http://www.academia.edu/3279532/alevis_rights_and-the_freedom_of_religion_in_turkey. Also "Members of Alevi Community Stage Demo in Turkey," Press *TV*, 4 November 2013 at: http://www.presstv.ir/2013/11/04/332842/alevis-stage-demonstrations-in-turkey. The conditions of the Alevis have deteriorated under Erdoğan partly because of tensions in Syrian-Turkish relations following Turkey's call for Bashar Al Assad's removal and its help to his opponents. On general human rights issues and their impact on EU-Turkey relations, also see Senem Aydin-Düzgit and E. Fuat Keyman, "EU-Turkey Relations and the Stagnation of Turkish Democracy," *Global Turkey in Europe*, Working Paper No. 2, 4 December 2012.

45. "Jethro Mullen, "Pope Francis Uses 'Genocide' to Refer to Mass Killings of Armenians," *CNN*, 13 April, 2015, at: http://www.cnn.com/2015/04/13/europe/pope-francis-turkey-armenia-genocide-reference; and "Turkey Anger at Pope Francis Armenian Genocide Claim," *BBC News/Europe*, 12 April 2015 at: http://www.bbc.com/news/world-europe-32272604.

46. For a discussion of the question of minority rights in EU-Turkish relations, see Gözde Yilmaz, "From EU Conditionality to Domestic Choice for Change: Exploring Europeanization of Minority Rights," in eds. Cigdem Nas and Yonca Özer, *Turkey and the European Union: The Process of Europeanization* (UK: Ashgate, 2012).

47. "EU Raises Concerns on Media Freedom in Turkey After Baydar Fired," *Today's Zaman*, 25 July 2013. Also Robert Fisk, "Has Recep Tayyip Erdoğan Gone from Model Middle East Strongman to Tin Pot Dictator?" *The Independent*, 10 April 2014.

48. Emmott, "EU Chastises Turkey Over Interference in Courts, Freedom of Speech." For more details on the EU Commission's assessment of Turkey's human rights record, see the Commissions' 2014 Turkey Progress Report.

49. Safak Timur & Tim Orango, "Turkey Seized Newspaper *Zaman* as Press Crackdown Continues," *New York Times*, 4 March 2016.

50. Jack Moore, "France, Germany and EU Officials Condemn Turkey's Seizure of *Zaman* Newspaper," *Newsweek*, 7 March, 2016, at: http://www.newsweek.com/france-germany-turkey-zaman-erdogan.

51. Kardaş, "Turkey's New Drive to Reenergize EU Accession: Moving beyond the Suboptimal Equilibrium."

52. Meltem Müftüler-Baç and E. Fuat Keyman, "Turkey's Unconsolidated Democracy: The Nexus between Democratization and Majoritarianism in Turkey," *Global Turkey in Europe*, Policy Brief, No. 19, January 2015.

53. Based on author's conversations with Marc Pierini.

54. See Yilmaz, "From EU Conditionality to Domestic Choice for Change," 121.

55. Emre Peker, "Turkish Police Seize Two TV Stations of Government Critics, *The Wall Street Journal*, 28 October 2015.

56. De Mattei, *Turkey in Europe: Benefit or Catastrophe*, 16.

57. For more details, see "The EU Council Progress Report on Turkey," October 2014.

58. Daniel Dombey, "Turkey's Economy Slows to 2.4% in 2014," *Financial Times*, 31 March 2015.

59. For a discussion of these countervailing economic arguments regarding Turkey's EU membership in the case of East European countries, see Armağan Emre Çakir and Angelika Gergelova, "Tug of War or Lifeline? Central European Views on Turkey's Accession to the EU," in eds. Lucy Tunkrova and Pavel Saradin, *The Politics of EU Accession: Turkish Challenges and Central European Experiences* (London: Routledge, 2010), 119–20.

60. For a discussion of some of these issues, see Katinka Barysch "The Economics of Turkish Accession," *Centre For European Reform*, 5 July 2011, at: http://www.cer.org.uk/sites/default/files/publications/attachements/pdf/2011/turkey-july   05-2161.pdf.essay_economics.

61. Zia Öniş, "Turkey, Europe, and Paradoxes of Identity: Perspectives on the International Context of Democratization," *Mediterranean Quarterly*, 10.3. 1997, at: https://muse.jhu.edu/journals/mediterranean_quarterly/v010/10.3onis.html.

62. De Mattei, *Turkey in Europe: Benefit or Catastrophe?* 1.

63. Celsen Oner, *Turkey and the European Union: The Question of European Identity* (Lanham, MD: Lexington Books, 2011), 3.
64. Oner, *Turkey and the European Union*, 4.
65. For a full discussion of these issues, see Gerard Delanty, *Inventing Europe: Idea, Identity, Reality* (New York: St. Martin's Press, 1995).
66. Statement at a conference in 2004, entitled "EU and Turkey: Beyond 2004."
67. For a discussion of these issues, see Elzbieta Stadmüller and Klaus Bachmann (eds.), *The EU's Shifting Borders: Theoretical and Policy Implications in the New Neighborhood* (London & New York: Routledge, 2012).
68. Oner, *Turkey and the European Union: The Question of European Identity*, 7.
69. The idea of Europe as a construct of imagination is reflected in the title of the following book by Chiara Bottici and Benoit Challand, *Imagining Europe: Myth, Memory and Identity* (Cambridge: Cambridge University Press, 2013).
70. On these questions, see Bahar Rumellili, "Transforming Conflicts on EU Borders: The Case of Greek-Turkish Relations," *Journal of Common Market Studies*, 45. 1. March 2007.
71. Quoted in Oner, *Turkey and the European Union: The Question of European Identity*, 15.
72. Bottici and Challand, *Imagining Europe*, 18.
73. Bottici and Challand, *Imagining Europe*, 19.
74. In fact, these countries hope one day to join Europe.
75. However, it should be noted that Europe already is vulnerable to the consequences of these local conflicts, and that Turkey's EU membership would guarantee that it would not pursue policies in these areas contrary to European positions.
76. "Deputy Bozkir: Cyprus Is Used as Excuse to Block Turkey's EU Accession."
77. A former high-level EU diplomat told the author that the EU's policy in regard to Ukraine, which was seen in Moscow as provocation, was inordinately influenced by Poland which, because of its historical experience, has a particularly negative view of Russia.
78. Quoted in David Kushner, "Self-Perception and Identity in Contemporary Turkey," *Journal of Contemporary History*, 32.2 (1997), 232.
79. On the question of different layers of European identity and their coexistence and conflict, see Andrew C. Gould and Anthony M. Messina, *Europe's Contending Identities: Supranationalism, Ethnoregionalism, Religion and Nationalism* (Cambridge: Cambridge University Press, 2014).
80. Asa Lundgren, "The Case of Turkey: Are Some Countries More 'European' Than Others," in ed. Helen Sjursen, *Questioning EU Enlargement: Europe in Search of Identity* (London: Routledge, 2006), 134.
81. Lundgren, "The Case of Turkey," 135.
82. Lundgren, "The Case of Turkey," 134.
83. Kardaş, "Turkey's New Drive to Reenergize EU Accession: Moving Beyond the Suboptimal Equilibrium."
84. The leader of the French right wing political party Front National, Marine Le Pen, is of this view.
85. See, for example: "How Tories Can Avoid the Fate We Want Least: David Cameron Must Bring Forward EU Referendum to Six Months After Elections," *Daily Mail*, 5 November 2014, at: http://www.dailymail.co.uk/news/article-2822795/DAILY_MAIL-COMMENT. Tories-avoid-fate-want-David-Cameron. And "UK Should Leave EU to Control Immigration Within Country," *RT QUESTION MORE*, 24 October 2014, at: http://www.rt.com/op-edge/198952-uk-eu-immigration-referendum-Cameron. Also, "The Rise of Anti-EU Parties and the Crisis of Confidence," *EU Observer*, 7 January 2014, at: http://www.euobserver.com/political/122156.
86. Ingrid Kylstad, "Turkey and the EU: A 'New' European Identity in the Making?" LEQS Paper No. 27, October 2010.
87. For more detailed discussion of these issues, see François Foret, *Religion and Politics in the European Union: The Secular Canopy* (Cambridge, Cambridge University Press, 2014), 13–37.

88. On the importance of historical memory, see Thomas Pedersen, *When Culture Becomes Politics: European Identity in Perspective* (Aarhus, Denmark: Aarhus University Press, 2008), 83–116.

89. See Anthony D. Smith, *National Identity* (Reno: University of Nevada Press, 1991).

90. José Casanova, "The Long, Difficult and Tortuous Journey of Turkey into Europe and the Dilemmas of European Civilization," *Constellations*, 13. 2. 2006, 236.

91. An example of backsliding is the rise of religious militancy and obscurantism in many Muslim countries, despite decades of modernization.

92. The rise of religious fundamentalism and militancy is at least partly the consequence of the process of imported modernity.

93. Gerard Delanty, "Islam and European Modernity in Historical Perspective: toward a Cosmopolitan Perspective," in eds. Hakan Yilmaz and Çağla E. Aykaç, *Perceptions of Islam in Europe: Culture, Identity and the Muslim "Other"* (London: I. B. Tauris, 2012), 13–29.

94. S. N. Eisenstadt, *The Origins and Diversity of Axial Civilizations* (New York: SUNY Press, 1986).

95. Britain is still in the process of converting to decimal units in some parts of the economy.

96. Kalypso Nicolaidis, "Turkey Is European . . . for Europe's Sake," in *Turkey and the European Union: From Association to Accession*. Netherlands: Ministry of Foreign Affairs, January 2004, 5.

97. Perry Anderson, "Kemalism," *London Review of Books*, 30. 17. 2008.

98. See de Mattei, *Turkey in Europe: Benefit or Catastrophe*, 38–49.

99. Debate continues about how much of this problem relates to economic difficulties in recent years and how much derives from factors related to the end of the Cold War, especially the opening of frontiers to "European" countries that had missed more than forty years of social, economic, and political development, as well as factors such as the falling birthrate in Western Europe which has required an upsurge in immigration, including from countries that are not part of the European experience in any meaningful sense. This is an offshoot of the long-standing debate between "deepening" and "widening." Is the former necessary to enable the latter to have a chance to succeed without destroying any EU identity that is more than just a sophisticated customs union?

100. For a discussion of these issues, see Ali Tekin, "Future of Turkey-EU Relations: A Civilizational Discourse," *Futures*, 37. 2005, at: http://www.sciencedirect.com.

101. Helene Ahrweiler, "Roots and Trends in European Culture," in ed. Soledad Garcia, *European Identity and Search for Legitimacy* (London: Pinter Publishers, 1993), 34.

102. Ahrweiler, "Roots and Trends," 35. This view dismisses the Persian Achaemenid Empire, the first world empire and the model for Alexander's world empire, and it also treats the highly sophisticated Sassanid Empire as uncivilized.

103. Alexander Rosenthal Pubul, "A Reflection on European Unity: The EU and the Memory of Christendom," *EU Perspectives*, 13 June 2014 at: http://www.euperspectives.blogactiv.eu/2014/06/13/a-reflection-on-european-unity-the-eu-and-the-memory-of-christendom.

104. The French consider the conversion and baptism of Clovis, the King of the Franks, to Christianity in the ninth century as marking France's birth. In 1996 the government celebrated the 1,000th anniversary of his baptism. See Gail Russel Chaddok, "Ancient Hero Clovis Stirs French Debate," *Christian Science Monitor*, 18 September 1996.

105. John Hale, "The Renaissance Idea of Europe," in ed. Soledad Garcia, *European Identity and Search for Legitimacy*, 46.

106. For a brief chronology of the gradual change from Christendom to Europe, see M. E. Yapp, "Europe in the Turkish Mirror," *Past & Present*, 137. November 1992, 142–46.

107. Pubul, "A Reflection on European Unity." On these issues, also see Daniel Philpot and Timothy Samuel Shah, "Faith, Freedom and Federation: The Role of Religious Ideas and Institutions in European Political Conversion," in eds. Timothy A. Byrnes and Peter J. Katzenstein, *Religion in an Expanding Europe* (Cambridge: Cambridge University Press, 2006), 34–63.

108. Quoted in Pubul, "A Reflection on European Unity," 34–63.

109. For a discussion of these issues, see Wolfram Kaiser, *Christian Democracy and the Origins of European Union* (Cambridge: Cambridge University Press, 2007).
110. Delanty, "Islam and European Modernity in Historical Perspective," 16.
111. A prominent critic of philosophers was Imam Ghazali. In his book *Ehyaye al Din* (the Revival of Religion), he attacked philosophers.
112. Delanty, "Islam and European Modernity in Historical Perspective," 17.
113. His full name was Charles Louis de Secondat, Baron de la Brede et de Montesquieu.
114. Karl Lowith is a scholar who believed that modernity is in effect a secularized version of Christianity. See his *Meaning in History: The Theological Presumptions of the Philosophy of History* (Chicago: Chicago University Press, 1949).
115. Matthew 22:21, *King James Version*.
116. Based on author's interview with him. He is a professor at the Free University of Brussels and a prolific author on the subject of religion in European politics and institutions.
117. Samuel P. Huntington, *The Clash of Civilizations and the Remaking of the World Order* (New York: Simon & Schuster, 1996), 21. For a more detailed analysis of the concept of the other and its manifold manifestations, see Vilho Harle, *The Enemy with a Thousand Faces* (Bridgeport, CT: Praeger, 2000).
118. Ahrweiler, "Roots and Trends in European Culture," 34.
119. Turkish President Erdoğan in 2016 said that for a long time all Muslims were considered as Turks.
120. A later edited version is by Charles Schefer, entitled *Petit Traité de L'origines des Turcs par Theodore Spandouyn Cantacasim*, Paris, 1896.
121. Hakan Yilmaz, "Giris: Turkiye'yi Avrupa Haritasina Sokmak," in ed. Hakan Yilmaz, *Avrupa Haritsanida Turkiye* (Istanbul: Bosphorus University Press, 2005), p. 17.
122. On Blacque, see Orhan Kologlu, "Alexandre Blacque: *Defenseur de L'Etat Ottoman Pour l'Amour des Libertés*," in eds. Batu and Bacque Grammont, *Empire Ottoman, La Republique de Turquie et La France* (Istanbul: ISIS Publishers, 1986), 179–95.
123. Yapp, "Europe in the Turkish Mirror," 155.
124. The Constitution has so far been ratified by eighteen members. France and the Netherlands rejected the constitution in a referendum.
125. On attacks in Paris in 2015, see *"Charlie Hebdo Attacks: Three Days of Terror," BBC NewsEurope*, 14 January 2015, at: http://www.bbc.com/news/world-europe-30708237.
126. For the involvement of European Muslims in ISIL and operations in Syria, see Michael Holden, "Up to 5,000 European Fighters in Syria Pose Risk," *Reuters*, 31 January 2015.
127. Based on conversations with Marc Pierini.
128. De Mattei, *Turkey in Europe: Benefit or Catastrophe*," 53.
129. "Swiss Voters Back Ban on Minarets," *BBC News*, 29 November 2009, at: http://www.news.bbc.co.uk/2/hi/europe/838509.
130. Quoted in Andrew Higgins, "A More Secular Europe Divided by the Cross," *New York Times*, 17 June 2013.
131. Higgins, "A More Secular Divided."
132. For a discussion of these issues, also see Philip Jenkins, *God's Continent, Christianity, Islam and Europe's Religious Crisis* (Oxford: Oxford University Press, 2007).
133. See David Gibson, "A 'Christian' Europe Without Christianity," *Religion News Service*, 13 August 2013.
134. Gibson, "A 'Christian' Europe."
135. Gibson, "A 'Christian' Europe." Pope Benedict XVI wrote the foreword to the book.
136. Quoted in Gibson, "A 'Christian' Europe."
137. "David Cameron Says the UK Is a Christian Country," *BBC News/UK Politics*, 16 December 2011, at: http://www.bbc.com/nnews/uk-politics-16224394?print=true. Also Steven Swinford, "David Cameron Says Christians Should Be 'More Evangelical,'" *Daily Telegraph*, 16 April 2014, at: http://www.telegraph.co.uk/news/religion/10770245/David-Cammeron-says-Christians-should-be-more-evangelical.html.
138. De Mattei, *Turkey in Europe: Benefit or Catastrophe*, 50–62.
139. Quoted in de Mattei, *Turkey in Europe*, 50–62.
140. Foret, *Religion and Politics in the European Union; The Secular Canopy*, 242.

141. Foret, *Religion and Politics*, 244.

142. For a detailed analysis of the position of various EU member states on Turkish membership, see Sait Aksit, Özgehan Şenyuva, Çiğdem Üstün, "Turkey Watch: EU Member States' Perceptions on Turkey's Accession to the EU," November 2009, available at: http://www.academia.edu/839822/Turkey_Watch_EU_Member_States_Perceptions_on_Turkey's_Accession_to_the_EU.

143. Kardaş, "Turkey's New Drive to Reenergize EU Accession: Moving Beyond the Suboptimal Equilibrium."

144. Pinar Dost-Niyego, "Europe-Turkey Tensions Rise as Russia Seeks Partnership with Ankara," *Atlantic Council*, 22 December 2014, at: http://www.atlanticcouncil.org/blogs/new-atlanticist/europe-turkey-tensions-rise-as-russia-seeks-partnership-with-ankara?tmpl=component&print=1.

145. Alex Barker and Daniel Dombey, "EU and Turkey Look to Deepen Trade Ties," *Financial Times*, 23 March 2015, at: http://www.ft.com/cms/s/)/b03abe4e-d07e-11e4-982a-00144feab7de.html.

146. See Aksit, Senyura, and Üstün, "Turkey Watch: EU Member States' Perceptions on Turkey's Accession to the EU."

147. See Hannah Q. Young, "Turkish Accession to the European Union: Shaped by Perception or Reality," *Claremont-UC Undergraduate Conference on the European Union*, 11. 2013, 147. Also see Antonia M. Ruiz-Jimenez and Jose I. Torreblanca, "European Public Opinion and Turkey's Accession: Making Sense of Arguments For and Against," *European Institutes Network*, Working Paper No. 16, May 2007, at: www.CEPS.eu/files/book/1494.pdf.

148. Foret, *Religion and Politics in the European Union*, 243.

Conclusion

The analysis in this study, in particular in the three case studies, has yielded several important conclusions about religion's role in shaping the behavior of international actors, especially as compared to other determinants of their actions. Through this analysis, it has also assessed religion's relative influence in determining the dynamics and character of international affairs in comparison to other factors such as the pursuit of power and interests, security, economic gain, and prestige. This work has sought to dispel erroneous assumptions about the approach which the international relations discipline takes to the study of religion's role in international affairs. In particular, it has shown the invalidity of the thesis of the discipline's secular bias and that of the inadequacy of existing theoretical schools of international relations to properly addressing religion's role in and impact on international affairs. It has shown that an accurate assessment of religion's relative role in determining the behavior of international actors, as well as its impact on international affairs, requires two essential steps. First, religion needs to be defined more rigorously and less expansively than is often the case. Second, it is necessary to clarify how and in what ways religion's impact is different from that of other value systems and ideational and cultural factors on international actors' behavior and, hence, on the dynamics of international affairs. The study has further shown that assessing the role of religion in international affairs requires identification of the principal agents and channels through which religion's influence is transmitted to international affairs.

The following are the most significant conclusions drawn from this study:

IMPORTANCE OF AGENCY

To assess religion's impact on international affairs as accurately as possible, the question of *agency* should receive greater attention. As with other forces affecting the character and dynamics of international affairs, religion's influence is transmitted through the actions of such agents, namely both state and non-state actors. Thus it is necessary first to identify the *range and characteristics of various agents* through whose intermediary religion's influence is transmitted to international affairs. Further, it is important to identify *the principal international actors and their characteristics* because it is through their agency that religion's influence is mostly transmitted to international affairs.

CONTINUED IMPORTANCE OF STATE ACTORS

Despite the erosion of the power of nation-states, especially that of small and weak states, nation-states still remain the main units of the international system. Their actions most shape the dynamics and character of international affairs. Meanwhile, the impact of non-state actors is less significant, partly because most of them are either formed by the coming together of states or they need the support of state actors. This is especially true of most violent non-state actors. Only in those societies where state structures have been shattered by civil war or foreign military intervention do non-state actors operate fairly independently. Thus what is sometimes interpreted as the obsolescence of nation-states is really about the weakness of states and their inequality in terms of their power and ability effectively to manage their societies.

IMPORTANCE OF IDENTIFYING PRINCIPAL DETERMINANTS OF INTERNATIONAL ACTORS' BEHAVIOR

Assessing religion's relative role in shaping the behavior of various actors requires that the range of factors that determine the actions of both state and non-state actors be clearly established and their relative impact be weighed.

IMPORTANCE OF FOCUSING ON SPECIFIC CASES

This assessment is best done by focusing on specific cases. Only by analyzing specific cases can the interplay of various determinants of international actors' behavior, including that of religion, be properly observed and their relative influence measured. Otherwise, analysis risks being lost in generalities.

FALLACY OF INTERNATIONAL RELATION'S SECULAR BIAS

There is no validity to claims of a secular bias in the international relations discipline and that analysts have willfully ignored religion's role. If it has not received adequate attention, that is not because of international relations scholars' secular biases. Rather, the neglect of religion's role has been due to the fact that, until the last four decades, religion's role in politics, even in religious societies, had declined and was replaced by various secular ideologies, such as nationalism, socialism, and liberalism.

ADEQUACY OF EXISTING THEORETICAL SCHOOLS OF INTERNATIONAL RELATIONS

Despite the view of some scholars in the field, existing theoretical schools of the international relations discipline are well equipped to address religion's role in analyzing the behavior of international actors, along with other factors which affect the dynamics and character of international relations. This judgment is based on evidence that religion exercises its influence mostly by being part of various international actors' value systems and cultures, as well as by constituting a key component of their collective identities. Consequently, religion's role can be addressed in the framework of analyzing the impact of value/ideational factors and identity-related influences on actors' behavior.

This observation implies that religion's impact on the behavior of those actors whose societies are religious or where religion forms a key component of their national identities is stronger than in societies that are less religious or not at all. Yet even those state actors whose societies are religious and where religion is an important identity-marker are forced to balance the demands of values and identities against more tangible material considerations. Because all theoretical schools of international relations allow for factoring in the impact of ideas/ideals and identity-related factors in analyzing various actors' behavior, they can also accommodate the study of the role of religion.

CONTINUED PRIMACY OF SECURITY AND MATERIAL INTERESTS

The case studies of Turkish and Russian approaches to the Bosnian War illustrate the continued centrality of security- and interest-related factors in determining state actors' behavior, as compared to pressures of ideas, ideals, and identity. They also validate a basic premise of the realist school of international relations theory that security is a fundamental driver of states' behavior. In the final analysis, in both the Russian and Turkish cases, considerations of security, political, and economic interests prevailed over impulses generated by factors of religious solidarity with their respective Muslim and Orthodox co-religionists or bonds of ethnicity and culture.

The exception to this rule is when decisions regarding an issue related to actors' external behavior has highly significant internal political dimensions and raises fundamental identity-related questions. A good example is the case of Turkish efforts to join the European Union. Because potential Turkish admission to the EU raises fundamental questions about European identity, identity-related and religio-cultural arguments have played a larger role in the EU decision to so far deny Turkey membership. However, the fact that Turkey's EU membership has not been absolutely necessary from the security perspective of European states has made it easier for the EU to reject Turkey's requests to join.

CENTRAL ROLE OF CAPABILITIES

The case studies demonstrated that, regardless of their desires or preferences, states' ability to pursue value/identity-related policies is largely determined by their capabilities. Pursuit of such objectives is subject to the same resource constraints as are more materially inspired goals. For example, if Russia's economy had been stronger at the time of the Bosnian crisis and its need for Western assistance less urgent, Moscow might have taken bolder actions in defense of fellow Orthodox Serbs. But because of its economic weakness, Russia had to be more cautious. A similar situation prevailed in Turkey. Its concern to preserve its security and political connections with Europe and the United States, along with its dependence on Western military and economic assistance, argued against a bold Turkish policy in defense of Bosnian Muslims.

RELIGION IS MORE EFFECTIVE IF USED AS IDEOLOGY

Religion's impact on the behavior of international actors is stronger when it is ideologized and serves as the foundation of political legitimacy. In its ideologized form religion develops a close linkage to power. However, generally ideologized religions are so far removed from the traditional religions, defined as theological and/or spiritual systems of belief, or even traditional cultural patterns, that their characterization as religion is problematic. In its ideologized version, religion performs functions similar to that of secular ideologies or values systems. It is thus more appropriate that it be treated in the same manner as secular ideologies and its influence on international actors' behavior be addressed and assessed in the same way as the impact of other value/ideational/cultural and identity-related factors.

INDIRECT NATURE OF RELIGION'S INFLUENCE

Religion's influence is generally felt indirectly, that is, through its role in shaping various actors' identities and their self-perceptions and world-views, as well as being part of their cultures and value systems. Religion affects their behavior by virtue of being "a diffuse influence or symbolic material."[1] Thus religion clearly impacts actors' perceptions of their interests and hence their behavior, including perceptions of who are their friends and who are their enemies. In this way it also affects the dynamics of international relations. However, religion's role in shaping actors' behavior in specific cases is fairly limited or at any rate not decisive, especially when security concerns and significant political and economic interests are at stake.

INTERNAL POLITICS AS THE PRINCIPAL CONDUIT FOR RELIGION'S INFLUENCE

Religion influences international affairs largely by affecting the internal development of various state actors, especially in states whose societies are still highly or significantly religious. In such states, there is a greater linkage and interaction between religion and politics than in predominantly secular societies where the level of popular religiosity is not very high. Internal political changes within states, especially of a dramatic and fundamental character, often alter the pattern and character of their external behavior. Consequently, such dramatic changes also alter the dynamics of regional and at times even of international relations. If caused by religious factors, such internal changes serve as one channel through which religion's influence is felt on international affairs.

Alterations in the external behavior of countries undergoing dramatic political changes occur when they change their value systems or political ideologies and hence the pattern of power relations to the character of political elites. A good example is the 1979 Iranian Revolution, which brought down the country's secular monarchy, ushered in an avowedly Islamic political system, and changed the composition of Iran's political elites. The impact of religion on Iran's post-revolution political system was strong because it was of an ideologized variety. This was especially true of the new regime's world-view, which was shaped more by Marxist and Third Worldist notions than by traditional and theological Islam. Following these changes, Iran's external behavior was dramatically altered which, in turn, deeply affected the dynamics of regional and even to some degree international politics.

The emergence and growing influence of Islamically oriented political elites in Turkey in the 1990s affected the behavior of the Turkish state. But because Turkey's political and, especially, foreign policy community remained essentially secular at the time of the Bosnian crisis, the Islamic elites' influence in shaping Turkish policy remained limited. It is conceivable but unlikely that Turkey's behavior would have been different if the country had been ruled by an Islamist party. The coming to power in 2003 of an Islamically oriented political party, Justice and Development (AKP), did have significant implications for Turkish foreign policy, especially from 2011 to 2015. Islamically influenced views regarding Turkey's foreign policy impacted on its relations with the European Union and altered the dynamics of the Turkish desire to join the EU, as well as European views about the wisdom of Turkey's admission. The Islamist party's accession to power also affected the Turkish government's perception of its interests and views of its friendships and enmities in neighboring regions, especially the Middle East. In particular, it injected a sectarian note into Turkey's regional policies and thus significantly contributed to changes in the dynamics of regional relations.

IMPORTANCE OF DOMESTIC STRUCTURES OF ACTORS AS CHANNELS OF INFLUENCE

Religion's influence on international affairs is largely transmitted through the domestic political structures of international actors. They include the character of domestic political systems of actors, in particular whether they are autocratic or participatory, and the nature and characteristics of their political leaders. In participatory political systems, party politics and rivalries could be an important channel for religion's influence on international actors' behavior because competing political parties often use value-related and ideational elements, of which religion is a part, as means to advance more worldly goals and objectives. This interaction was clearly demonstrated in Russian and Turkish policies toward the Bosnian War. Religion was used by competing political players to advance their own positions in electoral politics and to undermine those of their rivals. Although their use of religion was essentially instrumental, serving as a tool to advance their own particular objectives and ambitions, it nevertheless made religion a more significant factor in deliberations regarding appropriate state policies toward the Bosnia conflict. For example, the instrumental use of religion by the Russian opposition forced President Boris Yeltsin's government to adopt a relatively more pro-Serb posture than it would possibly have done otherwise, without however altering the underlying principles of Russia's approach to the conflict. Similarly, Turkey's secular government had to show its commitment to helping the

Bosnian Muslims, partly out of competition with the rival Islamist party, *Refah*.

CIVIL SOCIETY AND PUBLIC OPINION AS CHANNELS FOR RELIGION'S INFLUENCE

Another channel for transmitting religion's influence to international actors and hence to international affairs is through the activities of civil societies, including various religious groups and institutions. Public opinion, especially the degree of the public's willingness to make sacrifices for the sake of religious considerations, also influences the extent of religion's impact on state actors' behavior. This was clearly demonstrated in Russian and Turkish approaches to the Bosnian conflict. In both cases, lack of widespread popular support for unilateral intervention, especially of a military nature, on behalf of their respective fellow religionists in Bosnia and Serbia, contributed to the Turkish and Russian governments' ability to pursue essentially pragmatic policies determined by their security and other interests rather than by religious sympathies.

POLITICAL LEADERS' PROCLIVITIES

Political leaders' character, their ideational and value orientations, including the level of their religiosity, and their self-perceptions and world-views are also important channels for transmitting religion's influence. A recent example of how leaders' ideational/value inclinations and their self- and world-views affected the behavior of key state actors, significantly impacting the dynamics of regional and international relations, was the 2003 decision by the United States and the United Kingdom to invade Iraq. The leaders of these two states, U.S. president George W. Bush and British prime minister Tony Blair, both had strong religious beliefs which influenced their respective world-views. In particular, both leaders saw the international arena as a battlefield on which forces of good and evil contended and that it was necessary for good to triumph. Because they saw Iraq's Saddam Hussein as representing evil, they believed he must be removed. However, had there not been other important security-related, economic, and political arguments in favor of invading Iraq, the two leaders' religious inclinations and their shared Manichean view of the world might not have been sufficient to tip the balance of the argument in favor of invasion. Certainly, in the absence of such security and other pragmatic considerations it would have been much more difficult to convince the British and American publics of the wisdom of engaging in large-scale military operations. By contrast, the fact that neither President Boris Yeltsin nor the Turkish prime minister, Tansu Çiller, was particularly religious contributed to their adopting policies toward the Bosnian War which were essentially pragmatic and based on their views of Turkish and Russian national interests.

RELIGION AS INSTRUMENT OF POLICY

Religion influences international affairs more by being used as an instrument to advance various actors' policy goals than by playing a key role in their formulation. This is particularly true where the indirect channels of religion's influence on actors, such as being part of their value systems, collective identity, culture, and historical experience, are excluded from analysis of their motivations. Yet even the instrumental use of religion affects the dynamics of international affairs and enhances its role in shaping their character and dynamics. For example, the Taliban's behavior might not have been motivated solely or even predominantly by religion. Nevertheless, in the last two decades their instrumentalization of religion as a tool of their power game has deeply affected the dynamics of regional and to some degree international affairs.

RELIGION'S COMPARATIVELY LIMITED ROLE AS A DETERMINANT OF ACTORS' BEHAVIOR

Compared to other determinants of actors' behavior, religion's influence is limited. This is especially so when the pursuit of religiously inspired or influenced goals risks endangering actors' security and other vital political and economic interests. By contrast, if the pursuit of religiously motivated objectives, as indeed with all other value-determined goals, is seen as advancing actors' more material interests, its influence is enhanced. This observation may explain both the rise of religion's profile as an influential factor in international affairs and its actual impact: the instrumentalization of religion as a policy tool has enhanced its influence.

THE NEED FOR MORE ANALYSIS OF RELIGION'S ROLE AS A DETERMINANT OF INTERNATIONAL ACTORS' BEHAVIOR AND AS AN INFLUENCE IN INTERNATIONAL AFFAIRS

It is clear that religion's role in determining the behavior of various international actors and its uses as an instrument of policy and their consequences need to receive greater attention. In particular, more attention should be paid to religion's role as a variable in the domestic politics of actors—in other words, within the internal context of foreign policymaking—as well as to its role as a factor influencing the external environments within which actors operate. In short, religion's role in the nexus between the internal and external determinants of international actors' behavior should be further studied. At the same time, it is important not to exaggerate religion's impact as a factor separate from other ideational and value-related determinants of actors' behavior. In particular, religion has a fairly limited direct impact as a set of theological and/or spiritual precepts, rather than its indirect influence through its becoming part of identity, culture, self-perceptions, and worldviews of actors. Likewise, it is not warranted to qualify as "religion" essentially secular notions rooted in religion and the ideologized religions. For example, America's sense of its exceptionalism might be rooted in religion, but in its current version its influence on U.S. actions in the world cannot be cited as evidence of religion's impact. In other words, the past neglect of religion's role in international affairs should not be overcompensated for by inflating its impact. Indeed, exaggerating religion's role could result in ignoring or underestimating the influence of other factors, which, in turn, would risk obscuring real motives behind international actors' behavior and the real causes of conflicts and thus inevitably complicating resolution of regional and international problems.

To summarize, religion has become an important factor affecting the dynamics of international affairs and the character of international relations. Religion's more salient international profile has resulted from its growing role in the domestic politics of many, including hitherto totally secular, countries. Religion's more systematic and frequent use as an instrument of policy by international actors has further enhanced its influence on international affairs. Consequently, religion's role in international affairs and the channels through which this influence is transmitted should receive more thorough attention and analysis. Its relative impact should also be adequately assessed. At the same time, however, its role should not be exaggerated. Despite the growing importance of ideas, ideals, and identities and value systems based upon them, power and interest remain the principal drivers of international relations and ideas and ideals often serve as justification for the pursuit of power and interests. The nature of the international system also remains more anarchical than law-based, which also puts premium on power.

NOTE

1. For details, see A. Capelle Pogaceam and P. Michel (eds.), *Religion(s) et Identité(s) en Europe: L'epreuve de pluriel* (Religion[s] and Identities[ies] in Europe: Testing Plurality). Paris: Presse de Sciences Po, 2008.

Appendix

Yugoslavia's Unraveling and Its Internecine Wars

The Socialist Federal Republic of Yugoslavia came into being in 1946. It succeeded the Kingdom of the Serbs, Croats, and Slovenes. The Kingdom was established in December 1918 following the end of the Austria-Hungarian Empire, by joining the states of Slovenes and Croats and Serbs with the formerly independent Kingdom of Serbia. The Serbian royal house became the dynasty of the newly created kingdom. In July 1923, the newly formed kingdom gained international recognition. In July 1929, its name was changed to the Kingdom of Yugoslavia, the country of "Southern Slavs" in order to reflect its new composition.[1] In April 1941, the Axis powers invaded the country and caused the emergence of two resistance movements. Of the two movements, that of socialist forces under the leadership of Josip Broz Tito was the most important and successful.[2] In 1943, his movement declared the establishment of a Democratic Yugoslavia. In 1945, the monarchy was abolished and in 1946 the establishment of the People's Republic of Yugoslavia was announced.

Initially, as a socialist government, Yugoslavia had close links with the USSR, but the two drifted apart. This parting of the ways can be attributed to the fact that Yugoslavia was the only country in Eastern Europe that had had a major resistance movement and thus, while liberated in part by Soviet and Bulgarian forces, it was not as beholden and subservient to Moscow as other countries in the region. By the late 1940s, Yugoslavia developed its own independent version of socialism and mode of socialist development. It also distanced itself from the USSR's international positions, and in 1961 it became one of the founding members of the Non-Aligned Movement (NAM). In 1963, the country's name was changed once more to the Socialist Federal

THE FORMER YUGOSLAVIA

Republic of Yugoslavia. The SFRY consisted of six republics (Bosnia and Herzegovina, Croatia, Macedonia, Montenegro, Serbia, and Slovenia) and two autonomous regions (Kosovo and Vojvodina).[3]

FRAGILITY OF STATE: CULTURAL DIVISIONS

Because of its history and its ethnic and religious make up, the Yugoslav state under its various forms was a fragile political entity. Despite their common Slavic roots, peoples of Yugoslavia had developed different cultural traditions and identities, largely because they had come under the influence of different religions and empires. For example, the Slovenes and the Croats are Catholic while the Serbs are Orthodox Christians. Croatia and Slovenia had been mostly under Habsburg rule and therefore were influenced by Germanic culture. Because of their adherence to Catholicism they also felt the influence of Latin culture. The Serbs, by contrast, were influenced by Russian culture, largely because of their shared adherence to Orthodox Christianity. Those Slavs who had become Muslims following Ottoman control over the country were influenced by Turkish-Ottoman culture. Policies adopted by the Axis powers toward Yugoslavia, such as the Nazis' creation of an Independent Croat state, exacerbated these cultural and ethnic divisions. In short,

Yugoslavia's internal divisions coupled with actions of some external powers prevented the consolidation of the Yugoslav state prior to the outbreak of World War II.

After the formation of the Federal Republic of Yugoslavia in 1946, Marshal Tito, a Croat, endeavored to submerge the country's many differences by encouraging a common socialist identity. The promotion of a common socialist identity might have generated some sense of unity among Yugoslavia's diverse peoples. However, the survival of the Yugoslav Federation for more than four decades after its establishment was mainly due to Tito's personality and his iron rule over the country. Tito's iron rule held Yugoslavia together for some time, but it also generated resentment on the part of many of Yugoslavia's people.[4] This resentment contributed to Yugoslavia's eventual unraveling once Tito's grip on the country was removed after his death in 1980.

ECONOMIC DIVISIONS

In addition to ethnic and cultural divisions, Yugoslavia suffered from significant economic disparities among its constituent republics and regions. These disparities predated the creation of the Yugoslav Federation, and reflected differences among republics and regions in regard to size, economic structure, the level of industrialization and modernization, and the level of productivity. For example, in 1952, Slovenia had the highest rate of per capita GDP and Kosovo, an autonomous region, the lowest. Serbia occupied a middle position between the two. These disparities did not disappear in the following decades, and some republics fell behind even more.[5]

Because richer republics were called upon by Belgrade to finance the development of less advanced areas, existing economic disparities created deep resentments in the economically better off republics and led to complaints. At times, they even caused political crisis, as it happened in Croatia in 1970–1971. In response to these complaints, in 1974 the federal government adopted a new constitution, and it granted more powers to regional governments. According to some sources, the provisions of the 1974 Constitution "provided for the effective devolution of all real power away from the federal government and to the autonomous republics." It also established "a collective presidency of the eight provincial representatives and a federal government with little control over economic, cultural, and political policy."[6] The result was a significant weakening of the Federal institutions. Consequently, when, after Tito's death in 1980, a political crisis broke in the country, the 1974 constitution's characteristics contributed to Yugoslavia's speedy unraveling.

EMERGING IDEOLOGICAL VACUUM

By the time of Tito's death, socialism's appeal in the country had eroded considerably, and thus had created an ideological vacuum. The anti-socialist trend was strongest in the economically advanced and culturally more Western-oriented republics of Slovenia and Croatia. These republics did not want to continue to bear the burdens of poorer republics and regions, and wanted to establish market economies and liberal democratic systems. In order to achieve their goals, they started to establish their own direct links to Western countries independent of the Federal Government.[7]

Over the following years, this ideological vacuum was filled by ethnocentric nationalism, which further deepened existing ethnic, religious, and cultural cleavages. Yugoslavia's nationalists were encouraged by the emergence of similar movements in the Central and East European countries and in the USSR. The Yugoslav nationalists argued that if the Baltic States could become independent, why not also Slovenia, Croatia, and, as it turned out, Bosnia-Herzegovina, Macedonia, Montenegro, and (eventually) even Kosovo. Centrifugal trends were intensified in Yugoslavia by the end of the Cold War, German unification, the end of communist regimes in Central and Eastern Europe and the gradual disintegration of the USSR. In particular, the USSR's collapse eliminated a potential, albeit unlikely, security threat to Yugoslavia, thus undermining "a powerful incentive for unity and cooperation."[8]

Meanwhile, the evolution of events in the USSR and the East European countries diverted the West's attention away from Yugoslavia, and it did not provide "the extensive financial and economic support necessary to preserve a Yugoslav economy already close to collapse."[9] This Western neglect further exacerbated Yugoslavia's other problems and thus contributed to its dissolution.

ELECTIONS OF 1990: ROAD TO INDEPENDENCE AND WAR

In the 1990 elections of the local governments of Yugoslavia's constituent parts, the Communist Party was defeated, but the communists retained their control over the Federal Government. These electoral results indicated that nationalist and independence-seeking tendencies had reached a tipping point. The intensification of these sentiments was largely responsible for Slovenia's and Croatia's decision to declare their independence in June 1991. In response, and in order to retain the Federal structure, the Federal Government sent the Yugoslav National Army (JNA) to Slovenia and Croatia, which led to relatively limited wars in both republics. The war in Slovenia was very short, and the war in Croatia, although it lasted longer, also ended relatively soon. By January 1992, a truce was signed under United Nations auspices, and a United Nations' Protection Force (UNPROFOR) was established. Shortly after the end of hostilities, the European Community (EC, the EU's predecessor) recognized both Slovenia and Croatia. Because of its historic ties with Croatia, Germany had unilaterally recognized Croatia's independence. There was no broad agreement among EC members regarding how to approach the Yugoslav crisis and whether to recognize the breakaway republics. Eventually, however, the EC recognized them. The EC members also disagreed on the question of who was the real culprit in unleashing Yugoslavia's disintegrative process: the Germans tended to attribute all responsibility to Serbia and its ultra-nationalist leader, Slobodan Milošević, whereas France, which had historic ties to Serbia, along with Britain believed that responsibility for the crisis was shared by all republics.[10]

THE WAR IN BOSNIA

The most serious, longest-lasting, and most-violent crisis began when, in February 1992, Bosnia-Herzegovina held a referendum on independence. Shortly afterward it, too, seceded from the Yugoslav Federation. However, Bosnia's case was different from those of other republics because the Bosniaks, or Muslim Bosnians, formed only 44 percent of Bosnia-Herzegovina's population, which also included significant numbers of Serbs and Croats. The Bosnian Muslims were prompted to declare independence partly because they feared that, with other members of the federation having become independent, they would become a mere vassal of Belgrade. Some observers, however, have attributed Bosnia's decision to declare independence to the desire of its leader, Alija Izetbegovic, to create an Islamic state in Bosnia, while others have refuted this claim.[11]

Regardless of whether Izetbegovic wanted to establish an Islamic state or not, the Serbs were unwilling to tolerate Yugoslavia's further disintegration and the shrinking of their own territory. The Croats, too, did not favor the emergence of an independent Bosnia-Herzegovina. According to some observers, the Serbs and the Croats had agreed to divide Bosnia between themselves.[12] The result was the outbreak of hostilities between Bosnia-Herzegovina and, first, the Bosnian Serbs, then Serbia itself, and eventually also Croatia.

Stages of the Conflict

The Bosnian War went through several stages and involved different and shifting alliances. The first stage of the war was triggered by the Bosnian Serbs' decision to break away from the newly independent republic of Bosnia-Herzegovina. It involved the Bosnian Serbs on the one hand and Bosnian government forces on the other. The latter were made up of an alliance between Bosniaks and Croats living in Bosnia-Herzegovina. Meanwhile, the Yugoslav National Army (JNA) helped the Bosnian Serbs.

Trying to stop the war, the United Nations imposed an arms embargo on the combatants. Because the Serbs were more heavily armed than the Muslims and because the Bosnian Serbs had a common border with Serbia, the UN arms embargo ultimately benefited them and was harmful to the Bosnians. The United Nations also established Safe Areas for the refugees and placed UNPROFOR units in them. In 1993, the Croats changed sides and turned on the Bosniaks, thus creating a three-way war. Meanwhile, there were various European-level and international efforts to end hostilities. Despite these efforts and various peace plans, notably those presented by the Europeans under the leadership of Lord Carrington and Ambassador José Cutileiro,[13] and later the so-called Vance-Owen plan,[14] the conflict continued. The main reason for the failure of these plans was that they were all rejected by different parties to the conflict.

Meanwhile, several of the UN-established Safe Areas to protect the refugees were attacked by Bosnian Serb forces. Part of the reason for the Serbs' success was NATO's inability to provide air support to UNPROFOR because of the United Nations' refusal to give its necessary agreement. The worst of these killings happened in Srebrenica in July 1995 when more than 8,000 Bosnian men and boys were killed. This incident finally galvanized both some reluctant NATO allies and the United Nations secretary general, Boutros Boutros-Ghali, to agree to use NATO air power effectively for the first time in the war, thus implementing earlier UN-sanctioned and -mandated NATO decisions. Pursuant to UN resolutions, NATO had earlier declared that no fixed-wing aircraft of any of the belligerent parties (plus Serbia) could fly over Bosnia, and it conducted more than 100,000 air sorties to enforce this rule. NATO had also agreed to help protect the UN Safe Areas, but there was never agreement either among all the NATO allies (with Britain being most reticent) or all the permanent members of the UN Security Council to implement this policy, except on a very limited, sporadic ("pinprick") basis. NATO also had a policy to respond with ground attacks if UNPROFOR forces came under fire, but that provision was never called upon.[15]

Following the Srebrenica massacre, all NATO allies agreed to a major application of air power if there were a further Serb provocation. The United Nations secretary general, Boutros-Ghali, also agreed that the UN would "turn its key" and permit NATO action.[16] There was a provocation (a Bosnian Serb mortar attack on a Muslim market in Sarajevo), NATO used airpower (*Operation Deliberate Force*), and twenty-one days later the Bosnian War came to an end.[17]

Efforts and Plans to End the War

As early as 1991, efforts were undertaken to find ways of solving the Yugoslav crisis and preventing further deterioration of the situation.

Vance Plan

The first of the peace plans was developed by the former U.S. secretary of state, Cyrus Vance, in November 1991 during the Croatian war of independence; it was aimed at ending the war between Croatia and the Yugoslav government. The plan failed because of Serbian opposition. According to some reports, the Bosnian leader, Alija Izetbegovic, who initially had accepted the plan, also changed his mind. Reportedly, he did so at the suggestion of the U.S. ambassador to Yugoslavia, who promised him that the United States would recognize an independent Bosnia.[18]

Carrington-Cutileiro Plan

The first plan dealing specifically with the Bosnian crisis was developed under EC (now EU) auspices, and was called the Carrington-Cutileiro Plan. It provided for power-sharing among Bosnia-Herzegovina's different ethnic groups at all administrative levels, the devolution of the powers of the federal government to local ethnic communities, and the classification of all areas of Bosnia-Herzegovina as Bosniak, Serb, or Croat, even where ethnic majority was not evident. On 18 March 1992, all three parties—Serbs-Croats and Bosniaks—signed the agreement. However, ten days later the Bosnian leader, Alija Izetbegovic, withdrew his signature and said he would not agree to Bosnia's partition into its ethnic components.[19]

Vance-Owen Plan

This plan was the outcome of a conference held in London in August 1992. It shared some of the characteristics of the Carrington-Cutileiro Plan. It, too, recommended a decentralized setup for Bosnia-Herzegovina, with a large degree of autonomy for its Serb and Croat communities, while at the same time trying to divide it into provinces within which there would be a significant degree of ethnic homogeneity.[20]

The Contact Group and the Dayton Accords

A Contact Group on Bosnia was established in April 1994. It was composed of the representatives of France, Germany, the United Kingdom, the United States, and the Russian Federation. The idea was that its informal, less public, and thus confidential nature would allow the United States and Russia to discuss ways of ending the crisis.[21] In July 1994, the group presented a map on the delineation of the borders between the Bosnia-Croat Federation and the Serbs on a 51 percent to 49 percent basis of division of territory and presented it to the Serbs and the Bosnian Serbs; the former accepted the plan but the latter rejected it. The Contact Group's efforts continued, but partly because of differences between the United States and some of the group's other members, it did not progress very far.[22]

The U.S. position on some issues, such as the creation of a Serb Republic within Bosnia, changed in 1995 and its approach to Milošević also softened. With the success of the NATO bombing campaign, which produced Serbian defeat, as well as loss of territory by the Serbs to a Croat-Bosniak ground campaign,[23] the Contact Group began to discuss the framework for peace talks in Dayton, Ohio. Once the talks started, the United States took over and negotiated the Dayton Peace Agreement.[24] The Dayton Accords ultimately worked to the detriment of the Muslim Bosniaks, with its Serb population creating its own republic, called Respublika Srpska, and holding on to the ethnically cleansed territories.[25]

NOTES

1. For more details, see John R. Lampe, *Yugoslavia as History: Twice There Was a Country* (Cambridge: Cambridge University Press, 2000).
2. See *Yugoslav Partisans* at https://en.wikipedia.org/wiki/Yugoslav_Partisans. The rival, monarchist resistance group, the Chetniks, was led by Draža Mihailović, which often collaborated with the Axis powers and, after a brief period of cooperation, was in conflict with Tito's partisans. At the end of the war, Mihailović was tried and executed by the SFRY. See *Chetniks*, at https://en.wikipedia.org/wiki/Chetniks.
3. See *Socialist Federal Republic of Yugoslavia,* at https://en.wikipedia.org/wiki/Socialist_Federal_Republic_of_Yugoslavia.
4. Tito said that "I am the leader of one country which has two alphabets, three languages, four religions, five nationalities, six republics, surrounded by seven neighbours, a country in which live eight ethnic minorities." See http://tvtropes.org/pmwiki/pmwiki.php/UsefulNotes/Yugoslavia. This saying was sometimes amended to refer to "one Party" or "one Tito."
5. See John B. Allcock, "Rural-Urban Differences and the Break-up of Yugoslavia," *Balkanologie*, VI. 1 & 2 December 2002, 108.
6. "The Breakup of Yugoslavia: Milestones: 1989–1992, *Office of the Historian, U.S. Department of State,* Last Update, October 2013, at http://www.history.state.gov/milestones/1989-1992/breakup-yugoslavia.
7. Branislav Radeljic, "Europe 1989–2009: Rethinking the Break-up of Yugoslavia," 2009, at http://www.desk.c.u-tokyo.ac.JP/downloads/es_a_Radeljic.pdf.
8. "The Breakup of Yugoslavia, Milestones: 1989–1992."
9. "The Breakup of Yugoslavia."
10. Dejan Marolov, "The EU Policy toward the Dissolution of Yugoslavia: Special Emphasis on the EU Policy toward the Republic of Macedonia," *Analytical Journal*, 4.2 (2011). For a more detailed treatment, see Sonia Lucarelli, *Europe and the Breakup of Yugoslavia: A Political Failure in Search of a Scholarly Explanation*, The Hague: Kluwer Law International, 2000.
11. See Alan F. Fogelquist, "The Yugoslav Breakup and the War in Bosnia-Hercegovina: Implications for Kosovo? *Eurasia Research Center*, April 1995, at http://www.globalgeopolitics.net/arcgg/arc/1995-04Bosnia.htm.
12. "What happened to Yugoslavia? The War, the Peace and the Future," *Center for European Studies,* UNC-Chapel Hill, 2004, 7.

13. Lord Carrington had been Secretary General of NATO (1984–1988) and Portuguese ambassador José Cutileiro was later Secretary General of the Western Europe Union. See *From the Carrington-Cutileiro Plan to War, February–March 1992; Was there an alternative for Bosnia?* at https://www.academia.edu/2629914/_From_the_Carrington-Cutileiro_Plan_to_war_February-March_1992_was_there_an_alternative_for_Bosnia.

14. This plan was named for former U.S. Secretary of State Cyrus Vance (1911–1980) and former UK Secretary of State for Foreign and Commonwealth Affairs (1977–1979), Lord Owen. For a discussion of all the Bosnia peace plans before the Dayton Accords, see *Peace plans offered before and during the Bosnian War*, at https://en.wikipedia.org/wiki/Peace_plans_offered_before_and_during_the_Bosnian_War.

15. For details of the NATO decisions on the use of airpower, see Robert E. Hunter, *Education Never Ends*, Washington, DC, Association for Diplomatic Studies and Training, 2012, pp. 204–208. (Downloadable at http://www.ebook-dl.co/dl-ton/education-never-ends.) The full story is at Hunter, *Education Never Ends*, 195–238.

16. Under arrangements between NATO and the United Nations, both had to agree to a use of force to protect the UN-mandated Safe Areas. That is, both had to "turn their key" to permit NATO bombing.

17. Hunter, *Education Never Ends*, pp. 232–33.

18. See Geert-Hinrich Ahrens, *Diplomacy on the Edge: Containment of Ethnic Conflicts and the Minorities Working Groups of the Conferences on Yugoslavia*, Washington, DC, Woodrow Wilson Center Press, 2007.

19. Ahrens, *Diplomacy on the Edge*.

20. For details, see David Owen (ed.), *Bosnia-Herzegovina: The Vance-Owen Peace Plan* (Liverpool: University of Liverpool Press, 2013).

21. For an analysis of the genesis and operation of the Contact Group, see Helen-Leigh Phippard, "The Contact Group on (and in) Bosnia: An Exercise in Conflict Mediation?" *International Journal*, 53. 2. (Spring 1998).

22. Phippard, "The Contact Group," 2.

23. The ground campaign more or less established a division of territory on a 51/49 percent basis, as previously envisioned under the Contact Group plan.

24. The ground campaign, also: *Dayton Accords*, The U. S. Department of State, Diplomacy in Action, at: http://www.state.gov/eur/rls/or/Dayton.

25. On the developments leading to Dayton and the Dayton Accords, see Christopher Schwegman, "The Contact Group and its Impact on the European Institutional Structure," *Institute for Security Studies, Western European Union, Occasional Paper*, No. 16, 2000.

Bibliography

BOOKS

Ajami, Fuad. *The Vanished Imam*. Ithaca: Cornell University Press, 1996.
Alagha, Joseph Elie. *The Shifts in Hizbullah's Ideology: Religious Ideology, Political Ideology and Political Action*. Institute for the Study of the Islamic World (ISIM), Amsterdam: The University of Amsterdam Press, 2005.
Altunişik, Meliha, and Tür, Özlem. *Turkey: Challenges of Continuity and Change*. London: Routledge, 2005.
Ayubi, Nazih. *Political Islam: Religion and Politics in the Arab World*. New York: Routledge, 1991.
Bal, Idris (ed.) *Turkish Foreign Policy in the Post-Cold War Era*. Boca Raton, Florida: Brown Walker Press, 2004.
Bennigsen, Alexander, and Broxup, Marie. *The Islamic Threat to the Soviet State*. New York: St. Martin's Press, 1983.
Bennett, A. L. *International Organizations: Principles and Issues*. Englewood Cliffs, NJ: Prentice Hall, 1991.
Berdyaev, Nicolai. *The Origins of Russian Communism*. London: Geoffrey Bless, 1994.
Berger, Peter L. *Sacred Canopy: Elements of a Sociological Theory of Religion*. New York: Anchor Books, 1990.
———. *Desecularization of the World: Resurgent Religion and World Politics*. Grand Rapids, MI: William B. Eerdmans, 1997.
Bottici, Chiara, and Challand, Benoit. *Imagining Europe, Myth, Memory and Identity*. Cambridge: Cambridge University Press, 2013.
Bozdoğan, Sibel, and Kasaba, Reşat (eds.). *Rethinking Modernity and National Identity in Turkey*. Seattle: University of Washington Press, 1997.
Bozman, Ada. *Politics and Culture in International History: From the Ancient Near East to the Opening of the Modern World*. New Brunswick, USA: Transaction Publishers, 1994.
Brown, Archie. *New Thinking in Soviet Politics*. New York: St. Martin's Press, 1992.
Brown, Seyom. *New Forces, Old Forces, and the Future of World Politics*. New York: Harper Collins College Publishers, 1995.
Brzezinski, Zbigniew. *Ideology and Power in Soviet Politics*. Westport, CT. Greenwood Press, 1976.
Bull, Hedley. *The Anarchical Society: A Study of Order in World Politics*. New York: Columbia University Press (4th edition), 2012.

Byrnes, R. F. *V. O. Kliuchevskii, Historian of Russia*. Bloomington: Indiana University Press, 1995.

Byrnes, Timothy A., and Katzenstein, Peter J. (eds.) *Religion in an Expanding Europe*. Cambridge: Cambridge University Press, 2006.

Chapman, Peter. *Bananas: How the United Fruit Company Shaped the World*. New York: Canongate, 2008.

Cohen, Sami. *The Resilience of the State: Democracy and the Challenges of Globalization* (translated by Jonathan Derrick). Boulder/London: Lynne Rienner, 2006.

Curanovic, Alicja. *The Religious Factor in Russia's Foreign Policy*. London: Routledge, 2012.

Dedman, Martin (ed.). *The Origins and Development of the European Union: 1945–2008*. London: Routledge, 2010.

Delanty, Gerard. *Inventing Europe: Idea, Identity, Reality*. New York: St. Martin's Press, 1995.

Donaldson, Robert, and Nogee, Joseph. *The Foreign Policy of Russia: Changing Systems, Enduring Interests*. Armonk, NY: M. E. Sharpe, 1998.

Düzgit, Senem Aydin. *Construction of European Identity*. New York: Palgrave Macmillan, 2012.

Eisenstadt, S. N. *The Origins and Diversity of Axial Civilizations*. New York, SUNY Press, 1986.

Foret, François. *Religion and Politics in the European Union: The Secular Canopy*. Cambridge: Cambridge University Press, 2014.

Fox, Jonathan, and Sandler, Shumel. *Bringing Religion into International Relations*. New York: Palgrave Macmillan, 2004.

Fuller, Graham. *From Eastern Europe to Western China: The Growing Role of Turkey in World Affairs and Its Implications for Western Interests*. Santa Monica: RAND, 1993.

Garcia, Soledad (ed.) *European Identity and Search for Legitimacy*. London: Pinter Publishers, 1993.

Geertz, Clifford. *The Interpretation of Cultures*. New York: Basic Books, 1973

Goldstein, J. S. *International Relations*. 3rd ed. New York: Longman, 1999.

Goldstein, Judith, and Keohane, Robert (eds.). *Ideas and Foreign Policy: Beliefs, Institutions, and Political Change*. Ithaca: Cornell University Press, 1993.

Gould, Andrew C., and Messina, Anthony M. *Europe's Contending Identities: Supranationalism, Ethnoregionalism, Religion and Nationalism*. Cambridge: Cambridge University Press, 2014.

Groom, A. J. R., and Light, Margot (eds.). *Contemporary International Relations: A Guide to Theory*. London: Pinter Publishers, 1994.

Gutierrez, Gustavo. *Liberation Theology* (translated by Mary Knoll). New York: Orbis Books, 1973.

Haass, Richard N. *War of Necessity, War of Choice: A Memoir of Two Iraq Wars*. New York: Simon & Shuster, 2009.

Hale, William. *Turkish Foreign Policy, 1774–2000*. London: Frank Cass, 2000.

Harle, Vilho. *The Enemy with a Thousand Faces*. Bridgeport, CT: Praeger, 2000.

Hatzopolous, Pavlos, and Petito, Fabio. *Religion in International Relations: Return from Exile*. New York: Palgrave Macmillan, 2003.

Haynes, Jeffrey. *An Introduction to International Relations and Religion*. Harlow, England: Pearson/Longman, 2007.

———. *Religion, Politics and International Relations: Selected Essays*. London: Routledge, 2011.

Hermann, Charles F., Kegley Jr., Charles W., and Roseneau, James N. (eds.). *New Directions in the Study of Foreign Policy*. Boston: Allen and Unwin, 1987.

Holsti, K. J. *International Politics*. Englewood Cliffs, NJ: Prentice Hall, 1995.

Howard, Lise Marje. *UN Peacekeeping in Civil Wars*. Cambridge: Cambridge University Press, 2008.

Hughes, Edel. *Turkey's Accession to the European Union: The Politics of Exclusion*. London: Routledge, 2010.

Hunter, Robert E. *Education Never Ends*. Washington, DC: Association for Diplomatic Studies and Training, 2012.

Hunter, Shireen T. *Islam in Russia: The Politics of Identity and Security.* Armonk, NY: M. E. Sharpe, 2004.

———. (ed.) *Reformist Voices of Islam: Mediating Islam and Modernity.* Armonk, NY: M. E. Sharpe, 2008.

———. *Iran and the World: Continuity in a Revolutionary Decade.* Bloomington, Indiana University Press, 1990.

———. *Iran Divided: The Historical Roots of Iranian Debates on Identity, Culture and Governance in the Twenty-First Century.* Lanham, MD: Rowman & Littlefield, 2014.

Huntington, Samuel P. *The Clash of Civilizations and the Remaking of the World Order.* New York: Touchstone, 1997.

Idinopulos, Thomas A., and Courtney, Brian Wilson. *What Is Religion: Origins, Definitions and Explanations.* Champaign, IL: Human Kinetic Books, 1998.

Immerman, R. H. *The CIA in Guatemala: The Foreign Policy of Intervention.* Austin: University of Texas Press, 1982.

Jaber, Hala. *Hizbollah: Born with a Vengeance.* New York: Columbia University Press, 1996.

Jenkins, Philip. *God's Continent: Christianity, Islam and Europe's Religious Crisis.* Oxford: Oxford University Press, 2007.

Kaiser, Wolfram. *Christian Democracy and the Origins of European Union.* Cambridge: Cambridge University Press, 2007.

Karns, Margaret P., and Mingst, Karen A. (eds.). *The United States and Multilateral Institutions: Patterns of Changing Instrumentality and Influence.* Boston: Unwin Hyman, 1990.

Kegley Jr., W., and Wittkopf, Eugene R. (eds.). *The Global Agenda: Issues and Perspectives.* New York: McGraw-Hill Inc., 1995.

Kennedy, Emmett. *Secularism and Its Opponents: From Augustine to Solzhenitsyn.* New York: Palgrave Macmillan, 2006.

Keohane, Robert, and Nye, Joseph. *Transnational Relations and World Politics.* Cambridge, MA: Harvard University Press, 1971.

Kortunov, S. V. *National Identity: Understanding the Meaning.* Moscow: Aspect Press, 2009.

Kushner, David. *The Rise of Turkish Nationalism, 1876–1908.* London: Frank Cass, 1977.

Landau, Jacob. *Pan-Turkism in Turkey: A Study in Irredentism.* Hamden, CT: Archon Books, 1981.

———. *Pan-Turkism: From Irredentism to Cooperation.* Bloomington, IN: Indiana University Press, 1995.

———. *The Politics of Pan-Islam: Ideology and Organization.* Oxford: Oxford University Press, 1990.

———. *Radical Politics in Modern Turkey.* Leiden: E. J. Brill, 1974.

Laqueur, Walter. (ed.). *The Middle East in Transition.* New York: Praeger, 1958.

Leatherborrow, W. J., and Offord, D. S. (eds. & trs.). *A Documentary History of Russian Thought.* Ann Arbor, MI: Ardis Publishers, 1987.

Lerner, Daniel. *The Passing of Traditional Society: Modernizing the Middle East.* Glencoe, IL: Free Press, 1958.

Lukashevich, Stephen. *Ivan Aksakov, 1832–1886: A Study in Russian Thought and Politics.* Cambridge, MA: Harvard University Press, 1965.

Mackenzie, David Clark. *A World Beyond Borders: An Introduction to the History of International Organizations.* Tonawanda, NY: University of Toronto Press, 2010.

Mackenzie, David. *Serbs and Russians.* New York: Columbia University Press, 1996.

Maley, William (ed.). *Fundamentalism Reborn: Afghanistan and the Taliban.* New York: New York University Press, 2001.

Mango, Andrew. *Turkey: The Challenge of a New Role.* Washington Paper 163, Washington, D. C.: CSIS/Praeger, 1994.

Mardin, Serif. *Religion and Social Change in Turkey: The Case of Bediuzzaman Nursi.* Albany: SUNY Press, 1989.

Mazlish, Bruce. *Leviathans: Multinational Corporations and the New Order.* New York: Simon & Schuster, 1994.

Mattei, Roberto de (translator John Laughland). *Turkey in Europe: Benefit or Catastrophe.* UK: Gracewing, 2009.

McDaniel, Timothy. *The Agony of the Russian Idea.* Princeton: Princeton University Press, 1996.
Mendelson, Sarah. *Changing Course: Ideas, Politics, and the Soviet Withdrawal from Afghanistan.* Princeton, NJ: Princeton University Press, 1998.
Miller, L. H. *Global Order: Values and Power in International Politics.* Boulder, CO: Westview Press, 1994.
Morgenthau, Hans J. *Politics Among Nations: The Struggle for Power and Peace.* New York: McGraw-Hill Education.
Nas, Cigdem, and Ozer, Yonca. *Turkey and the European Union: The Process of Europeanization.* UK: Ashgate, 2012.
Northedge, F. S. (ed.). *The Foreign Policies of the Powers.* London: Faber & Faber, 1968.
Norton, Augustus R. *AMAL and the Shia: Struggle for the Soul of Lebanon.* Austin: University of Texas Press, 1987.
Olson, Robert. *The Emergence of Kurdish Nationalism and the Sheikh Said Rebellion, 1880–1925.* Austin: University of Texas Press, 1989.
Oner, Celsen. *Turkey and the European Union: The Question of European Identity.* Lanham, MD: Lexington Books, 2011.
Osgood, Robert Endicott. *Ideals and Self-Interest in America's Foreign Policy.* Chicago: The University of Chicago Press, 1953.
Paz, Estrella Tolentino. *Multi-national Corporations: Emergence and Evolution.* London: Routledge, 2000.
Pedersen, Thomas. *When Culture Becomes Politics: European Identity in Perspective.* Aarhus, Denmark: Aarhus University Press, 2008.
Pogaceam, A. Capelle, and Michel, P. (eds.). *Religion(s) et Identité(s) en Europe: L'epreuve de Pluriel* (Religion[s] and Identity[ies] in Europe: Testing Plurality). Paris: Presse de Sciences Po., 2008.
Reinalda, Bob (ed.). *Non-State Actors.* Surrey, England: Ashgate Publishing, 2011.
Riasanovsky, Nicholas V. *Russian Identities: A Historical Survey.* Oxford: Oxford University Press, 2005.
Robbins, Phillip. *Turkey and the Middle East.* London: Pinter Publishers (for the Royal Institute of International Affairs). 1990.
Rosenau, James. *Turbulences in World Politics: A Theory of Change and Continuity.* Princeton, NJ: Princeton University Press, 1990.
Roy, Olivier. *Islam and Resistance in Afghanistan.* Cambridge: Cambridge University Press, 1990.
Saikal, Amin. *Modern Afghanistan: A History of Struggle and Survival.* London: I. B. Tauris, 2004.
Sandal, Nukhet A. and Fox, Jonathan. *Religion in International Relations Theory.* London: Routledge, 2013.
Schwab, George (ed.). *Ideology and Foreign Policy: A Global Perspective.* New York: Cyro Press, 1978.
Sezer, Duygu Bazoğlu. *Turkish Security in the Shifting Balkans.* New York: Columbia University Pres, 1996.
Shahabi, H. B. (ed.). *Distant Relations: Iran and Lebanon in the Last 500 Years.* London: I. B. Tauris, 2006.
Shakman Hurd, Elizabeth. *The Politics of Secularism in International Politics.* Princeton, NJ: Princeton University Press, 2008.
Shiraev, Eric, and Terrio, Deone (eds.). *International Public Opinion and the Bosnian Crisis.* Lanham, MD: Lexington Books, 2006.
Sjursen, Helen (ed.). *Questioning EU Enlargement: Europe in Search of Identity.* London: Routledge, 2006.
Smith, Anthony D. *Ethnic Origins of States.* Oxford: Basil Blackwell, 1986.
———. *National Identity.* Reno, NV: University of Nevada Press, 1991.
———. *The Cultural Foundations of Nations.* Oxford: Basil Blackwell, 2008.
Snyder, Jack (ed.). *Religion and International Relations Theory.* New York: Columbia University Press, 2011.

Surkan, Vahide. *Islam in Modern Turkey: An Intellectual Biography of Bediuzzaman Said Nursi*. Albany: SUNY Press, 2005.
Thomas, Scott M. *The Global Resurgence of Religion and the Transformation of International Relations*. New York: Palgrave Macmillan, 2005.
Tunkrova, Lucy, and Pavel Saradin (eds.). *The Politics of EU Accession: Turkish Challenges and Central European Experiences*. London: Routledge, 2010.
Tyerman, Christopher. *The Crusades*. New York: Sterling Publishing Company, 2007.
Ullman, Richard H. (ed.), *The World and Yugoslavia's Wars*. New York: Council on Foreign Relations, 1996.
Vital, David. *The Inequality of States: A Study of Small Power in International Relations*. London: Clarendon Press, 1972.
Walicki, Andrzej. *The Slavophile Controversy* (translator Hilda Andrews Rusiecka). Oxford: Clarendon Press, 1975.
Wallander, Celeste (ed.), *The Sources of Russian Foreign Policy after the Cold War*. Boulder, CO: Westview Press, 1996.
Waltz, Kenneth. *Theories of International Politics*. New York: Random House, 1979.
Watson, Adam. *The Evolution of International Society*. New York. NY: Routledge, 2009.
Weber, Max. *The Sociology of Religion*. 5th edition, Boston: Beacon Press, 1969.
Williams, Michael C. *Culture and Security: Symbolic Power and the Politics of International Security*. London: Routledge, 2007.
Yavuz, Hakan. *Islamic Political Identity in Turkey*. Oxford: Oxford University Press, 2003.
———. *Towards an Islamic Enlightenment: The Gülen Movement*. Oxford: Oxford University Press, 2013.
Yilmaz, Hakan, and Aykaç, Çağla E. (eds.), *Perceptions of Islam in Europe: Culture, Identity and the Muslim "Other."* London: I. B. Tauris, 2012.

JOURNAL ARTICLES / REPORTS / ANALYSES

Aktar, Cengiz. "The Positive Agenda and Beyond: A New Beginning for the EU-Turkey Relations?" *Insight Turkey*. vol. 16, no. 3, Summer 2014.
Anderson, Perry. "Kemalism." *London Review of Books*, vol. 30, no. 17, 2008.
Ardic, Nurullah. "Civilizational Discourse, the 'Alliance of Civilization' and Turkish Foreign Policy." *Insight Turkey*, vol. 16, no. 3, Summer 2014.
Areljić, Dušan. "Turkish Interests and Involvement in the Western Balkans: A Score Card." *Insight Turkey*, vol. 13, no, 3, 2011.
Aydin Düzgit, Senem, and Keyman, Fuat E. "EU-Turkey Relations and the Stagnation of Turkish Democracy," *Global Turkey in Europe*, Working Paper no. 2, 4 December 2012.
Balci, Tamer. "From Nationalization of Islam to Privatization of Nationalism: Islam and Turkish National Identity." *History Studies: International Journal of History*, vol. 1, no. 1, 2009.
Barkey, Karen. "Political Legitimacy and Islam in the Ottoman Empire: Lessons Learned." *Philosophy and Social Criticism*, vol. 40, nos. 4–5, 2014.
Barysch, Katinka. "The Economics of Turkish Accession." *Centre for European Reform*, 5 July 2011.
Baudner, Jorge. "The Evolution of Turkish Foreign Policy under the AK Party Government." *Insight Turkey*, vol. 16, no. 3, Summer 2014.
Bulakbashi, Suha. "Behind the Turkish-Israeli Alliance: A Turkish View." *Journal of Palestine Studies*, vol. 29, no. 1, Autumn 1999.
Bulut, Esra. "The Role of Religion in Turkish Reactions to Balkan Conflicts." *Turkish Policy Quarterly*, Spring 2004.
Byman, Daniel L., and Pollack, Kenneth J. "Let Us Praise Great Men: Bringing the Statesman Back." *International Security*, vol. 52, no. 4, 2001.
Casanova, José. "The Long, Difficult and Tortuous Journey of Turkey into Europe and the Dilemmas of European Civilization." *Constellations*, vol. 13, no. 2, 2006.
Cohen, Lenard J. "Russia and the Balkans: Pan-Slavism, Partnership and Power." *Canadian Journal of International Affairs*, vol. 49, no. 4, Autumn 1994.

Crow, Suzanne. "Competing Blueprints for Russian Foreign Policy." *RFE/RL Research Report*, vol. 1, no. 50, 1992.
———. "Ambarsumatov's Influence on Russian Foreign Policy." *RFE/RL Research Report*, vol. 2, no. 19, 7 May 1993.
———. "Reading Moscow's Policies Towards Rump Yugoslavia." *RFE/RL Research Report*, vol. 1, no. 44 November, 1992.
Demirtaş Cokşun, Birgul. "Turkish Foreign Policy Towards the Bosnian War (1992–1995): A Constructivist Analysis." *Journal of Black Sea Research*, no. 28, Winter 2011.
Dyson, Stephen Benedict. "Personality and Foreign Policy: Blair's Iraq Decisions." *Foreign Policy Analysis*, no. 2, 2006.
Ekinci, Didem. "The War in Bosnia-Herzegovina (1992–1995) and Turkish Parliamentary Debates." *Ulusrarasi Iliskiller*, vol. 6, no. 22, Summer 2004.
Evans, Andrew. "Forced Miracles: The Russian Orthodox Church and Postsoviet International Relations." *Religion, State & Society*, vol. 30, no. 1, 2002.
Gangloff, Sylvie. "The Impact of the Ottoman Legacy on Turkish Policy in the Balkans 1991–1999," *Centre Nationale de la Recherche Scientific* (National Center for Scientific Research), 2005.
———. "The Weight of Islam in Turkish Foreign Policy in the Balkans." *Turkish Review of Balkan Studies*, 2011.
Göle, Nilüfer. "Secularism and Islamism in Turkey: The Making of Elites and Counter-Elites." *Middle East Journal*, vol. 5, no. 1, Winter, 1997.
Goulding, Marrack. "The Evolution of United Nations Peacekeeping." *International Affairs*, vol. 69, no. 3, July 1993.
Guzzini, Stefano. "A Reconstruction of Constructivism in International Relations." *European Journal of International Affairs*, vol. 6, no. 2, 2000.
Gvosdev, Nicholas K. "The New Emperors? Post-Soviet Presidents and Church-State Relations in Ukraine and Russia." Sophia Institute, Columbia University, *Studies on Orthodox Theology*, 2010.
Hakimov, Raphael. "Russia and Tatarstan at a Crossroads of History." *Anthropology and Archeology of Eurasia*, vol. 37, no. 1.
Hoffmann, Stanley. "Obstinate or Obsolete? The Fate of the Nation State and the Case of Western Europe." *Daedalus*, vol. 95, no. 3, Summer, 1996.
Hunter, Shireen T. "Bridge or Frontier: Turkey's Post-Cold War Geopolitical Posture." *International Spectator*, vol. 34, no. 1, 1991.
İçner, Erhan, and Phinnemore, David. "Turkey and the EU: Looking Beyond pessimisms." *Insight Turkey*, vol. 16, no. 3, Summer 2014.
Judis, John B. "The Chosen Nation: The Influence of Religion on U.S. Foreign Policy." Carnegie Endowment for International Peace, *Policy Brief*, no. 37, March 2005.
Kaariainen, Kimmo, and Furman, Dmitri. "Orthodoxy as a Component of Russian Identity." *East-West Church and Ministry Report*, no. 10, Winter 2002.
Kardaş, Şaban. "Turkey's New Drive to Reenergize EU Accession: Beyond Suboptimal Equilibrium?" German Marshall Fund of the United States, *Analysis on Turkey*, 13 March 2013.
Kohen, Sami. "Contacts with Central Asian States: A Foundation for Pan-Turkism." *The Washington Report on Middle East Affairs*, August–September 1992.
Kushner, David. "Self-Perception and Identity in Contemporary Turkey." *Journal of Contemporary History*, vol. 32, no. 2, 1997.
Kuzio, Taras. "Historiography and National Identity among the Eastern Slavs: Towards a New Framework." *National Identities*, vol. 3, no. 2, 2001.
Kylstad, Ingrid. "Turkey and the EU: A 'New' European Identity in the Making?" *LEQS Paper*, no. 27, October 2010.
Laciner, Sedat. "Turgut Özal Period in Turkish Foreign Policy: Özalism." *The Journal of Turkish Weekly*, March, 2009.
Lake, Anthony. "Confronting Backlash States." *Foreign Affairs*, vol. 73, no. 2, Spring 2003.
Lewis, Bernard. "The Roots of Muslim Rage." *The Atlantic*, 1990.
Lynch, Allen C. "The Realism of Russian Foreign Policy." *Europe-Asia Studies*, vol. 53, no. 1, 2001.

Makowsky, Alan. "How to Deal with Erbakan." *Middle East Quarterly*, vol. 4, no. 1, March 1997.
Masker, John Scott. "Signs of a Democratized Foreign Policy? Russian Politics, Public Opinion and the Bosna Crisis." *World Affairs*, vol. 160, no. 4, Spring 1998.
Morelli, Vincent L. "European Union Enlargement: A Status Report on Turkey's Accession Negotiations." *Congressional Research Service*, no. 7-5700, 5 August 2013.
Müftüler-Baç, Meltem, and Keyman, Fuat E. "Turkey's Unconsolidated Democracy: The Nexus between Democratization and Majoritarianism in Turkey." *Global Turkey in Europe*, Policy Brief, no. 19, January 2015.
Nicolaidis, Kalypso. "Turkey Is European . . . for Europe's Sake." In *Turkey and the European Union: From Association to Accession*. Ministry of Foreign Affairs, Netherlands, January 2005.
Nye, Joseph S. "Neorealism and Neoliberalism." *World Politics*, vol. 40, no. 2, January 1988.
Ocak, Ahmet Yaşar. "Islam in the Ottoman Empire: A Sociological Framework for a New Interpretation." *International Journal of Turkish Studies*, vol. 9, nos. 1–2, 2003.
Önis, Zia. "Turkey, Europe, and Paradoxes of Identity: Perspectives on the International Context of Democratization." *Mediterranean Quarterly*, vol. 10, no. 3, 1997.
Pain, E. M. "Dynamics of Russian National Identity." *Ethnopanorama*, no. 1, 2002.
Phippard, Helen-Leigh. "The Contact Group on (and in) Bosnia: An Exercise in Conflict Mediation." *International Journal*, vol. 53, no. 2, Spring 1998.
Rice, Condoleezza. "Promoting National Interest." *Foreign Affairs*, vol. 79, no. 1, Winter 2000.
Rowley, David G. "Imperial versus National Discourse in the Case of Russia." *Nations and Nationalism*, vol. 6, no, 1, 2000.
Ruble, Blair. "The Orthodox Church and Russian Politics." Kennan Institute, Woodrow Wilson Center for International Scholars, 2011.
Rumellili, Bahar. "Transforming Conflicts on EU Borders: The Case of Greek-Turkish Relations." *Journal of Common Market Studies*, vol. 45, issue 1, March 2007.
Sayari, Sabri. "Turkish Foreign Policy in the Post-Cold War Era." *Journal of International Affairs*, vol. 54, no. 1, Fall 2002.
———. "La Turquie et la Crise Yugoslave" (Turkey and the Yugoslav Crisis). *La Politique Etrangere*, no. 2, 1992.
Schwegman, Christopher. "The Contact Group Made Its Impact on the European Institutional Structure." Institute for Security Studies, Western European Union, *Occasional Paper*, no. 6.
Sherr, J., and Matin, J. S. "Russian and Ukrainian Perceptions of Events in Yugoslavia." *Conflict Studies Research Center*, 1994.
Stankevich, Sergei. "Russia in Search of Itself." *National Interest*, Summer 1992.
Suvarierol, Samin. "The Cyprus Obstacle on Turkey's Road to Membership in the European Union." *Turkish Studies*, vol. 4, Issue 1, 2003.
Tekin, Ali. "Future of Turkey-EU Relations: A Civilizational Discourse." *Futures*, no. 37, 2005.
Tolz, Vera. "Forging the Nation: National Identity and Nation Building in Post-Communist Russia." *Europe-Asia Studies*, vol. 50, no. 6, 1998.
Veremis, Thanos. "Greek-Turkish Relations and the Balkans." *The South-Eastern European Yearbook*, 1991.
Waxman, Dov. "Islam and Turkish National Identity." *The Turkish Yearbook*, vol. XXX, 2009.
Wolf, Martin. "Will the Nation State Survive Globalization?" *Foreign Affairs*, vol. 80, no. 1, 2001.
Yaşli, Fatih. "The Long Road that Led to the AKP's 'New Turkey.'" *The Turkey Analyst*, vol. 28, no. 1, January 2015.
Yavuz, Hakan. "Turkish Identity and Foreign Policy in Flux: The Rise of Neo-Ottomanism." *Critique*, Spring 1998.
Zevelev, Igor. "The Russian World Boundaries." *Russia in Global Affairs*, June 2014.
Zubeida, Sami. "Turkish Islam and National Identity." *Middle East Report*, April–June 1996.

Index

Abarinov, W., 122
Abdullah, Abdullah, 88n1
Adelman, Kenneth, 71
Afghanistan: religion and policies on, 9–10; Soviet invasion of, 49–51; U.S. invasion of, 4, 178. *See also* Taliban
agency, 31; importance of, 222
aggression, prevention of, and state behavior, 76
Ahrweiler, Helene, 197, 202
AKP. *See* Justice and Development Party
Aksiuchits, Victor, 101, 103
Albania, 177
Albright, Madeleine, 68
Alevis, 182, 216n44
Alexy II, patriarch, 108, 125–126
Allende, Salvador, 39
Al Qaeda, 4–5, 34, 54
Altunisik, Meliha, 155
AMAL, 45
Ambartsumov, Yevgenii, 117, 121
Amnesty International, 62
Anderson, Perry, 196
anti-colonial movements, 33, 44
Arab Afghans, 60n71
Arab Spring, 16
Arbenz, Jacobo, 39
Armenia, 149, 188
Armenian Genocide, 182–183
Assad, Bashar Al, 44, 176
Assad, Hafiz al, 46

Atatürk (Mustafa Kemal), 139–140; and foreign policy, 145–146; limits to reform project of, 140–142
Atli, Ilhan, 164
authority: Islam and, 139, 142; Orthodox Christianity and, 101–102; religion and, 17–18
autonomy, and state behavior, 78
Averroes, 18
Avicenna, 18, 199
Azerbaijan, 149

Babar, Naseerullah, 48, 53
Bagis, Egemen, 175
Baker, James, 52
Balci, Tamer, 141
Balkans, 153–154, 177; Ottoman legacy and, 154–156; Turkey and, 145
behavior. *See* determinants of behavior
Belarus, 107, 112
Bennigsen, Alexander, 101
Berdyaev, Nicolai, 106
Berger, Peter, 29n48
Bhutto, Benazir, 53
bin Laden, Osama, 4, 54
Bin Saud, Turki Bin Faisal, 48
Black September, 44
Blair, Tony, 71
Boko Haram, 34
Bosnia-Herzegovina, 234, 235

Bosniaks: Russia and, 110, 115, 125; Turkey and, 136–137, 157–159, 161–164
Bosnian Turks, 156
Bosnian War, 235–238; Russia and, 94, 98, 113, 114–123; Turkey and, 135–167. *See also* Yugoslav crisis
Boutros-Ghali, Boutros, 236
Bozkir, Volkan, 180, 189
Brexit debate, 38, 175, 193
Britain, 37–38, 175, 236; population of, 189; resource base and, 69
Broxup, Marie, 101
Brzezinski, Zbigniew, 73
Bulgaria, 104, 112, 154, 177
Bush, George H. W., 96
Bush, George W., 27n10, 71, 81
Byman, Daniel L., 70
Byzantium, 105, 109

Cameron, David, 206
Çandar, Cengiz, 151
capabilities: central role of, 224; versus intentions, 81–82
Carrington, Peter, 236
Carrington-Cutileiro Plan, 237
Casanova, José, 194
case studies, 25, 26; importance of, 222
Catherine the Great, 105
Catholicism, 199, 232
Cedar Revolution, 46
Central Asia, Turkey and, 138
Central Europe, and EU, 205, 206
Central Intelligence Agency, 58n43
Çetin, Hikmet, 160
Chaadev, Pyotr Yakovlevich, 105–106
Charlemagne, king of the Franks, 198
Charter of Russian-American Partnership, 115
Chechenya, 82, 110, 120
Cheney, Richard, 71
China, 29n41, 69
Christianity: in Balkans, 154–155; and European boundaries, 186; and European culture, 197–202; and government, 17–18; and Other, 202–203. *See also* Orthodox Christianity
Churkin, Vitaly, 119

Çiçek, Cemil, 160
Çiller, Tansu, 152, 153, 159, 163
civil society: and religious influence, 227; in Russia, and Bosnian War, 123–125; Turkey and, 182
clash of civilizations theory, 3–4
Clinton administration, 52, 80, 81, 90n51
Clovis, king of the Franks, 218n104
Cohen, Sami, 43
Cold War: and corporations, 39; and interational system, 75; and stability, 90n38. *See also* Soviet Union collapse
Commonwealth of Independent States. *See* Russia
communism: and Afghanistan, 51; discrediting of, and study of religion and international affairs, 2; and religion, 29n41
Comte, Auguste, 35
Congress for Cultural Freedom, 58n43
constructivism, 23, 72–73
Contact Group on Bosnia, 237–238
cosmopolitanism, EU and, 193
Council of Europe, 146
Crimean War, 102
Croatia, 98, 119, 160, 164, 232, 233, 234, 234–235
Crow, Suzanne, 120
Cuba, 29n41
culture: and EU refusal of Turkey, 190–191; and European identity, 192; and Orthodox Christianity, 108; and public opinion on Europe and Turkey, 210–211; religion as, 197–202; and Turkey and Bosnian War, 136–137; and Yugoslav crisis, 232–233
Cutileiro, José, 236
Cyprus, 174, 179–180, 215n25

DAESH. *See* Islamic State
Davies, Glyn, 54
Davutoğlu, Ahmet, 182
Dayton Accords, 237–238
Delanty, Gerard, 199–200
Demirel, Suleiman, 151–152, 155, 165
democracy, Turkey and, 181
determinants of behavior, 24, 61–88; identification of, 26, 222; religion as, need for research on, 228–229; term,

63. *See also* motivations
Diran, Salaheddin, 164
Dole, Robert, 148
domestic affairs: and EU refusal of Turkey, 180–183; versus influence of religion, 8; and religious influence, 225–227; and Russia and Yugoslav crisis, 94, 97–98, 115, 120–123; and Turkey and Bosnian War, 157–159, 166–167
Dostoevsky, Fyodor, 102
Dostum, Abdul Rashid, 51
Durkheim, Émile, 11

East: as inferior Other, 177–204; versus West, 202
East Asia, secularization in, 18
Eastern Europe, and EU, 205, 206
Ecevit, Bülent, 143, 158
economic issues: and EU popularity, 218n99; and EU refusal of Turkey, 176, 184–186, 185; and Russia and Yugoslav crisis, 95, 113, 120–123; and state behavior, 77; and Turkey, 144; and Yugoslav crisis, 233
Edwards, Jonathan, 67
Eggert, Konstantin, 123
Egypt, 20, 176
ends, 81–82
English School, 25
Enlightenment, 10, 16, 197, 200
equilibrium, in international system, 75–76, 90n38
Erbakan, Necmettin, 142–143, 151, 155, 158, 180
Erdoğan, Recep Tayyip, 29n51, 167n1, 175, 178, 181–182
Erduran, Refik, 164
ethnic issues: and Russian identity, 102, 103–104, 109–111; and Taliban, 54, 83–84; and terrorism, 82; and Turkish foreign policy, 156; and Turkish identity, 138, 154; and Yugoslav crisis, 232–233. *See also* Yugoslav crisis
EU. *See* European Union
Eurasia: and Taliban, 52; and Turkey, 186–190
Eurasianism: Russia and, 104, 114, 116–117; Turkey and, 151–152

Euro-Atlanticist School, 111, 113, 114, 115, 118–119, 122
Europe: culture of, Christianity and, 197–202; identity of, 190–196; Other and, 202–204
European, term, 198
European Community, 173; boundaries of, 186–190; and Turkey, 151; and Yugoslav crisis, 235
European Council, 173–174
Europeanization, 10
European Union (EU), 57n28; boundaries of, 186–190; deepen versus widen debate, 193; development of, 37–38, 173, 211–212; expansion of, 204–208; identity of, 190–196, 211–212; objectives of, 61–62; population of, 189; principles of, 179–180; and Turkey, 146, 153, 162, 167n1, 173–213
exceptionalism, 66; Russia and, 111–112, 114, 116–117; and state behavior, 66–68; Turkey and, 151
external determinants of behavior, 74–76; nature of, 63

Fallaci, Oriana, 206
Fatih, Mehmet, 154
Ferguson, Niall, 206
foreign investment: Russia and, 52, 120; Turkey and, 176, 185
Foret, François, 202, 207
Fox, Jonathan, 24
France, 113, 144, 174, 208; population of, 189
Francis, pope, 182
Francisco de Vitoria, 201

Gangloff, Sylvie, 159
Ganswein, Georg, 206
Geertz, Clifford, 11, 28n21
gender issues, Turkey and, 182, 191
geography: Eurasianist School and, 116, 117; and Russia, 64, 65; and state behavior, 64–65; and Turkey, 152, 186–190
Georgia, 188
Germany, 160, 174, 182–183, 235; population of, 189

Ghazali, Abu Hamed Muhammad ibn Muhammad al, 17, 219n111
Giscard d'Estaing, Valéry, 186
global arrogance, 86, 88n11
Gonzales, Felipe, 96
Gorbachev, Mikhail, 114, 122; opposition to, 97–98; and Yugoslav crisis, 94–95, 95–96
government-organized NGO (GNGO), 43
Greece: ancient, legacy of, 197, 202; and EU, 177; and Turkey, 138, 156, 174
Guatemala, 39
Gül, Abdullah, 181
Gülen, Fethullah, 141, 182
Gülen movement, 147

Hakimov, Raphael, 131n32
Hale, John, 198
Halliday, Fred, 85
HAMAS, 44, 82
Hanafi schools, 49
Hariri, Rafiq, 46
Haussmann, Ricardo, 65
Hazaras, 83
Hekmatyar, Gulbudin, 48
hijab, 209
history: Christianity and, 201–202; and national identity, 201; and Russian identity, 99–106; and state behavior, 65–66
Hizb e Vahdat, 51
Hizbullah, 5, 46–47; emergence of, 34, 45; Iran and, 45–46; motivations of, 82–83, 85–87
Hoffmann, Stanley, 34, 35
Holbrooke, Richard, 162
human rights, and EU refusal of Turkey, 180–183
Human Rights Watch, 62
Huntington, Samuel P., 3–4, 202
Hussein, Saddam, 149

ideals: versus interests, 78; Russian debate on, 117; and state behavior, 72–74
ideologies: relation to religion, 12, 13–14, 21, 74, 224–225; and state behavior, 72–74; and Yugoslav crisis, 234
IGOs. *See* inter-governmental organizations

immigrants, 160, 204–208; Russia and, 110
imperialism: Russia and, 99–100; Turkey and, 137, 139–140
independence, and state behavior, 78
influence of religion: factors affecting, 204–205, 225–228; as indirect, 225; limitations of, 228; mechanisms of, 7, 22; need for research on, 7, 228–229; return of, 204–208; secularism and, 21
instruments of policy, 81–82; need for research on, 7; religion as, 7, 21–22, 167, 228
intentions, versus capabilities, 81–82
interests, 72; versus ideals, 78; primacy of, 223–224; Russian debate on, 114, 117; and Turkey and Bosnian War, 159–160, 166
inter-governmental organizations (IGOs), 33, 35–37, 61
internal determinants of behavior, 63–74; nature of, 63
international actors, 31–55; differentiating impact of religion on, 23; identification of, 26; and international system, 31–33; motivations of, 61–88
international affairs, religion and, 1–27, 221–229; balance in, 5–8; interest in, 1; lack of resources on, xi–xii, 23; as new paradigm, 3–5; research topics in, 6–8
International Labor Organization, 61
international organizations, 32–33, 35–37
international system: as anarchic, 72, 75, 229; characteristics of, 31–32; evolution of, 31–33; multipolar, 116–117; Russia and, 115; states and, 35
Iran, 10, 21, 80; economic issues, 77; geography and, 65; history and, 66; and Hizbullah, 45–46, 85–87; religion and authority in, 17, 18; and Taliban, 84; TNCs and, 39; and Turkey, 143, 152
Iraq, and terrorist groups, 62
Iraq War, 4–5; ends and means and, 81; and EU rejection of Turkey, 178; leader personalities and, 71–72; motivations for, 79–81
Islam: and EU rejection of Turkey, 178; and European culture, 199–200; and

foreign policy, 153–154; and government, 17, 142–144; Huntington on, 3–5; and ideology, 13; influence of, 204; Iran and, 143; as Other, 202–203; and religious versus secular spheres, 15; and Turkey, 135–137, 139–140, 142–144, 147, 151–154, 158; and Turkish identity, 140–142, 208–210; and Yugoslav crisis, 232; *See also under* Muslim; Shias; Sunnis
Islamic State (IS), 5, 27n9, 34, 55, 56n10, 205, 210
Islamo-fascism, term, 27n10
Israel, Turkey and, 150
Italy, population of, 189
Ivan the Terrible, 102
Izetbegovic, Alija, 155, 162, 235, 237

Jamiat e Islami, 50–51
Japan, 69
John Paul II, pope, 19
Jordan, 20
journalists, Turkey and, 183
Judaism: and European culture, 199–200; and ideology, 13; and religious versus secular spheres, 15
Judis, John, 67–68
Justice and Development Party (AKP), 143, 180, 183; and domestic affairs, 181, 182; and EU refusal, 183

Keder, Caglar, 141
Kemalism, 135. *See also* Atatürk
Keohane, Robert, 34
Khalis, Malavi Muhammad Yunus, 51
Khamenei, Ali, 70–71, 85–86
Khomeini, Rouhollah, 21, 76, 88n11
Kievan Rus, 100, 101, 101–102
Kirill, metropolitan, 126
Kirişi, Kemal, 187
Kmalkak, Mustafa, 169n44
Kortunov, S. V., 108
Kosovo, 177, 233, 234; Battle of, 154, 155, 170n49; crisis, Russia and, 113, 119
Kozyrev, Andrei, 114, 115, 118, 119, 121, 122, 129
Kurds, 82, 140, 159–160, 168n18, 182
Kushner, David, 137–138, 208
Kylstad, Ingrid, 193

labor issues, Turkey and, 190
Lake, Anthony, 80, 81
Laqueur, Walter, 8
Larrabee, Stephen, 156
Lashkar e Taiba, 62
leader personality: and religious influence, 227–228; and state behavior, 70–72
leadership, Turkey and, 162–163
League of Arab States, 61
League of Nations, 32–33
Lebanon, Hizbullah and, 45–46, 85–87
legislature: European, representation in, 189; Russian, 121–122; Turkish, 142–143
Le Pen, Marine, 217n74
Lerner, Daniel, 8
Lesser, Ian O., 156
Lewis, Bernard, 3
liberalism, 23; on motivation, 72–73
Liberation Theology, 14
Ligachev, Igor, 97
Light, Margot, 63
Lincoln, Abraham, 68
Locke, John, 18, 19
Lowith, Karl, 219n114
Lukin, Vladimir, 121

Macedonia, 234
Malaysia, 40
Mango, Andrew, 140
Manichaeism, 71
Marx, Karl, 11–12
Marxism: and Islam, 14, 29n52, 86; and Liberation Theology, 14; and religion, 19; and Turkey, 143
Masood, Ahmad Shah, 50, 53
McCain, John, 27n10
means, 81–82
media, Turkey and, 183
Merkel, Angela, 174
Middle East, Turkey and, 150, 176, 210
Mihailović, Draža, 238n2
military, Turkey and, 180
Miller, Aaron David, 64, 65
Milošević, Slobodan, 96, 97–98, 156, 170n49
mission: as motivation, 68; Russia and, 68, 102, 111–112, 113, 115, 116
MNCs. *See* multinational corporations

modernization, 10; Christianity and, 219n114; European identity and, 194–195; Russia and, 105–106; theory on, 5–6, 9; Turkey and, 140, 195–196
Montenegro, 177, 234
Montesquieu, C. L. de, 200
Morgenthau, Hans, 24, 72
Morocco, 20
Morsi, Muhammad, 176
Mortimer, Edward, 147
Mossadegh, Mohammad, 39
motivation(s), 61–88; categories of, 63–64; examples of, 78–81; need for research on, 7; religion as, 21–22; of state behavior, 76–78; and Taliban, 54; term, 63; of violent non-state actors, 62–63, 82–87
Mujahedin, 48, 50, 51
Mukharev, Alexander, 125
multiculturalism, 205
multinational corporations (MNCs), 32, 33, 34, 39–40, 58n37; objectives of, 62; and Taliban, 53–54
multipolarity, characteristics of, 116–117
Muscovite State, 102
Muslim(s): Balkan, Turkey and, 155–156; Bosnian. *See* Bosniaks; as immigrants, 204–208; Soviet, Turkey and, 147; *See also under* Islam
Muslim population: and EU rejection of Turkey, 178; and influence of religion, 205
Muslim world: history and, 66; religion and authority in, 18; and secularism, 20

Naim, Qasim, 85
Napoleon Bonaparte, 65
Nasrallah, Seyyed Hassan, 59n58
National Endowment for Democracy, 43, 58n42
national identity: definition of, 99; and foreign policy, 146; history and, 201; Other and, 202–204; security and, 73; Turkey and, 130n18, 137–139, 140–144, 147, 175; Yugoslavia and, 232–233. *See also* Russian identity
nationalism: and Europe, 196; Gorbachev and, 96; Orthodox Church and, 126; Russia and, 98, 121; Turkey and, 138, 139
nation-state(s), 32; determinants of behavior, 63–74; motivations of, 76–78; relevance of, 33–35, 222; Russia as, 99–100, 101–102
NATO. *See* North Atlantic Treaty Organization
neo-liberalism, 25
neo-Ottomanism, 151
Netherlands, population of, 189
New Thinking, 94–95, 114, 129n2
Nigeria, 40
Non-Aligned Movement, 66, 231
non-governmental organizations (NGOs), 32, 41–43, 58n43; definition of, 41–43; objectives of, 62; Turkey and, 164
non-state actors, 34; motivations of, 61–63; term, 32
North Atlantic Treaty Organization (NATO), 57n17, 57n26, 113, 119, 124; and Bosnian War, 236–237, 239n16; and Turkey, 142, 146, 161, 162
Northedge, Frederick, 63, 76
North Korea, 29n41
Nursî, Bediuzzaman Said, 141, 168n19
Nye, Joseph, 34, 72

Organisation for Economic Co-operation and Development, and Turkey, 146
Organization of African Unity, 61
Organization of American States, 61
Organization of Islamic Cooperation, 163
Orthodox Christianity, 108, 199; and foreign policy, 109, 125–126; reforms and, 105–106; and Russian identity, 98, 100, 100–102, 108–109; and Slavism, 103; and Yugoslav crisis, 97, 232
Oschlies, Wolf, 129
Ottoman Empire, 102, 209; and Bosnian Muslims, 136–137; and Europe, 187; legacy of, 154–156; and Slavs, 104; and Turkish identity, 137, 139
Owen, David, 239n14
Özal, Turgut, 136, 143–144, 147, 151, 157, 158, 163
Özal Doctrine, 150

Pakistan, 10; and Taliban, 47–49; and terrorist groups, 62

Palestinian Liberation Organization, 44, 82
Pan-Slavism, 98, 104, 106
Pan-Turkism, 145, 151
Pashtuns, 48, 60n70, 83–84
Pera, Marcello, 206
Perle, Richard, 71
Perry, William, 53
Persia, 202
Persian Gulf War, 135; and EU rejection of Turkey, 178; Turkey and, 149–150
Peter the Great, 105–106
Pius II, pope, 198
Poland, 65, 208, 217n77
Polikarpov, Mikhail, 124
political system, and state behavior, 69–70
Pollack, Kenneth J., 70
Pomaks, 154
Portugal, 177
power, justification of pursuit of, religion and, 24
press freedom, Turkey and, 183
prestige, and state behavior, 77
Primakov, Yevgeny, 116
prosperity, and state behavior, 77
Protestantism, 199
Protestant Reformation, 18, 200
public opinion: on EU rejection of Turkey, 175, 210–211, 211; NGOs and, 43; and religious influence, 227; in Russia, and Bosnian War, 123–125; in Turkey, and Bosnian War, 157–159, 165
Pubul, Alexander Rosenthal, 198
Putin, Vladimir, 102

Qutb, Seyyed Muhammad, 14

Rabbani, Burhaneddin, 51
radicalization, 178, 205
Rahman, Maulana Fazlur, 48
Raphel, Robin, 54
Rashid, Ahmed, 48
Reagan, Ronald, 71
realism, 23, 24; modified, 25; on motivation, 72
Reason, Age of, 10, 16
refugees, 178, 207
regional organizations, 32, 37–39; objectives of, 61–62
Rehn, Ollie, 179–180

religion: as culture, 197–202; decline of, 10–11, 16, 28n39; definitional issues, 6–7, 11–15, 28n21; differentiating impact on international actors, 23; and EU rejection of Turkey, 173, 207–208; and European identity, 190–191, 196; and exceptionalism, 66–68; as instrument of policy, 7, 21–22, 228; and international affairs, 1–27, 221–229; as motivation, 21–22; and national identity, 99; need for research on, 6–7; as new paradigm in international relations, 3–5; and public opinion on Europe and Turkey, 210–211; relation to government, history of, 17–18; relation to ideology, 12, 13–14, 21, 74, 224–225; relation to secularism, 19–21; and Russia and Yugoslav crisis, 128–129; versus secular sphere, 15–16. *See also* Christianity; influence; Islam; Orthodox Christianity
religious freedom, Turkey and, 182
Renaissance, 18, 197
resource base, and state behavior, 68–69
Rice, Condoleezza, 79–80
Rocard, Michel, 188
Rodman, Peter, 150
Romanenko, Sergei, 121
Romania, 164, 177; population of, 189
Rome, ancient, legacy of, 197
Roosevelt, Franklin, 71
Rowley, David, 100
Royal Dutch Shell, 40
Russia: geography and, 64, 65; history and, 65; and mission, 68, 102, 111–112, 113, 115, 116; and Turkey, 138, 185, 210; and Yugoslav crisis, 93–129, 237. *See also* Soviet Union
Russian identity, 98; and foreign policy, 98–99, 107–112; history and, 99–106; religion and, 67

Saadat Party, 169n26, 169n44
Sadr, Musa, 45, 47
Safavids, 139, 168n12
Saikal, Amin, 48
Samarin, Yuri, 106
Sandal, Nukhet A., 24
Sarkozy, Nicolas, 174, 178–179

Saudi Arabia, 10; ideology and religion in, 21; and Lebanon, 46; religion and authority in, 18; and Taliban, 48–49, 51
Sayari, Sabri, 155
Schuman, Robert, 199
secular bias, 5, 6, 8–11; as fallacy, 223
secularism, 12; challenges for, 204–208; Christian roots of, 200–201; definition of, 15; development of, 17–18; and European identity, 190; relation to religion, 19–21; versus religious sphere, 15–16; Turkey and, 20, 136–137, 139–140, 143–144, 152; types of, 19, 20
security: and identity, 73; as motivation, 72; primacy of, 223–224
self-preservation, and state behavior, 76
Sepah e Sahaba, 62
September 11, 2001, 4–5
Serbia, 163, 177, 233; Russia and, 112–113
Serbs, 232; and Bosnian War, 235, 238; Orthodox Church and, 125–126; Ottomans and, 154; Russia and, 93, 96, 104, 112–113, 119, 123, 124, 126; Turkey and, 137, 155
sexual orientation, Turkey and, 191
Shanghai Cooperation Organization, 175
Shariati, Ali, 14, 21, 29n52
Shcherbatov, Mikhail, 106
Shias, 5, 10; in Afghanistan, 51, 83–84; and Hizbullah, 46–47; and terrorist groups, 55. *See also* Islam
Shiraev, Eric, 120
Slavism: and foreign policy, 111; and Russian identity, 103–104, 109–111
Slavophilism, 104, 106
Slovenia, 98, 160, 232, 233, 234
Snyder, Jack, 23
Solidarity (Poland), 43
Solzhenitsyn, Alexander, 107
Soros, George, 43
Soviet Union: invasion of Afghanistan, 49–51; and Turkey, 145; and Yugoslav crisis, 94–98. *See also* Russia
Soviet Union collapse: consequences of, 52; and EU rejection of Turkey, 178; and influence of religion, 204; international effects of, 148–149; and NGOs, 41; and study of religion and international affairs, 1–3; and Turkey, 135, 146–147; and Yugoslav crisis, 98
Spain, 177; population of, 189
Spandugino, Theodoro, 203
speech freedom, Turkey and, 183
Srebrenica massacre, 236
stability, in international system, 75–76, 90n38
Stankevich, Sergei, 116
state. *See* nation-state
Stiftungen, 43, 58n42
Sufi brotherhoods, 141
Sunnis, 5, 10; in Afghanistan, 50–51; and terrorist groups, 55, 62. *See also* Islam
Surkov, Vladislav, 111–112
Syria, 45–46, 176; civil war, 178, 212

Taliban, 5; emergence of, 34; global politics and, 49–54; motivations of, 82–85; Pakistan and, 47–49
Tatars, 102, 131n32, 138
territorial issues: EU and, 180; Greek-Turkish, 180; and state behavior, 76
terrorism, 205; and EU rejection of Turkey, 178
terrorists. *See* violent non-state actors
theory in international affairs, 25–27; as adequate, 223; critique of, 5–8; religion and, 3–5, 23–25
Thomas, Scott, 5
Thomas Aquinas, 18, 200
Tillich, Paul, 12
Tito, Josip Broz, 231, 233, 238n4
Tolz, Vrea, 107
transnational corporations (TNCs), 32, 33, 39–40; objectives of, 62
Tür, Özlem, 155
Turk, term, 137–138
Turkey: and Bosnian War, 135–167; geography and, 152, 186–190; international role of, 208–210; and national identity, 130n18, 137–139, 140–144, 147, 175, 208–210; as Other, 203–204; population of, 188–190, 189; and secularism, 20; size of, 188; and Yugoslav crisis, 159–160
Turkish application to European Union, 146, 153, 162, 167n1, 173–213; history of, 173–177; religion and, 207–208

Turkish foreign policy: Atatürk and, 145–146; and Bosnian War, 161–164; and EU appliation, 175–176; Islam and, 153–154; new framework for, 149–151; Soviet collapse and, 148–149
Turkism, 138, 209

Ukraine, 98, 107, 112, 208, 210, 217n77
unipolarity, 148
United Nations, 32–33, 119; and Bosnian War, 239n16; and enforcement, 36–37; and NGOs, 41; objectives of, 61; and Turkey, 162; and Yugoslav crisis, 235, 236
United States: and Afghanistan, 50, 51; and Bosnian War, 237–238; and exceptionalism, 66, 67–68; geography and, 64; history and, 66; and ideals versus interests, 78; motivations for Iraq War, 79–81; and Persian Gulf War, 149–150; and Russia, 115; and Taliban, 53–54; and Turkey, 142, 148, 152
universalism, EU and, 193
Ural Turks, 138

value systems, 12; and state behavior, 72–74
Vance, Cyrus, 237, 239n14
Vance-Owen Plan, 236, 237, 239n14
Vance Plan, 237
Velayti, Ali Akbar, 89n21
Vietnam, 29n41
violent non-state actors, 32, 44–49; emergence of, 34; motivations of, 62–63, 82–87

Vladimir, prince, 101
volunteers, in Yugoslav conflict: Russian, 124–125; Turkish, 164

Wahhabism, 21, 49
Waltz, Kenneth, 90n35
Weber, Max, 11, 16, 73
Welfare Party (Turkey), 136, 142, 158, 164
West: and secularization, 10; and Yugoslav crisis, 234
Westernization: Russia and, 105–106, 111, 113, 114, 115, 118–119, 122; Turkey and, 140, 151–154
Westphalia, Treaty of, 31
Wilson, Woodrow, 90n42
Winthrop, John, 89n15
Wolf, Martin, 35
World Health Organization, 61

Yasli, Fatih, 143
Yavuz, Hakan, 140, 141
Yeltsin, Boris, 97, 98, 107, 120; and Bosnian War, 117–123
Yildrim, Bulent, 164
Yilmaz, Hakan, 203
Yugoslav crisis, 93, 231–238, 232; elections of 1990 and, 234–235; fear of contagion from, 95–96; Russia and, 93–129; Turkey and, 135, 159–160. *See also* Bosnian War

Zagrebov, Alexander, 124
Zhirinovsky, Vladimir, 121, 124
Zinoviev, Alexander, 110
Zvolensky, Stanislav, 206

About the Author

Shireen T. Hunter is research professor at the Prince Alwaleed Bin Talal Center for Muslim-Christian Understanding at Georgetown University. Her books include *Iran Divided: The Historical Roots of Iranian Debates on Identity, Culture, and Governance in the Twenty-First Century*, a *Choice* Outstanding Academic title.

CPSIA information can be obtained at www.ICGtesting.com
Printed in the USA
BVOW01s0350280916

463491BV00001B/1/P

9 781442 272583